Exam Ref 70-247 Configuring and Deploying a Private Cloud

Orin Thomas

PUBLISHED BY
Microsoft Press
A Division of Microsoft Corporation
One Microsoft Way
Redmond, Washington 98052-6399

Library of Congress Control Number: 2014946866
ISBN: 978-0-7356-8618-2

Printed and bound in the United States of America.

First Printing

Microsoft Press books are available through booksellers and distributors worldwide. If you need support related to this book, email Microsoft Press Book Support at mspinput@microsoft.com. Please tell us what you think of this book at http://aka.ms/tellpress.

Acquisitions Editor: Alison Hirsch
Developmental Editor: Karen Szall
Editorial Production: Troy Mott, Martin Murtonen
Technical Reviewer: Telmo Sampaio
Copyeditor: Christina Rudloff
Indexer: Judy Hoer
Cover: Twist Creative • Seattle

Contents at a glance

Contents

What do you think of this book? We want to hear from you!

Microsoft is interested in hearing your feedback so we can continually improve our
books and learning resources for you. To participate in a brief online survey, please visit:

www.microsoft.com/learning/booksurvey/

Chapter 2: Configure System Center infrastructure   83

Chapter 3: Configure the fabric   153

What do you think of this book? We want to hear from you!

Microsoft is interested in hearing your feedback so we can continually improve our
books and learning resources for you. To participate in a brief online survey, please visit:

www.microsoft.com/learning/booksurvey/

Introduction

The 70-247 exam deals with advanced topics that require candidates to have an excellent working knowledge of both Windows Server 2012 R2 and the products in the System Center 2012 R2 suite. Much of the exam comprises topics that even experienced systems administrators may rarely encounter unless they work with Virtual Machine Manager, Orchestrator, Service Manager, Data Protection Manager, and Operations Manager on a day-to-day basis. To be successful in taking this exam, a candidate not only needs to know how each of these products works when used by itself, but how the products in the System Center suite work together when used to monitor and operate a private cloud.

Candidates for this exam are Information Technology (IT) Professionals who want to validate their advanced Windows Server 2012 R2 operating system and System Center 2012 R2 management skills, configuration skills, and knowledge. To pass this exam, candidates require strong understanding of how to design a System Center deployment, configure System Center infrastructure, configure fabric resources, configure System Center integration, and how to configure and deploy virtual machines and services. To pass, candidates require a theoretical understanding, as well as meaningful practical experience implementing the technologies involved.

This book covers every exam objective, but it does not cover every exam question. Only the Microsoft exam team has access to the exam questions themselves and Microsoft regularly adds new questions to the exam, making it impossible to cover specific questions. You should consider this book a supplement to your relevant real-world experience and other study materials. If you encounter a topic in this book that you do not feel completely comfortable with, use the links you'll find in text to find more information and take the time to research and study the topic. Great information is available on TechNet, through MVA courses, and in blogs and forums.

Microsoft certifications

Microsoft certifications distinguish you by proving your command of a broad set of skills and experience with current Microsoft products and technologies. The exams and corresponding certifications are developed to validate your mastery of critical competencies as you design and develop, or implement and support, solutions with Microsoft products and technologies both on-premises and in the cloud. Certification brings a variety of benefits to the individual and to employers and organizations.

Free ebooks from Microsoft Press

From technical overviews to in-depth information on special topics, the free ebooks from Microsoft Press cover a wide range of topics. These ebooks are available in PDF, EPUB, and Mobi for Kindle formats, ready for you to download at:

http://aka.ms/mspressfree

Check back often to see what is new!

Errata, updates, & book support

We've made every effort to ensure the accuracy of this book and its companion content. You can access updates to this book—in the form of a list of submitted errata and their related corrections—at:

http://aka.ms/ER247/errata

If you discover an error that is not already listed, please submit it to us at the same page.

If you need additional support, email Microsoft Press Book Support at *mspinput@ microsoft.com*.

Please note that product support for Microsoft software and hardware is not offered through the previous addresses. For help with Microsoft software or hardware, go to *http://support.microsoft.com*.

We want to hear from you

At Microsoft Press, your satisfaction is our top priority, and your feedback our most valuable asset. Please tell us what you think of this book at:

http://aka.ms/tellpress

The survey is short, and we read every one of your comments and ideas. Thanks in advance for your input!

Stay in touch

Let's keep the conversation going! We're on Twitter: *http://twitter.com/MicrosoftPress*.

Preparing for the exam

Microsoft certification exams are a great way to build your resume and let the world know about your level of expertise. Certification exams validate your on-the-job experience and product knowledge. While there is no substitution for on-the-job experience, preparation through study and hands-on practice can help you prepare for the exam. We recommend that you round out your exam preparation plan by using a combination of available study materials and courses. For example, you might use this Exam Ref and another study guide for your "at home" preparation and take a Microsoft Official Curriculum course for the class-room experience. Choose the combination that you think works best for you.

Note that this Exam Ref is based on publically available information about the exam and the author's experience. To safeguard the integrity of the exam, authors do not have access to the live exam.

CHAPTER 1

Design and deploy System Center

One of the first steps in deploying a private cloud using Microsoft technologies is the deployment of the System Center products that you will use to manage that private cloud. In this chapter you will learn which System Center products are appropriate for particular tasks within the private cloud, how to install those products, how to make those products highly available, how to back up and recover those products, and how to upgrade some of those products from previous versions.

IMPORTANT
Have you read page xv?
It contains valuable information regarding the skills you need to pass the exam.

Objectives in this chapter:

- Objective 1.1: Design a scalable System Center architecture
- Objective 1.2: Install the System Center infrastructure
- Objective 1.3: Upgrade System Center components

Objective 1.1: Design a scalable System Center architecture

This objective deals with knowing which System Center products you would deploy to accomplish specific goals in a private cloud deployment, how you can make those System Center products highly available, and how to back up and recover those System Center products.

This objective covers the following topics:
- Understanding System Center 2012 R2 products
- Examining System Center 2012 R2 high availability
- Backing up and recovering VMM

Understanding System Center 2012 R2 products

Each System Center 2012 R2 product plays a different role within a private cloud environment. Understanding which product you would leverage to complete each task is an important part of the 70-247 exam. The following pages provide a brief description of the basic purpose of each System Center 2012 R2 product in a private cloud deployment.

Virtual Machine Manager

Virtual Machine Manager (VMM) allows you to manage your organization's virtualization infrastructure, including virtualization hosts, storage, and networking resources. You can use VMM to create, manage, deploy, and update VMs. You can also use VMM to create, manage, deploy, and update applications and services that are hosted within your organization's private cloud. VMM supports management of virtualization hosts running Hyper-V, VMware ESX and ESXi, as well as Citrix Xen.

You can use VMM to perform the following tasks:

- Automatically place new VMs on virtualization hosts that have the most available resources. This feature is termed intelligent placement.
- Automatically move virtual machines between cluster nodes based on cluster node workload and available resources. This includes evacuating VMs off of host cluster nodes so that VMM can shut those nodes down to preserve electricity.
- Deploy and manage Server App-V applications.
- Manage the process of VM live migration between virtualization hosts.
- Manage software updates for VMM infrastructure, including VMM servers and virtualization hosts.

> *MORE INFO*   **VIRTUAL MACHINE MANAGER**
>
> You can learn more about Virtual Machine Manager at *http://technet.microsoft.com /library/gg610610.aspx.*

App Controller

App Controller includes a Self-Service Portal. You can grant access to this Self-Service Portal to allow users to deploy services and applications to your organization's private cloud, as well as to the Microsoft Azure public cloud. You grant access by delegating the appropriate roles and permissions. App Controller allows an application's owner to scale out, or scale back in, an application. Scaling out allows the application to have access to increased resources as demand for those resources escalates. In System Center 2012 R2, App Controller functions as VMM's Self-Service Portal. Previous versions of VMM had their own Self-Service Portal.

Orchestrator

Orchestrator provides a drag-and-drop interface, allowing you to build complicated automation runbooks. A runbook is a branching automation workflow. You create runbooks by connecting together Orchestrator tasks. Integration packs are collections of tasks. Microsoft provides integration packs for each of the System Center products. Using the tasks contained within these integration packs, you can build complicated runbooks that enact intricate tasks. For example, you could create a runbook that deploys a VM from a template using VMM in response to an alert raised in Operations Manager, and then configures protection for that VM using Data Protection Manager. You use Orchestrator runbooks to automate activities in a private cloud deployment.

Operations Manager

Operations Manager allows you to monitor the performance and availability of private cloud elements, from being able to monitor individual virtualization hosts, through to monitoring specific virtual machines, and applications that run on those virtual machines and within the private cloud. Operations Manager supports automatic remediation of some problems. You can enhance the capability of Operations Manager by importing product-specific management packs.

Service Manager

Service Manager is a service management product that you can use to manage incidents and problems in a manner consistent with ITIL (Information Technology Infrastructure Library) or MOF (Microsoft Operations Framework) practices. You can configure Service Manager with connectors to Operations Manager.

You can configure Service Manager to trigger Orchestrator runbooks and publish this to the Service Manager Self-Service Portal as a service offering. For example, you could create an Orchestrator runbook that places a designated SQL Server database hosted in the private cloud into protection using Data Protection Manager. You could use Service Manager to publish this runbook automation as a service offering on the Self-Service Portal. Users could then use the Self-Service Portal to interact with the service offering, putting their SQL Server workload into protection without having to directly interact with Orchestrator or Data Protection Manager.

> **MORE INFO** **SERVICE MANAGER**
>
> You can learn more about Service Manager at *http://technet.microsoft.com/library/hh305220.aspx.*

Data Protection Manager

Data Protection Manager (DPM) is Microsoft's backup and recovery solution. You use Data Protection Manager to provide protection for your private cloud workloads. In addition to providing protection for physically deployed workloads, DPM supports backup and recovery of virtual machines running on Hyper-V virtualization hosts. This can take the form of fully recovering a VM to the original or a different Hyper-V host, or allows for item level recovery of elements within the protected VM. You can use DPM to perform the following tasks:

- Perform bare metal recovery of protected Windows servers and desktops.
- Back up and recover from disk, tape, or Microsoft Azure.
- Manage multiple DPM servers from a single console.

Configuration Manager

Configuration Manager provides you with the ability to manage the configuration of computers and devices, including virtual machines deployed in a private cloud. You can use Configuration Manager to:

- Deploy operating systems, software applications, software,updates, and operating system updates.
- Monitor and correct operating system and application compliance settings.
- Collect hardware and software inventory.
- Perform remote administration.

In a private cloud environment, you would use VMM to manage virtual machine deployment, but might use Configuration Manager to manage software updates and monitor configuration drift for existing virtual machines.

EXAM TIP

Remember that you use VMM to manage the software updates of your virtualization infrastructure, which includes the virtualization hosts and VMM servers. You could do this with Configuration Manager, but doing it with VMM has the benefit of ensuring that VMs are properly dealt with before a virtualization host is updated. You would use Configuration Manager to manage the software updates of the virtual machines that were deployed and running within your organization's private cloud.

MORE INFO   CONFIGURATION MANAGER

You can learn more about Configuration Manager at *http://technet.microsoft.com/library/gg682129.aspx.*

Examining System Center 2012 R2 high availability

The most straightforward method of making the server that hosts a System Center product highly available is to deploy that product within a highly available virtual machine. Additional protection is possible by configuring a replica virtual machine hosted on a second failover cluster.

You can make the databases for each System Center product highly available by deploying the databases on:

- A SQL Server instance hosted on a highly available virtual machine
- A SQL Server failover cluster
- SQL Server availability groups

Using availability groups with System Center product databases involves substantial configuration of SQL Server prior to the deployment of the System Center product. You'll have to specify the availability group listener name during product setup.

Beyond deploying the product on a highly available virtual machine, Table 1-1 lists additional high availability strategies for each System Center product.

TABLE 1-1 System Center high availability options

Product	High availability options
VMM	■ Install VMM on an existing failover cluster. VMM supports being installed as highly available when deployed on an existing failover cluster. In this configuration, the Virtual Machine Manager service account must be a domain account. You must also configure distributed key management to store VMM encryption keys in AD DS. ■ Deploy the VMM database to a SQL Server failover cluster. This failover cluster should be separate from the failover cluster that hosts the VMM failover cluster.
App Controller	■ Install multiple App Controller servers behind a load balancer. ■ Deploy the App Controller database on a SQL Server failover cluster or highly available virtual machine.
Orchestrator	■ Install multiple runbook servers. ■ Install the Orchestrator web service on multiple web servers in a load-balanced configuration. ■ Deploy the Orchestrator database on a SQL Server failover cluster or highly available virtual machine. ■ You cannot deploy multiple management servers. When the management server is unavailable, you will be unable to publish new runbooks. You will be able to start, stop, and monitor existing runbooks using the Orchestration console.
Operations Manager	■ Deploy multiple management servers. ■ Deploy the Service Manager databases on a SQL Server failover cluster or highly available virtual machine.
Service Manager	■ Deploy multiple load-balanced management servers. ■ Deploy the Service Manager databases on a SQL Server failover cluster or highly available virtual machine. ■ Deploy multiple web content and portal servers.
Data Protection Manager	■ Deploy DPM on a highly available virtual machine. ■ Configure a second DPM server as a replica. ■ Deploy the DPM database on a SQL Server failover cluster or highly available virtual machine.
Configuration Manager	■ Deploy each Configuration Manager site database on a SQL Server failover cluster or highly available virtual machine. ■ Deploy a hierarchy of sites, with a CAS and multiple primary sites. ■ Install multiple instances of the management point, distribution point, state migration point, system health validator point, application catalog web service point, application catalog website point, software update point site system roles. ■ Install multiple instances of the SMS Provider at each site.

Backing up and recovering VMM

Perhaps the simplest method of protecting System Center products is to deploy them in virtual machines. Once you've done that, you can then configure DPM to protect those virtual machines. When recovering a VM protected by DPM, you can choose to recover the VM, or you can perform item level recovery. When recovering a VM, you can choose to recover the VM to its original location or to a separate Hyper-V host that has the DPM agent deployed.

Item level recovery allows you to choose to recover specific files or folders from a VM, rather than having to recover the VM in its entirety.

> **MORE INFO**   **VIRTUAL MACHINE RECOVERY**
>
> You can learn more about virtual machine recovery at *http://technet.microsoft.com/en-us/ library/hh757981.aspx.*

VMM

In order to recover a VMM deployment, you need to have a backup of the VMM database. You should also have a backup of the files stored in the VMM library. Microsoft recommends that you perform a full back up of the VMM database every 7 days and perform an incremental back up of the VMM database every day. You should back up at least one VMM library server whenever you substantially modify content stored on the server.

You can back up the VMM database using the VMM console, by using SQL Server Management Studio, or by configuring protection for the database using DPM. To back up the VMM database using the VMM console, perform the following steps:

1. In the Settings workspace of the VMM console, click Backup in the ribbon.
2. In the Virtual Machine Manager Backup dialog box, specify the location that will store the backup file.

You can restore the VMM database using SQL Server Management Studio, DPM, or by using the SCVMMRecover.exe utility from an elevated command prompt on the server that hosts VMM.

After restoring the VMM database, you will need to perform the following steps:

- Manually remove any virtualization hosts that you had removed from VMM subsequent to when you performed the backup.
- Manually remove any VMs that you had removed from VMM subsequent to when you performed the backup.
- Manually add any virtualization hosts that had been added to VMM subsequent to when you performed the backup.

If you restore the VMM database to a separate computer, you may need to reassociate any virtualization hosts and library servers that display an Access Denied message.

> **MORE INFO**   **BACKING UP AND RESTORING VMM**
>
> You can learn more about backing up and restoring a VMM deployment at *http://technet. microsoft.com/en-us/library/hh882397.aspx.*

App Controller

All App Controller settings are stored within the App Controller database. You can use SQL Server Management Studio or DPM to back up the App Controller database. To be able to recover the database, you'll need to ensure that you back up the App Controller AES key. You can back up the App Controller AES key using the Export-SCACAesKey cmdlet.

If your App Controller deployment is otherwise functioning, you can restore the App Controller database using either the SQL Server Management Studio tools or by using DPM. In the event that you are reinstalling App Controller on a new computer, you'll need to restore the App Controller database and have access to the App Controller AES key before running the App Controller Installation Wizard and specifying that you want to perform recovery using an existing database.

> **MORE INFO** **APP CONTROLLER BACKUP AND RESTORE**
>
> You can learn more about backing up and restoring App Controller at *http://technet. microsoft.com/en-us/library/hh771092.aspx*.

Orchestrator

Backing up Orchestrator involves backing up the following elements:

- Backup of the Orchestrator database
- SQL instance service master key
- File backup of the Orchestrator management server
- File backup of each runbook server
- File backup of each Orchestrator web server

Orchestrator runbooks are stored within the Orchestration database. As the Orchestration database uses encryption, you will also need to back up the service master key. Without the service master key, you will not be able to access the encrypted data stored in the Orchestration database if recovered to a separate instance. You back up a service master key with the BACKUP SERVICE MASTER KEY TO FILE Transact SQL statement.

On the management server, ensure that you back up the settings.dat file. This file stores information that allows the Orchestrator program files to access the Orchestration database. For Orchestrator web servers, ensure that the web.config files are being protected. DPM supports standard file backups of Orchestrator.

> **MORE INFO** **BACK UP ORCHESTRATOR**
>
> You can learn more about backing up Orchestrator at *http://technet.microsoft.com/en-us/ library/hh852622.aspx*.

Operations Manager

If you have not deployed Operations Manager within a VM, or if you want to just protect an Operations Manager deployment without requiring that the host computer or VM also be able to be recovered in its entirety, you should ensure that you regularly back up the following elements:

- Operational database
- Data warehouse database (if deployed)
- Audit Collection Services (ACS) database (if deployed)
- Custom management packs
- Custom report definition files
- Computer certificates

Microsoft recommends the backup schedule listed in Table 1-2 for an Operations Manager deployment.

TABLE 1-2 Operations Manager data protection

Feature	Full backup	Incremental backup
Operational database	Every 7 days	Daily
Data warehouse database	Every 28 days	Every 7 days
Reporting Server	<ul><li>Frequency depends on how often reports change</li><li>Perform full backup after substantial changes</li></ul>	Full backup only
Audit Collection Services (ACS) Database	Every 28 days	Every 7 days
SQL instance Master database	<ul><li>After deployment</li><li>When changes are made to SQL logons or security</li></ul>	Full backup only
Msdb database	After deployment	When changes are made to Operations Manager related SQL Server Agent jobs
Custom management packs	When changes are made to management packs	Full backup only

You can use SQL Server Management Studio to configure regular database backups. In a private cloud environment where you have deployed DPM, you should configure a custom DPM protection group to manage backups for Operations Manager. You back up custom management packs by exporting them using the Management Packs node of the Administration workspace of the Operations Manager console.

You perform recovery by restoring the appropriate databases, either using SQL Server Management Studio or by using DPM. You recover custom management packs by importing them using the Operations Manager console.

Service Manager

Backing up Service Manager involves backing up the following elements:

- Service Manager encryption keys
- Service Manager database
- Service Manager data warehouse database

You can back up the Service Manager encryption keys using the SecureStorageBackup. exe command line utility from an elevated command prompt. You can back up the Service Manager database and the data warehouse database using SQL Server Management Studio or by using DPM.

To recover a Service Manager deployment, perform the following general steps:

1. Restore the encryption key.
2. Install the new Service Manager management server on a computer that has the same name as the original management server.
3. In the event that SQL Server was also installed on the Service Manager management server, install SQL Server and restore the Service Manager database.
4. Run the Service Manager Installation Wizard, and select the Use An Existing Database option, providing the details of the SQL instance that hosts the Service Manager database.

Data Protection Manager

Just because DPM functions as a data protection solution for other elements of your private cloud deployment, doesn't mean that you don't need to back up the DPM server itself. Your protection strategy for the DPM server should include backing up:

- The DPM database
- All local volumes and application data on the computer that hosts DPM
- All replicas on the DPM server protected by that DPM server

There are two general strategies that you can use to protect a DPM server. These are:

- **Back up the DPM server using a second DPM server** When you configure DPM in this way, the second DPM server functions as a replica of the first DPM server. In the event that the first DPM server fails, the secondary server will start protecting all of the workloads that were previously protected by the primary DPM server. Should it be necessary, you can configure a tertiary DPM server that will function as a replica of the secondary DPM server.

- **Back up the DPM database to tape** You can configure DPM to back up the DPM database to a tape library. To recover the DPM database from tape, you'll need to uninstall DPM from the original server, remove the DPM database that you want to restore using SQL Server Management Studio, reinstall DPM, perform a tape inventory, re-catalog the imported tape, recover the database to a network folder, and then use the DPMSync.exe utility to attach the database to DPM. You'll need to then reestablish protection for all computers that were protected by the DPM server. You can do this by running the setdpmserver.exe command on each protected computer.

> *MORE INFO* **BACKING UP DPM**
>
> You can learn more about backing up DPM at *http://technet.microsoft.com/en-us/library/jj244607.aspx*.

Configuration Manager

Configuration Manager includes a backup maintenance task that runs on a schedule. This task, shown in Figure 1-1, is available through the Site Maintenance item on the ribbon, which you can open when you select the Sites node in the Administration workspace of the Configuration Manager console. The Configuration Manager Backup Site Server site maintenance task backs up the following:

- Site database
- Configuration Manager registry keys
- Configuration Manager files and folders

DPM supports protecting Configuration Manager as a workload. When creating a DPM protection group for Configuration Manager, ensure that you select the SMS Writer Service item, and the site database on the Configuration Manager server.

> *MORE INFO* **CONFIGURATION MANAGER BACKUP AND RECOVERY**
>
> You can learn more about Configuration Manager backup and recovery at *http://technet.microsoft.com/en-us/library/gg712697.aspx*.

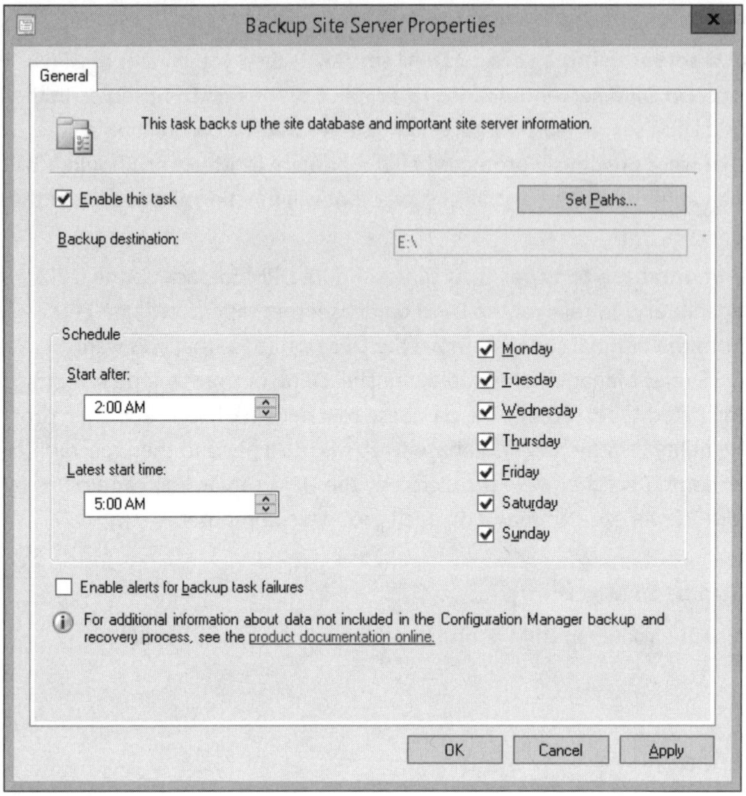

FIGURE 1-1 Backup site server task

If your organization uses custom Reporting Services reports with Configuration Manager, you will need to ensure that the following are protected:

- Report Server database
- Source files for reports and models
- Encryption keys
- Custom assemblies or extensions
- Configuration files
- Custom SQL views
- Custom stored procedures

The backup site server scheduled maintenance task does not backup content files for software updates, applications, or operating system deployment. You should back up the SCCMContentLib folder on the Configuration Manager site server, using file backup to backup the content library. You will also need to ensure that you have taken a file backup of package source files. If you have not kept track of the location of package source files, you can determine the location by using the following Transact SQL query against the Configuration Manager database as shown in Figure 1-2:

```
SELECT PackageID, Name, PkgSourcePath FROM v_Package
```

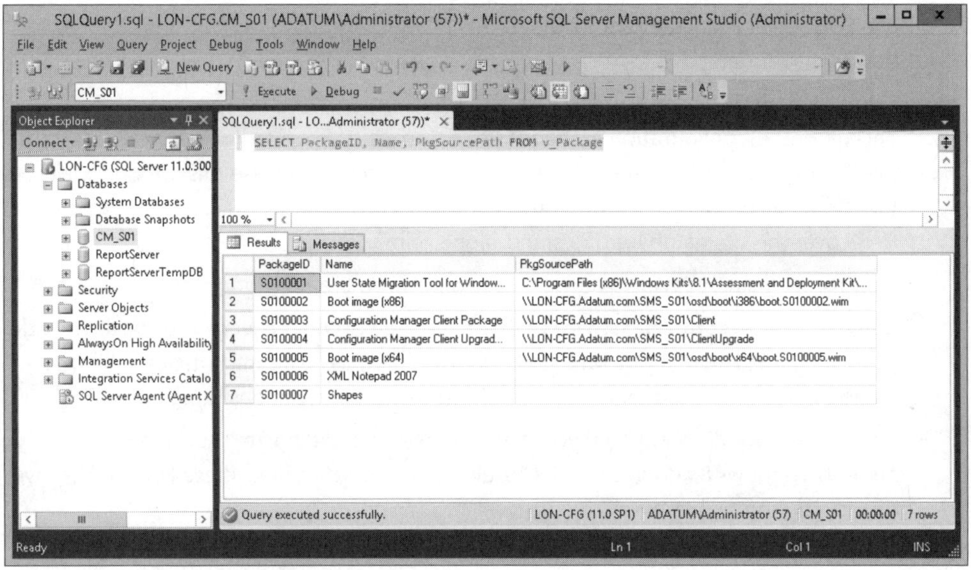

FIGURE 1-2 Package source location

When recovering a site server, you can choose one of the following options:

- **Recover the site server using an existing backup**   You can leverage this option if you have created a backup using the scheduled maintenance task.

- **Reinstall the site server**   Only use this option if you don't have a backup of the site server. When using this option, ensure that you use the same site code and site database name as the original site server.

It will be necessary to recover the Configuration Manager database if the database becomes corrupted or if the data is otherwise lost. If you are recovering a database in a hierarchy, any changes made to the site database since the backup will be retrieved from the central administration site if you are recovering a primary site database, or from a primary site database if you are recovering the central administration site. If you are recovering the database of a stand alone primary site, all changes made subsequent to the backup will be lost.

When performing database recovery, you have the following recovery options:

- **Recover the site database using a backup set**   This option allows you to restore the database using the backup created using the scheduled maintenance task.

- **Use a site database that has been manually recovered**   You use this option if you use SQL Server Management Studio, DPM, or another tool to back up the Configuration Manager database.

- **Create a new database for this site**   Use this option if you do not have access to a backup of the Configuration Manager site database. This option is only available if the site is part of a Configuration Manager hierarchy. You cannot use this option to recover the site database of a CAS if no primary sites are present and you can't use this option to recover the site database of a stand-alone primary site.

After performing site recovery, you will need to perform the following steps:

- **Reenter user account passwords**   The final page of the recovery wizard will provide you with information about which accounts require password information. This information is also saved to the file C:\ConfigMgrPostRecoveryActions.html.

- **Reenter sideloading keys**   If you have entered sideloading keys for software deployment to Windows 8 and Windows 8.1 devices, you must reenter these keys, as they will be reset during site recovery.

- **Configure SSL for site system roles that use IIS**   You will also need to reconfigure IIS to use the appropriate SSL certificate for site system roles after performing recovery.

- **Recover custom reports**   If you have custom Configuration Manager reports, you will need to recover these reports after performing site recovery.

- **Recover content files**   You will need to recover content files to the same locations as they used on the site server prior to the failure that triggered the recovery process.

- **Update Microsoft Azure management certificates**   If your organization uses Microsoft Azure for cloud-based distribution points, you will need to update these management certificates for the newly recovered site server.

If you need to recover a computer that hosts a Configuration Manager secondary site, ensure that you configure the computer with the same name as the original computer that hosted the secondary site. Recovery of a secondary site requires that the primary site server is available. Configuration Manager secondary sites aren't backed up by scheduled maintenance tasks.

EXAM TIP

Remember the additional elements of each product that require backup beyond the product's database to be able to perform full recovery.

Thought experiment

Highly available System Center infrastructure planning at Contoso

In this thought experiment, apply what you've learned about this objective. You can find answers to these questions in the "Answers" section at the end of this chapter.

You are in the process of integrating the VMM and DPM products into the plan for a private cloud deployment at Contoso. You want to avoid deploying the VMM management server and the Data Protection Manager server in a VM. Given these constraints:

1. What steps can you take to make VMM highly available?

2. What steps can you take to make DPM highly available?

Objective summary

- Virtual Machine Manager allows you to manage your private cloud's virtualization infrastructure.
- App Controller allows you to manage both private and public clouds.
- Orchestrator allows you to configure automation for private cloud processes.
- Operations Manager provides you with performance and availability monitoring for private cloud workloads.
- Service Manager provides a framework based on ITIL and MOF for private cloud management.
- Data Protection Manager allows you to configure backup and recovery for private cloud workloads.
- Configuration Manager allows you to deploy applications as well as managing and monitoring the configuration of virtual machines running in private clouds.
- Protecting System Center products primarily involves ensuring that the product database is backed up on a regular basis.

Objective review

Answer the following questions to test your knowledge of the information in this objective. You can find the answers to these questions and explanations of why each answer choice is correct or incorrect in the "Answers" section at the end of this chapter.

1. Which System Center product would you deploy to monitor software update compliance for Windows 8.1 virtual machines hosted in your organization's private cloud?

   A. Virtual Machine Manager

   B. Operations Manager

   C. Configuration Manager

   D. Orchestrator

2. Which of the following steps can you take to make System Center 2012 R2 Orchestrator more highly available?

   A. Deploy multiple management servers.

   B. Deploy multiple runbook servers.

   C. Deploy the Orchestration database on a SQL Server failover cluster.

   D. Deploy the management server on a highly available virtual machine.

3. A failure occurs in your datacenter and the computer hosting the Service Manager management service is lost. This computer also hosted the SQL Server instance that hosted the Service Manager database. You have backups of the database and the encryption key. The computer hosting the Service Manager data warehouse and the computer hosting the Service Manager Self-Service Portal is unaffected. Which of the following steps must you take prior to using the Service Manager installation media to recover Service Manager?

   A. Restore the existing encryption key from backup.

   B. Create a new encryption key.

   C. Ensure that the replacement server has the same name as the failed Service Manager management server.

   D. Install SQL Server and recover the Service Manager database.

Objective 1.2: Install the System Center infrastructure

This objective deals with the hardware requirements and software requirements for each System Center product. You'll then learn how to install each system center product.

> **This objective covers the following topics:**
> - Understanding hardware requirements
> - Software prerequisites
> - Installing System Center 2012 R2

Understanding hardware requirements

Each product in the System Center 2012 R2 suite has separate hardware requirements. These hardware requirements are just for the product itself, and don't include items such as the SQL Server program files required to support the product, or the amount of disk space required to host elements such as the VMM library or Configuration Manager distribution points.

VMM

Table 1-3 describes the hardware or virtual machine resource requirements for the different elements of a VMM deployment where there are less than 150 users.

TABLE 1-3 VMM hardware requirements

	VMM manage-ment server	VMM database	VMM console	VMM library server
Minimum Processor	Pentium 4, 2 GHz	Pentium 4, 2.8 GHz	Pentium 4, 1 GHz	Pentium 4, 2.8 GHz
Recommended Processor	Pentium 4, 2 GHz	Dual core 2 GHz x64	Pentium 4, 2 GHz	Dual core 3.2 GHz x64
Minimum RAM	2 GB	2 GB	2 GB	2 GB
Recommended RAM	2 GB	4 GB	2 GB	2 GB
Minimum storage	2 GB	20 GB	2 GB	Varies based on de-ployment
Recommended storage	2 GB	150 GB	2 GB	Varies based on de-ployment

Table 1-4 describes the hardware or virtual machine resource requirements for the different elements of a VMM deployment where there are more than 150 users. The requirements for VMM library servers do not change based on the number of users, only based on the amount of content to be stored on the library server.

TABLE 1-4 VMM hardware requirements for large deployments

	VMM management server	VMM database	VMM console
Minimum Processor	Pentium 4, 2 GHz	Dual core 2 GHz x64	Dual core 2 GHz x64
Recommended Processor	Dual core 2 GHz x64	Dual core 2.8 GHz x64	Dual core 2 GHz x64
Minimum RAM	4 GB	4 GB	4 GB
Recommended RAM	4 GB	8 GB	4 GB
Minimum storage	4 GB	50 GB	4 GB
Recommended storage	4 GB	200 GB	4 GB

App Controller

An App Controller server requires the following hardware or virtual machine resource allocation:

- Minimum processor: 2 GHz Pentium 4
- Recommended processor: 2.8 GHz dual core x64 processor
- Minimum RAM: 1 GB
- Recommended RAM: 4 GB
- Minimum program file storage: 512 MB
- Recommended program file storage: 1 GB

Orchestrator

Orchestrator has several elements: the management server, the runbook server, the runbook designer, and the web service. You can deploy these elements on separate computers or on the same computer. The elements require the following hardware or virtual machine resource allocation:

- Minimum processor: 2.1 GHz dual core x64 CPU
- Recommended processor: 2.1 GHz dual core x64 CPU
- Minimum RAM: 1 GB
- Recommended RAM: 2 GB
- Minimum program file storage: 200 MB
- Recommended program file storage: 200 MB

Operations Manager

Instead of having set minimum hardware requirements, you calculate the hardware requirements for Operations Manager using the Operations Manager Sizing Helper. The sizing helper is an Excel spreadsheet that takes into account the particular nature of your organization's Operations Manager deployment, making hardware allocation recommendations based on that deployment. You can download the Operations Manager Sizing Helper files from Microsoft's website.

Service Manager

The Service Manager management server and the Service Manager data warehouse management server must be deployed on separate computers or virtual machines. The requirements for the computer that host the Service Manager database exceed the requirements for the computer that hosts the management server or data warehouse management server roles. Table 1-5 describes the hardware or virtual machine resource requirements for the different elements of a Service Manager deployment.

TABLE 1-5 Service Manager hardware requirements

	Management server	Management server database	Data warehouse management server	Data warehouse databases
Minimum Processor	4 Core 2.66 GHz x64 CPU	8 Core 2.66 GHz x64 CPU	4 Core 2.66 GHz x64 CPU	8 Core 2.66 GHz x64 CPU
Recommended Processor	4 Core 2.66 GHz x64 CPU	8 Core 2.66 GHz x64 CPU	4 Core 2.66 GHz x64 CPU	8 Core 2.66 GHz x64 CPU
Minimum RAM	8 GB	8 GB	8 GB	8 GB
Recommended RAM	8 GB	32 GB	16 GB	32 GB
Minimum storage	10 GB	80 GB	10 GB	400 GB
Recommended storage	10 GB	80 GB	10 GB	400 GB

Data Protection Manager

A Data Protection Manager server requires the following hardware or virtual machine resource allocation:

- Minimum processor: 1 GHz dual core x64 CPU

- Recommended processor: 2.33 GHz quad core x64 CPU

- Minimum RAM: 4 GB

- Recommended RAM: 8 GB

- Minimum program file storage: 3 GB

- Recommended program file storage: 3 GB

Configuration Manager

Minimum and recommended Configuration Manager hardware configuration depends on the number of clients that need to be supported on the site system roles deployed. Table 1-6 lists different site configurations and the minimum recommended hardware configuration.

TABLE 1-6 Configuration Manager hardware requirements

Site configuration	Minimum recommended hardware
Central administration site using SQL Server standard edition. ■ SQL Server deployed on site server ■ Supports up to 50,000 clients	■ 8 core Intel Xeon 5504 or comparable CPU ■ 32 GB RAM ■ 300 GB storage for program files and database files
Central administration site using SQL Server enterprise edition ■ SQL Server deployed on site server ■ Supports up to 400,000 clients	■ 16 core Intel Xeon L5520 or comparable CPU ■ 64 GB RAM ■ 1.6 TB storage for program files and database files
Stand alone primary site ■ SQL Server deployed on site server ■ Supports up to 100,000 clients	■ 8 core Intel Xeon 5504 or comparable CPU ■ 32 GB RAM ■ 550 GB storage for program files and database files
Primary site in hierarchy ■ SQL Server deployed on site server ■ Supports up to 50,000 clients	■ 4 core Intel Xeon 5140 or comparable CPU ■ 16 GB RAM ■ 300 GB storage for program files and database files
Primary site in hierarchy ■ SQL Server deployed on remote computer ■ Supports up to 100,000 clients	Site server ■ 4 core Intel Xeon 5140 or comparable CPU ■ 16 GB RAM ■ 200 GB storage for program files and database files Remote SQL Server ■ 8 core Intel Xeon 5504 or comparable CPU ■ 32 GB RAM ■ 550 GB storage for program files and database files
Secondary site ■ SQL Server deployed on site server ■ Supports up to 5,000 clients	■ 4 core Intel Xeon 5140 or comparable CPU ■ 8 GB RAM ■ 100 GB storage for program files and database files

The hardware requirements for remote site system servers are listed in Table 1-7.

TABLE 1-7 Site system server requirements

Site system role	Minimum recommended hardware
Management point	<ul><li>4 core Intel Xeon 5140 or comparable CPU</li><li>8 GB RAM</li><li>50 GB storage for OS and program files</li></ul>
Distribution point	<ul><li>2 core Intel Xeon 5140 or comparable CPU</li><li>8 GB RAM</li><li>Storage varies based on content deployed to distribution point</li></ul>
Application catalog with web service and web-site on computer hosting site system	<ul><li>4 core Intel Xeon 5140 or comparable CPU</li><li>16 GB RAM</li><li>50 GB storage for OS and program files</li></ul>
Other site system roles	<ul><li>4 core Intel Xeon 5140 or comparable CPU</li><li>8 GB RAM</li><li>50 GB storage for OS and program files</li></ul>

> *MORE INFO* **CONFIGURATION MANAGER HARDWARE REQUIREMENTS**
>
> You can learn more about the hardware requirements for Configuration Manager at *http://technet.microsoft.com/en-us/library/hh846235.aspx.*

Software prerequisites

The software prerequisites for each product in the System Center 2012 R2 suite are varied. In most cases, any roles or features that are already included with the host operating system will be installed automatically as part of the product's installation routine, and do not need to be installed prior to commencing installation.

Some products in the System Center 2012 R2 suite can only be installed on computers running Windows Server 2008 R2 SP1 and are not supported on computers running Windows Server 2008 R2.

A minimum of four separate computers are required if you want to deploy all products in the System Center 2012 R2 suite. This is because some products cannot coexist on the same computer as others. In production environments, Microsoft generally advises that each System Center 2012 R2 element be deployed on a separate computer.

SQL Server requirements

Each product in the System Center 2012 R2 suite uses a SQL Server database to host configuration and product data. SQL Server support is as follows:

- **App Controller**   SQL Server 2008 R2 SP2, SQL Server 2012 (RTM and SP1)

- **DPM**   SQL Sever 2008 R2 (SP1 and SP2), SQL Server 2012 (RTM and SP1)

- **Operations Manager Data Warehouse**   SQL Server 2008 R2 (SP1 and SP2), SQL Server 2012 (RTM, SP1, and SP2)

- **Operations Manager Operational Database**   SQL Server 2008 R2 (SP1 and SP2), SQL Server 2012 (RTM, SP1, and SP2)

- **Operations Manager Reporting Server**   SQL Server 2008 R2 (SP1 and SP2), SQL Server 2012 (RTM, SP1, and SP2)

- **Orchestrator Management Server**   SQL Server 2008 R2 (SP1 and SP2), SQL Server 2012 (RTM and SP1)

- **Service Manager Database**   SQL Server 2008 R2 (SP1 and SP2), SQL Server 2012 (RTM and SP1)

- **Service Manager Data Warehouse Database**   SQL Server 2008 R2 (SP1 and SP2), SQL Server 2012 (RTM and SP1)

- **Virtual Machine Manager**   SQL Server 2008 R2 SP2, SQL Server 2012 (RTM and SP1)

In testing environments it is possible to use one SQL Server Database Engine element to host the databases for all System Center 2012 R2 products. The performance impact of this configuration means that it is not recommended for production environments. System Center R2 products cannot share an Reporting Services instance, and separate instances must be deployed for each product that uses Reporting Services.

> *MORE INFO*   **SYSTEM CENTER SQL SERVER REQUIREMENTS**
>
> You can learn more about the System Center 2012 R2 SQL Server requirements at *http://technet.microsoft.com/library/dn281933.aspx*.

VMM

You can install the System Center 2012 R2 VMM management server on computers running the following operating systems:

- Windows Server 2012

- Windows Server 2012 R2

You must install the Windows ADK for Windows 8.1 on the computer that will host the management server role.

The SQL Server instance that supports VMM should have the following:

- The SQL Server instance must allow for case-insensitive database objects.
- The Database Engine Services And Management Tools - Complete features must be installed. Collation is configured during deployment.
- Analysis server and reporting server elements should be deployed.

Other than SQL Server, a VMM management server has no external dependencies.

> **MORE INFO** **VMM SOFTWARE REQUIREMENTS**
>
> You can learn more about the VMM software prerequisites at *http://technet.microsoft.com/library/dn771747.aspx*.

App Controller

You can install System Center 2012 R2 App Controller on computers running the following operating systems:

- Windows Server 2008
- Windows Server 2008 R2
- Windows Server 2012
- Windows Server 2012 R2

App Controller has the following software prerequisites:

- .NET Framework 4.5
- VMM console
- Supported version of SQL Server
  - SQL Server 2008 R2 (Standard, Enterprise, Datacenter) SP2
  - SQL Server 2012 (Standard, Enterprise)
- Virtual Machine Manager 2012 R2 console

Installing App Controller will automatically install the Web Server (IIS) role and the following features:

- Static Content
- Default Document
- Directory Browsing
- HTTP Errors
- ASP.NET
- .NET Extensibility
- ISAPI Extensions
- ISAPI Filters

- HTTP Logging
- Request Monitor
- Tracing
- Basic Authentication
- Windows Authentication
- Request Filtering
- Static Content Compression
- IIS Management Console

> **MORE INFO** **APP CONTROLLER SOFTWARE REQUIREMENTS**
>
> You can learn more about the software requirements for App Controller at *http://technet.microsoft.com/en-us/library/dn771748.aspx*.

Orchestrator

You can install the System Center 2012 R2 Orchestrator management server, runbook server, web service, and Runbook Designer roles on computers running the following operating systems:

- Windows Server 2008 R2
- Windows Server 2012
- Windows Server 2012 R2

Orchestrator has the following software requirements:

- Internet Information Services (IIS)
- .NET Framework 3.5
- .NET Framework 4.5
- WCF HTTP Activation
- Microsoft Silverlight 4

> **MORE INFO** **ORCHESTRATOR SOFTWARE REQUIREMENTS**
>
> You can learn more about the software requirements for Orchestrator at *http://technet.microsoft.com/en-us/library/hh420348.aspx*.

Operations Manager

You can install the System Center 2012 R2 Operations Manager management server, data warehouse server, gateway server, reporting server, and web console roles on computers running the following operating systems:

- Windows Server 2008 R2 SP1
- Windows Server 2012
- Windows Server 2012 R2

When installed on Windows Server 2012 R2, Operations Manager has software prerequisites listed in Table 1-8.

TABLE 1-8 Operations Manager software requirements

Operations Manager element	Software prerequisites
Management server	- .NET Framework 4 or .NET Framework 4.5
Operations console	- Microsoft Report Viewer 2012 Redistributable Package
Web console	- .NET Framework 4 IIS Elements: - Static Content - Default Document - Directory Browsing - HTTP Errors - HTTP Logging - Request Monitor - Request Filtering - Static Content Compression - Web Server (IIS) Support - IIS 6 Metabase Compatibility - ASP.NET (version 2.0 and 4.0) - Windows Authentication
Operations Manager reporting	- SQL Server Reporting Services (native mode only)
Operations Manager data warehouse	- .NET Framework 4

> *MORE INFO* **OPERATIONS MANAGER SOFTWARE REQUIREMENTS**
>
> You can learn more about the software requirements for Operations Manager at *http://technet.microsoft.com/en-US/library/dn249696.aspx*.

Service Manager

You can install the System Center 2012 R2 Service Manager management server, data warehouse management server, database, and data warehouse database on computers running the following operating systems:

- Windows Server 2008 R2 SP1

- Windows Server 2012

- Windows Server 2012 R2

You can install the Service Manager Self-Service Portal on computers running:

- Windows Server 2008 R2

- Windows Server 2012

- Windows Server 2012 R2

Table 1-9 lists the software prerequisites for each System Center 2012 R2 Service Manager element when Service Manager is deployed on Windows Server 2012 R2.

TABLE 1-9 Service Manager software requirements

Element	Software prerequisites
Management server	- SQL Server 2008 R2 Native Client or SQL Server 2012 Native Client - Microsoft Report Viewer Redistributable
Console	- Microsoft Report Viewer Redistributable - Excel 2007 or later to view OLAP data cubes - SQL Server 2012 Analysis Management Objects
Self-Service Portal: web content server	- Internet Information Services with IIS 6 Metabase compatibility - SSL Certificate - SQL Server 2012 Analysis Management Objects
Self-Service Portal: SharePoint Web Parts	- Microsoft SharePoint Foundation 2010 with SP2 or Microsoft SharePoint Server 2010 with SP2 (Note that SharePoint 2013 is not supported for Service Manager 2012 R2) - SQL Server 2012 with SP1

> *MORE INFO* **SERVICE MANAGER SOFTWARE REQUIREMENTS**
>
> You can learn more about the software requirements for Service Manager at *http://technet.microsoft.com/en-us/library/hh519608.aspx.*

Data Protection Manager

You can install a System Center 2012 R2 Data Protection Manager server on computers running the following operating systems:

- Windows Server 2008

- Windows Server 2008 R2

- Windows Server 2012

- Windows Server 2012 R2

You can use DPM with both the Standard or Enterprise editions of SQL Server 2008 R2 SP1, and SQL Server 2012. DPM requires that the Database Engine services and Reporting Services elements of SQL Server be deployed.

The DPM server also has the following software prerequisites:

- Microsoft .NET Framework 4.0
- Windows Installer 4.5 or later
- Visual C++ 2008 Redistributable
- Windows PowerShell 3.0
- Windows Single Instance Store (SIS)
- Microsoft Application Error Reporting

Configuration Manager

You can install System Center 2012 R2 Configuration Manager on computers running the following operating systems:

- Windows Server 2008 SP2
- Windows Server 2008 R2
- Windows Server 2012
- Windows Server 2012 R2

The site server has the software requirements listed in Table 1-10 when deployed on Windows Server 2012 or Windows Server 2012 R2.

TABLE 1-10 Configuration Manager software requirements

Site system role	Prerequisites
Site Server	- .NET Framework 3.5 - .NET Framework 4.5 - Windows ADK
SMS provider	- Windows ADK
Application Catalog web service point	- .NET Framework 3.5 - HTTP Activation - .NET Framework 4.5 - ASP.NET 4.5 - IIS Configuration: Default Document, IIS 6 Metabase Compatibility, ASP.NET 3.5, .NET Extensibility 3.5
Application Catalog website point	- .NET Framework 3.5 - .NET Framework 4.5 - ASP.NET 4.5 - IIS Configuration: Default Document, Static Content, ASP.NET 3.5, ASP.NET 4.5, .NET Extensibility 3.5, .NET Extensibility 4.5, Windows Authentication, IIS 6 Metabase Compatibility

Asset Intelligence synchronization point	■ .NET Framework 4.5
Certificate registration point	■ .NET Framework 4.5 ■ HTTP Activation ■ IIS Configuration: ASP.NET 3.5, ASP.NET 4.5, IIS 6 Metabase Compatibility, IIS 6 WMI Compatibility
Distribution point	■ Remote Differential Compression ■ Windows Deployment Services ■ Microsoft Visual C++ Redistributable ■ IIS Configuration: ISAPI Extensions, Windows Authentication, IIS 6 Metabase Compatibility, IIS 6 WMI Compatibility
Endpoint Protection point	■ .NET Framework 3.5
Enrollment point	■ .NET Framework 3.5 ■ HTTP Activation ■ .NET Framework 4.5 ■ ASP.NET 4.5 ■ IIS Configuration: Default Document, ASP.NET 3.5, .NET Extensibility 3.5, IIS 6 Metabase Compatibility
Enrollment Proxy point	■ .NET Framework 3.5 ■ .NET Framework 4.5 ■ IIS Configuration: Default Document, Static Content, ASP.NET 3.5, ASP.NET 4.5, .NET Extensibility 3.5, .NET Extensibility 4.5, Windows Authentication, IIS 6 Metabase Compatibility
Fallback Status point	■ IIS Configuration: IIS 6 Management Compatibility
Management point	■ .NET Framework 4.5 ■ BITS Server Extensions ■ IIS Configuration: ISAPI Extensions, Windows Authentication, IIS 6 Metabase Compatibility, IIS 6 WMI Compatibility
Out of band service point	■ .NET Framework 4.5
Reporting service point	■ .NET Framework 4.5 ■ SQL Server Reporting Services
Software Update point	■ .NET Framework 3.5 SP1 ■ .NET Framework 4.5 ■ Windows Server Update Services
Windows Intune connector	■ .NET Framework 4.5

The Configuration Manger setup downloader is a stand-alone application that retrieves prerequisite files used for Configuration Manager setup. When you use this application, files are downloaded form Microsoft's website to a directory that you specify. You run the setup downloader by running the setupdl.exe executable located in the \SMSSETUP\BIN\X64 folder of the Configuration Manager installation media. Figure 1-3 shows the setup downloader window with a folder that will store the setup downloader files.

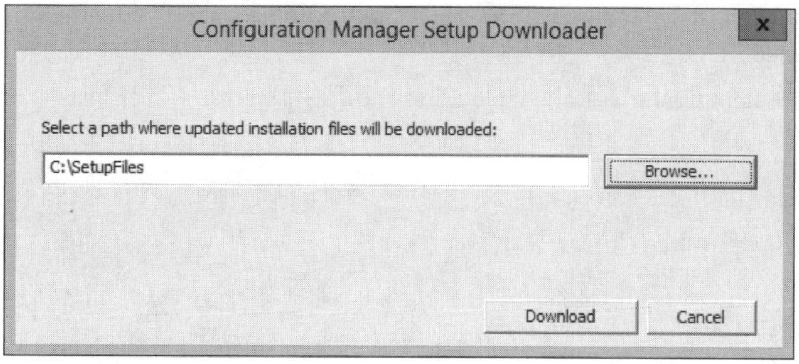

FIGURE 1-3 Setup downloader

When you run Configuration Manager setup, you have the opportunity of specifying the location of these files. You don't have to run the setup downloader prior to installing Configuration Manager. You'll need to allow Configuration Manager to connect to the Internet to retrieve these files if you haven't run the setup downloader.

> **MORE INFO** **CONFIGURATION MANAGER SOFTWARE REQUIREMENTS**
>
> You can learn more about the software requirements for Configuration Manager at *http://technet.microsoft.com/en-us/library/gg682077.aspx*.

Installing System Center 2012 R2 products

System Center 2012 R2 comes with a unified installer that allows you to use a single interface to deploy all System Center products in a specially prepared environment. The unified installer deploys products on a one-server per-product basis. It does not allow for complex deployments. You should only use the unified installer to deploy lab and proof of concept environments.

> **MORE INFO** **SUPPORTED CONFIGURATIONS FOR CONFIGURATION MANAGER**
>
> You can learn more about the software requirements for Configuration Manager at *http://technet.microsoft.com/en-us/library/gg682077.aspx*.

In the next few pages, you'll learn the process for installing each of the System Center 2012 R2 products on a computer that has the necessary software prerequisites, including an appropriately configured SQL Server instance, deployed.

VMM

Once you have deployed the necessary software prerequisites, including the SQL Server instance that will host the VMM database and Windows ADK, you can install VMM by performing the following steps:

1. Run Setup.exe on the installation media. This will happen automatically if you mount the installation media ISO.

2. In the Microsoft System Center 2012 R2 dialog box, shown in Figure 1-4, click Install.

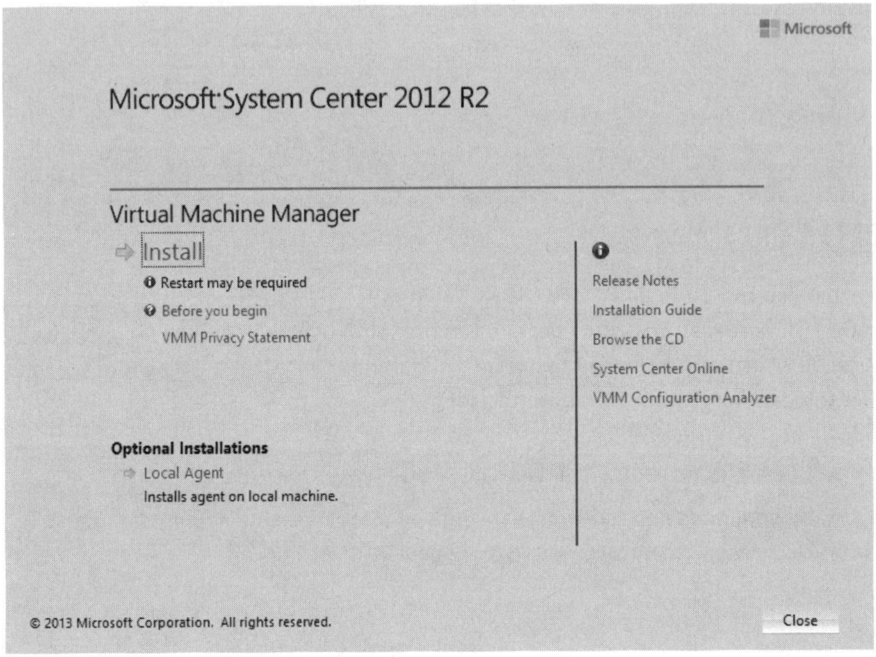

FIGURE 1-4 VMM installation dialog box

3. On the Select Features to install page, select VMM Management Server. VMM Console will automatically be selected.

4. On the Product Registration Information page, enter your product key. If you don't enter your product key, VMM will be installed as an evaluation edition.

5. On the Please Read This License Agreement page, agree with the terms of the license agreement.

6. On the Customer Experience Improvement Program (CEIP) page, choose if you want to participate in this program.

7. On the Microsoft Update page, choose whether you want to use Microsoft Update to check for updates. The recommended choice is On.

8. On the Installation location page, select the installation location. The recommended location is C:\Program Files\Microsoft System Center 2012 R2\Virtual Machine Manager.

   The prerequisite check will run.

1. On the Database Configuration page, shown in Figure 1-5, specify the connection settings for the VMM Database, including the Server Name, Port, Instance Name, and

Database Name and then click next. You will not have to specify the port if you are using a local SQL Server instance.

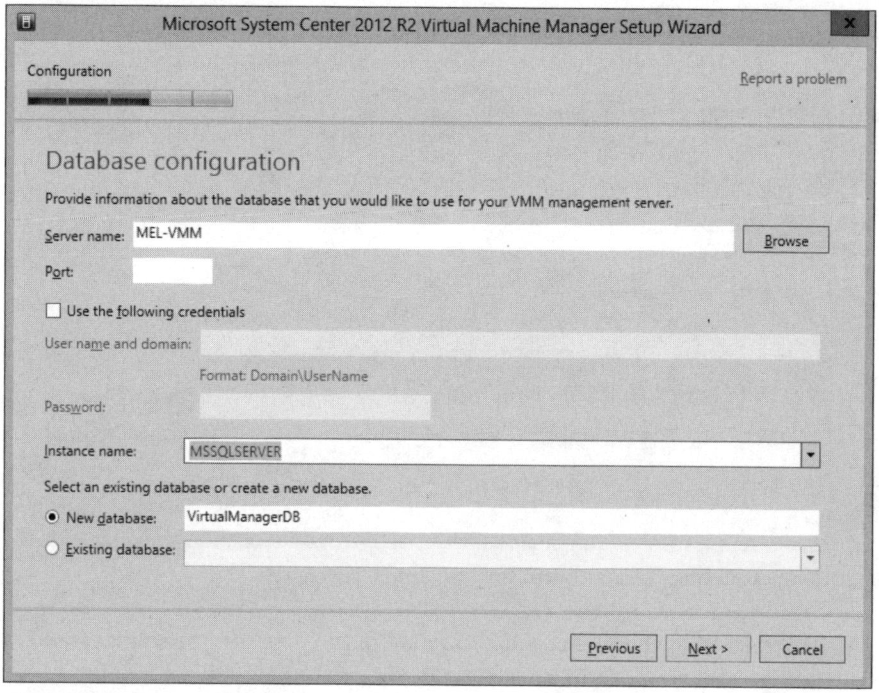

FIGURE 1-5 Database configuration

2. On the Configure Service Account And Distributed Key Management page, specify whether to use a Local System Account or a Domain Account and then click next. If choosing a Domain Account, the account must be a member of the Local Administrators group on the VMM management server. You also use this page to specify whether encryption keys are stored locally or in Active Directory. If you are configuring a highly available VMM installation, you must store the encryption keys in Active Directory and must specify service account credentials that are members of the domain. Figure 1-6 shows this page of the installation wizard.

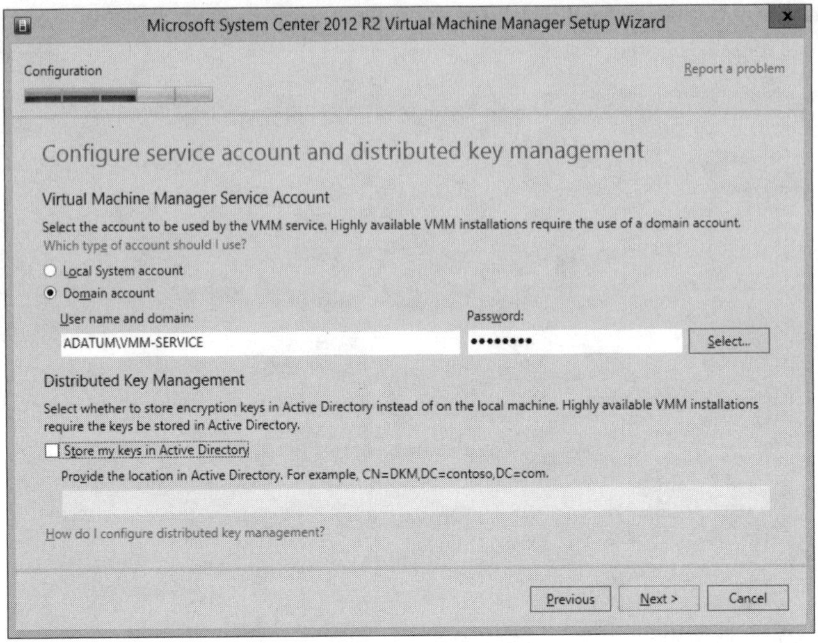

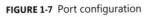

FIGURE 1-6 Service account and distributed key management

3. On the Port Configuration page, shown in Figure 1-7, review the configuration for the management server and then click Next.

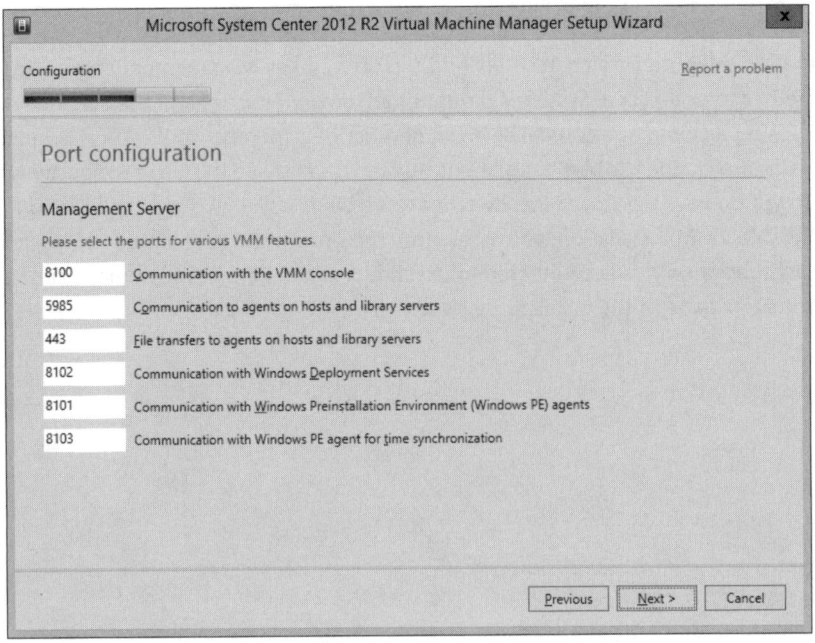

FIGURE 1-7 Port configuration

4. On the Library Configuration page, shown in Figure 1-8, specify the location of the VMM library.

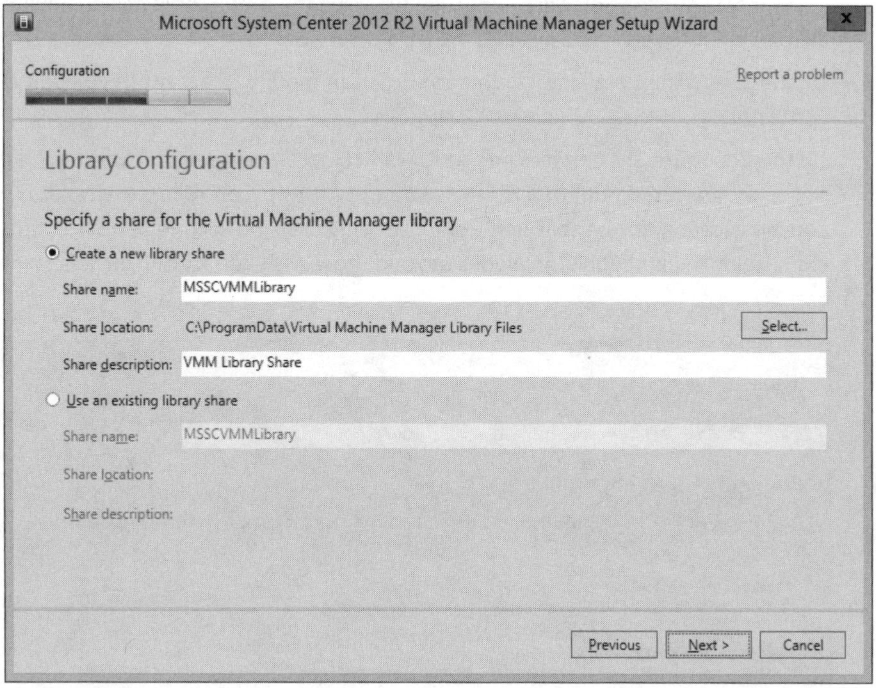

FIGURE 1-8 Library configuration

5. On the Installation Summary page, review the installation settings, and click Install.

6. When the installation completes, open the VMM console to verify that the installation has completed correctly.

> **MORE INFO DEPLOYING VMM**
>
> You can learn more about deploying VMM at *http://technet.microsoft.com/en-US/library/gg610669.aspx*.

App Controller

To install App Controller once you have installed and configured the appropriate prerequisite software, perform the following steps:

1. Mount the App Controller installation media and run Setup.exe.

2. On the App Controller Setup dialog box, click Install.

3. On the Enter Your Product Registration Information page, provide a product key. If you don't provide a product key, App Controller will install as an evaluation version.

4. You must agree to the license terms on the Review The Software License Terms page before you can continue the installation.

5. In the Install Missing Software page, you will have the option of installing any missing IIS role and role services, as well as WCF Data Services 5.0.

6. On the Select The Installation Path page, you can modify or accept the default installation path.

7. On the Configure The Services page, shown in Figure 1-9, select between using the Network Service Account or a Domain Account for App Controller services. If using a domain account, ensure that App Controller only uses the account. This account does not require any additional privileges beyond those assigned by default to a standard user account.

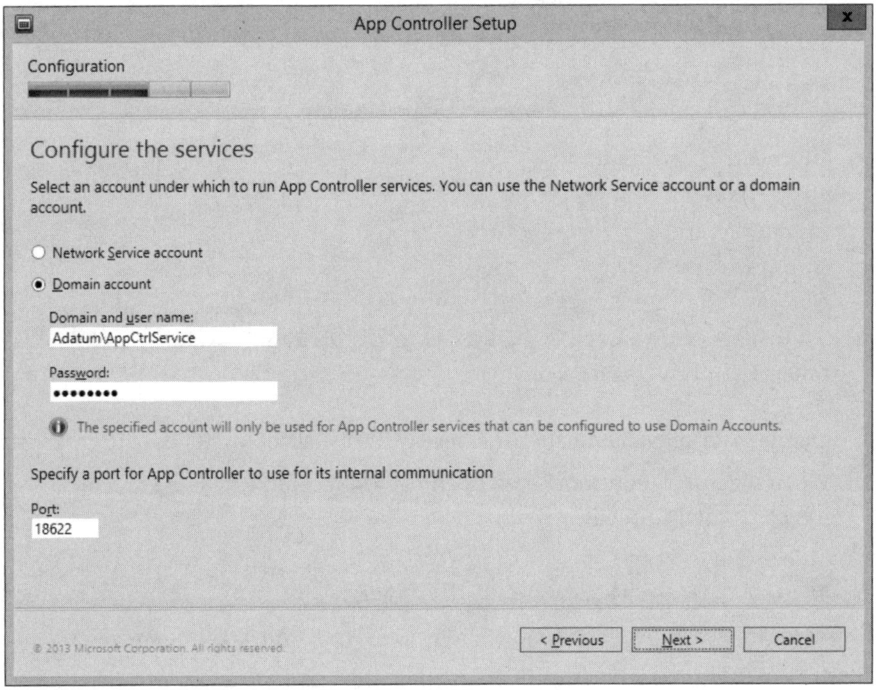

FIGURE 1-9 Service account setup

8. On the Configure The Website page, select an existing SSL certificate that has been installed on the web server, or choose to have the computer generate a self-signed certificate. You should use a certificate from a trusted CA, either internal or external third party, unless the App Controller server is only being used in a test environment. Figure 1-10 shows this page.

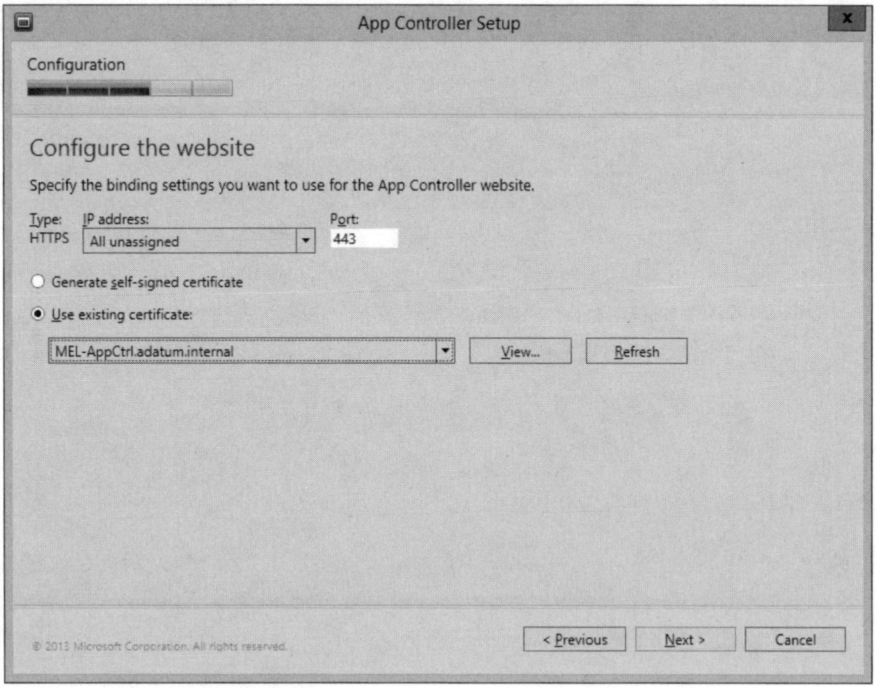

FIGURE 1-10 Website configuration

9. On the Configure The SQL Server Database page, shown in Figure 1-11, specify the details of the SQL instance that will host the App Controller database.

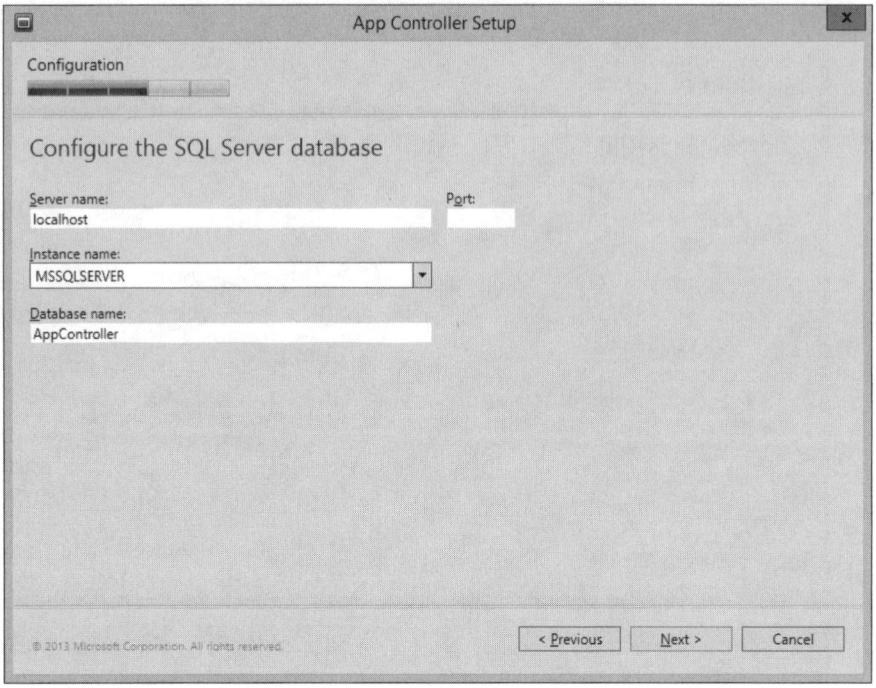

Figure 1-11 Database configuration

10. On the Help Improve App Controller For System Center 2012 R2 page, select whether you want to participate in the CEIP, and whether you want to use Microsoft Update to receive program updates.

11. On the Confirm The Settings page, review the settings, and click Install.

> *MORE INFO* **INSTALL APP CONTROLLER**
>
> You can learn more about installing App Controller at *http://technet.microsoft.com/en-us/library/gg696046.aspx*.

Orchestrator

Once you have deployed the necessary prerequisites, you can deploy Orchestrator by performing the following steps:

1. Mount the installation media, or run SetupOrchestrator.exe.

2. On the System Center 2012 R2 Orchestrator Setup dialog box, click Install.

3. On the Product Registration page, enter your product key and your organization name. If you do not enter a product key, Orchestrator will be installed as an evaluation edition.

4. On the License Terms page, accept the license terms to proceed with the installation.

5. On the Select Features To Install page, shown in Figure 1-12, select which features you will install. If no management server is present in the environment, the management server feature will be installed. On a single server deployment, you'd install each of these services. The web service feature is required if you will be configuring cross-product integration features such as the Orchestrator connector for Service Manager. You would also deploy this element if you want to use a web console to manage Orchestrator runbooks.

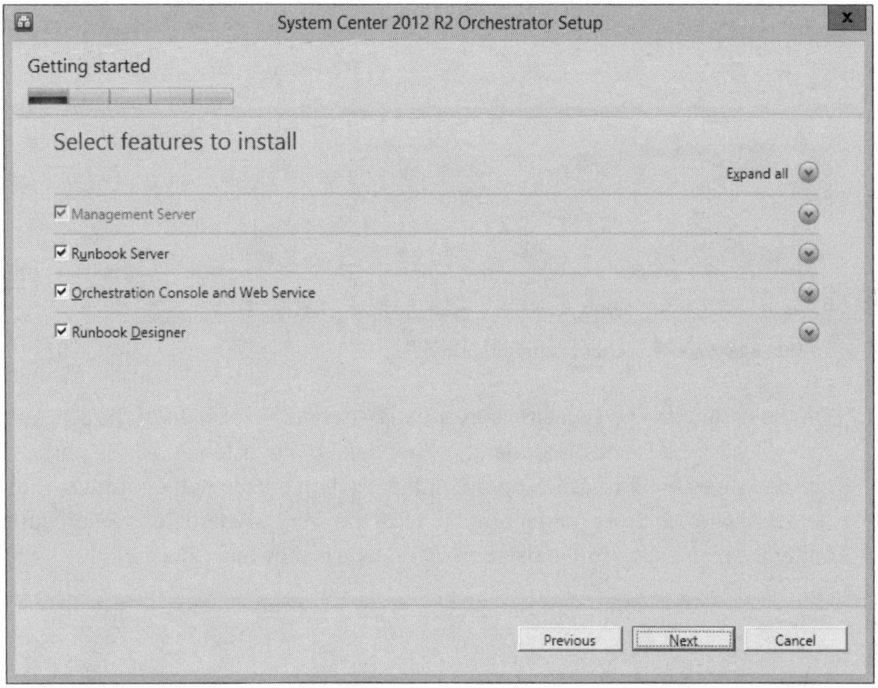

FIGURE 1-12 Feature installation

The setup routine will check for missing prerequisites. At this stage any Windows Server roles or features that haven't been installed will be installed on the server.

6. On the Configure The Service Account page, specify which account will be used by Orchestrator to run runbooks and access remote system resources. This account should not have Domain Admin privileges but should have the "Log On As A Service" right. This right will be granted if not already assigned. Figure 1-13 shows this page. Click Test to verify that the credentials work.

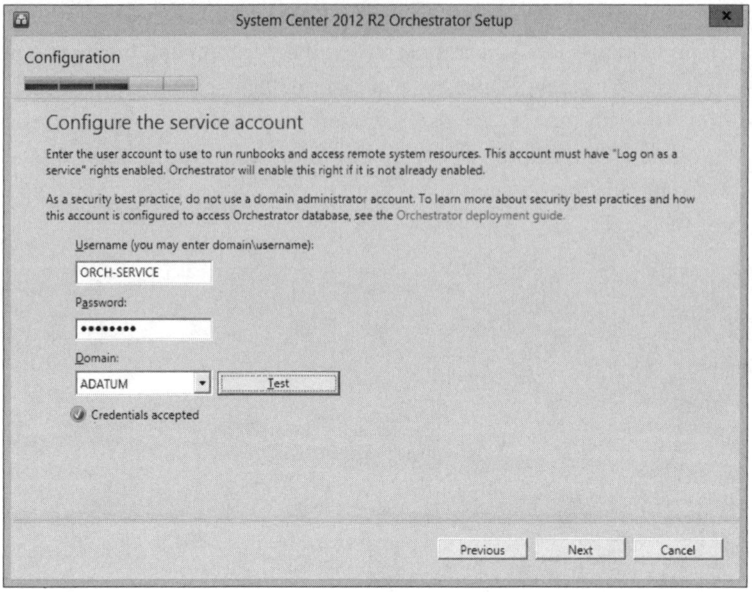

FIGURE 1-13 Service account configuration

7. On the Configure The Database Server page, specify the location of the SQL Instance that will host the Orchestrator database. By default this instance will use port 1433. You can choose whether to use Windows Authentication or SQL Authentication, with the default being Windows Authentication. Click the Test Database Connection button to verify the connection to the database. This page is shown in Figure 1-14.

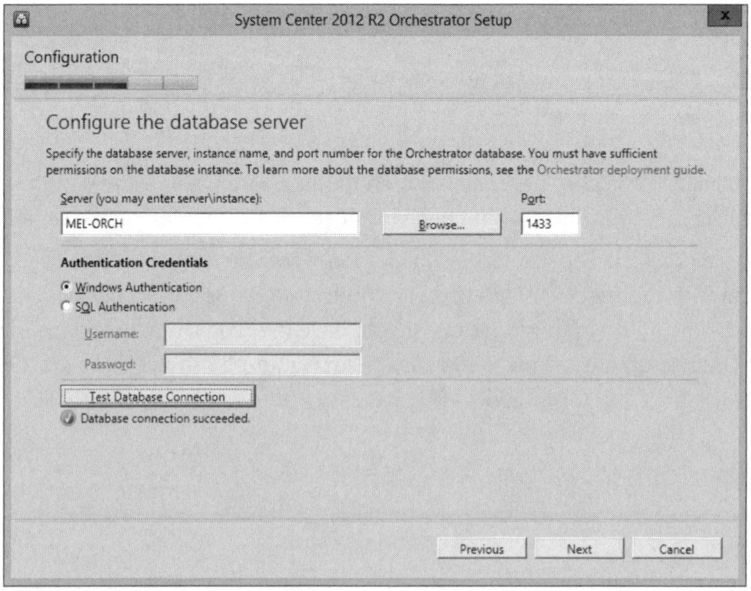

FIGURE 1-14 Database configuration

8. On the Configure The Database page, select to create a new database, or to use an existing database. This page is shown in Figure 1-15.

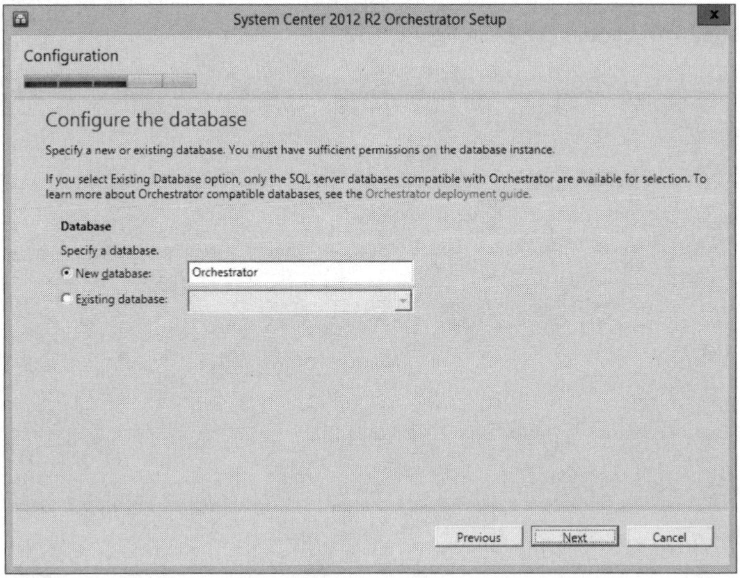

FIGURE 1-15 Orchestrator database

9. On the Configure Orchestrator Users Group page, specify which users will have access to the Runbook Designer and Deployment Manager. Figure 1-16 shows access granted to the ADATUM\OrchestratorUsers group. You also have the option to grant remote access to the Runbook Designer for this group.

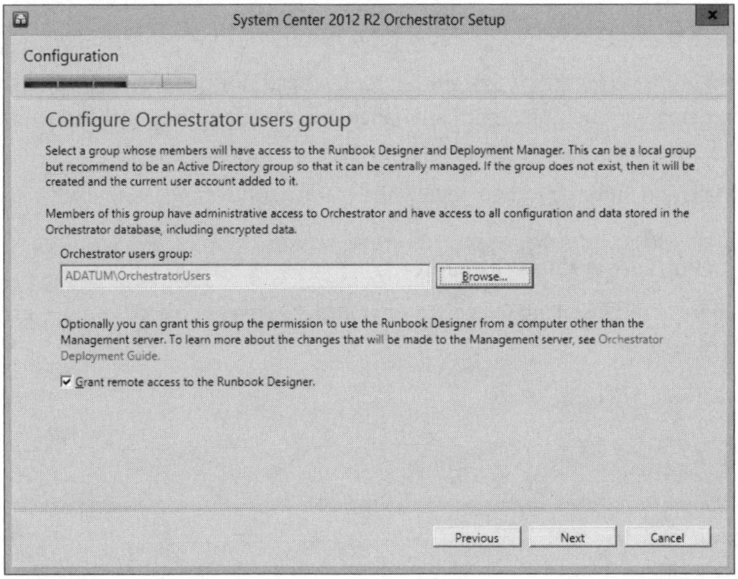

FIGURE 1-16 Orchestrator user group

10. On the Configure The Ports For The Web Services page, review the ports assigned for the web service port and the Orchestration console port. You will need to use port information when configuring connectors, such as the Orchestrator connector for Service Manager. This page is shown in Figure 1-17.

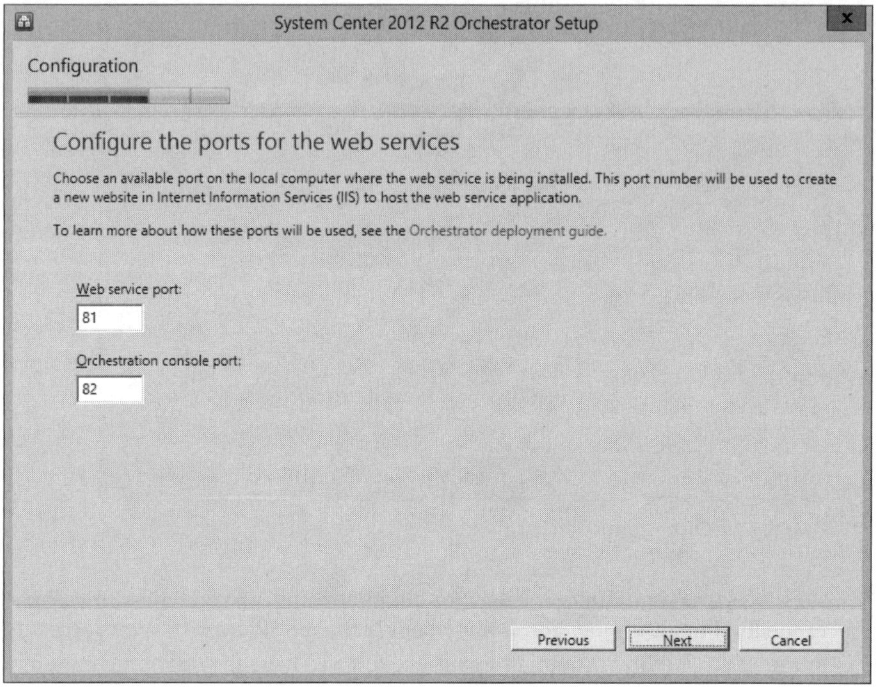

FIGURE 1-17 Orchestrator ports

11. On the Select The Installation page, review the location for the program files.

12. On the Help Improve Microsoft System Center Orchestrator page, select whether you want to participate in the Customer Experience Improvement Program and whether you want to send error data to Microsoft.

13. On the Installation Summary page, review the installation settings, and click Install.

> **MORE INFO**   **INSTALLING ORCHESTRATOR**
>
> You can learn more about installing Orchestrator at *http://technet.microsoft.com/en-us/library/hh420336.aspx*.

Operations Manager

To install Operations Manager, ensure that you have deployed the necessary software prerequisites installed, and then perform the following steps:

1. Mount the Operations Manager installation media, or run Setup.exe.

2. In the Operations Manager Installation dialog box, click Install.

3. On the Select Features To Install page, shown in Figure 1-18, select the features that you want to install.

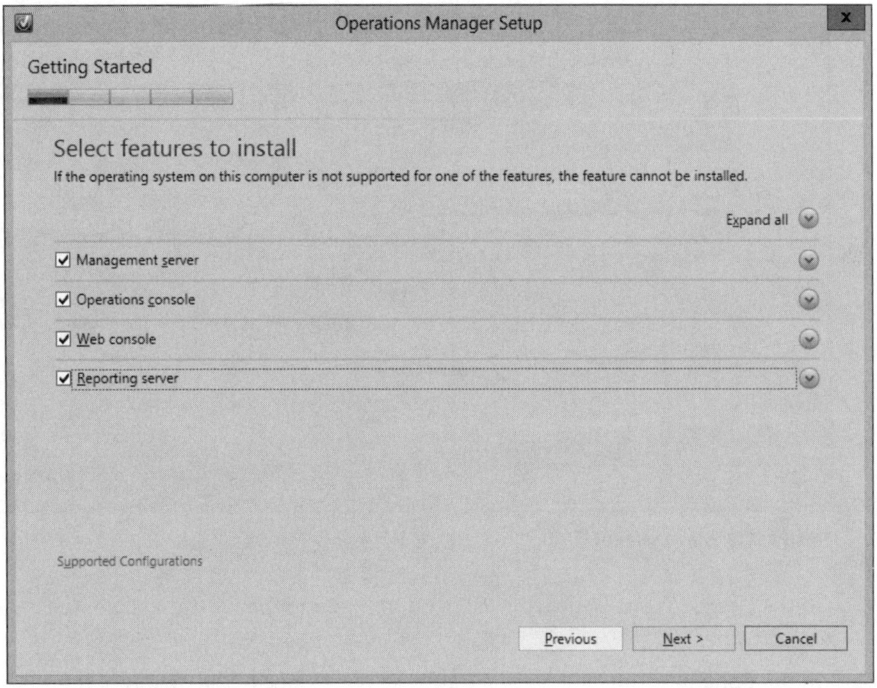

FIGURE 1-18 Feature selection

4. On the Select Installation Location page, review the installation location, and specify an alternative if appropriate.

5. On the Prerequisites page, verify that all necessary prerequisites are installed, and click Next.

6. On the Specify An Installation page, you can choose to create a new Operations Manager Management Group, or to add the management server to an existing Management Group. Figure 1-19 shows the creation of the Melbourne Management Group.

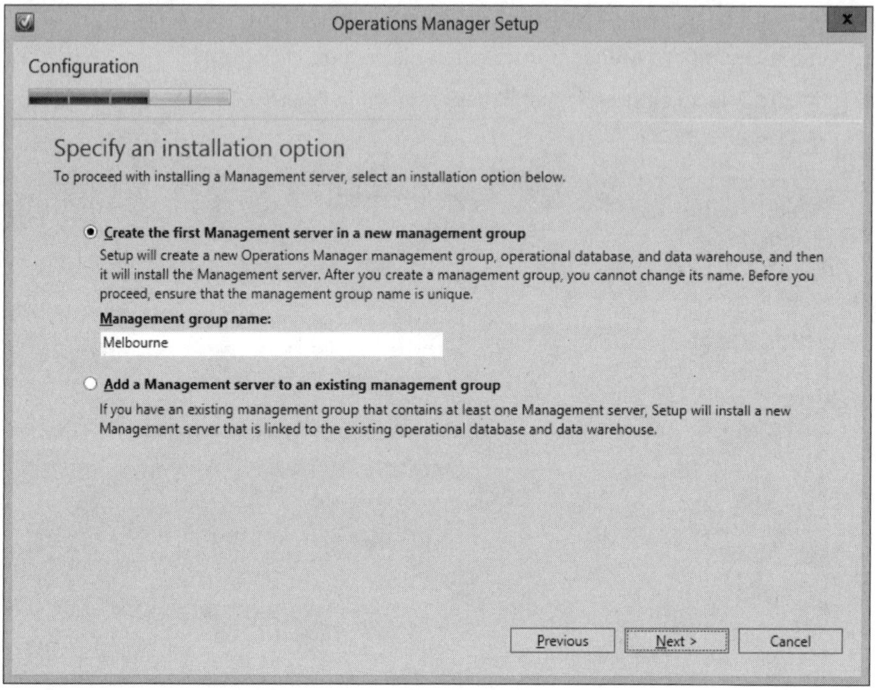

FIGURE 1-19 Management Group

7. On the License Terms page, you will need to agree to the license to continue installing the software.

8. On the Configure The Operational Database page, specify the details of the SQL Instance that will host the database. Figure 1-20 shows the database will be hosted on the server MEL-OPSMGR. The default name for the database is OperationsManager. You can also configure the database file and log file location in this dialog box.

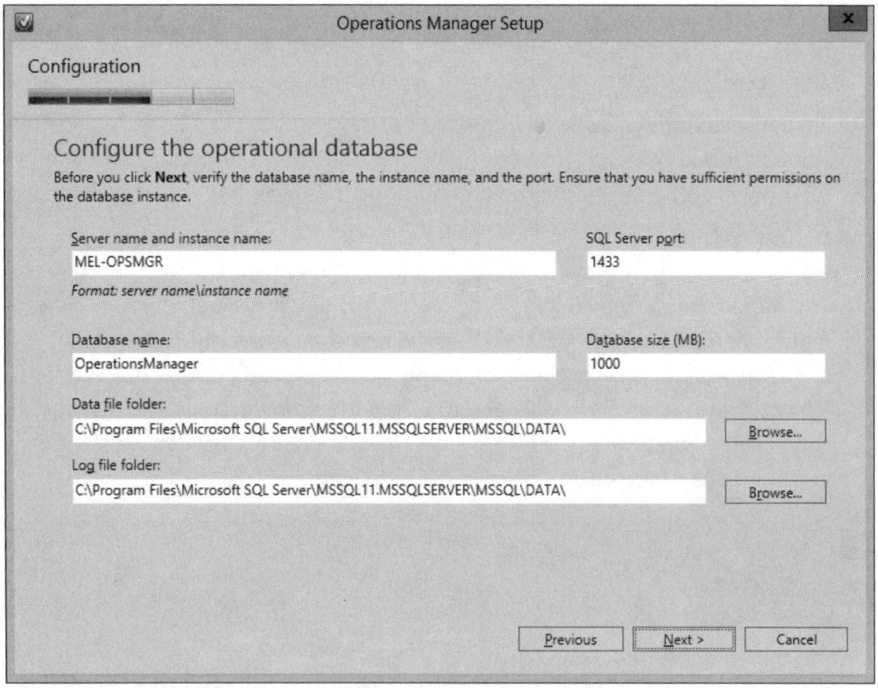

FIGURE 1-20 Operational database

9. On the Configure The Data Warehouse Database page, you specify the details of the data warehouse database. This can be co-located on the same instance as the Operations Manager database, but with larger deployments, for performance reasons, should be located on a separate computer. The default database name is Operations-ManagerDW.

10. On the SQL Server Instance For Reporting Service page, select the SQL instance with Reporting Services installed that will function as the reporting server for Operations Manager. The SQL Server Agent must be running on the instance that hosts Reporting Services.

11. On the Specify A Web Site For Use With The Web Console page, specify which website to use for the web console. The default is the default IIS website. You can select an alternative website. If an SSL certificate is installed, you can choose to enable SSL.

12. On the Select An Authentication Mode For Use With The Web Console page, select whether to use Mixed or Network Authentication. Mixed Authentication is appropriate for intranet scenarios. Network Authentication is appropriate for users accessing the web console from an external location.

13. On the Configure Operations Manager Accounts page, specify the service accounts. You should use low-privileged domain accounts that are a member of the local Performance Monitor Users group and has the Allow Log On Locally Permission. If you want to enable Agentless Exception Monitoring, you'll need an account that has local Administrator privileges. You will need to assign the action account the Manage Auditing and Security Log privilege if management packs require access to the security event log. This page of the setup wizard is shown in Figure 1-21.

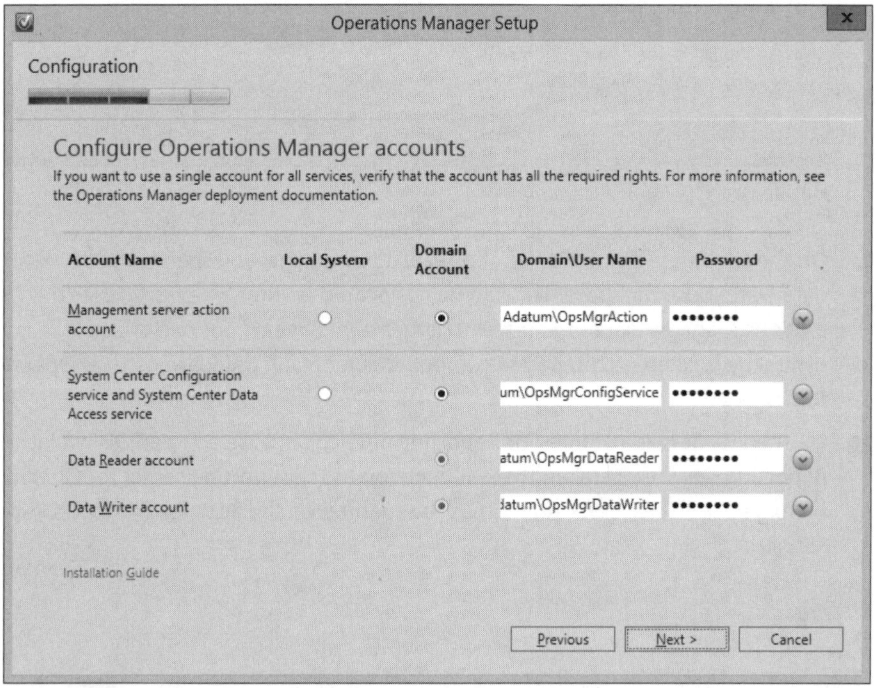

FIGURE 1-21 Service Account configuration

14. On the Help Improve Operations Manager page, select whether you want to participate in the Customer Experience Improvement Program, Error Reporting, and Operational Data Reporting programs.

15. On the Microsoft Update page, select whether you want to use Microsoft Update to check for updates.

16. On the Installation Summary page, review the installation settings, and click Install.

> **MORE INFO** **INSTALLING OPERATIONS MANAGER**
>
> You can learn more about installing Operations Manager at *http://technet.microsoft.com/ en-us/library/hh457006.aspx.*

Service Manager

There are three main elements to a Service Manager deployment. These are: the Service Manager management server, Service Manager data warehouse, and Service Manager Self-Service Portal.

SERVICE MANAGER MANAGEMENT SERVER

To install the Service Manager management server, ensure that you have deployed the necessary software prerequisites and then perform the following steps:

1. Mount the Service Manager installation media, and run Setup.exe from the AMD64 folder.

2. In the Microsoft System Center 2012 R2 Service Manager dialog box, shown in Figure 1-22, click Service Manager Management Server, under Install.

FIGURE 1-22 Service Manager setup

3. On the Product Registration page, enter your name, organization, product key, and agree to the license terms.

4. On the Installation Location page, verify the program files location, and click Next.

5. On the Prerequisites page, verify that the computer meets the prerequisite requirements.

6. On the Configure The Service Manager Database page, specify the details of the SQL instance that will host the database. The default database name is ServiceManager. Figure 1-23 shows this page.

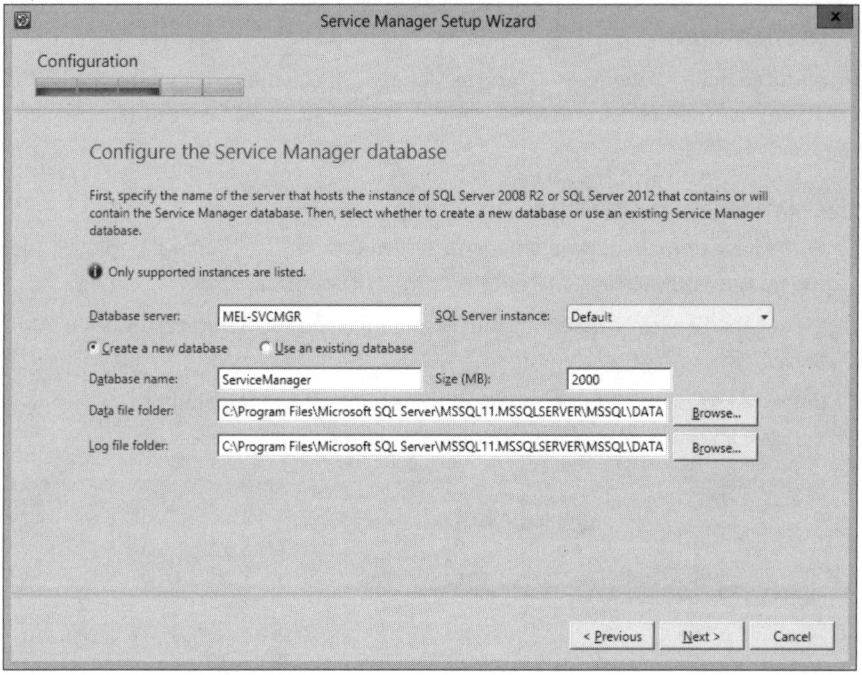

FIGURE 1-23 Database setup

7. On the Configure The Service Manager Management Group page, specify a name for the Management Group. Also specify a security group for Management Group administrators. You should create a domain security group for this purpose and not use an existing security group, such as the Domain Admins group. Figure 1-24 shows this page where the Management Group Name is set to Melbourne and the Management Group Administrators is set to Service_Manager_Admins.

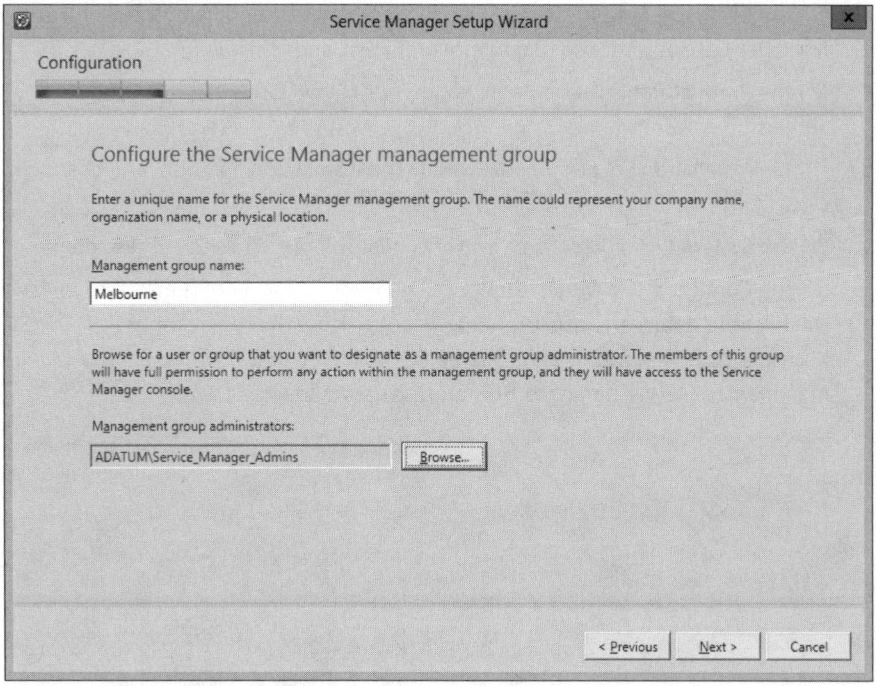

FIGURE 1-24 Management Group name

8. On the Configure The Account For Service Manager services, choose to use the Local System account, or a domain account that has local Admin privileges on the Service Manager server.

9. On the Configure The Service Manager Workflow page, choose to either use the Local System account, or a domain account that is a member of the local Users security group on the server.

10. On the Help Improve Microsoft System Center 2012 R2 Service Manager page, choose whether to participate in the CEIP.

11. On the Use Microsoft Update To Help Keep Your Computer Secure And Up-To-Date page, select whether or not you wish the server to use Microsoft Update to retrieve updates.

12. Review the installation summary, and click Install.

SERVICE MANAGER DATA WAREHOUSE

To install the Service Manager data warehouse server, ensure that you have deployed the necessary software prerequisites, and then perform the following steps:

1. Mount the Service Manager installation media. In the AMD64 folder, run Setup.exe.

2. On the Microsoft System Center 2012 R2 Service Manager dialog box, click Service Manager Data Warehouse Management Server, under install.

3. On the Product Registration page, enter your Name, Organization, Product Key, and agree to the license terms.

4. On the Installation Location page, review the installation location, and change if necessary.

5. On the System Check Results page, verify that the prerequisite checks complete.

6. On the Configure The Data Warehouse Databases page, configure which instance will host the data warehouse. It is important to note that you cannot host the Service Manager data warehouse on the same SQL instance that host the Service Manager management server database. This page is shown in Figure 1-25.

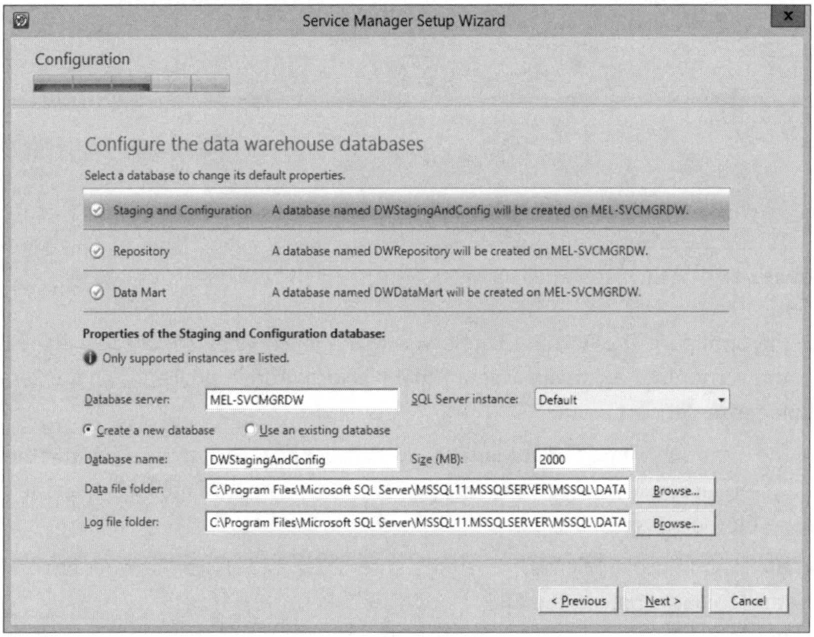

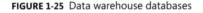

FIGURE 1-25 Data warehouse databases

7. On the Configure Additional Data Warehouse Datamarts page, configure which instance will host data warehouse datamart databases. Datamart databases can be co-located with the data warehouse database.

8. On the Configure The Data Warehouse Management Group page, specify the data warehouse Management Group name, and specify which security group will be delegated the Management Group administrator permission. Figure 1-26 shows this page

where the Management Group name is set to DW_Melbourne, and the Management Group administrators is set to ADATUM\Service_Manager_Admins.

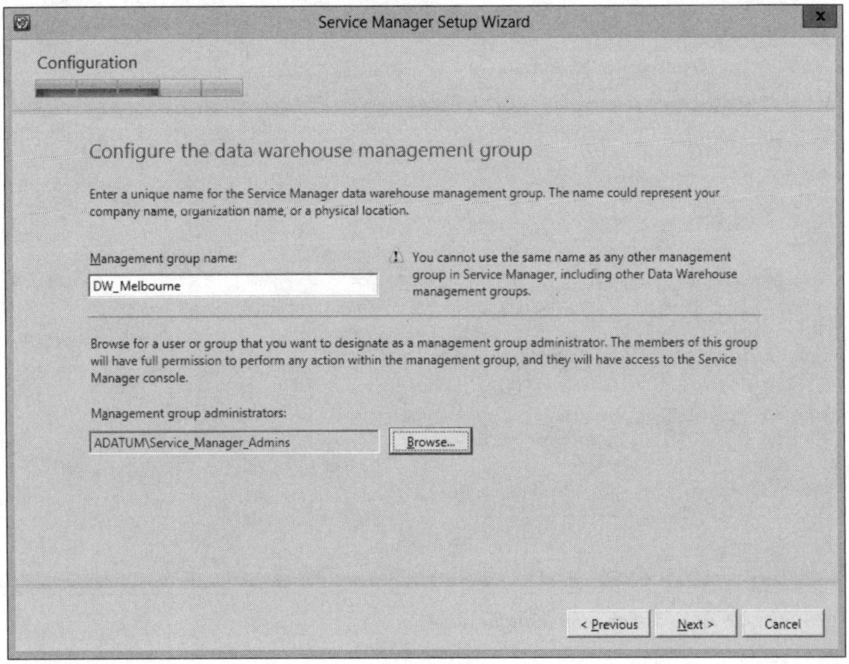

FIGURE 1-26 Data Warehouse Management Group

9. On the Configure The Reporting Server For The Data Warehouse page, verify the configuration of the SQL Server Reporting Services instance that will be used by the data warehouse.

10. On the Configure The Account For Service Manager services, you can choose to use the Local System account, or a domain account that is a member of the local Administrators group on the server hosting the data warehouse. If using a domain account, this account can be the same account as the one used for the Service Manager service on the Service Manager management server.

11. On the Configure The Reporting account, specify the account that will be used to read data warehouse reporting data sources, and be used to generate reports. This should be an unprivileged domain account.

12. On the Configure Analysis Services For OLAP Cubes, specify an Analysis Services instance. Figure 1-27 shows this page.

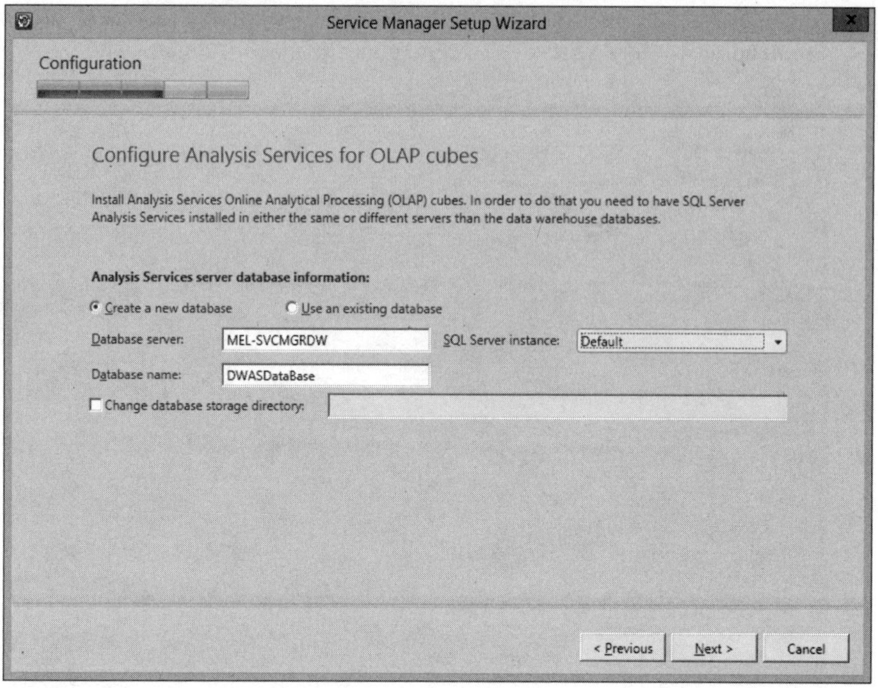

FIGURE 1-27 Analysis Services configuration

13. On the Configure Analysis Services credential page, specify the credentials on a non-privileged domain account that can be used to communicate with the datamarts.

14. On the Help Improve Microsoft System Center 2012 R2 Service Manager page, specify whether you want to participate in the CEIP program.

15. On the Use Microsoft Update To Help Keep Your Computer Secure And Up-To-Date page, select whether you want to use Microsoft Update as the source of updates for the server.

16. On the Installation Summary page, review the installation settings, and click Install to begin the installation.

Once the installation has completed, you can connect the Service Manager management server to the data warehouse by performing the following steps:

1. Open the Service Manager console using the credentials of a user that has administrative privileges on the data warehouse management server.

2. In the Administration workspace of the Service Manager console, click Register With Service Manager Data Warehouse.

3. On the Data Warehouse page of the Data Warehouse Registration Wizard, enter the name of the data warehouse server, and click Test Connection.

4. On the Credentials page, select or create a Run As account that has credentials to connect to the data warehouse server.

5. On the Summary page, click Create, to create the connection. Verify that data warehouse registration has been successful as shown in Figure 1-28.

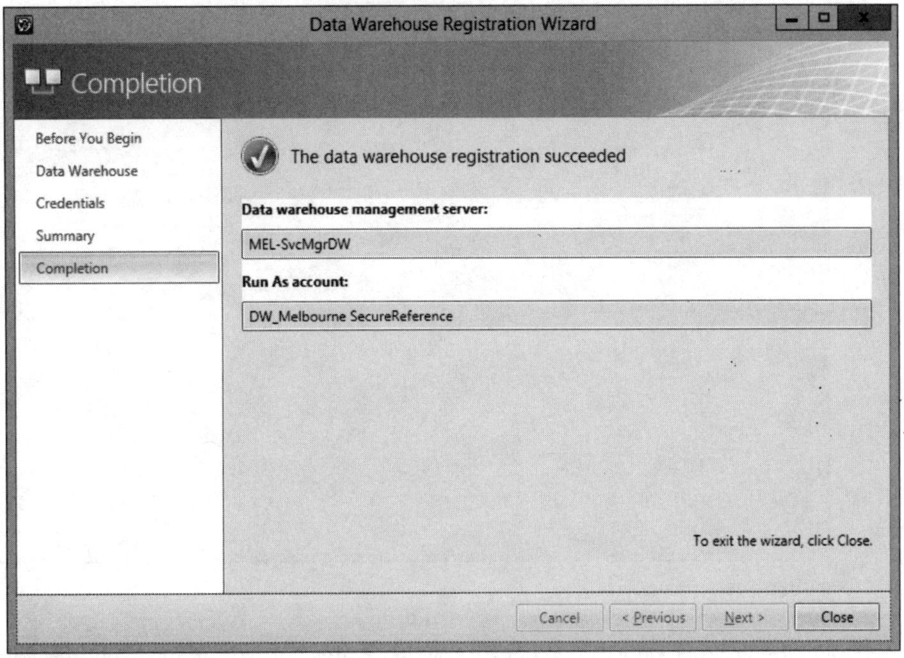

FIGURE 1-28 Data warehouse registration

SERVICE MANAGER SELF-SERVICE PORTAL

To install the Service Manager Self-Service Portal, ensure that you have deployed the necessary software prerequisites, including SQL Server and SharePoint 2010 SP2, and then by performing the following steps:

1. Mount the Service Manager installation media. In the AMD64 folder, run Setup.exe.

2. On the Service Manager Setup Wizard dialog box, click Service Manager Web Portal under Install (Optional).

3. On the Portal Parts page, select Web Content Server, and SharePoint Web Parts, as shown in Figure 1-29.

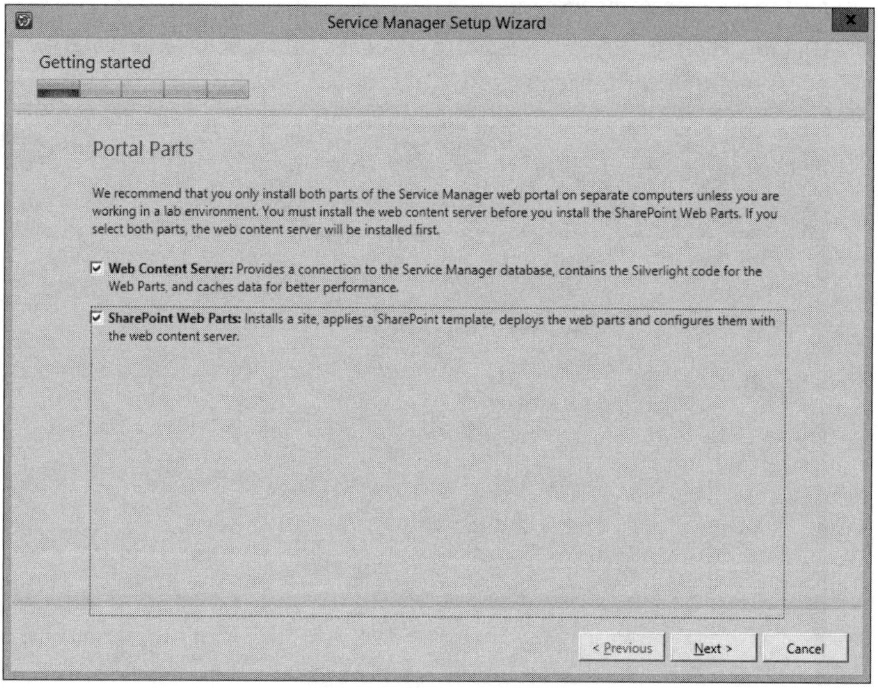

FIGURE 1-29 Portal parts

4. On the Product Registration page, provide a Name, Organization Name, and agree to the license terms.

5. On the Installation Location page, review the installation location. This will be the website that will host the portal. Figure 1-30 shows this page.

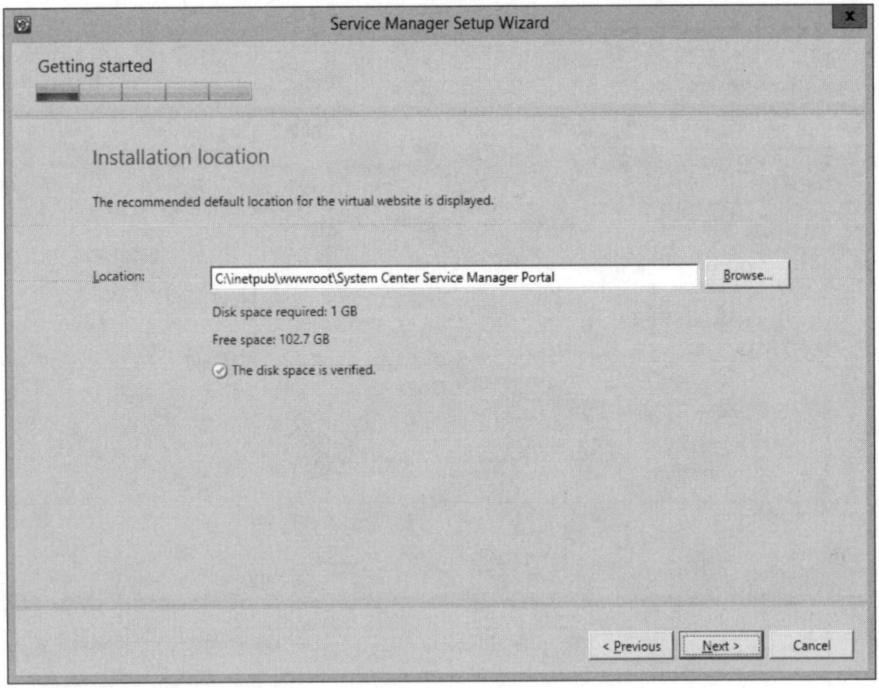

Service Manager Setup Wizard

Getting started

Installation location

The recommended default location for the virtual website is displayed.

Location: C:\inetpub\wwwroot\System Center Service Manager Portal   Browse...

Disk space required: 1 GB

Free space: 102.7 GB

✓ The disk space is verified.

< Previous   Next >   Cancel

FIGURE 1-30 Installation location

6. On the System Check Results page, review the prerequisite check.

7. On the Configure The Service Manager Self-Service Portal name and port, select whether to use SSL, and configure the website name.

8. On the Select The Service Manager Database page, specify the location of the Service Manager database. To connect to this database, you'll need to be signed on as a member of the Administrators user role on the Service Manager management server.

9. On the Configure The Account For The Self-Service Portal page, specify the account that will be used to connect to the Service Manager database. This account will be added to the Service Manager Administrators user role.

10. On the Configure The Service Manager SharePoint Web Site page, configure the properties of the Service Manager SharePoint website, including whether SSL encryption will be used. Figure 1-31 shows this page.

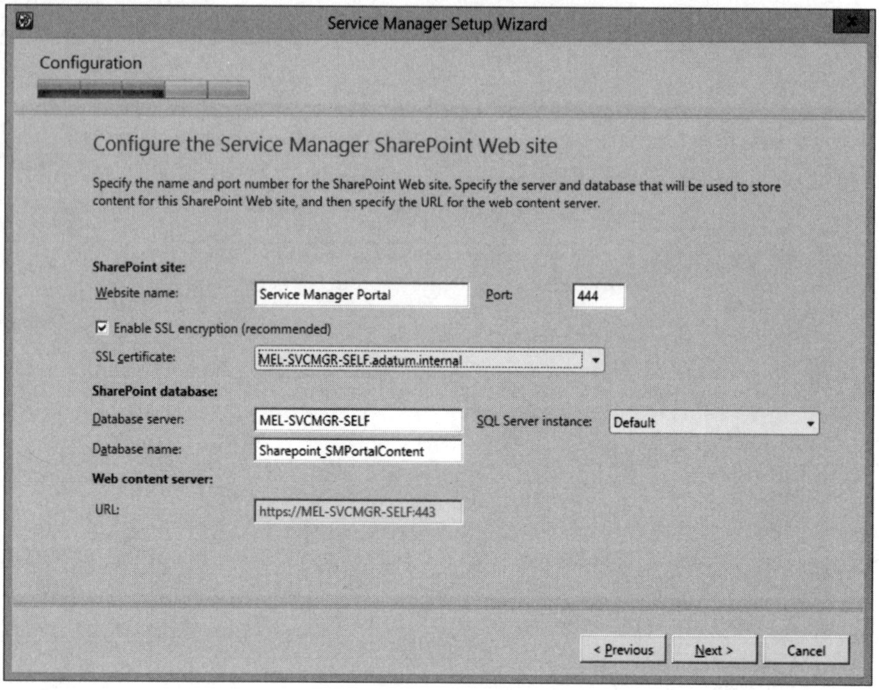

FIGURE 1-31 Service Manager SharePoint Web site

11. On the Configure The Account For The Service Manager SharePoint application pool, specify a domain account that will be used to run the application pool. This account does not require special credentials or group membership.

12. On the Help Improve Microsoft System Center 2012 R2 Service Manager page, choose whether to participate in the CEIP program.

13. On the Use Microsoft Update To Help Keep Your Computer Secure And Up-To-Date page, choose whether to use Microsoft Update to provide updates to the server.

14. On the Installation Summary page, click Install to complete the installation.

MORE INFO **INSTALLING SERVICE MANAGER**

You can learn more about installing Service Manager at *http://technet.microsoft.com/en-us/library/hh495575.aspx.*

Data Protection Manager

To install DPM, ensure that you have deployed the necessary software prerequisites and then perform the following steps:

1. Mount the DPM installation media, or run Setup.exe from the \SCDPM folder.
2. On the Data Protection Manager screen, shown in Figure 1-32, click Data Protection Manager, under Install.

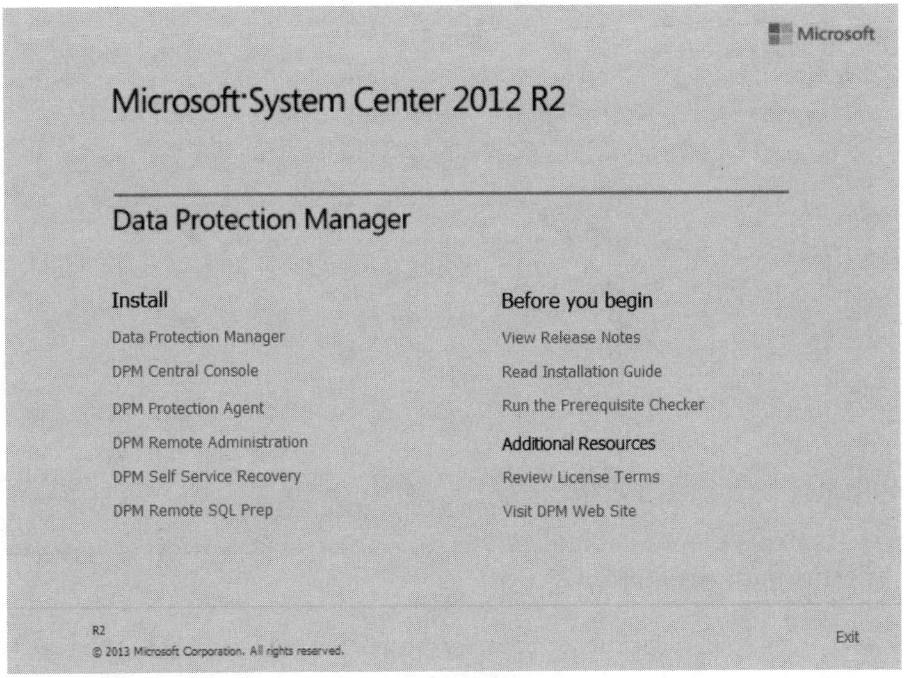

FIGURE 1-32 Data Protection Manager installation dialog box

3. On the Microsoft Software License Terms page, accept the license terms to continue the installation.
4. On the Welcome page of the Data Protection Manager Setup Wizard, click Next.
5. On the Prerequisites Check page, specify the details of the SQL Server instance that will support DPM. Figure 1-33 shows this set to MEL-DPM. Click Check, and install to perform the prerequisite check, and to install any missing elements. If elements are missing, it may be necessary to restart the computer after the missing elements are installed and to rerun the installation wizard.

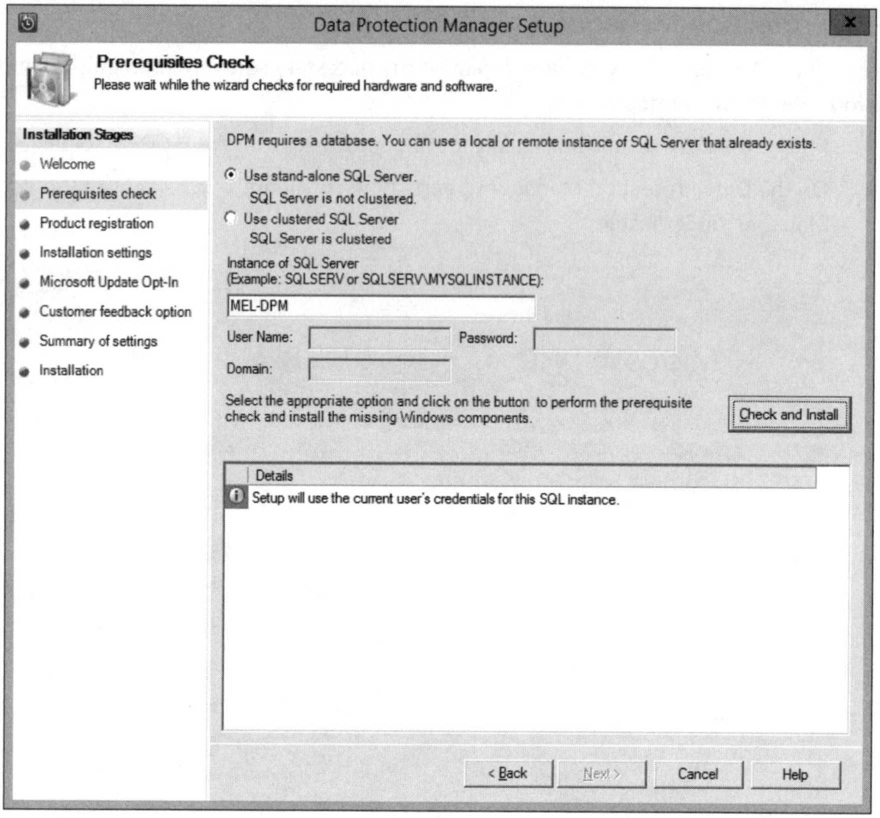

FIGURE 1-33 Prerequisites check

6. On the Product Registration page, specify the User Name, Company Name, and Product Key.

7. On the Installation Settings page, review the location specified for the DPM program files.

8. On the Microsoft Update Opt-In page, choose whether or not to use Microsoft Update to check for updates.

9. On the Customer Experience Improvement Program page, select whether you want to participate in the Customer Experience Improvement Program.

10. On the Summary Of Settings page, review the installation settings, and click Install to deploy DPM.

> **MORE INFO** **INSTALLING DATA PROTECTION MANAGER**
>
> You can learn more about installing Data Protection Manager at *http://technet.microsoft.com/en-us/library/hh758153.aspx.*

Configuration Manager

To install a Configuration Manager stand alone primary site, ensure that you have deployed the necessary software prerequisites installed, and then perform the following steps:

1. Mount the Configuration Manager installation media.

2. On the System Center 2012 R2 Configuration Manager Setup dialog box, click Install.

3. On the Before You Begin page, click Next.

4. On the Available Setup Options page, shown in Figure 1-34, select Install A Configuration Manager Primary Site. A primary site is appropriate for the majority of private cloud deployments. You would consider deploying a central administration site and multiple primary site if you needed to support more than 50,000 clients, or had multiple separate administration teams in a large national/regional or international deployment.

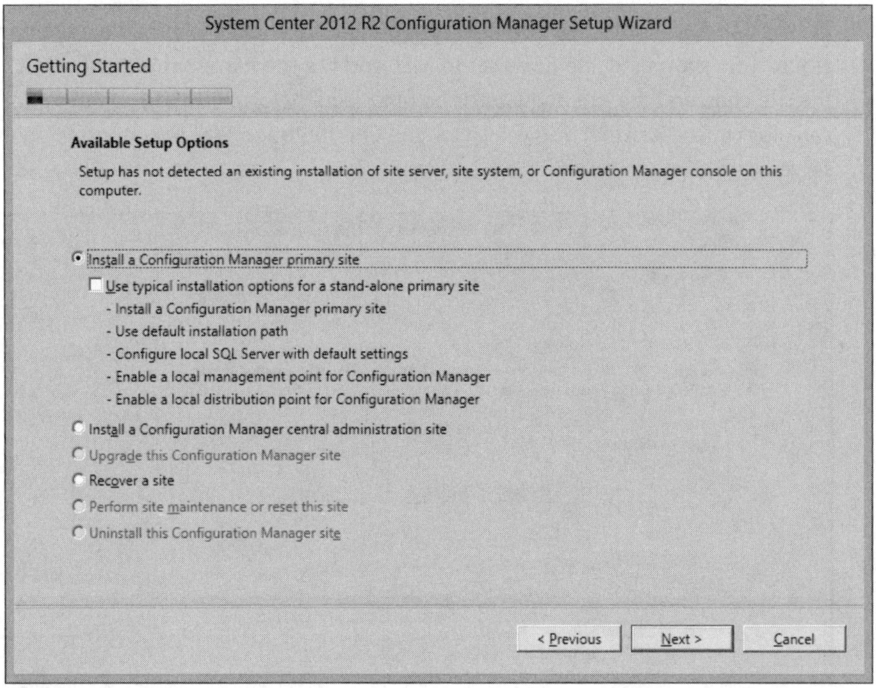

FIGURE 1-34 Available setup options

5. On the Product Key page, enter a product key, or choose to install the evaluation version of the product.

6. On the Microsoft Software License Terms page, you will need to accept the license terms to continue the installation process.

7. On the Prerequisite Licenses page, you will need to accept each of the prerequisite licenses to continue the installation process.

8. On the Prerequisite Downloads page, you can choose to download prerequisite files, or, if you've used the Prerequisite Download Tool, use the previously downloaded files, as shown in Figure 1-35.

9. On the Language Selection page, choose the languages that Configuration Manager will display in the console and in reports.

10. On the Client Language Selection page, choose the client languages that Configuration Manager will support.

11. On the Site And Installation settings, configure a site code, and provide a site name. Figure 1-36 shows the Site Code set to MEL and the site name set to Melbourne. Both the site code and the site name must be unique in the organization. On this page you can also choose whether you will install the Configuration Manager console on this server.

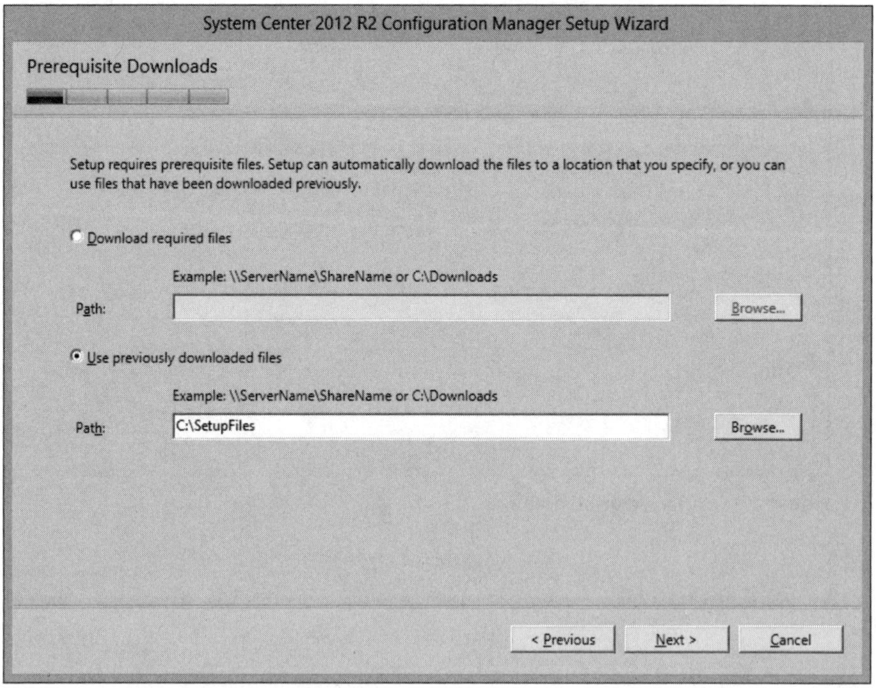

FIGURE 1-35 Use previously downloaded files

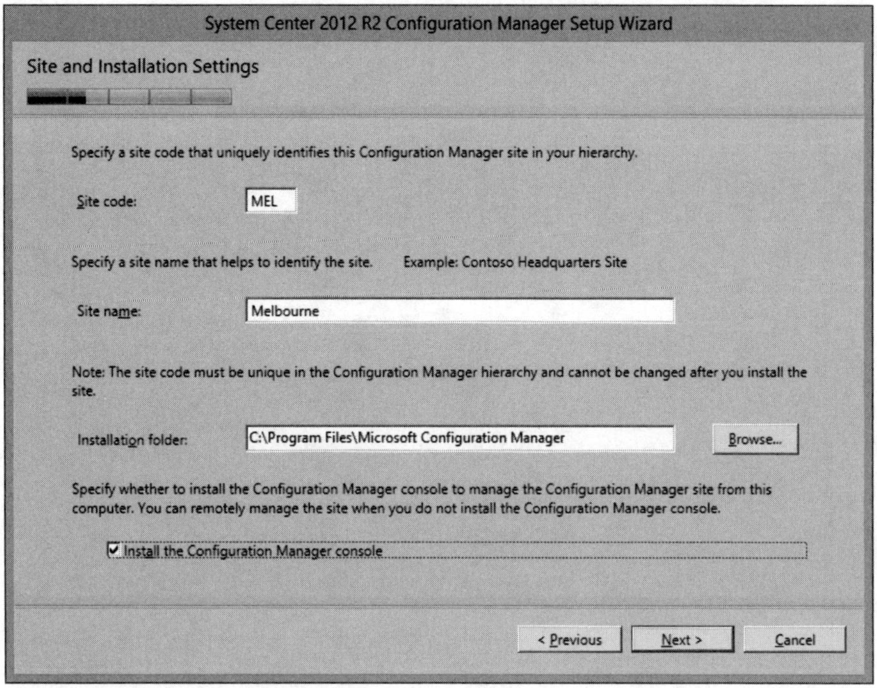

FIGURE 1-36 Site code and site name

12. On the Primary Site Installation page, you choose whether you want to join the site to an existing hierarchy, in which case you specify the address of the central administration site server, or if you are going to install the primary site as a stand alone site. With System Center 2012 R2 Configuration Manager, you can install a primary site as stand alone, and then later add a central administration site if it becomes necessary to add additional sites. Figure 1-37 shows this page.

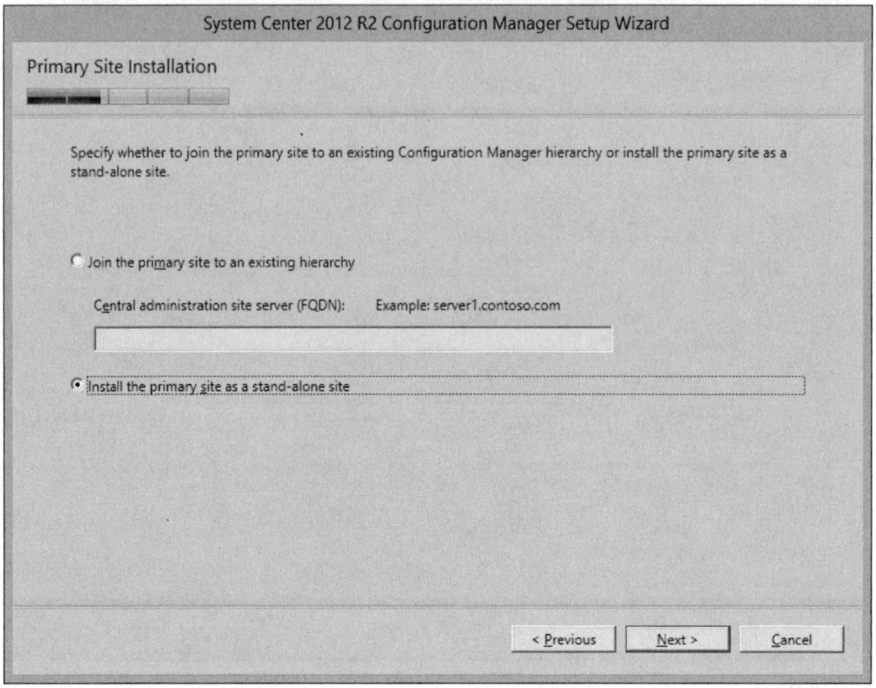

FIGURE 1-37 Primary site installation

13. On the Database Information page, shown in Figure 1-38, specify the settings of the SQL Server instance information. The database will be named CM_xxx, where xxx is the site code of the primary site.

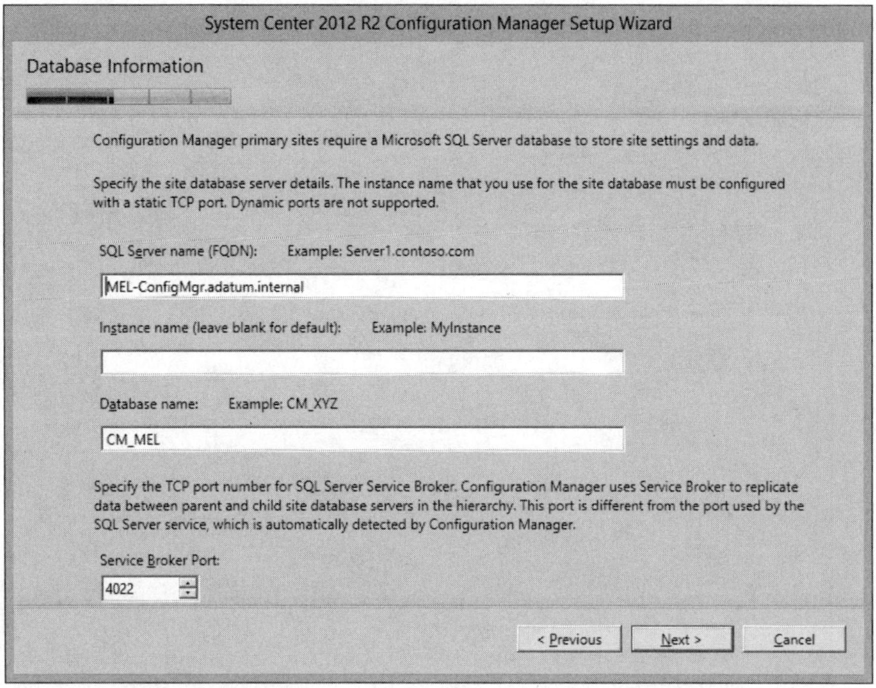

FIGURE 1-38 Database information

14. On the Database Information page, specify the location of the Configuration Manager database's database and log files.

15. On the SMS Provider Settings page, specify the details of which server will host the SMS Provider. The SMS Provider facilitates communication between the Configuration Manager console and the Configuration Manager site database. Generally the SMS Provider is installed on the site server. Figure 1-39 shows this page.

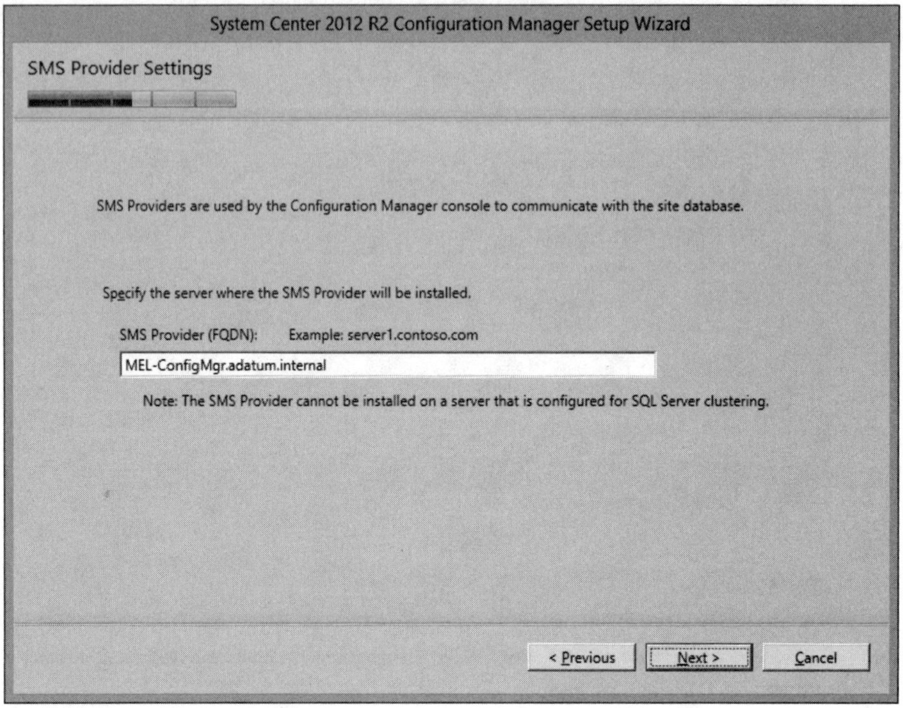

FIGURE 1-39 SMS Provider Settings

16. On the Client Computer Communication Settings page, select whether all site system roles will only accept HTTPS communication from clients, or whether you will configure the communication method on a per-role basis. If choosing to require HTTPS communication from clients, you will need to ensure that clients trust the Certification Authority that issued the certificate. If choosing to configure communication for each site system role, you can also select the option for clients to use HTTPS when available and to fall back to insecure application when a certificate is not available.

17. On the Site System Roles page, specify whether to install a management point and a distribution point. If deploying a single Configuration Manager server, you would add these roles. If deploying multiple servers, you might host these roles on separate servers. This page is shown in Figure 1-40.

System Center 2012 R2 Configuration Manager Setup Wizard

Site System Roles

Specify whether to have Setup install a management point or distribution point.

A management point provides clients with policy and content location information. It also receives configuration data from clients.

☑ Install a management point.

FQDN:

MEL-ConfigMgr.adatum.internal

Client connection:

HTTP

A distribution point contains source files for clients to download and lets you control content distribution by using bandwidth, throttling, and scheduling controls.

☑ Install a distribution point.

FQDN:

MEL-ConfigMgr.adatum.internal

Client connection:

HTTP

The site server's computer account is used to install the selected site system roles. Ensure that this account is a member of the local administrators group for the specified servers.

You can install additional site system roles from the Configuration Manager console after Setup finishes.

Site system roles configured to use HTTPS must have a valid PKI server certificate.

< Previous   Next >   Cancel

FIGURE 1-40 Site System Roles

18. On the Customer Experience Improvement Program page, choose whether to join the Customer Experience Improvement Program.

19. Review the installation settings. Configuration Manager will perform the prerequisite check to verify that all necessary prerequisite elements are installed. As long as the prerequisite check only shows Warnings, you will be able to begin the installation.

After you complete the installation, you may choose to extend the Active Directory schema so that Configuration Manager clients that are members of the Configuration Manager server's Active Directory environment can query Active Directory to locate site servers.

MORE INFO **INSTALLING CONFIGURATION MANAGER**

You can learn more about installing Configuration Manager at *http://technet.microsoft. com/en-us/library/gg712320.aspx.*

EXAM TIP

Remember which products have the Windows ADK as a prerequisite.

> ### Thought experiment
> #### Planning Service Manager deployment at Fabrikam
>
> In this thought experiment, apply what you've learned about this objective. You can find answers to these questions in the "Answers" section at the end of this chapter.
>
> You are in the process of planning a service manager deployment at Fabrikam. You are in the planning the number of SQL Server instances necessary to support the deployment. You also want to ensure that you have access to any necessary software prerequisites prior to performing deployment. With this information in mind, answer the following questions:
>
> 1. Which software prerequisites for the Service Manager management server are not roles or features already included with Windows Server 2012 R2?
>
> 2. How many SQL instances will you need to support the Service Manager management database and the Service Manager data warehouse database?

Objective summary

- The processor, RAM, and storage requirements for each System Center product, and each element within that product vary. You should avoid using the minimum specified hardware required in production environments.

- Each System Center product has a unique set of software requirements. To simplify the deployment process, you should deploy software prerequisites prior to performing installation.

- Some System Center products have multiple elements, which must be installed in a specific order. Some products, such as Service Manager's management server and data warehouse server, cannot be installed on the same host server.

- While it is possible to deploy the databases for different System Center products on the same SQL Server instance, Microsoft recommends this configuration only for test environments.

Objective review

Answer the following questions to test your knowledge of the information in this objective. You can find the answers to these questions and explanations of why each answer choice is correct or incorrect in the "Answers" section at the end of this chapter.

1. You are preparing to deploy App Controller on a computer running Windows Server 2012 R2. Which of the following System Center 2012 R2 consoles must be present on the server before you can deploy App Controller?

   A. Service Manager console

   B. Orchestrator console

   C. Operations Manager console

   D. VMM console

2. You are preparing to deploy VMM. You are in the process of preparing a domain account that will function as the service account for the VMM service. Which of the following local groups on the server that hosts VMM must the account used by the VMM service be a member of?

   A. Administrators

   B. Virtual Machine Manager servers

   C. Hyper-V Administrators

   D. Backup Operators

3. You want to deploy the System Center 2012 R2 Service Manager Self-Service Portal on a computer running Windows Server 2012 R2. Which version of SharePoint server must you deploy to support this configuration?

   A. SharePoint Server 2013 SP1

   B. SharePoint Server 2010 SP1

   C. SharePoint Server 2010 SP2

   D. SharePoint Server 2013 RTM

4. You are planning on deploying System Center 2012 R2 Virtual Machine Manager as a highly available role on a Windows Server 2012 R2 failover cluster. Which of the following configuration choices must you make when deploying this configuration?

   A. Use the Local System account for the VMM Service.

   B. Use a domain account for the VMM Service.

   C. Store the encryption keys in Active Directory.

   D. Deploy the SQL Server instance on a highly available virtual machine.

Objective 1.3: Upgrade System Center components

This objective deals with transitioning from one version of a System Center product to the System Center 2012 R2 version. It provides general detail about how you can transition from one version of a product, such as Virtual Machine Manager 2008 R2, to Virtual Machine Manager 2012 R2. This section also provides links to more detailed documentation that details the more intricate complexities that must be taken into account when transitioning between product versions.

> **This objective covers the following topics:**
>
> - Upgrading or migrating from versions prior to System Center 2012.
> - Upgrading from System Center 2012 or System Center 2012 SP1.

Upgrading or migrating from versions prior to System Center 2012

Depending on the product and the versions involved, you can perform an in-place upgrade, or a migration from a pre-System Center 2012 version of a product, to the System Center 2012 R2 version of that product. In this section you'll learn about transitioning from pre-System Center 2012 versions of products, such as VMM 2008 R2 SP1, or Configuration Manager 2007 SP2. Later in the chapter, you'll learn about upgrading from the System Center 2012 or System Center 2012 SP1 version of a product, to the System Center 2012 R2 version of the product.

VMM

VMM supports performing an in-place upgrade from VMM 2008 R2 SP1, to VMM 2012 R2. In-place upgrades involve performing the upgrade on the existing server. When the upgrade is complete, the server that hosted the previous version of the product now hosts the new version of the product. When you perform an in-place upgrade from VMM 2008 R2 SP1 to VMM 2012 R2, you will retain the configuration and settings of the VMM 2008 R2 SP1 deployment in the new VMM 2012 R2 environment.

You can perform this in-place upgrade as long as the following conditions are met:

- You continue to use Windows Server 2008 R2 as the host operating system. If VMM 2008 R2 SP1 is installed on Windows Server 2008 with SP2, you will need to upgrade the host operating system to Windows Server 2008 R2 before you can upgrade VMM 2008 R2 SP1 to VMM 2012 R2.
- You continue to use SQL Server 2008 R2 SP2 to host the VMM database. VMM 2012 R2 can use SQL Server 2008 R2 SP2 to host the VMM database. If the database used with

VMM 2008 R2 SP1 is running an earlier version of SQL Server, you will need to update to SQL Server 2008 R2 SP2 before upgrading to VMM 2012 R2.

- You will need to ensure that Windows AIK for Windows 7 is installed on the VMM 2008 R2 SP1 server.

- Library servers running Windows Server 2003 must be upgraded to Windows Server 2008 R2, as VMM 2012 R2 does not support library servers running on Windows Server 2003.

You also have the option of performing an upgrade where you install VMM 2012 R2 on a separate computer, and upgrade the database from the VMM 2008 R2 SP1 installation. As an alternative, you can backup the VMM 2008 R2 SP1 database from the original SQL Server instance and restore it on a newly deployed instance of SQL Server. You can then use this restored instance as part of the upgrade process when deploying VMM 2012 R2 on a new computer.

During the upgrade process you will be asked to specify which account to use for the System Center Virtual Machine Manager Service, and whether you want to use distributed key management to store encryption keys within the AD DS database. You can choose to use the Local System account or a domain account. If the VMM 2008 R2 deployment is configured to use a domain account for the VMM service, you must use the same domain account for the VMM 2012 R2 VMM service; otherwise encrypted data will not be preserved. Encrypted data will be preserved if the VMM 2008 R2 service account was configured to use the Local System account, and you choose to use a domain account for the VMM 2012 R2 service only if you choose to use distributed key management.

The VMM 2012 R2 upgrade process includes an automatic rollback function in the event that the upgrade fails. This will return the deployment to VMM 2008 R2.

> **MORE INFO** **UPGRADING VMM**
>
> You can learn more about upgrading VMM at *http://technet.microsoft.com/en-us/library/dn469623.aspx*.

Orchestrator

System Center 2012 Orchestrator was the first version of Orchestrator. Prior to the release of System Center 2012 Orchestrator, the product was known as Opalis. You cannot perform an in-place upgrade from Opalis 6.3 to System Center 2012 R2 Orchestrator. You can perform a migration of Opalis policies to Orchestrator runbooks. To migrate, perform the following general steps:

1. Export the Opalis Integration Server 6.3 policies and global settings.

2. Import the policies on a computer where the Orchestrator Runbook Designer is installed. When prompted for a password, leave the Password option blank.

MORE INFO **MIGRATING FROM OPALIS TO ORCHESTRATOR**

You can learn more about migrating from Opalis to Orchestrator at *http://technet.
microsoft.com/en-us/library/hh420350.aspx.*

Operations Manager

You can perform an in-place upgrading from Operations Manager 2007 R2 CU4 to Operations Manager 2012 R2 as long as all of the servers in the Management Group support Operations Manager 2012 R2.

When performing an in-place upgrade, you must upgrade servers in the Management Group in the following order:

1. Upgrade manually deployed agents, secondary management servers, and gateways, before you upgrade the Management Group.

2. Perform the Management Group upgrade on the Operations Manager 2007 R2 CU4 server that hosts the RMS. The exceptions to this rule include if the RMS is deployed on a 32-bit operating system, or if the RMS server is clustered. In these scenarios it is necessary to upgrade from a secondary server.

Prior to performing the upgrade, perform the following steps:

1. Import the Upgrade Helper Management Pack.

2. Back up the RMS encryption key.

3. Disable Notification Subscriptions.

4. Disable Connectors.

5. Verify that the Operational Database has more than 50 percent free space. Increase free space if needed.

6. Verify that the SQL Server collation is supported.

7. Backup the Operations Manager database.

8. Restore the RMS encryption key on a secondary management server if the RMS cannot be directly upgraded.

9. Upgrade SQL Server Reporting Services if SQL Server 2008 R2, or SQL Server 2008 R2 SP1 is not currently being used for the Reporting Services instance.

Once you have completed the pre-upgrade tasks, perform the following steps:

1. Upgrade all manually deployed Operations Manager agents.

2. Upgrade the secondary management servers.

3. Upgrade the gateway servers.

4. Perform the Management Group upgrade on the server that hosts the Operations Manager 2007 R2 CU4 RMS role.

5. Upgrade push-installed management agents.

Service Manager

You can upgrade from Service Manager 2010 SP1 to System Center 2012 R2 Service Manager. To perform an in-place upgrade, the source server needs to be able to support System Center 2012 R2 Service Manager. Upgrading involves performing the following general steps:

1. Back up the Service Manager management database and the data warehouse database.

2. Determine which data warehouse jobs are running.

3. Disable the data warehouse job schedules.

4. Verify that data warehouse jobs are no longer running.

5. Stop the Self-Service Portal.

6. Upgrade the data warehouse management server by performing an in-place upgrade.

7. Upgrade the Service Manager management server by performing an in-place upgrade.

8. Upgrade the Service Manager console on any computers that host the Service Manager 2012 SP1 console.

Data Protection Manager

You can upgrade from DPM 2010 with QFE4 to System Center 2012 R2 DPM as long as DPM 2010 is deployed on Windows Server 2008 R2 or a 64-bit version of Windows Server 2008. DPM 2012 R2 can be deployed on Windows Server 2008 as long as it is the x64 version. Prior to performing the upgrade, ensure that the following pre-requisites are met:

1. Ensure that at least 4.5 GB is available.

2. Back up the DPM 2010 database.

3. Stop sharing any tape libraries.

4. Upgrade agents on protected computers.

5. Add MicrosoftDPMACCT to the Access Control List (ACL) for the DPMDB folder, assigning the Full Control permission.

Once these steps have been taken, starting the DPM 2012 R2 installation process will trigger the upgrade, as the installation process detects the installation of DPM 2010.

MORE INFO **UPGRADE FROM DPM 2010**

You can learn more about upgrading from DPM 2010 at *http://technet.microsoft.com/ en-us/library/hh848301.aspx.*

Configuration Manager

You cannot perform an in-place upgrade of Configuration Manager 2007 SP2 to Configuration Manager 2012 R2. Instead you must create a new Configuration Manager 2012 R2 hierarchy and migrate objects from the Configuration Manager 2007 SP2 hierarchy to the new hierarchy. Once the migration is complete, you decommission the original hierarchy. When performing a migration, you specify a Configuration Manager 2007 SP2 source hierarchy, choosing a top-level site in that hierarchy as the source site. A migration job can migrate data from one or more source sites. You can only migrate data from Configuration Manager 2007 SP2 primary sites.

To perform the migration:

- The account used to perform the migration must be a member of the Infrastructure Administrator security role in the destination site. This role has the necessary permissions to manage migration operations.

- Configure the Source Site Account. This account needs read permission on all objects in the Configuration Manager 2007 R2 site. To upgrade distribution points, this account needs Read, Execute, and Delete permissions on the Site class on the Configuration Manager 2007 site server.

- Configure the Source Site Database Account. This account is used to query the SQL Server site database of the source site. This account needs Connect, Execute, and Select permissions on the source site database.

- Before migrating software updates, deploy a software update point in the Configuration Manager 2012 R2 hierarchy.

The data gathering process identifies objects in the source site that can be migrated. You can migrate the following objects from a Configuration Manager 2007 hierarchy to a Configuration Manager 2012 R2 hierarchy:

- Collections
- Advertisements
- Boundaries
- Software distribution packages
- Virtual application packages
- Software updates:

- Deployments
- Deployment packages
- Templates
- Software update lists
- Operating system deployment:
  - Boot images
  - Driver packages
  - Drivers
  - Images
  - Packages
  - Task sequences
- Desired configuration management:
  - Configuration baselines
  - Configuration items
- Asset Intelligence customizations
- Software metering rules

The following objects cannot be migrated from a Configuration Manager 2007 R2 hierarchy to a Configuration Manager 2012 R2 hierarchy:

- Queries
- Security rights and instances for the site and objects
- Configuration Manager 2007 reports from SQL Server Reporting Services
- Configuration Manager 2007 web reports
- Client inventory and history data
- AMT client provisioning information
- Files in the client cache

Once the data gathering process is complete, you configure migration jobs to migrate specific objects to the Configuration Manager 2012 R2 environment. You should only migrate Configuration Manager clients after all objects that the client uses have been migrated. For example, you might have an advertisement for a program that is deployed to a custom collection that contains a specific client. Migrate the advertisement, program, and the custom collection before migrating the client.

MORE INFO **MIGRATION TO CONFIGURATION MANAGER**

You can learn more about migrating to System Center 2012 R2 Configuration Manager at the following address: *http://technet.microsoft.com/en-us/library/gg681981.aspx.*

Upgrading between System Center 2012, System Center 2012 SP1, and 2012 R2

Some organizations will have deployed System Center 2012, or System Center 2012 SP1, and will wish to upgrade to System Center 2012 R2. This is more straightforward than migrating from an earlier version as software and hardware configurations that support System Center 2012, and System Center 2012 SP1 support System Center 2012 R2. You can perform in-place upgrades to transition from the System Center 2012 R2 or System Center 2012 R2 SP1 version of a product to the System Center 2012 R2 version of a product.

If you have multiple System Center 2012 or System Center 2012 SP1 products deployed in your environment, you need to ensure that you upgrade them in the following order:

1. Orchestrator
2. Service Manager
3. DPM
4. Operations Manager
5. Configuration Manager
6. VMM
7. App Controller

Upgrading Orchestrator

If you plan to install Service Manager Automation to your environment, you should install it prior to upgrading Orchestrator to 2012 R2. The general process of upgrading Orchestrator involves:

1. Backing up the Orchestrator database.
2. Stopping all Orchestrator runbooks.
3. Uninstalling the Orchestrator management server, runbook servers, the Web Service, and the Runbook Designer.
4. Installing the System Center 2012 R2 Orchestrator management server.
5. Install additional System Center 2012 R2 Orchestrator runbook servers.
6. Install the System Center 2012 R2 Runbook Designer.
7. Install Orchestrator Web Service.

If you have configured Orchestrator to be monitored by Operations Manager, you should place Orchestrator servers into maintenance mode prior to performing the upgrade, and take them out of maintenance mode once the upgrade is complete. To upgrade integration packs, uninstall the earlier version of the integration pack, and then install the newer integration pack.

Upgrading Service Manager

The general process of upgrading Service Manager from 2012 to 2012 R2 involves doing the following:

1. Backup the databases and management packs.

2. If Operations Manager is monitoring the Service Manager servers, place them into maintenance mode.

3. Remove the integration pack for Service Manager 2012 from Orchestrator.

4. Upgrade the SQL Server 2008 R2 AMO to the SQL Server 2012 AMO.

5. Upgrade the data warehouse management server. You will need to stop data warehouse jobs.

6. Upgrade the Service Manager management server.

Upgrading Data Protection Manager

The general process of upgrading Data Protection Manager from 2012 to 2012 R2 involves doing the following:

1. If Operations manager monitors the DPM servers, put them into maintenance mode prior to commencing upgrade.

2. If you are using the DPM integration pack for Orchestrator, remove this integration pack.

3. Remove any tape library sharing.

4. Perform the DPM upgrade by running Setup.exe from the installation media. The existing DPM installation will be detected and installer will run in upgrade mode.

5. Upgrade the DPM protection agents on protected computers and servers.

6. Run a replica consistency check as all replicas will be marked as inconsistent after the upgrade.

7. Re-enable tape library sharing.

Upgrading Operations Manager

The general process of upgrading Operations Manager from 2012 to 2012 R2 involves doing the following:

- If you are upgrading a single-server Management Group, you start the upgrade in the same manner as you would start Operations Manager installation, with the installation process detecting the existing deployment and entering upgrade mode. In upgrade mode, the Operations Manager Upgrade Wizard will perform a prerequisite check and offer solutions to allow you to resolve any blocking issues. If there are no blocking issues, you can perform the upgrade by completing the wizard.

- If upgrading a multi-server Management Group, you must upgrade the management servers first, followed by gateways, operations consoles, agents, the web console, reporting, and finally Audit Collection Services. Upgrading each server involves running setup from the installation media as you would when performing a new installation. As Operations Manager 2012 does not have an RMS, you don't have to upgrade any specific management server first.

Upgrading Configuration Manager

You can't perform a direct upgrade from Configuration Manager 2012 to Configuration Manager 2012 R2. You must instead upgrade to Configuration Manager 2012 SP1, and then perform a second upgrade to Configuration Manager 2012 R2.

Prior to performing the upgrade you should:

- Back up the site database.
- Disable all site maintenance tasks.
- Run the prerequisite checker for the new Configuration Manager version.
- Ensure that there are no pending restarts on any servers you will upgrade.
- Perform the installation of the new Configuration Manager version.
- Upgrade Configuration Manager clients.

You can configure automatic client upgrade through Site Settings Properties, as shown in Figure 1-41.

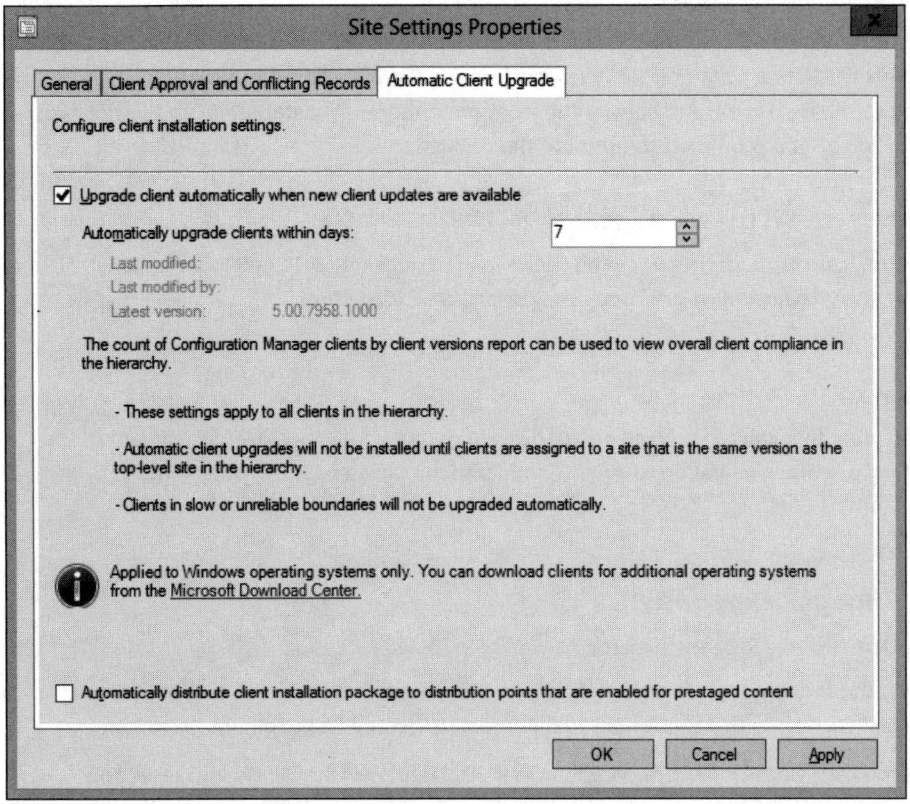

FIGURE 1-41 Upgrade Configuration Manager client

When upgrading from Configuration Manager 2012 or Configuration Manager 2012 SP1, to Configuration Manager 2012 R2, you must upgrade sites in the following order:

1. Upgrade Central Administration site

2. Upgrade primary sites

3. Upgrade secondary sites

Prior to performing the upgrade, ensure that you remove any instances of the Windows AIK, and replace them with the Windows ADK.

Upgrading VMM

The process of upgrading to System Center 2012 R2 VMM from System Center 2012 VMM, or System Center 2012 SP1 VMM, involves uninstalling the previous version of VMM and installing the 2012 R2 version of VMM. When uninstalling the previous version of VMM, ensure that you select the Retain Data option. When performing the installation of VMM 2012 R2, use the Existing Database option, and specify the location of the VMM database from the previous version. You will be prompted to upgrade the database.

> **MORE INFO SYSTEM CENTER 2012 TO 2012 R2 UPGRADE**
>
> You can learn more about upgrading between System Center 2012 and System Center 2012 R2 at *http://technet.microsoft.com/en-us/library/dn521010.aspx*.

> **EXAM TIP**
>
> Remember that you can't directly upgrade Configuration Manager 2007 SP2, and must instead perform a migration to a new Configuration Manager 2012 R2 hierarchy.

> ## *Thought experiment*
> ### Upgrading System Center at Tailspin Toys
>
> In this thought experiment, apply what you've learned about this objective. You can find answers to these questions in the "Answers" section at the end of this chapter.
>
> You have Opalis 6.3 and Service Manager 2010 deployed in your organization. You also want to upgrade your Service Manager deployment, which includes a data warehouse server, to Service Manager 2012 R2. You also want to retain the automation you created for Opalis 6.3 in Orchestrator 2012 R2. With this information in mind, answer the following questions:
>
> 1. Which should you upgrade first, the Service Manager data warehouse server, or the Service Manager management server?
>
> 2. What should you do to retain the automation you created for Opalis 6.3 in Orchestrator 2012 R2?

Objective summary

- In-place upgrades are supported for some pre-System Center 2012 products, such as Operations Manager 2007 R2, to the System Center 2012 R2 version as long as the operating system and hardware that hosts the source version of the product supports the upgraded product.

- Prior to upgrading each product, administrators must perform a set of product specific actions such as disabling certain SQL jobs.

- Prior to upgrading, you should always create a backup.

Objective review

Answer the following questions to test your knowledge of the information in this objective. You can find the answers to these questions and explanations of why each answer choice is correct or incorrect in the "Answers" section at the end of this chapter.

1. You are in the process of upgrading your System Center 2012 SP1 deployment to System Center 2012 R2. You have deployed App Controller, Configuration Manager, DPM, Operations Manager, Orchestrator, Service Manager, and VMM. Which of the following products should you upgrade first?

   A. DPM

   B. Service Manager

   C. Operations Manager

   D. VMM

2. Your VMM 2008 R2 deployment is configured to use a domain account for the VMM service. Which of the following steps must you take when performing an in-place upgrade to VMM 2012 R2?

   A. Use a new domain account for the VMM 2012 R2 VMM service

   B. Use the same domain account for the VMM 2012 R2 VMM service

   C. Use the Network Service account for the VMM 2012 R2 VMM service

   D. Use the Local System account for the VMM 2012 R2 VMM service.

3. You want to perform a direct upgrade of Operations Manager 2007 to Operations Manager 2012 R2. Which versions support this direct upgrade assuming other operating system, SQL Server, hardware, and software requirements are met?

   A. Operations Manager 2007

   B. Operations Manager 2007 R2 CU4

   C. You can't perform a direct upgrade of Operations Manager 2007 to Operations Manager 2012 R2.

   D. Operations Manager 2007 R2 CU3

Answers

This section contains the solutions to the thought experiments and answers to the objective review questions in this chapter.

Objective 1.1: Thought experiment

1. You can deploy VMM as a clustered role on a failover cluster, and the SQL database that supports it as a clustered role on a separate failover cluster. This meets the goal of making VMM highly available without deploying VMM on a highly available virtual machine.

2. You can configure a DPM secondary server as a replica. You can also deploy the DPM database on a SQL Server failover cluster. This meets the goal of making DPM highly available without deploying the workload in a virtual machine.

Objective 1.1: Review

1. **Correct answer:** C

    A. **Incorrect:** While VMM does include the ability to determine whether a VMM server or virtualization host is compliant against a software update baseline, VMM does not include the ability to monitor the software update compliance of other virtual machines running in the private cloud.

    B. **Incorrect:** Operations Manager does not include the ability to monitor software update compliance.

    C. **Correct:** You can use Configuration Manager to monitor software update compliance for Windows 8.1 virtual machines.

    D. **Incorrect:** Orchestrator does not include the ability to monitor software update compliance.

2. **Correct answers:** B, C, and D

    A. **Incorrect:** You can only deploy one Orchestrator management server.

    B. **Correct:** Deploying multiple runbook servers will make the Orchestrator deployment more highly available.

    C. **Correct:** Deploying the Orchestration database on a SQL Server failover cluster will make the Orchestrator deployment more highly available.

    D. **Correct:** Deploying the management server on a highly available virtual machine will make the Orchestrator deployment more highly available.

3. **Correct answers:** A, C and D

   A. **Correct:** The encryption key allows Service Manager to access the encrypted data in the Service Manager database.

   B. **Incorrect:** You will need to use the existing encryption key to access the data in the restored Service Manager database.

   C. **Correct:** The server that will function as the replacement Service Manager management server must have the same name as the originally failed server.

   D. **Correct:** You must install SQL Server and recover the Service Manager database before using the Service Manager installation media to recover Service Manager.

Objective 1.2: Thought experiment

1. The Service Manager management server requires the SQL Server 2008 R2 native client or the SQL Server 2012 native client, and the Microsoft Report Viewer Redistributable.

2. You will need at least two because the Service Manager management database and the Service Manager data warehouse database must be deployed on separate SQL Server instances.

Objective 1.2: Review

1. **Correct answer:** D

   A. **Incorrect:** The Service Manager console is not a software prerequisite for the App Controller console.

   B. **Incorrect:** The Orchestrator console is not a software prerequisite for the App Controller console.

   C. **Incorrect:** The Operations Manager console is not a software prerequisite for the App Controller console.

   D. **Correct:** The VMM console is a software prerequisite for the App Controller console.

2. **Correct answer:** A

   A. **Correct:** The domain account that will function as the VMM service account must be a member of the local Administrators group on the VMM server.

   B. **Incorrect:** The domain account that will function as the VMM service account does not need to be a member of the local Virtual Machine Manager Servers group on the VMM server.

   C. **Incorrect:** The domain account that will function as the VMM service account does not need to be a member of the local Hyper-V Administrators group on the VMM server.

   D. **Incorrect:** The domain account that will function as the VMM service account does not need to be a member of the local Backup Operators group on the VMM server.

3. **Correct answer:** C

   A. **Incorrect:** System Center 2012 R2 Service Manager's Self-Service Portal cannot be installed on SharePoint 2013 SP1.

   B. **Incorrect:** While System Center 2012 R2 Service Manager's Self-Service Portal can be installed on SharePoint 2010 SP1, SharePoint 2010 SP1 cannot be installed on Windows Server 2012 R2.

   C. **Correct:** SharePoint Server 2010 SP2 is the only version of SharePoint that can be installed on Windows Server 2012 R2, and which is also supported for the Service Manager 2012 R2 Self-Service Portal.

   D. **Incorrect:** System Center 2012 R2 Service Manager's Self-Service Portal cannot be installed on SharePoint 2013 RTM.

4. **Correct answers:** B and C

   A. **Incorrect:** You must use a domain account for the VMM service when deploying VMM as a highly available role on a Windows Server 2012 R2 failover cluster.

   B. **Correct:** You must use a domain account for the VMM service when deploying VMM as a highly available role on a Windows Server 2012 R2 failover cluster.

   C. **Correct:** You must store the encryption keys in Active Directory when deploying VMM as a highly available role on a Windows Server 2012 R2 failover cluster.

   D. **Incorrect:** While the SQL Server instance should be highly available, it is not necessary for the instance to be deployed on a highly available virtual machine. You could deploy the SQL Server instance on a failover cluster to accomplish the same goal.

Objective 1.3: Thought experiment

1. When upgrading from Service Manager 2010 to Service Manager 2012 R2, you must upgrade the data warehouse server before upgrading the Service Manager management server.

2. You will need to export the Opalis policies and import them as runbooks into Orchestrator 2012 R2.

Objective 1.3: Review

1. **Correct answer:** B

   A. **Incorrect:** You should upgrade Service Manager before DPM.

   B. **Correct:** Of the products listed, you should upgrade Service Manager first. You should upgrade Orchestrator before Service Manager, but Orchestrator was not listed as an answer.

   C. **Incorrect:** You should upgrade Service Manager and DPM before upgrading Operations Manager.

   D. **Incorrect:** You should upgrade Services Manager, DPM, and Operations Manager before upgrading VMM.

2. **Correct answer:** B

   A. **Incorrect:** If the VMM 2008 R2 deployment is using a specific domain account for the VMM service, you must use the same domain account for the VMM 2012 R2 service, otherwise encrypted data will not be retained.

   B. **Correct:** If the VMM 2008 R2 deployment is using a specific domain account for the VMM service, you must use the same domain account for the VMM 2012 R2 service, otherwise encrypted data will not be retained.

   C. **Incorrect:** If the VMM 2008 R2 deployment is using a specific domain account for the VMM service, you must use the same domain account for the VMM 2012 R2 service, otherwise encrypted data will not be retained.

   D. **Incorrect:** If the VMM 2008 R2 deployment is using a specific domain account for the VMM service, you must use the same domain account for the VMM 2012 R2 service, otherwise encrypted data will not be retained.

3. **Correct answer:** B

   A. **Incorrect:** You can perform a direct upgrade of Operations Manager 2007 R2 CU4 to Operations Manager 2012 R2. You cannot do this with previous versions of Operations Manager.

   B. **Correct:** You can perform a direct upgrade of Operations Manager 2007 R2 CU4 to Operations Manager 2012 R2.

   C. **Incorrect:** You can perform a direct upgrade of Operations Manager 2007 R2 CU4 to Operations Manager 2012 R2. You cannot do this with previous versions of Operations Manager.

   D. **Incorrect:** You can perform a direct upgrade of Operations Manager 2007 R2 CU4 to Operations Manager 2012 R2. You cannot do this with previous versions of Operations Manager.

CHAPTER 2

Configure System Center infrastructure

After you have deployed System Center, you need to configure additional elements to ensure that you can use System Center to manage your organization's private cloud. You'll need to configure Data Protection Manager to ensure that the infrastructure is being protected, and configure appropriate security roles and Run As accounts to ensure that tasks can be performed with least privilege. You'll also have to configure and manage portals and dashboards to grant access to users who are not directly responsible for managing System Center products.

Objectives in this chapter:

- Objective 2.1: Configure System Center components
- Objective 2.2: Configure portals and dashboards

Objective 2.1: Configure System Center components

This objective deals with several diverse elements of a System Center deployment, focusing initially on data protection using Data Protection Manager, but also covering how role-based permissions work through the use of roles, and how credentials work with Run As accounts.

> **This objective covers the following topics:**
> - DPM storage pools
> - DPM secondary servers
> - System Center agents
> - Run As accounts and profiles
> - User roles
> - Watcher nodes
> - Gateway servers

Understanding Data Protection Manager

Data Protection Manager (DPM) is the data protection, or backup and recovery element, of the System Center suite. Even though you are likely to deploy your private cloud workloads on to a fabric of highly redundant storage, network, and compute resources, hardware redundancy doesn't obviate the need for data protection. This is because you can lose critical data to other events like software errors, malware, or end users simply making mistakes.

DPM storage pools

A DPM storage pool is a collection of disks that DPM uses to store backup replicas and recovery points for the workloads that it protects. While DPM can also write data to tables, and store data in a Microsoft Azure recovery vault, the primary location for DPM to store protected data is within a storage pool.

DPM storage pools have the following requirements:

- DPM storage pools must be located on disks separate to the ones that host the system files, database files, and program files.
- A storage pool must exist before DPM can start protecting data.
- A storage pool can contain a single disk. You can add more disks to a storage pool at a later point in time.
- DPM storage pools do not support USB/1394 disks.
- DPM storage pools can only allocate space that exists in volumes it creates on disks. DPM ignores any existing volumes on a disk added to a storage pool.
- To maximize the amount of space allocated on a disk that you are going to add to a storage pool, delete any existing volumes prior to adding the disk to the pool.

To add disks to a DPM storage pool, perform the following steps:

1. In the Management workspace of the DPM console, click Disks, and then on the ribbon, click Add.

2. In the Add Disks To Storage Pool dialog box, shown in Figure 2-1, select the disks that you want to add, and click Add.

FIGURE 2-1 Adding disks to storage pool

3. If a warning dialog informs you that DPM will convert disks so that they are dynamic, and any existing volumes will be converted to simple volumes, click Yes.

4. Review the list of disks in the storage pool in the DPM console, as shown in Figure 2-2.

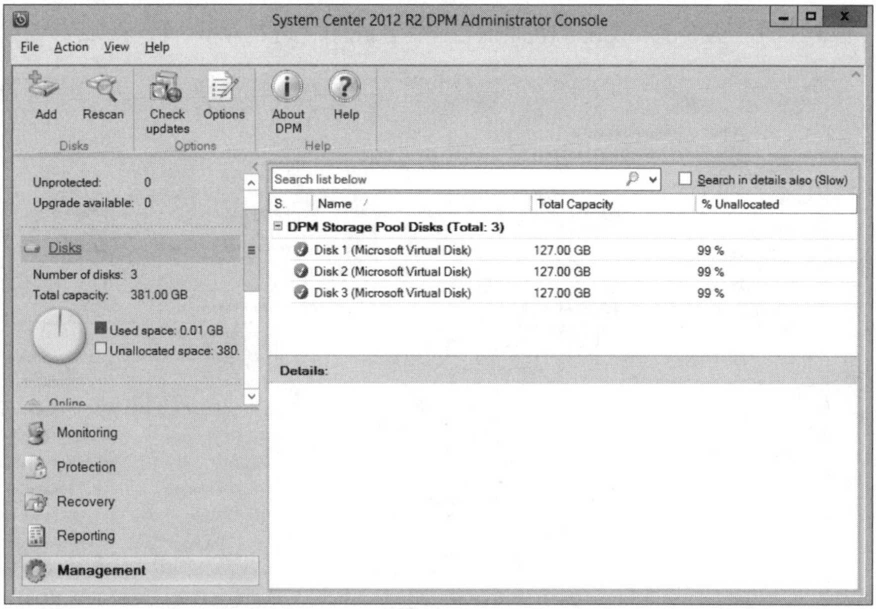

FIGURE 2-2 Disks in the storage pool

MORE INFO DPM STORAGE POOLS

You can learn more about DPM storage pools at *http://technet.microsoft.com/en-us/library/hh758075.aspx.*

DPM secondary servers

You can configure a second DPM server at the same site, or at another site, to protect the primary DPM server. The primary DPM server is the server that directly protects data sources. You configure the secondary DPM server to protect the backup replicas and databases on the primary DPM server. This allows you to use the secondary DPM server for recovery in the event that the primary fails. It's also possible to switch protected workloads from the primary server so that they are protected by the secondary (which becomes the new primary) if necessary.

To configure secondary protection, perform the following steps:

1. Deploy the DPM protection agent from the secondary server on the primary DPM server.

2. Add the primary DPM server to a protection group on the secondary DPM server. Configure protection for the following, as shown in Figure 2-3:

- The SQL Server database on the primary DPM server
- All volumes on the primary DPM server
- All protected workload replicas on the primary DPM server

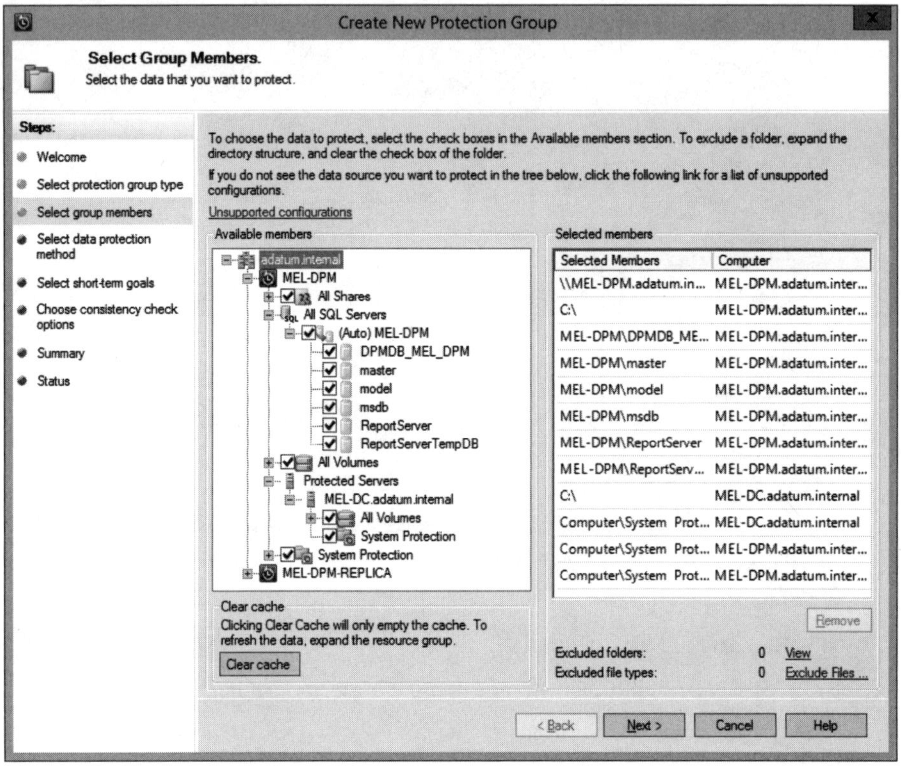

FIGURE 2-3 Select group members

Note that the following conditions apply when deploying this configuration:

- The primary and secondary DPM servers must be running the same operating system version, service packs, and software updates.
- The primary and secondary DPM servers must be running the same version of DPM, including service packs and software updates.
- You cannot configure file name extension exclusions when configuring the protection group.
- You can configure short-term disk-based protection, or short-term disk-based protection, and long-term tape-based protection. Figure 2-4 shows the selection of short-term protection.

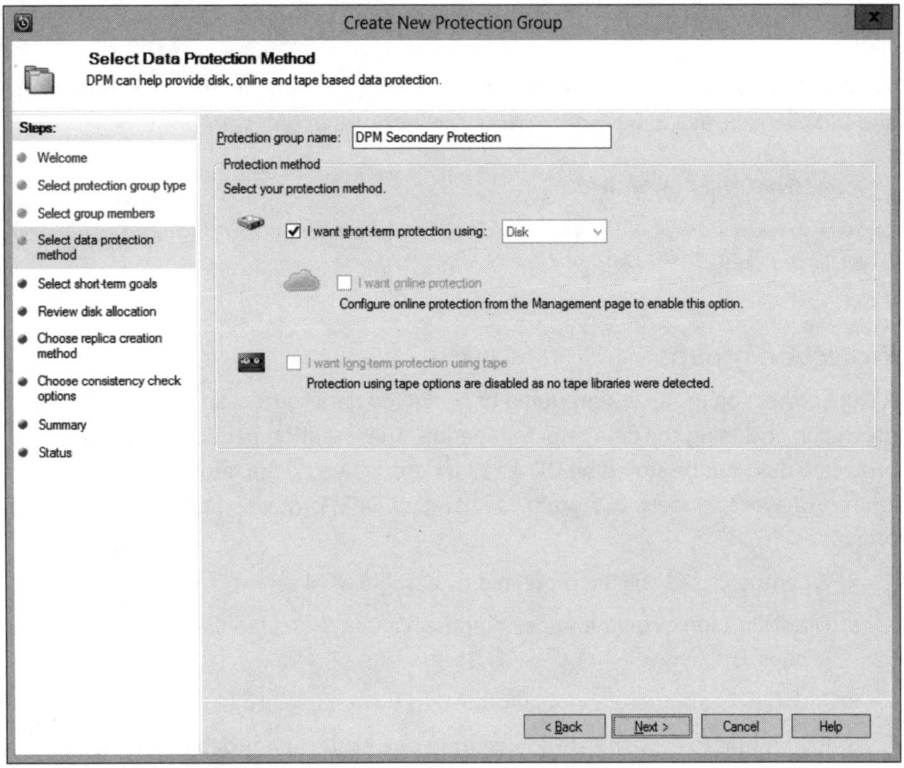

FIGURE 2-4 Short-term protection

MORE INFO DPM SECONDARY SERVERS

You can learn more about DPM secondary servers at *http://technet.microsoft.com/en-us/library/jj244598.aspx*.

DPM chaining

DPM chaining differs from a basic secondary DPM server configuration because not only does the second DPM server protect the first, but the first DPM server is configured to protect the second. Each DPM server has a set of workloads for which it functions as the primary DPM server. Those workloads are configured for secondary protection on the partner DPM server.

For example, you have two DPM servers, SYD-DPM and MEL-DPM. In a chaining configuration, you configure SYD-DPM to protect MEL-DPM, and configure MEL-DPM to protect SYD-DPM. If you configure SYD-DPM as the primary server protecting servers SYD-FS1 and SYD-FS2, you would configure secondary protection for SYD-FS1 and SYD-FS2 on MEL-DPM. Similarly, if you configure MEL-DPM as the primary server protecting servers MEL-FS3 and MEL-FS4, you would configure secondary protection for MEL-FS3 and MEL-FS4 on SYD-DPM.

In the event that one of the DPM servers fails, you can switch protection across to the partner server.

All DPM servers in a chained configuration need to be running the same operating system and DPM version, including service packs and software updates.

> **MORE INFO DPM CHAINING**
>
> You can learn more about DPM chaining at *http://technet.microsoft.com/en-us/library/hh758194.aspx*.

Protection groups

A DPM protection group is a grouping of protected data sources and the properties of that protection, including the data retention period. The retention period determines how long protected data can be stored by DPM and is determined by the frequency of backups and the amount of available space to store those backups. DPM protection groups have the following properties:

- A computer can only be protected by a single DPM server.
- Different sources on the same computer can be protected using different protection groups.
- A single data source cannot be protected by multiple protection groups.
- If you want to move a data source from one protection group to another, stop protecting it in the first protection group before initiating protection in the second protection group.
- A protection group can have multiple computers as members.
- All data sources within a protection group share the same retention settings.

To configure a protection group, perform the following steps:

1. In the Protection workspace of the DPM console, click New on the ribbon. This will launch the Create New Protection Group Wizard.
2. On the Select Protection Group Type page, choose between Servers and Clients. You should only choose the Clients option if you are backing up computers running a client operating system like Windows 8.1. This page is shown in Figure 2-5.

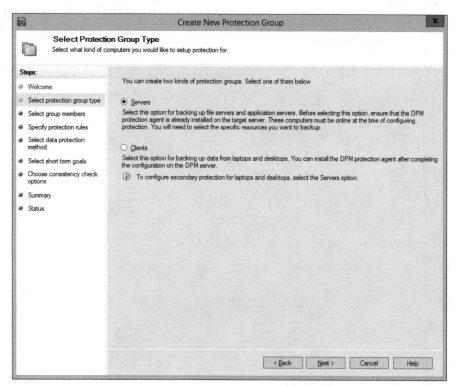

FIGURE 2-5 Protection group type

3. On the Select Group Members page, select the data sources that you want to protect. For example, in Figure 2-6, under MEL-OPSMGR, the following items are protected:

- **All Shares** This option protects all shares and any new shares that may be created on the computer.

- **All SQL Servers** This option protects all SQL instances and all databases hosted on those instances. This includes automatic protection for any new databases created on those instances.

- **All Volumes** This option protects all volumes and any new volumes added to the computer.

- **System Protection** This option protects the system state and also provides the option of performing a bare metal recovery of this server. Bare metal recovery is a complete recovery of the entire server, either to hardware or to a virtual environment.

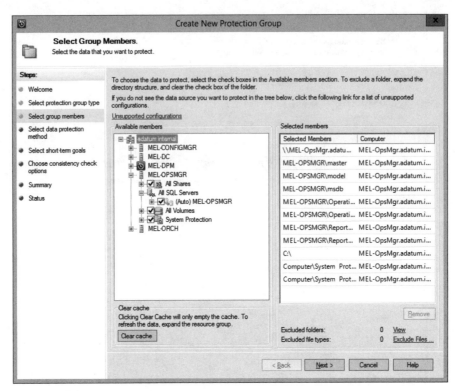

FIGURE 2-6 Select group members

4. On the Select Data Protection Method dialog box, you can select short-term protection using Disk. You can choose long-term protection if a tape drive has been configured. You can also configure online protection if online protection has been configured. Online protection is available if you have configured Microsoft Azure Backup.

5. On the Specify Short-Term Goals page, specify the Retention Range and the Synchronization Frequency. You also specify File Recovery and Application Recovery Points. Figure 2-7 shows the Specify Short-Term Goals page.

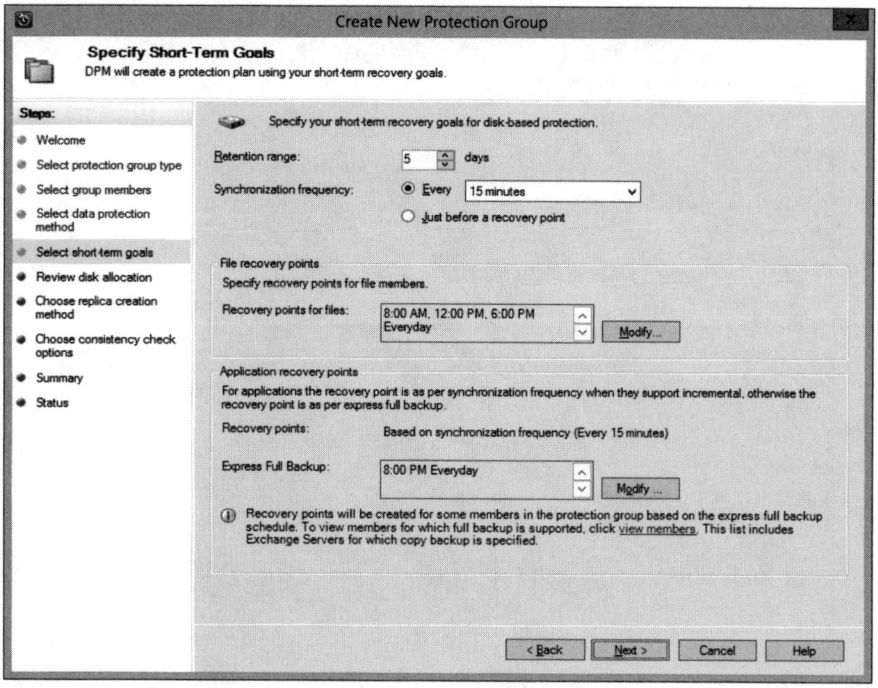

FIGURE 2-7 Short-term retention goals

6. On the Review Disk Allocation page, review how DPM has allocated storage space for the protected workload. Choose whether to co-locate data in the storage pool, which puts multiple data sources on replica volumes. Choose also whether to automatically grow the volumes. If you enable the option to grow volumes, ensure that you add capacity to the storage pool as necessary.

7. On the Choose Replica Creation Method, you specify how to create the initial replica of the protected data. You can configure DPM to create a replica immediately or at a later point in time over the network. Alternatively, you can transfer the data manually using removable media.

8. On the Consistency Check Options page, specify whether to automatically run a consistency check if a replica becomes inconsistent. You can also run daily consistency checks according to a schedule. Consistency checks are processor and disk intensive. Figure 2-8 shows this page.

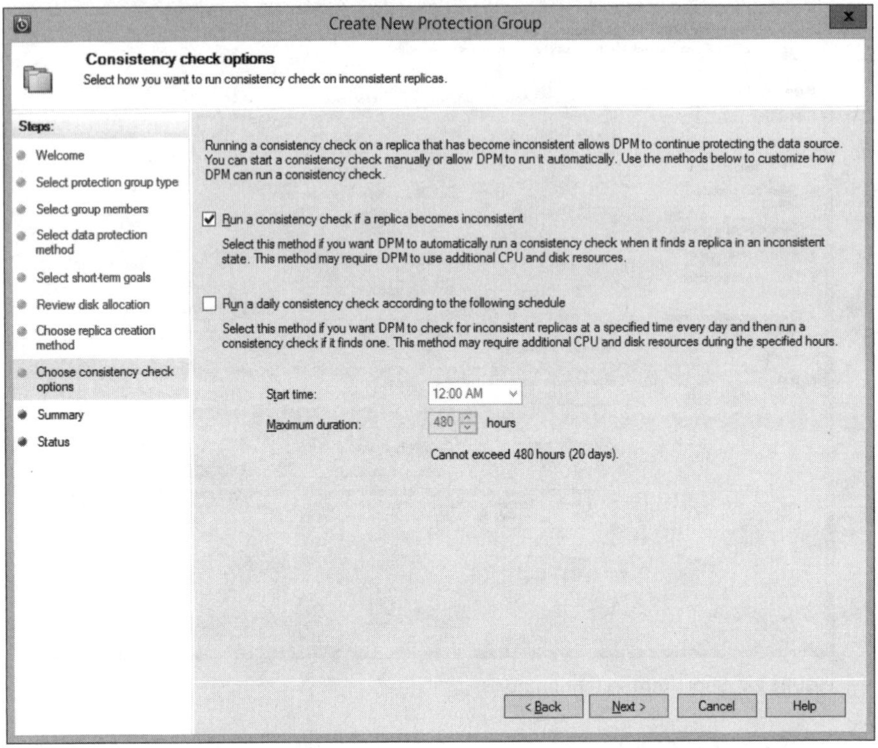

FIGURE 2-8 Consistency check options

9. On the Summary page, review the options, and then click Create Group. The protection group will be created. If you've specified that the replica be created immediately, DPM will create the replica.

MORE INFO DPM PROTECTION GROUPS

You can learn more about DPM protection groups at http://technet.microsoft.com/en-us/library/hh758123.aspx.

Understanding System Center agents

Agents are special software elements that allow certain System Center products to perform tasks on the computers on which they are installed. Each agent is specific to a separate product, and not all System Center products have an agent.

Operations Manager agent

The Operations Manager agent allows Operations Manager to monitor and interact with the computer on which it is installed. Although Operations Manager does support agentless monitoring, in the majority of private cloud scenarios, Operations Manager will monitor and manage computers that have the Operations Manager agent installed.

You can install the agent in three ways:

- Perform a push installation by running the Discovery Wizard from the Operations Manager console.

- Run the MOMAgent.msi Setup Wizard from the Operations Manager installation media on the computer on which you want to install the agent.

- Perform a command line installation on computers running Windows and supported UNIX and Linux operating systems. On computers running Windows operating systems, this involves using Msiexec.exe with the MOMAgent.msi installer.

You can deploy the Operations Manager agent by performing the following steps:

1. In the Administration workspace of the Operations Manager console, right-click on Device Management, and click Discovery Wizard.

2. On the Discovery Type page of the Computer And Device Management Wizard, shown in Figure 2-9, click Windows Computers, and click Next.

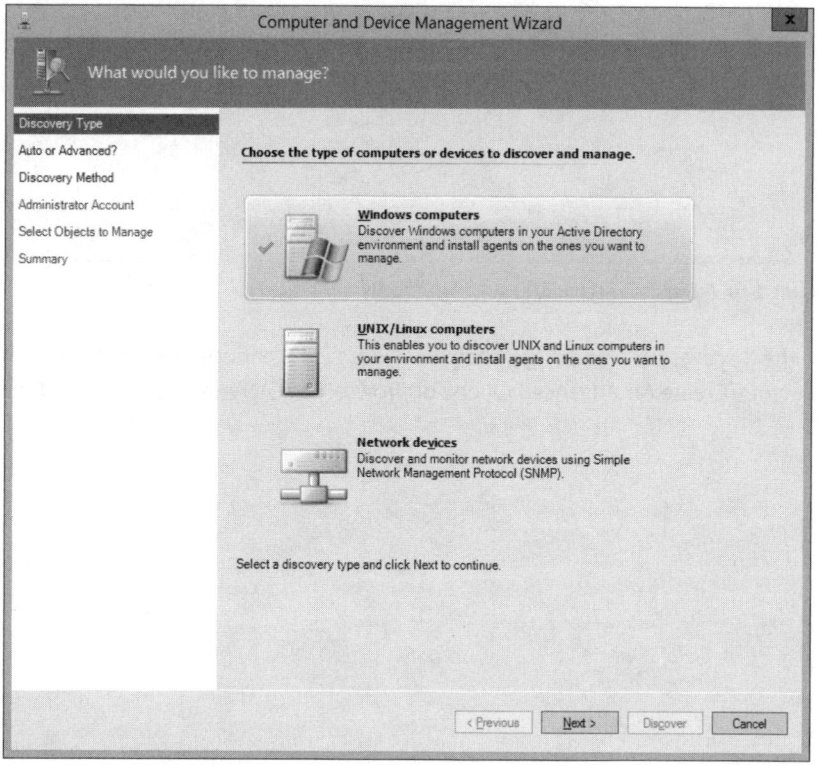

FIGURE 2-9 Discovery type

3. On the Auto Or Advanced page, choose between Automatic Computer Discovery, which will check the domain for all Windows-based computers, or Advanced Discovery, as shown in Figure 2-10, which allows you to choose between Clients, Servers, or Clients And Server.

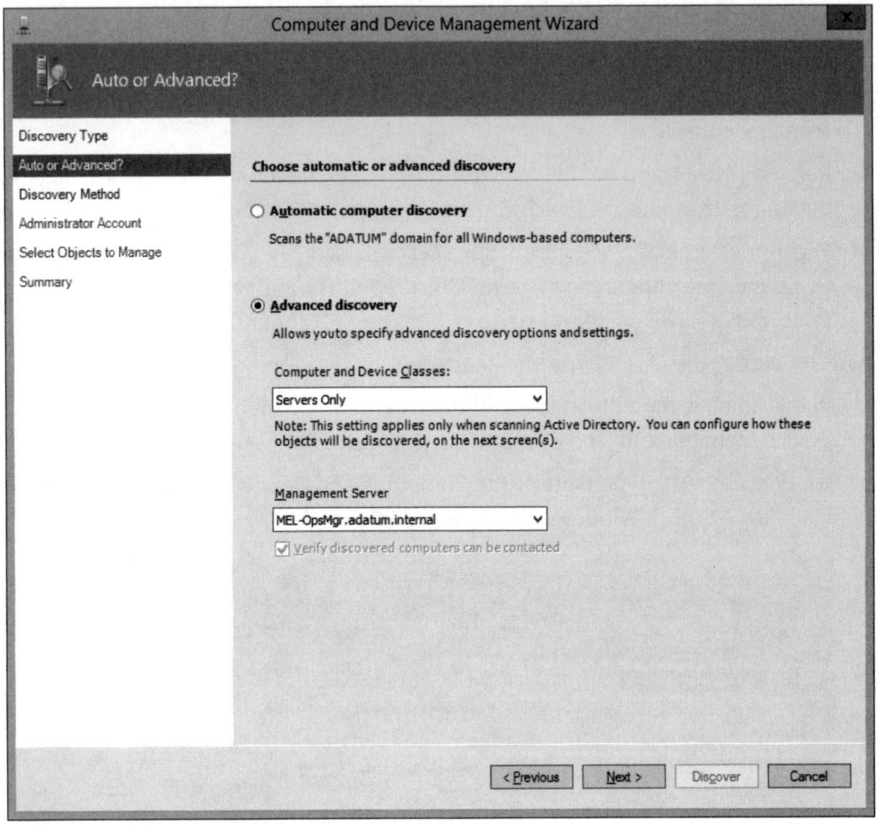

FIGURE 2-10 Advanced discovery

4. On the Discovery Method page, shown in Figure 2-11, choose whether to Scan Active Directory, Create An Advanced Query, or Browse For, Or Type-In Computer Names.

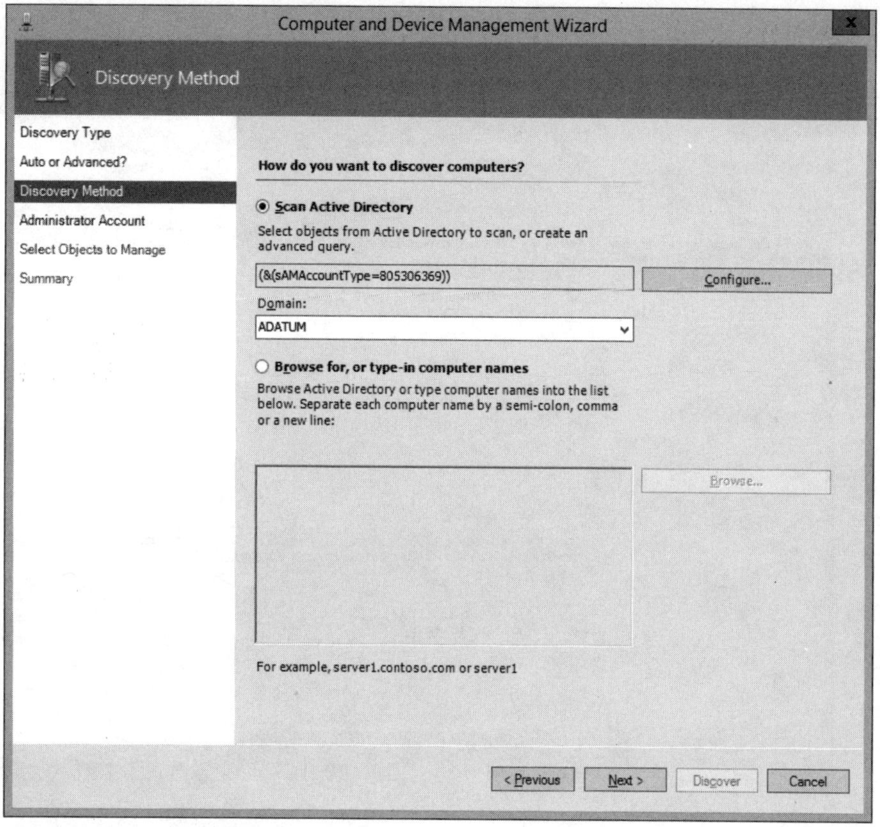

FIGURE 2-11 Discovery Method

5. On the Administrator Account name, choose whether to use the Management Server Action account or a specific user account. This account must have administrator rights on the computers to be scanned and to which you want to add agents.

6. On the Select Objects To Manage page, shown in Figure 2-12, select the computer to which you want to deploy the Operations Manager agent. If multiple management servers are present in the management group, you can select the management server to which the agent will report. You can also choose between Agent and Agentless Management Mode.

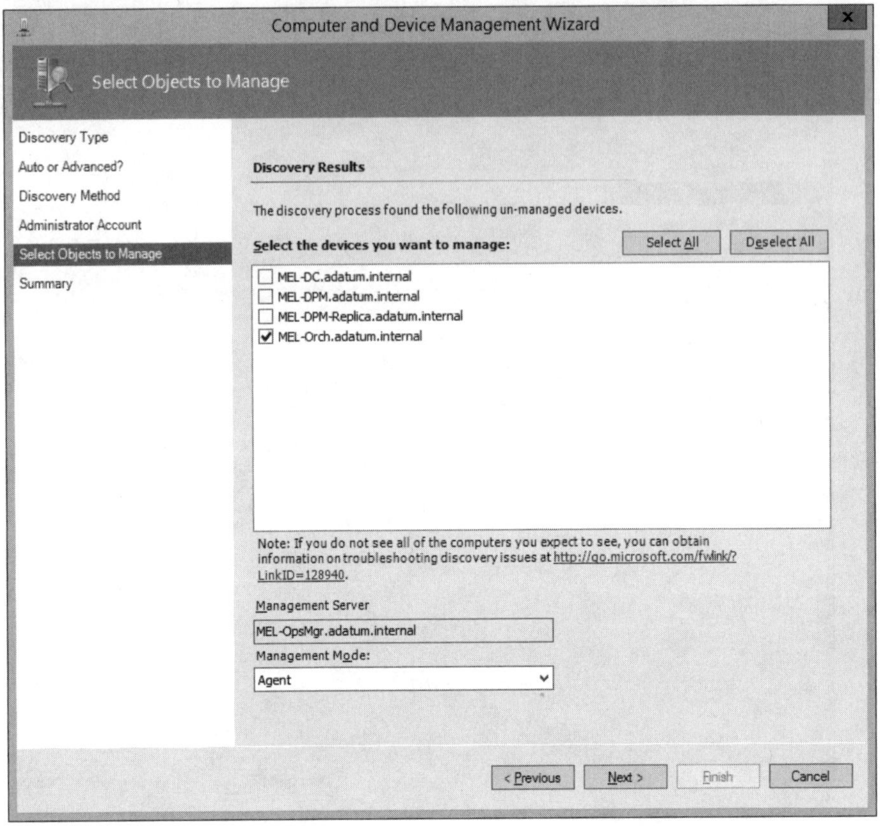

FIGURE 2-12 Select Objects To Manage

7. On the Summary page, shown in Figure 2-13, specify the location where the agent files should be deployed. You also specify the credentials that the agent will use when performing actions. The Local System account is used by default.

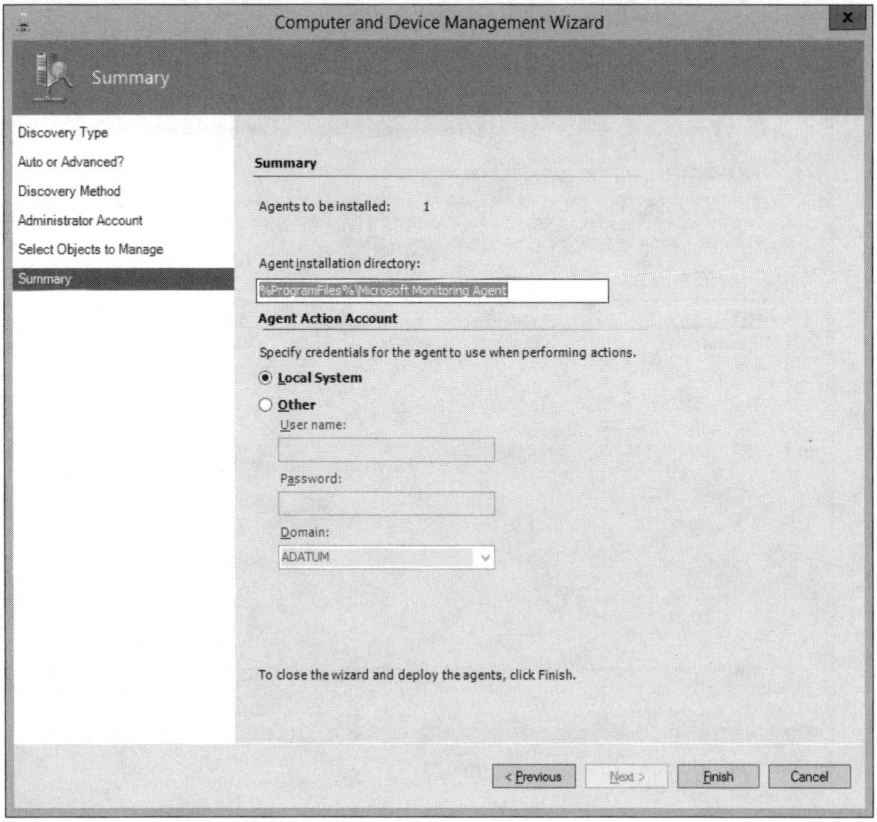

FIGURE 2-13 Account and installation directory

An Operations Manager agent can be a member of up to four separate management groups. When this is done, the agent sends back data to each management group. To configure the Operations Manager agent to be a member of more than one management group, perform one of the following actions:

- Open the Microsoft Monitoring Agent item in the control panel. On the Operations Manager tab, shown in Figure 2-14, click Add to add additional management groups.

- Run the Discovery Wizard from the Operations Manager console in each management group.

- Run MOMAgent.msi on the computer multiple times, specifying a new management group.

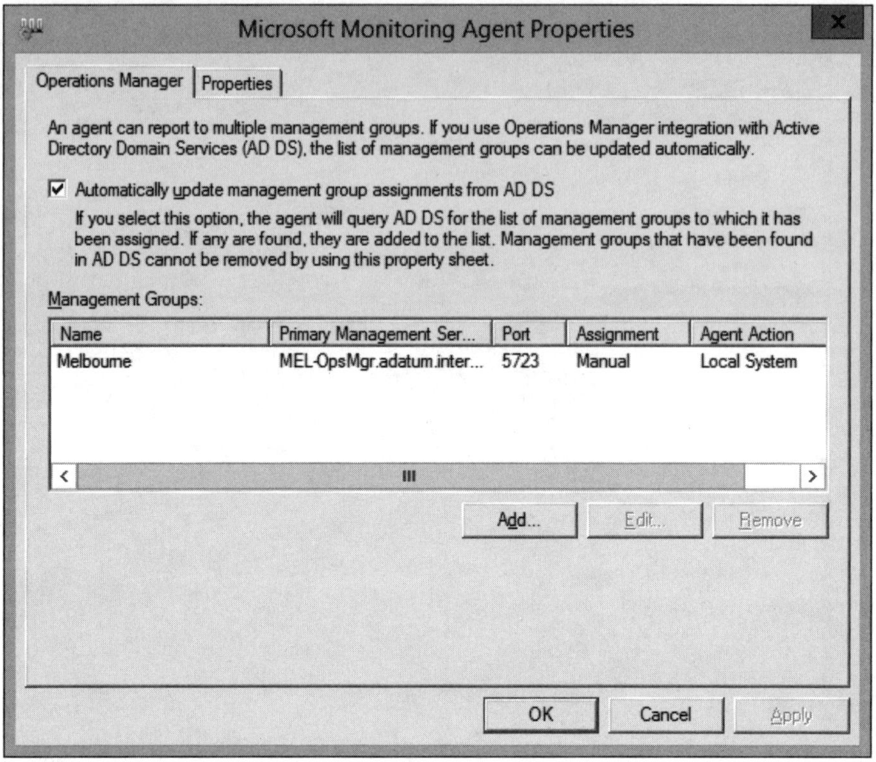

FIGURE 2-14 Additional management groups

> **MORE INFO OPERATIONS MANAGER AGENT**
>
> You can learn more about the Operations Manager agent at http://technet.microsoft.com/en-us/library/hh212883.aspx.

Configuration Manager client

The Configuration Manager client applies settings configured in Configuration Manager to the computer on which it is installed. The client is also responsible for reporting information back to the Configuration Manager site, such as providing inventory and compliance data.

The Configuration Manager client has two user interface elements, the Configuration Manager control panel item and the Software Center. The control panel item allows administrators to configure or troubleshoot Configuration Manager client settings. The Software Center allows users to request and install software made available through Configuration Manager, as well as to configure maintenance, power management, and remote assistance settings.

You can install the Configuration Manager client using the following methods:

- **Client Push from Configuration Manger** Allows you to deploy the client from the Configuration Manager console. This method is suitable when clients have already been deployed. You can configure automatic client push installation, which will deploy the Configuration Manager client to all specified computer resources. As Figure 2-15 shows, you can limit whether this targets servers, workstations, domain controllers, and Configuration Manager site systems servers.

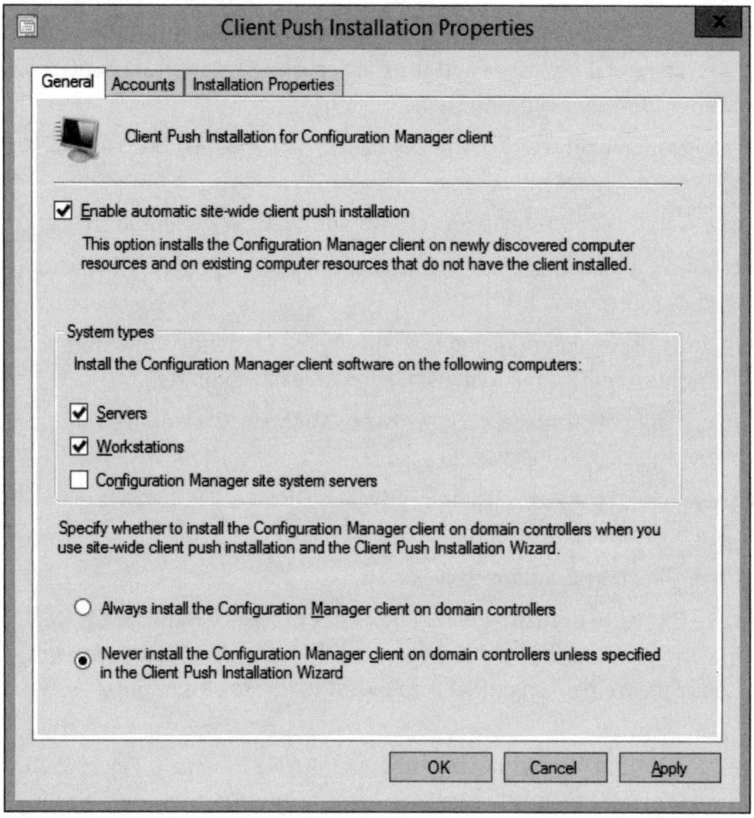

FIGURE 2-15 Client Push Installation Properties

- **Including the client in an operating system image** Rather than deploy the client after a computer has been deployed, this method allows you to include the Configuration Manager client in the operating system image. You would include the client when creating an operating system image deployed with a VMM template for a private cloud deployment. You could also configure a task sequence in an Operating System Deployment (OSD) sequence to include this client, and other System Center clients and agents when building the image.

- **Deployment from Windows Server Update Services** This method allows you to configure client deployment as a software update published through WSUS.

- **Manual installation** Use this method when you need to perform a small number of client installations.

- **Group Policy based installation** This method involves using Group Policy based software deployment to deploy the Configuration Manager agent.
- **Logon scripts** When you use this method, a logon script installs the Configuration Manager client software.

To install the Configuration Manager client using the client push method, you need to have first configured computer discovery and the client push installation account. To configure these elements, perform the following steps:

1. In the Administration workspace of the Configuration Manager console, click the Sites node under Site Configuration.
2. On the ribbon, click Client Installation Settings and then click Client Push Installation.
3. On the Accounts tab of the Client Push Installation Properties dialog box, click New, and then click New Account.
4. On the Windows User Account dialog box, specify the credentials of a user account that has the rights to perform agent installation on each computer.
5. In the Administration workspace, click Discovery Methods. Click Active Directory System Discovery, and click Properties.
6. On the General tab of the Active Directory System Discovery Properties dialog box, click Enable Active Directory System Discovery.
7. Next to Active Directory Containers, click New.
8. On the Active Directory Container dialog box, click Browse. On the Select New Container, select the container that will form the basis of your discovery search. For example, select the domain container if you want to locate all computers in a particular domain.
9. Specify an account that has permissions to search Active Directory. Figure 2-16 shows a scan of Active Directory that will search the Adatum.internal domain using the Adatum\Administrator account.

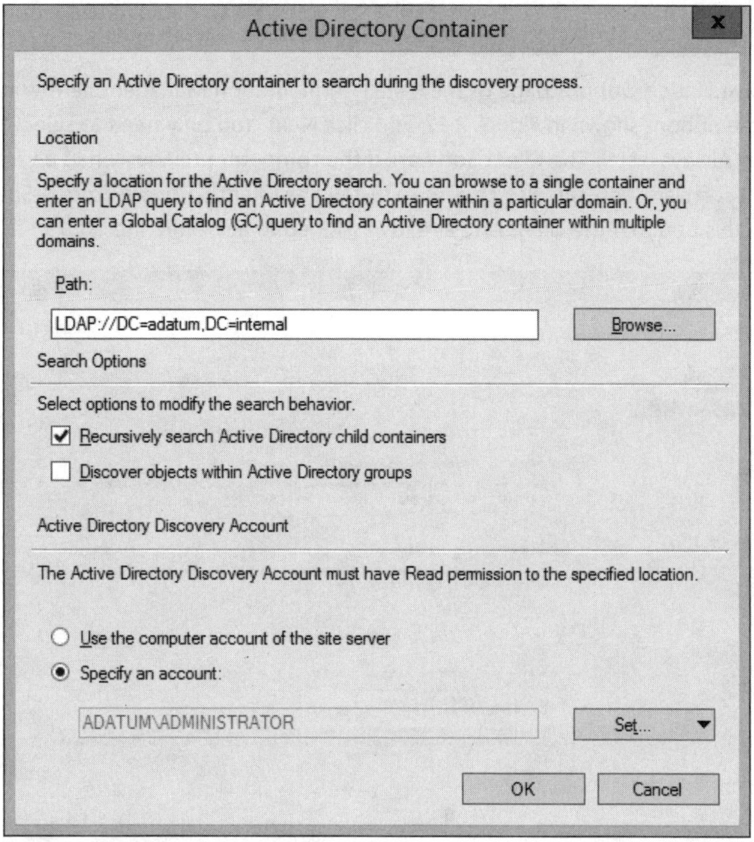

FIGURE 2-16 Scan Adatum domain

10. To trigger Active Directory System Discovery, select it from the list of discovery methods, and click Run Full Discovery Now on the ribbon.

11. In the Assets And Compliance workspace, click the Devices node.

12. In the list of devices, click the computer to which you want to deploy the agent and then click Install Client on the ribbon.

13. On the Installation Options page of the Install Configuration Manager Client Wizard, review the options shown in Figure 2-17, and click Next. You only need to select the option to Always Install The Client Software if the computer previously had a version of the client software. You can also choose to Install The Client Software From A Specific Site. Use this option if the client isn't already assigned to a specific site.

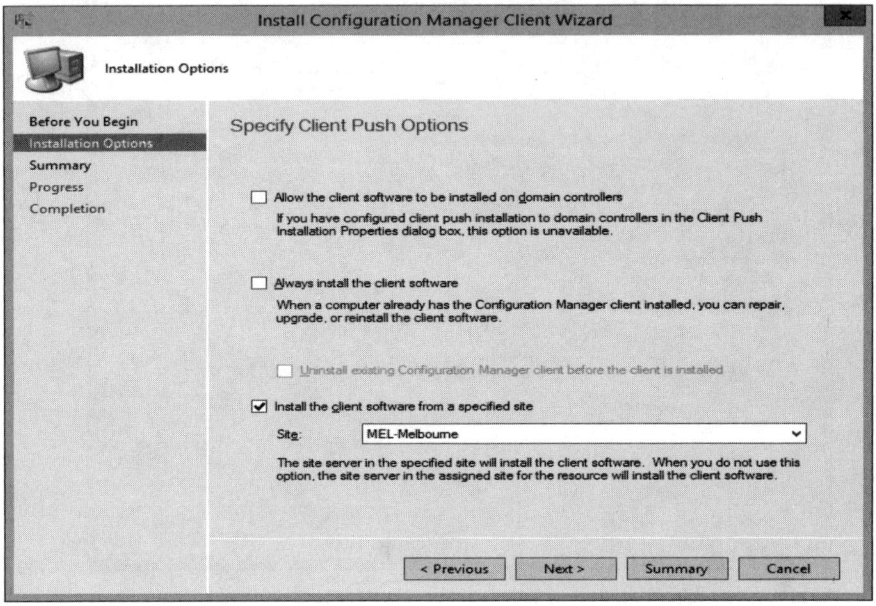

FIGURE 2-17 Client push options

14. Complete the wizard. You can verify that the client has installed by selecting the device in the Devices node of the Configuration Manager console, and verifying that the Client column says Yes, and that the Summary pane indicates that the client has communicated with the management point.

MORE INFO CONFIGURATION MANAGER CLIENT

You can learn more about Configuration Manager client at *http http://technet.microsoft. com/en-us/library/gg699391.aspx*.

DPM agent

The DPM agent allows DPM to discover and protect the workloads that are present on the computer that has the agent installed. You can perform a push installation of the agent from the DPM console, or install the agent from the command line. Installing the agent from the command line involves attaching the agent to a DPM management server. To do this, specify the DPM server name with the command line, either as:

```
DpmAgentInstaller_x64.exe <DPMServerName>
```

```
DpmAgentInstaller_x86.exe <DPMServerName>
```

The FQDN of the DPM server is <DPMServerName>. To perform a push installation of the agent from the DPM console, perform the following steps:

1. In the Management workspace of the DPM console, click Agents, and then on the ribbon, click Install.

2. On the Select Agent Deployment Method page of the Protection Agent Installation Wizard, shown in Figure 2-18, select Install Agents, and click Next. You would select the Attach Agents option if you had already deployed the agent software to the computers that you wanted to protect.

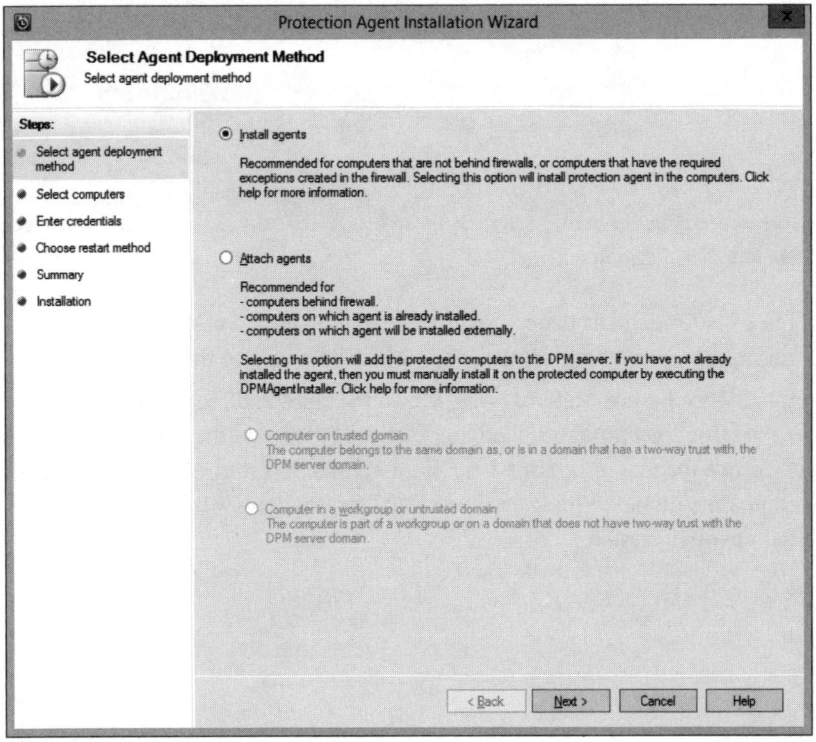

FIGURE 2-18 Install agents

3. On the Select Computers page, shown in Figure 2-19, select the computers on which you want to deploy the agent.

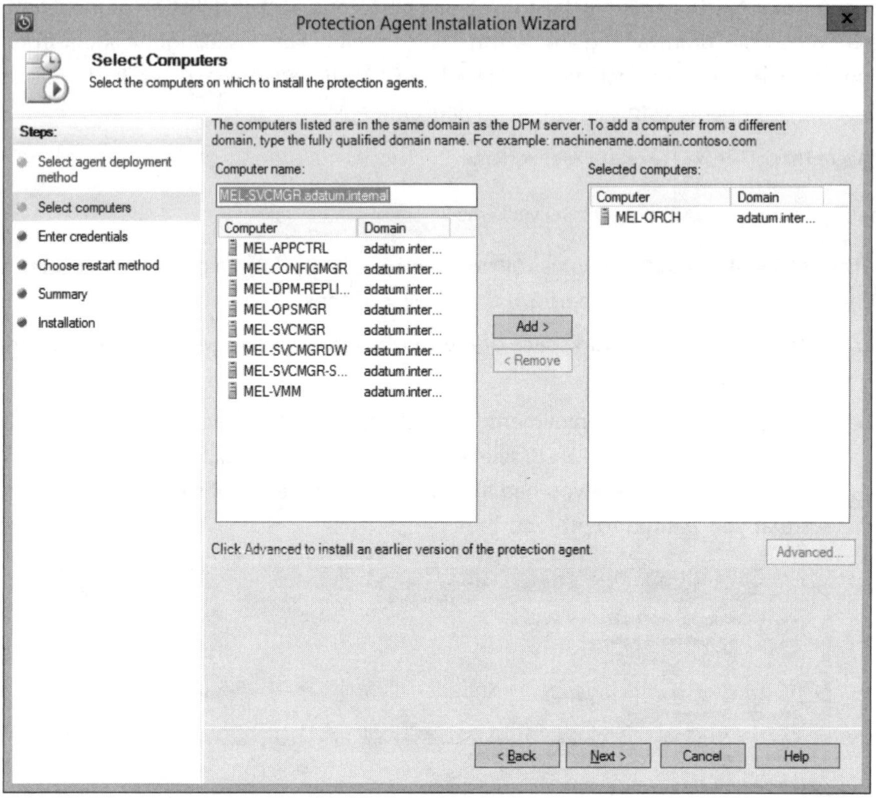

FIGURE 2-19 Select computers

4. On the Enter Credentials page, provide the credentials of a user account that has local administrator rights on the computers to which you want to deploy agents.

5. On the Choose Restart Method page, shown in Figure 2-20, select whether you want to have the target computer installed automatically (if required). The alternative is for you to perform a manual restart at a later point in time. A restart is generally only required for computers running Windows Server 2003 (or Windows XP which is no longer a supported operating system).

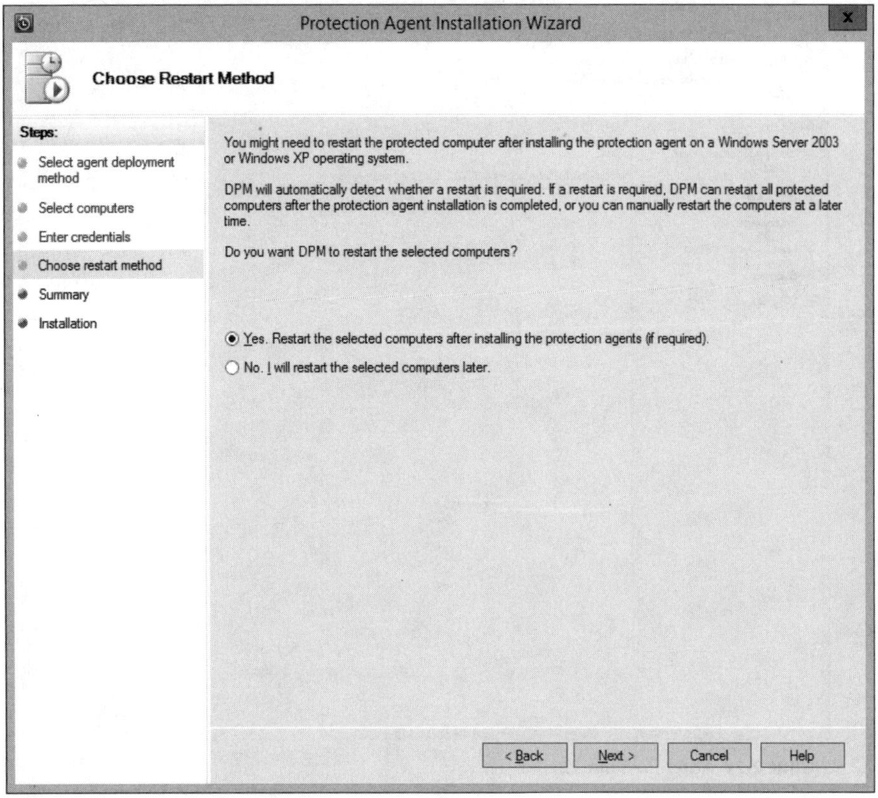

FIGURE 2-20 Choose restart method

6. On the Summary page, review the tasks that will be carried out by the Agent Installation Wizard.

7. On the Installation page, review the progress of the agent installation, as shown in Figure 2-21. Close the dialog box when the installation completes.

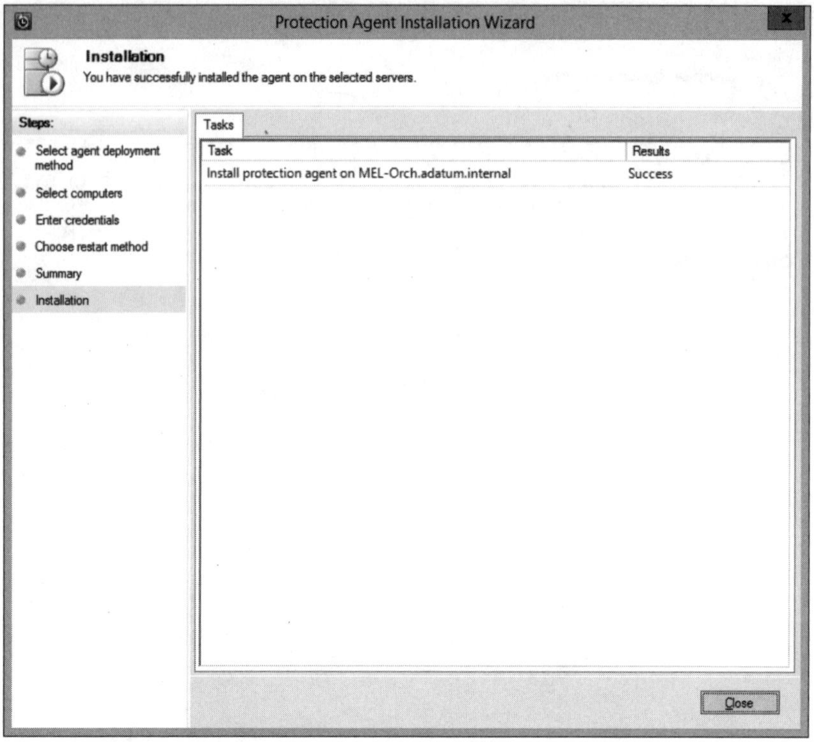

FIGURE 2-21 Agent Installation

> **MORE INFO DPM AGENT**
>
> You can learn more about the DPM agent at *http://technet.microsoft.com/en-us/library/hh758039.aspx.*

VMM agent

You deploy the VMM agent to virtualization hosts and virtualization host clusters that you want to manage using VMM. You can deploy the VMM agent directly to computers that are members of trusted Active Directory domains, to computers in untrusted domains, and stand-alone computers located on perimeter networks.

To add Hyper-V hosts in a disjoined namespace scenario, where the computer's primary DNS suffix does not match the domain name, you'll need to:

- Ensure that the VMM service has permission to register a Service Principal Name in Active Directory.

- Add the DNS suffix of the Hyper-V host to the TCP/IP connection settings on the VMM server.

To add Hyper-V hosts in an untrusted domain, ensure that you have local Administrator credentials on the target Hyper-V host, and then initiate a connection from the Fabric workspace of the VMM console using the FQDN or IP address of the target Hyper-V host. To add a Hyper-V host that is on a perimeter network, perform the following:

- Install the VMM agent locally on the computer running Hyper-V.

- Create an encryption key during installation.

- The key will be stored in a file, and the default name of this file is SecurityFile.txt.

- Transfer the file to the VMM server.

- Provide the path to the file that contains the key when adding the Hyper-V host using the VMM console.

To deploy the VMM agent on a Windows computer that is already a member of a trusted Active Directory domain, perform the following steps:

1. In the Fabric workspace of the VMM console, click Servers, and on the ribbon click Add Resources, and then click Hyper-V Hosts And Clusters.

2. On the Resource Location page of the Add Resource Wizard, select Windows Servers In A Trusted Active Directory Domain, as shown in Figure 2-22.

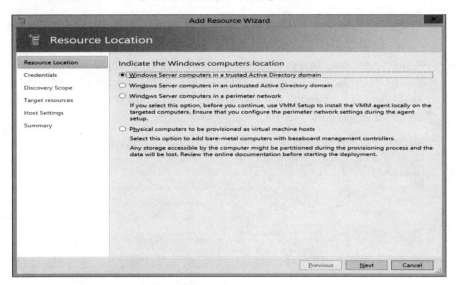

FIGURE 2-22 Add Resource Wizard

3. On the Credentials page, either select an existing Run As account, or manually provide credentials that are able to query Active Directory, and that have local Administrator permissions on the target computers.

4. On the Discovery Scope page, choose between specifying the Windows Server computers by NetBIOS name, FQDN, IPv4, or IPv6 address, or by querying Active Directory.

5.   On the Target Resources page, select the computer that you want to add as hosts, and click Next. Figure 2-23 shows Mel-hv1.adatum.internal selected.

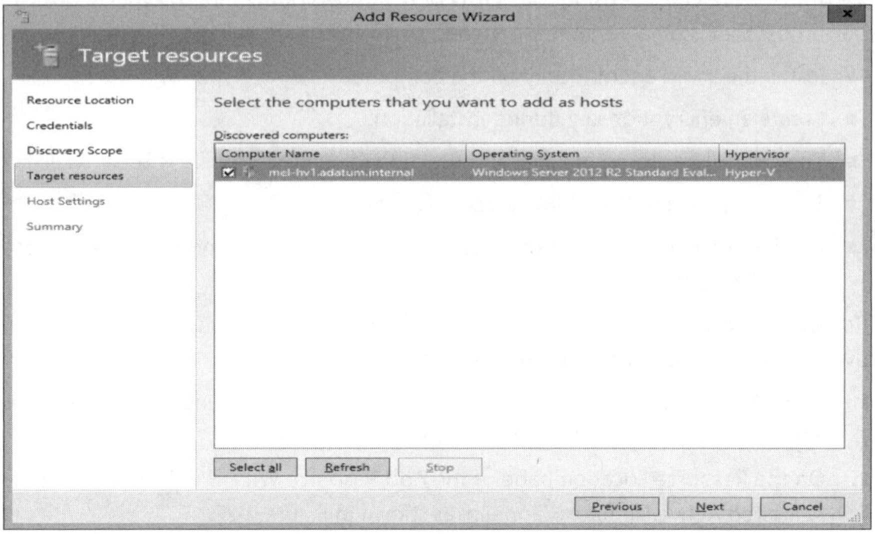

FIGURE 2-23 Target resources

6.   On the Host Settings page, specify the Host Group to which you want to add the new Hyper-V host. You can also specify the default virtual machine placement paths. If the computer needs to be reassociated with the VMM server, you'll need to select the Reassociate This Host With This VMM Environment option. Figure 2-24 shows the Host Group set to All Hosts, and VM placement set to volume D.

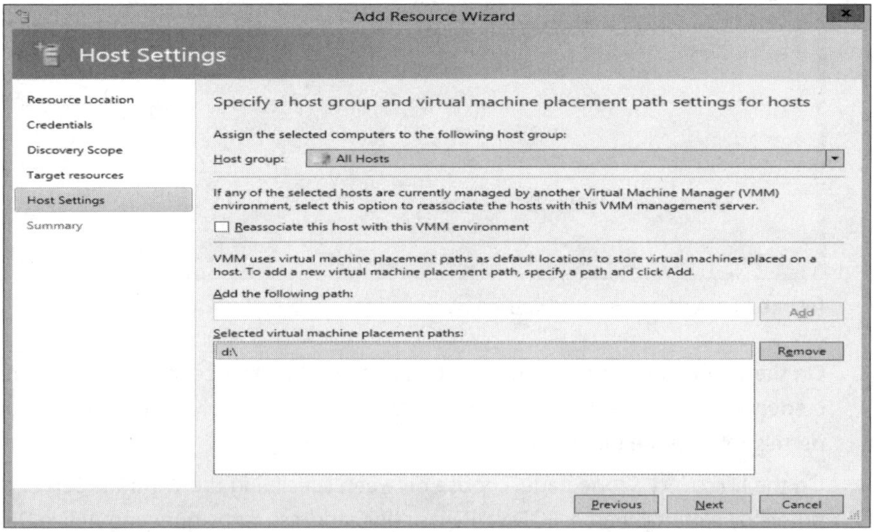

FIGURE 2-24 Host Settings

7. Complete the wizard, and verify agent deployment in the Jobs window.

> **MORE INFO VMM AGENT**
>
> You can learn more about the VMM agent at *http://technet.microsoft.com/en-us/library/gg610646.aspx*.

Run As accounts and Run As profiles

Run As accounts are used with Configuration Manager, Operations Manager, Virtual Machine Manager, and Service Manager. Run As accounts are stored sets of credentials that allow tasks to be performed, such as the installation of agents. Through a Run As account, a low privileged user can perform a specific task through an agent that would require elevated privileges without needing to have those tasks directly granted to them. For example, rather than add a user to the local Administrators group on a large number of servers, a Run As account can be configured that is a member of this group. When the user needs to perform a task on a remote computer with a specific System Center product that requires the permissions available to members of this group, they can use the Run As account to perform the task for them.

Operations Manager

Operations Manager uses Run As accounts and Run As profiles. A Run As account contains a single set of credentials. A Run As profile can have multiple Run As accounts associated with it. For example, you may need different sets of credentials to perform the same task on different computers. You could configure separate Run As accounts associated with those credentials, and then associate those Run As accounts with a specific profile.

Run As profiles are often defined in Operations Manager management packs. When configuring the management pack to function in your organization's private cloud, you'll need to create Run As accounts with credentials specific to your environment and associate them with the Run As profile that came with the management pack. Each Run As account in Operations Manager has a security classification, which can be set to More Secure or Less Secure. Setting a Run As account as More Secure allows you to limit which computers the Run As account credentials are distributed to.

To create a Run As account in Operations Manager for use with Windows based workloads, perform the following steps:

1. In the Administration workspace of the Operations Manager console, click Accounts under the Run As configuration node.
2. On the Tasks menu, click Actions, and then click Create Run As Account.
3. On the General Properties page of the Create Run As Account Wizard, specify the Run As account type, and a display name. The Run As account can be one of the following types:
   - Windows

- Community String
- Basic Authentication
- Simple Authentication
- Digest Authentication
- Binary Authentication
- Action Account
- SNMPv3 Account

4. On the Credentials page, specify a Username, Password, and Domain for the account.

5. On the Distribution Security page, specify whether you want to use the More Secure or Less Secure option. Figure 2-25 shows that the More Secure option selected.

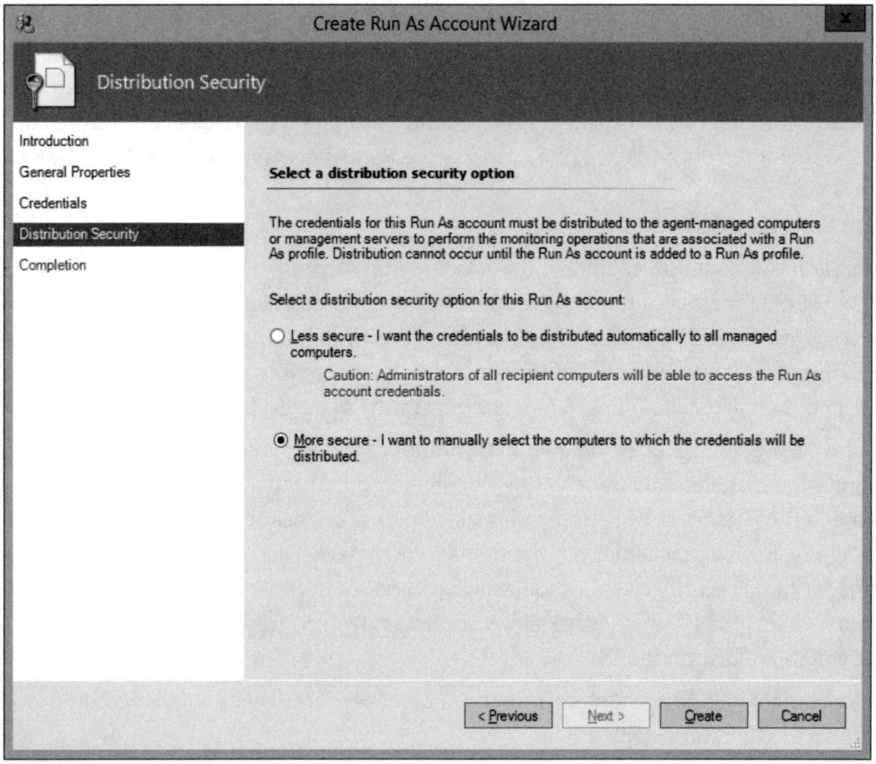

FIGURE 2-25 Distribution Security

6. Create the Run As account.

To create a Run As profile, perform the following steps:

1. In the Administration workspace of the Operations Manager console, click Profiles under Run As Configuration.

2. On the Tasks menu, click Actions, and then click Create Run As Profile.

3. On the General Properties page of the Run As Profile Wizard, provide a name for the Run As profile, and specify a management pack in which to save the Run As profile.

4. On the Run As Accounts page, add each Run As account that you want to associate with the Run As Profile. Figure 2-26 shows this page. Click Create to create the Run As profile.

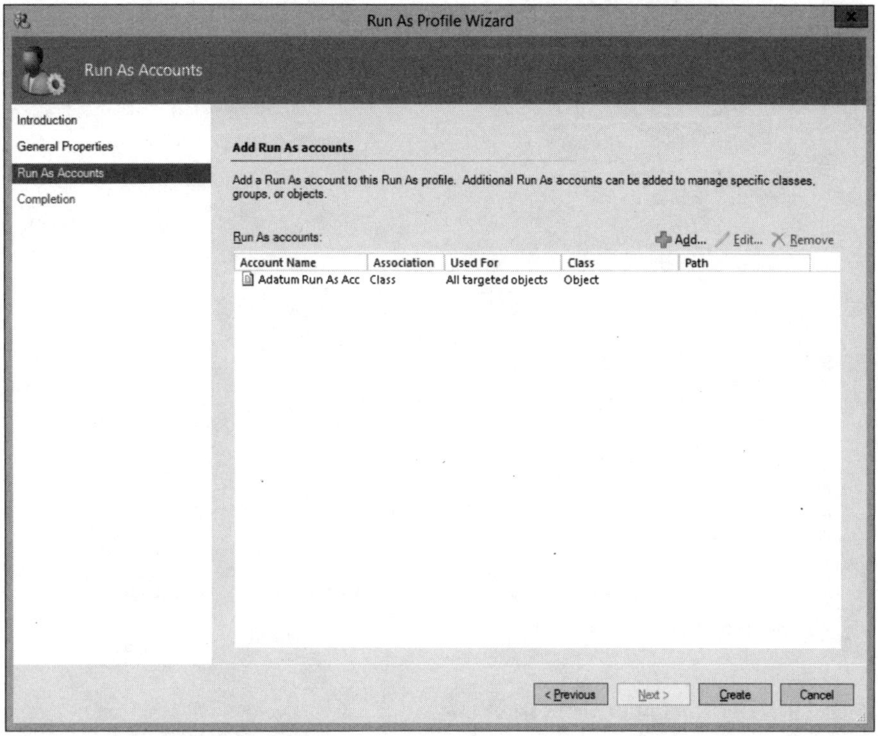

FIGURE 2-26 Run As Accounts

> **MORE INFO OPERATIONS MANAGER RUN AS ACCOUNTS AND PROFILES**
>
> You can learn more about Run As accounts and profiles at *http://technet.microsoft.com/ en-us/library/hh212714.aspx.*

Virtual Machine Manager

VMM has Run As accounts, but does not have Run As profiles. To create a Run As account in VMM, perform the following steps:

1. In the Settings workspace of the VMM console, click Create Run As Account on the ribbon.

2. On the Create Run As Account dialog box, provide a Name for the Run As account, the User Name that the Run As account is associated with, and the Password. Figure 2-27 shows this dialog box.

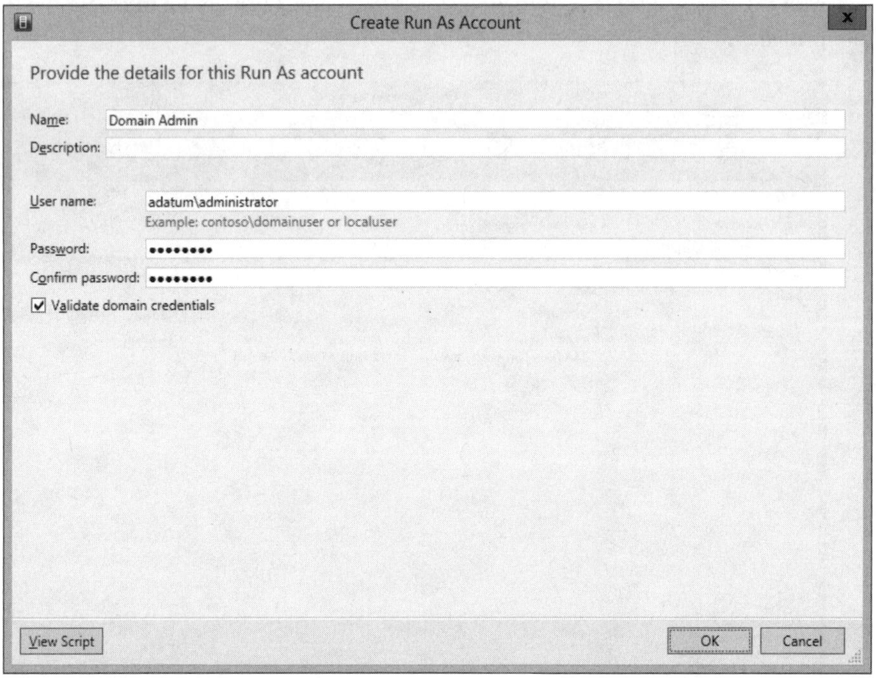

FIGURE 2-27 Create Run As Account

> **MORE INFO RUN AS ACCOUNTS IN VMM**
>
> You can learn more about Run As accounts in VMM at *http://technet.microsoft.com/en-us/library/gg675096.aspx.*

Service Manager

Unlike Operations Manager or VMM, where you configure Run As accounts on an as-needed basis, Run As accounts in Service Manger are configured during installation and only exist for the following purposes:

- Operational database account
- Workflow Run As account
- SQL Server Analysis Services account
- SQL Server Reporting Services account

Figure 2-28 shows some of the Service Manager Run As accounts.

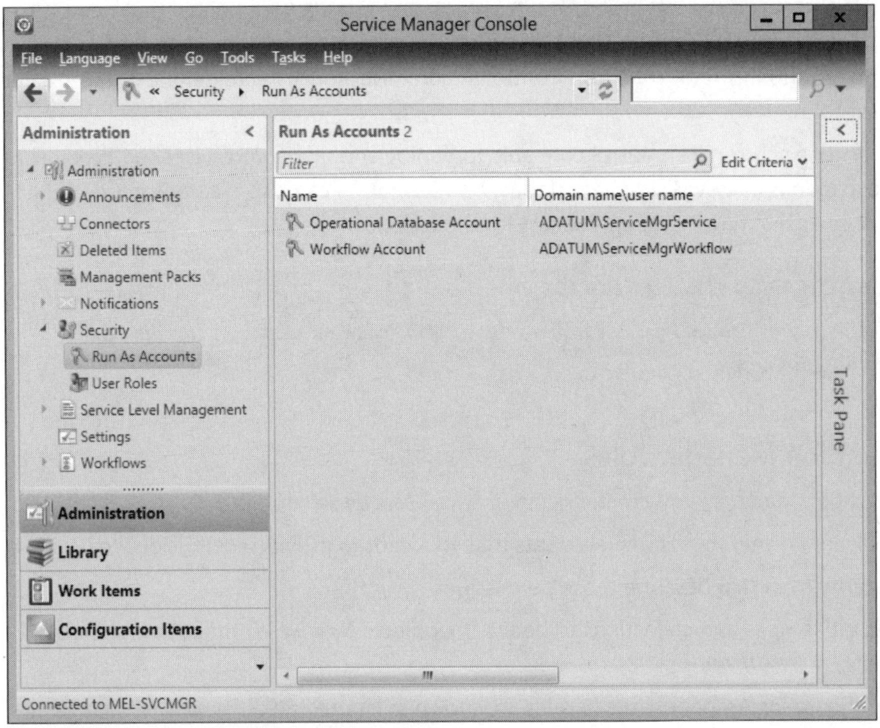

FIGURE 2-28 Service Manager Run As accounts

> **MORE INFO SERVICE MANAGER RUN AS ACCOUNTS**
>
> You can learn more about Service Manager Run As accounts at *http://technet.microsoft. com/en-us/library/hh495673.aspx.*

Configuration Manager

In Configuration Manager, the Accounts node of the Administration workspace stores accounts used as Run As accounts. Accounts differ from Configuration Manager Administrative Users. Configuration Manager Administrative Users are the way that you assign permissions and privileges in a Configuration Manager deployment.

Assigning user roles

Roles allow you to configure the permissions and privileges for users of System Center products. In general, you assign a security principle, usually a security group, but occasionally a user account to a role. You also often specify a scope, which limits the permissions and privileges assigned to a subset of product elements.

App Controller roles

App Controller has two separate roles. The Administrator role allows a person that holds it to perform all administrative actions. VMM administrators are not automatically added to the App Controller Administrator role. App Controller administrators can create one or more self-service user roles.

Members of a self-service user role are able to deploy and manage services to Microsoft Azure subscriptions or to VMM private clouds. Administrators can also create App Controller self-service roles that have read-only access for the scope.

> **MORE INFO APP CONTROLLER ROLES**
>
> You can learn more about App Controller roles at *http://technet.microsoft.com/en-us/library/hh221345.aspx.*

Configuration Manager roles

In Configuration Manager, you create administrative users by selecting:

- A security group to host the accounts that you want to provide permissions to.
- Security roles that describe those permissions.
- Security scopes and collections to define the objects over which those permissions apply.

The Configuration Manger security roles are shown in Figure 2-29.

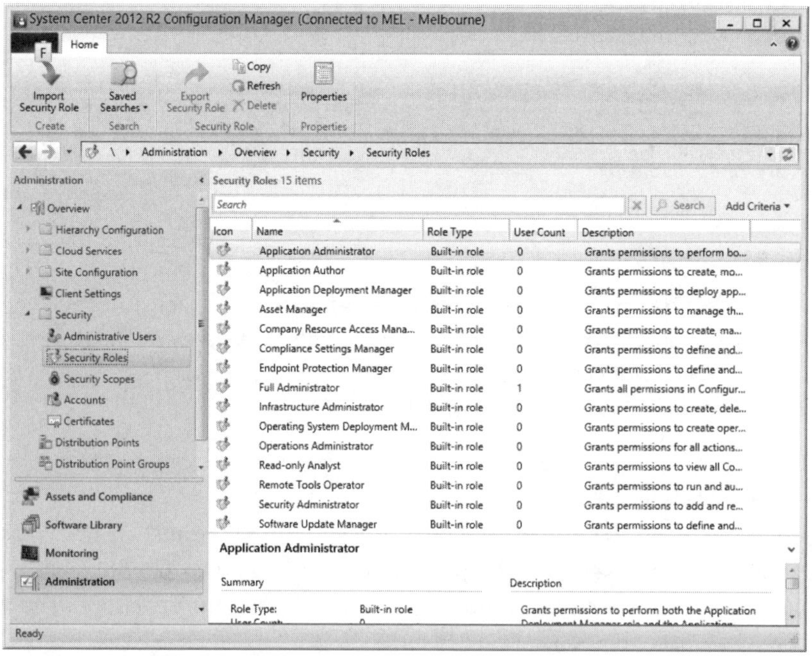

FIGURE 2-29 Security Roles

- **Application Administrator**   Includes the permissions of the Application Deployment Manager and Application Author roles. Allows management of queries, collections, user device affinity settings, and grants the ability to view site settings.

- **Application Author**   Provides permission to create, modify, and retire applications.

- **Application Deployment Manager**   Provides permissions to manage application deployment.

- **Asset Manager**   Provides permission to manage the asset intelligence synchronization point.

- **Company Resource Access Manager**   Provides permission to manage company resource access profiles.

- **Compliance Settings Manager**   Provides permission to manage compliance settings.

- **Endpoint Protection Manager**   Provides permission to manage Endpoint Protection security policies.

- **Full Administrator**   Provides all Configuration Manager permissions. Assigned to the user who performs installation of the first Configuration Manager site.

- **Infrastructure Administrator**   Provides permission to manage Configuration Manager infrastructure. Can also perform migration tasks.

- **Operating system Deployment Manager**   Provides permissions to create and deploy operating system images.

- **Operations Administrator**   Can perform any task in Configuration Manager, except for those related to managing security roles, administrative users, and security scopes.

- **Read-Only Analyst**   Can view settings for all Configuration Manager objects.

- **Remote Tools Operator**   Can run Remote Control, Remote Assistance, and Remote Desktop from the Configuration Manager console.

- **Security Administrator**   Provides permissions to manage security roles, collections, and security scopes.

- **Software Update Manager**   Provides permissions to define and deploy software updates.

MORE INFO CONFIGURATION MANAGER ROLES

You can learn more about the roles in Configuration Manager at *http://blogs.technet. com/b/hhoy/archive/2012/03/07/role-based-administration-in-system-center-2012-config- uration-manager.aspx.*

DPM roles

DPM has seven roles that you can use to control the assignment of permissions. These roles are:

- **DPM Admins**   Members of this role can perform all actions in DPM.
- **Recovery Operator**   Members of this role can perform recovery operations using DPM.
- **Reporting Operator**   Members of this role can run and manage reports.
- **Read-Only User**   Members of this role can view configuration items but cannot perform actions.
- **Tier-1 Support (help desk)**   Members of this role are able to resume backups and take automated recommended actions.
- **Tier-2 Support (escalation)**   Members of this role are able to run backups on demand and can enable and disable agents.
- **Tape Operator**   Members of this role can rerun backups and perform tape drive tasks.
- **Tape Admins**   Members of this role can perform any action related to tape drives.

> **MORE INFO DPM ROLES**
>
> You can learn more about DPM roles at *http://blogs.technet.com/b/dpm/archive/2011/09/08/dpm-2012-centralized-management-role-based-access-control.aspx*.

Operations Manager roles

You configure user roles in Operations Manager by selecting a profile and a scope. The scope defines the elements against which the permissions contained in the profile can be used. Figure 2-30 shows the available Operations Manager profiles.

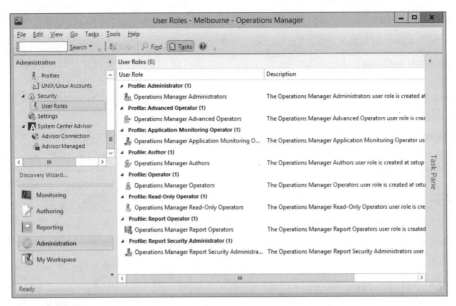

FIGURE 2-30 User Roles

These roles have the following permissions:

- **Administrator**   Has all privileges over the Operations Manager deployment.

- **Advanced Operator**   Has access to alerts, views, and tasks, and the ability to override the configuration of rules and monitors within the configured scope.

- **Application Monitoring Operator**   Grants members the ability to see Application Monitoring events.

- **Author**   Can create and manage monitoring configuration for targets and groups of targets within configured scope.

- **Operator**   Provides permission to interact with alerts, run tasks, and access views within their designated scope.

- **Read-Only Operator**   Provides read-only access to alerts and views within the designated scope.

- **Report Operator**   Provides access to reports within the designated scope.

- **Report Security Administrator**   Provides the ability to control access to reports.

MORE INFO OPERATIONS MANAGER USER ROLES

You can learn more about Operations Manager user roles at *http://technet.microsoft.com/en-us/library/hh230728.aspx.*

Orchestrator roles

Orchestrator has two different roles, the runbook author, and the runbook operator.

- **Runbook authors**   User accounts that are members of the Orchestrator Users group. You specify which group functions as the Orchestrator Users group during deployment. Members of this group have full administrator access to the Orchestrator deployment.

- **Runbook operators**   Runbook operators have permissions granted by runbook authors using the Orchestrator Runbook Designer. They can access the Orchestration console, can view and invoke runbooks to which they have been given permission.

> **MORE INFO ORCHESTRATOR ROLES**
>
> You can learn more about Orchestrator security groups at *http://technet.microsoft.com/en-us/library/hh912320.aspx*.

Service Manager roles

Service Manager includes 13 different built-in user roles that allow administrators to create additional user roles based on the built-in roles. These roles are available in the User Roles node of the Administration workspace, as shown in Figure 2-31, and have the following properties:

- **Activity Implementers**   Can edit manual activities in their queue scope. Have read-only access to other work items in their queue scope. Have read-only access to queue items in their group scope.

- **Administrators**   Full access to all elements of a Service Manager deployment.

- **Advanced Operators**   Are able to manage work items and configuration items in their queue scope. Can manage announcements in the Self-Service Portal.

- **Change Initiators**   Can create change requests and activities for configuration items in their group scope. Have read access to work items in their queue scope.

- **Service Request Analysts**   Can create and edit service requests and activity work items in their queue scope. Have read access to work items in their queue scope. Have read access to configuration items in their queue scope.

- **End Users**   Can create incidents, request software, view announcements and knowledge base articles in the Self-Service Portal.

- **Read-Only Operators**   Have read-only access to work items in their queue scope. Have read-only access to configuration items in their group scope.

- **Release Managers**   Can manage release records and activity work items in their queue scope. Have read-only access to other items in their queue scope. Have read-only access to items in their group scope.

- **Authors** Can manage work items in their queue scope. Can manage configuration items in their group scope. Can manage announcements in the Self-Service Portal.

- **Problem Analysts** Can manage problems in their queue scope. Have read-only access to other work items in their queue scope. Have read-only access to configuration items in their group scope.

- **Workflows** Can create and edit any configuration item or work item.

- **Incident Resolvers** Can manage incidents, problems, and manual activities in their group scope. Have read-only access to work items in their queue scope. Have read-only access to configuration items in their group scope.

- **Change Managers** Can manage change requests and activity work items in their queue scope. Have read-only access to work items in their queue scope. Have read-only access to configuration items in their group scope.

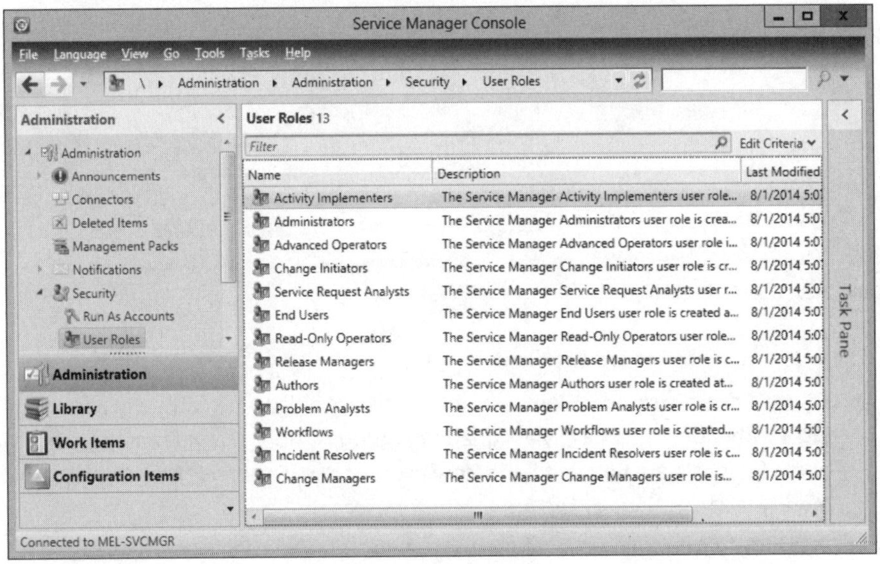

FIGURE 2-31 User Roles

MORE INFO SERVICE MANAGER USER ROLES

You can learn more about Service Manager user roles at http://technet.microsoft.com/en-us/library/hh524267.aspx.

Virtual Machine Manager roles

VMM has the built in Administrator role, which allows role members to perform any administrative action on all elements that VMM manages. Other roles in VMM are used when you create user roles. A user role consists of a profile, members, scope, library servers, and Run As accounts. Figure 2-32 shows the available user role profiles, which determine what actions a member of the user role can perform.

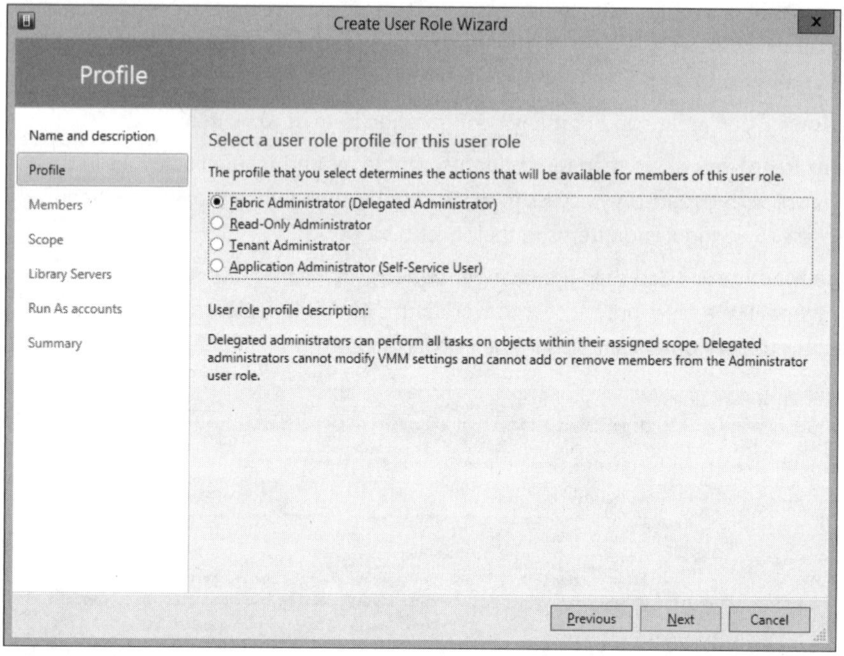

FIGURE 2-32 User Role Profiles

These user role profiles are as follows:

- **Fabric Administrator** Members of this role are able to perform any administrative tasks within their specifically assigned host groups, clouds, and library servers. Members of this role are unable to add XenServer or WSUS servers. They are also unable to modify VMM settings or the Administrator user role.

- **Read-Only Administrator** Members of this role can view the properties, status, and job status within their assigned host groups, clouds, and library servers. They are unable to modify these objects.

- **Tenant Administrator** Members of this role can manage self-service users and VM networks. They can also manage virtual machines and services as well as place quotas on resources.

- **Application Administrator** Called the Self-Service User Role in previous versions of VMM, allows the creation, deployment, and management of VMs and services.

> **MORE INFO VMM USER ROLES**
>
> You can learn more about VMM user roles at *http://technet.microsoft.com/en-us/library/gg696971.aspx.*

Understanding Operations Manager watcher nodes

An Operations Manager watcher node is a computer, a management server, or a device that hosts an Operations Manager agent that runs rules that probe an application or feature running on a third computer or device. For example, you might want to use Operations Manager to test the availability of a TCP port on a VPN appliance located on your organization's perimeter network. You could do this by using a computer deployed on the perimeter network, that has the Operations Manager agent installed, to probe the port of the VPN appliance to determine its availability. In this scenario, this computer on the perimeter network is functioning as the watcher node.

Operations Manager watcher nodes support synthetic transactions. Synthetic transactions are special tests that can be used to determine the availability or performance of the following:

- OLE DB Data Source
- Process
- TCP Port
- UNIX or Linux Log File
- UNIX or Linux Process
- Web Application Availability
- Web Application Transaction
- Windows Service

If you are planning on using watcher nodes to verify the availability of an application, consider using watcher nodes on different networks. This will allow you to determine whether the application is available from multiple locations.

The following management pack templates use watcher nodes:

- OLE DB Data Source
- TCP Port
- Web Application Transaction Monitoring

If necessary, you can configure the computer that hosts the application or feature that you want to monitor as the watcher node. You specify which agent managed computes will function as watcher nodes on the Watcher Node page of the Add Monitoring Wizard, as shown in Figure 2-33.

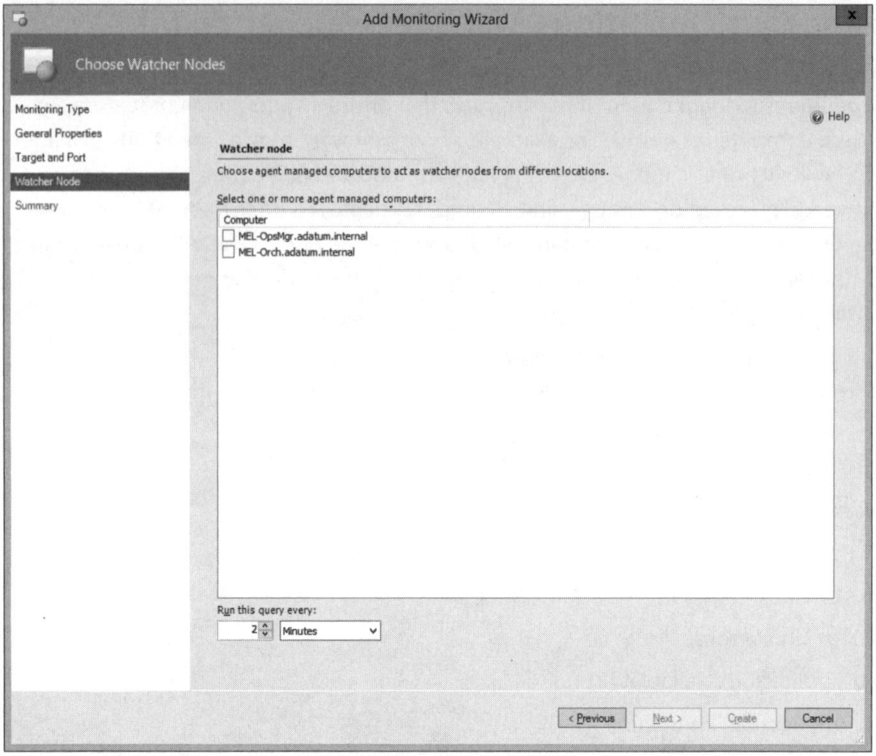

FIGURE 2-33 Watcher nodes

> **MORE INFO OPERATIONS MANAGER WATCHER NODES**
>
> You can learn more about Operations Manager watcher nodes at *http://technet.microsoft. com/en-us/library/hh457584.aspx*.

Operations Manager gateway servers

Mutual authentication must occur for an Operations Manager server to communicate with a computer or device that it manages. This is straightforward when the Operations Manager server, and the computer or device are members of the same Active Directory domain, or members of domains that have an existing trust relationship. Operations Manager gateway servers allow computers and devices that Operations Manager monitors, that do not have such a trust relationship, to perform authentication.

You deploy gateway servers within the trust boundary of the computer or devices that you want to monitor. For example, imagine two domains that don't have a trust relationship, Fabrikam.internal and Fabrikam.perimeter. An Operations Manager management server is deployed in the Fabrikam.internal domain. Computers that you want to monitor are located in the Fabrikam.perimeter domain. In this scenario, you would deploy an Operations Manager gateway server in the Fabrikam.perimeter domain. Authentication between the Operations Manager management server and the Operations Manager gateway server occurs using certificates.

To deploy a gateway server, you need to perform the following general steps:

1. Request certificates for computers or devices that have the Operations Manager agent installed, will function as the Operations Manager gateway server, or will function as the Operations Manager management server from a trusted certificate authority. This can be a third-party certificate authority, or an internal certificate authority.

2. Use the MOMCertImport.exe tool to import the certificates. The syntax of this command, used from an elevated command prompt, is:

```
momcertimport.exe /SubjectName <certificate subject name>
```

3. On the Operations Manager management server, use the Microsoft.EnterpriseManagement.GatewayApprovalTool.exe to configure communication between the management server and the computer that will function as the gateway server using the following syntax from an elevated command prompt:

```
Microsoft.EnterpriseManagement.gatewayApprovalTool.exe /ManagementServerName=<mana
gementserverFQDN> /GatewayName=<GatewayFQDN> /Action=Create
```

4. Install the gateway server using the Operations Manager installation media.

> **MORE INFO OPERATIONS MANAGER GATEWAY SERVERS**
>
> You can learn more about Operations Manager gateway servers at *http://technet.microsoft. com/en-us/library/hh212823.aspx.*

EXAM TIP

Remember the difference between roles and Run As profiles.

Objective summary

- DPM storage pools store backed up data. You must have a DPM storage pool configured before you can start protecting workloads with DPM.

- DPM secondary servers are DPM servers that back up all workloads on the primary server.

- DPM chaining involves spreading protected workloads across two or more DPM servers, with a separate DPM server providing a secondary backup location for each workload protected by any DPM server in the chain.

- Protection groups define which workloads are protected, the type of protection that is configured, and the retention period for that protection.

- Agents or clients are special software that some System Center products use to interact with computers.

- Operations Manager watcher nodes are used to perform synthetic transactions to monitor availability.

- Run As accounts allow operators of a System Center product to carry out a task using an alternate set of credentials.
- User roles define the permissions that an operator has when using a System Center product.
- Operations Manager gateway servers allow computers and devices that Operations Manager monitors that do not have such a trust relationship to perform authentication.

Objective review

Answer the following questions to test your knowledge of the information in this objective. You can find the answers to these questions and explanations of why each answer choice is correct or incorrect in the "Answers" section at the end of this chapter.

1. What is the minimum number of disks required for a DPM storage pool?
   - **A.** One
   - **B.** Two
   - **C.** Three
   - **D.** Four

2. How many Operations Manager management groups can a single Operations Manager agent report to?
   - **A.** One
   - **B.** Two
   - **C.** Four
   - **D.** Eight

3. Which of the following methods can you use to deploy the Configuration Manager client to virtual machines running Windows Server 2012 R2 in your organization's private cloud without requiring a logon to that VM?
   - **A.** Client push installation account
   - **B.** Deployment from Windows Server Update Services
   - **C.** Deployment from Windows Intune
   - **D.** Manual installation

4. Which of the following Operations Manager user roles has the ability to override the configuration of rules and monitors within the configured scope?
   - **A.** Operator
   - **B.** Report Security Administrator
   - **C.** Advanced Operator
   - **D.** Author

5. Which of the following Service Manager roles allow a user assigned the role the ability to create change requests for configuration items in their group scope?

   A. Service Request Analysts

   B. Read-Only Operators

   C. Problem Analysts

   D. Change Initiators

Objective 2.2: Configure portals and dashboards

In this section, you will learn about the different portals and dashboards that you can use to interact with and monitor your organization's private cloud environment.

This objective covers the following topics:
- App Controller
- Service Manager Self-Service Portal
- Operations Manager dashboards
- Application monitoring

Using App Controller

App Controller allows you to manage private clouds created with VMM, and public clouds running in Microsoft Azure. App Controller also functions as the Self-Service Portal for VMM. Administrators can use VMM to create services and service templates that they can then deploy to a private cloud. Users in the organization can use App Controller to manage and deploy those services.

> **MORE INFO CONFIGURING APP CONTROLLER**
>
> You can learn more about configuring App Controller at *http://technet.microsoft.com/en-us/library/gg696038.aspx*.

Deploying services and virtual machines

System Center App Controller provides users with self-service virtual machine deployment functionality for VMM 2012 SP1 and VMM 2012 R2. App Controller runs as a web application, shown in Figure 2-34. To perform self-service virtual machine deployment using App Controller, a user must be a member of a VMM self-service user role. This role is termed Application Administrator in VMM 2012 R2.

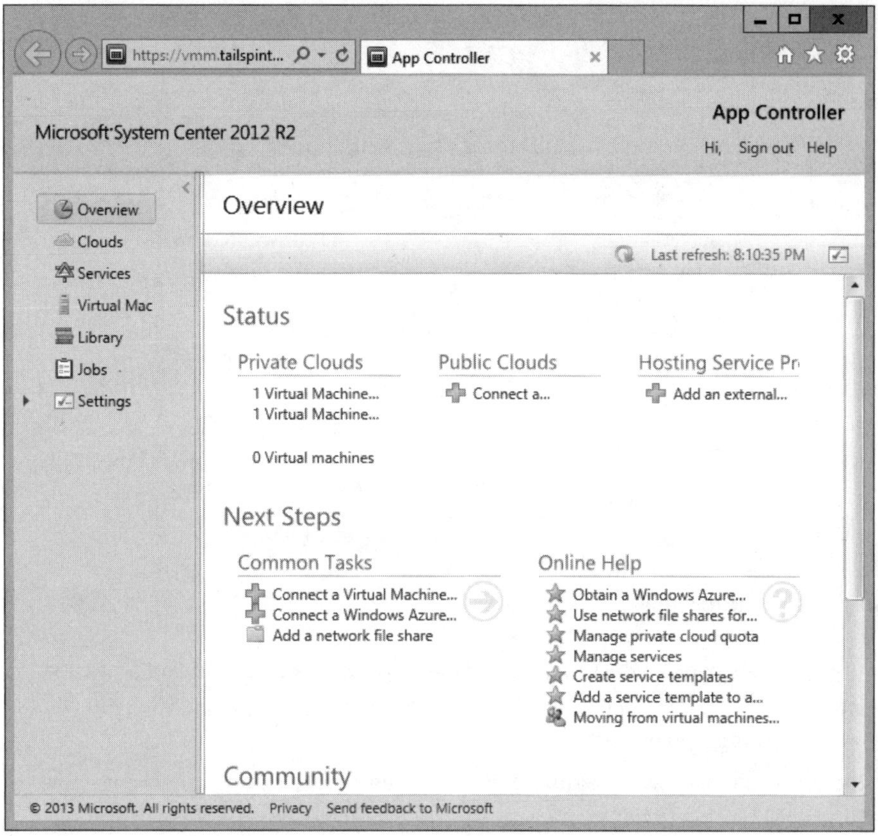

FIGURE 2-34 App Controller

To create a self-service user role in VMM, perform the following steps:

1. Click Create User Role on the ribbon when in the Settings workspace of the VMM console.

2. On the Name And Description page of the Create User Role Wizard, provide a name for the role and an optional description.

3. On the Profile page, click Application Administrator (Self-Service User), as shown in Figure 2-35.

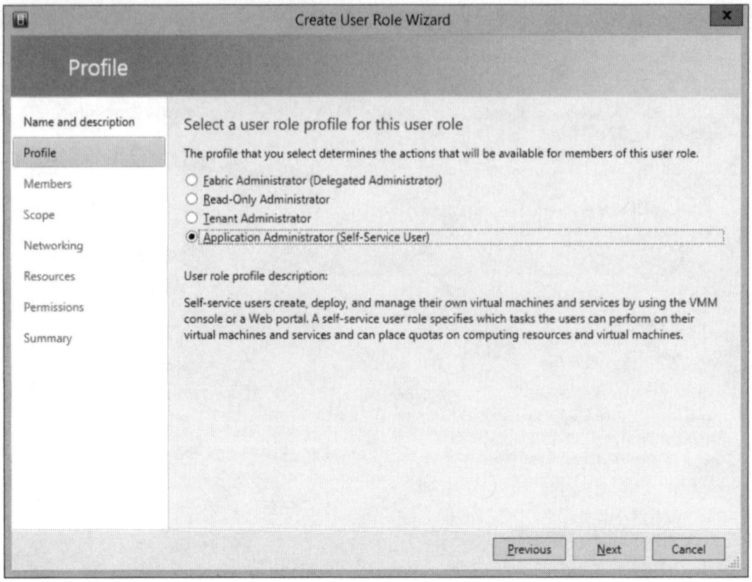

FIGURE 2-35 Create user role

4. On the Members page of the Create User Role Wizard, click Add, and add an Active Directory security group that will host the user accounts of the people who you want to grant self-service privileges to.

5. On the Scope page, shown in Figure 2-36, select the private cloud into which self-service users will be able to deploy VMs.

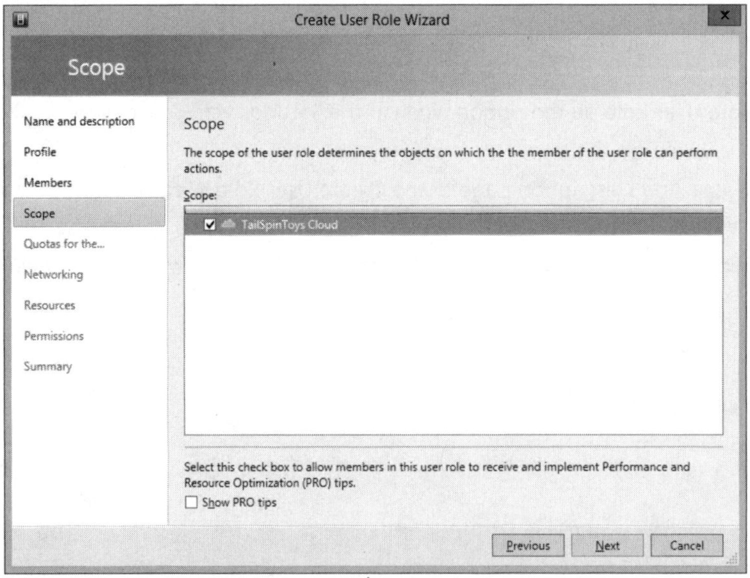

FIGURE 2-36 Create user role

6. On the Quotas page, specify the quotas for the self-service user role. You can configure role level quotas, which apply to all users of the role, or individual quotas, that apply to individual users. For example, Figure 2-37 shows member level quotas configured so that each role member can use a maximum of 2 virtual CPUs, 8192 MB of RAM, 50 GB of storage, and deploy a maximum of 2 virtual machines.

Create User Role Wizard ✕

Quotas for the TailSpinToys Cloud cloud

Name and description
Profile
Members
Scope
Quotas for the...
Networking
Resources
Permissions
Summary

Quotas for the TailSpinToys Cloud cloud

Role level quotas:
All members of this user role combined can use resources up to the specified limits.

Dimension	Available Capacity	Use Maximum	Assigned Quota
Virtual CPUs:	Unlimited	☑	Unlimited
Memory (MB):	Unlimited	☑	Unlimited
Storage (GB):	Unlimited	☑	Unlimited
Custom quota (points):	Unlimited	☑	Unlimited
Virtual machines:	Unlimited	☑	Unlimited

Member level quotas:
Each member of this user role combined can use resources up to the specified limits.

Dimension	Available Capacity	Use Maximum	Assigned Quota
Virtual CPUs:	Unlimited	☐	2
Memory (MB):	Unlimited	☐	8192
Storage (GB):	Unlimited	☐	50
Custom quota (points):	Unlimited	☐	10
Virtual machines:	Unlimited	☐	2

Previous   Next   Cancel

FIGURE 2-37 Member level quotas

7. On the Networking page, select which networks, if any, to which you will restrict the self-service users. If you don't specify any networks, self-service users can use any configured VM network.

8. On the Resources page, select which resources, if any, to which you will restrict the self-service users. If you don't specify any resources, self-service users can use any available VMM resources.

9. On the Permissions page, shown in Figure 2-38, configure the permissions that you want to assign to the users.

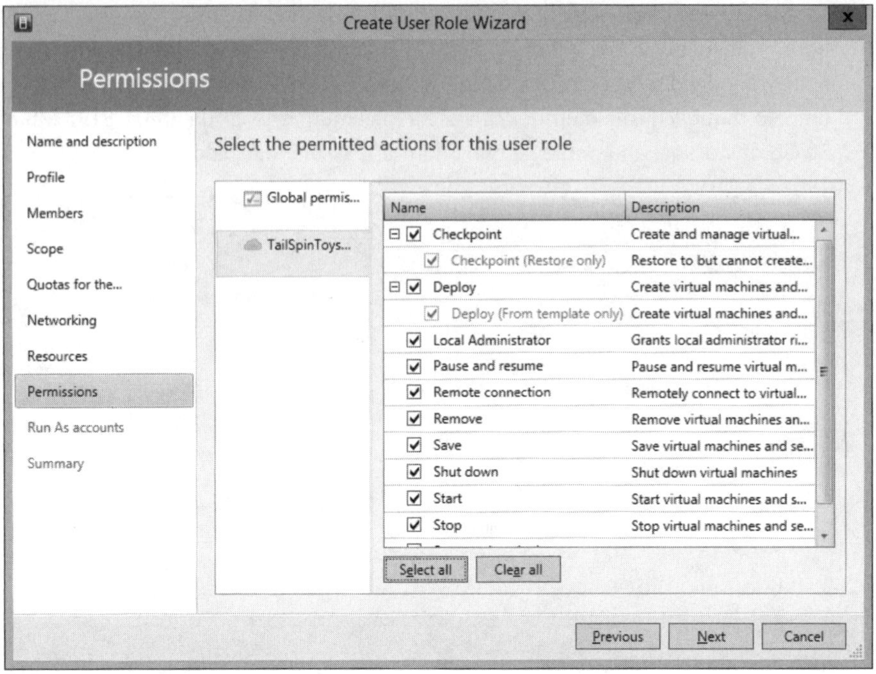

FIGURE 2-38 Permitted actions

10. On the Run As accounts page, select which VMM Run As accounts that members of the user role can utilize.

If a user is assigned the appropriate permissions through the VMM role they will be able to sign in to the App Controller portal. From there they will be able to connect to the private clouds hosted through VMM to which they have been assigned access, and deploy and manage virtual machines.

> **MORE INFO DEPLOYING SERVICES AND VIRTUAL MACHINES**
>
> You can learn more about deploying services and virtual machines at *http://technet. microsoft.com/en-us/library/gg696042.aspx*.

Managing services

You can use App Controller to manage services that you have deployed to your organization's private cloud.

To change the state of a deployed service, perform the following steps:

1. On the Services node of the App Controller console, click the Service Instance.

2. On the task bar, click the state that you want the service to enter. The available options are Start, Stop, Resume, Suspend, and Shut Down.

To change the properties of a service that is deployed to your organization's private cloud, click on the service in the Services node of the App Controller console, select Open Diagram from the task bar, and in the diagram, click the service to open the service's Properties page. Once you have made the necessary changes, click Update to modify the service.

> **MORE INFO MANAGING SERVICES AND VIRTUAL MACHINES**
>
> You can learn more about managing services and virtual machines at *http://technet. microsoft.com/en-us/library/gg696044.aspx*.

Using Service Manager Self-Service Portal

The Service Manager 2012 R2 Self-Service Portal is a SharePoint 2010 website that people in your organization can use to submit requests for service offerings and request offerings using their web browser. The Self-Service Portal leverages Service Manager user roles, meaning that users will be presented with different request and service offerings depending on role membership. Users are able to submit requests and view the status of those requests using the portal. Figure 2-39 shows the Service Manager 2012 R2 Self-Service Portal.

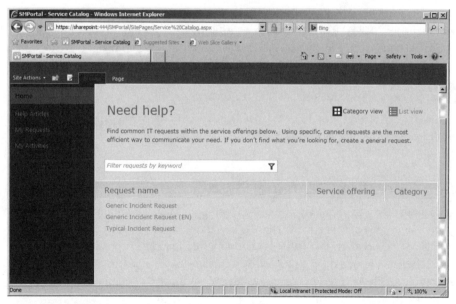

FIGURE 2-39 Self-Service Portal

When a user submits a request using the self-service website, the request is forwarded to the Service Manager server where the information submitted through the self-service website is processed. You can publish Service Manager requests and service offerings to the Self-Service Portal. Many organizations use the Self-Service Portal to allow users to submit their own incident tickets as an alternative to contacting the help desk.

This functionality is only the tip of the iceberg. If you integrate Service Manager with other System Center products, such as Operations Manager, Orchestrator, and Virtual Machine Manager, you can offer services that leverage these products through the Self-Service Portal. For example, you could create a service offering that:

- Allows users to request and deploy virtual machines through System Center Virtual Machine Manager, with the details of that request and subsequent deployment all logged within Service Manager.

- Allows users to put SQL Server databases into protection, or perform self-service recovery by leveraging Service Manager integration with Data Protection Manager and Orchestrator.

- Allows users to trigger Orchestrator runbooks. Since runbooks can be created to perform almost any task within your organization's Windows-based infrastructure, you can provide users with the ability, through the Self-Service Portal, to trigger any task for which you can build a runbook.

The Self-Service Portal can be hosted on a separate computer from the Service Manager server. One important thing to note is that you can only use SharePoint 2010 to host the Service Manager 2012 R2 RTM self-service website. You cannot use SharePoint 2013 to host the Service Manager 2012 R2 RTM self-service website. This is important as you cannot deploy versions of SharePoint 2010 prior to Service Pack 2 on computers running the Windows Server 2012 and Windows Server 2012 R2 operating systems.

> **MORE INFO SERVICE MANAGER SELF-SERVICE PORTAL**
>
> You can learn more about the Service Manager Self-Service Portal at *http://technet. microsoft.com/en-us/library/hh667344.aspx.*

Creating Operations Manager dashboards

Dashboards give you a way of quickly displaying Operations Manager information. Dashboards allow you to see pertinent information "at a glance," so that you can quickly ascertain whether an event has occurred that requires important information. Dashboards allow you to present multiple types of data in a single view. You can view dashboards in the Operations Manager console, or by using a web browser when the dashboard is published to SharePoint.

When creating a dashboard, you can choose from one of the following templates, as shown in Figure 2-40.

- **Column Layout** Column layouts consist of multiple columns of information.
- **Grid Layout** Grid layouts consist of multiple cells, each of which contains separate information.
- **Service Level Dashboard** A service level dashboard allows you to display information related to service level tracking.

- **Summary Dashboard** The summary dashboard will display the top selected number of performance counters for chosen values.

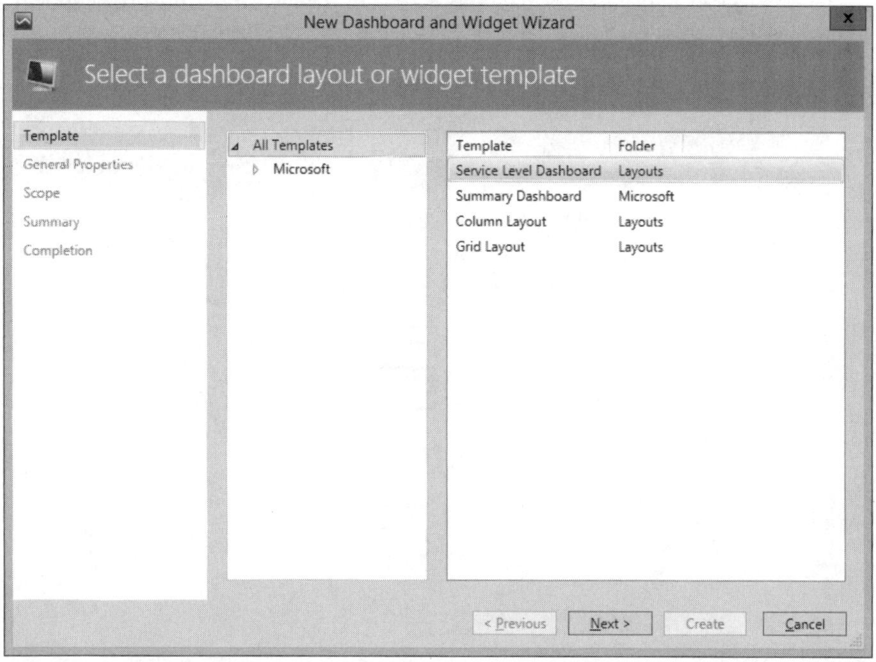

FIGURE 2-40 Dashboard layout

Once you choose a layout, you add widgets to the dashboard that display information that you are interested in viewing. You can add the following widget types to a dashboard:

- **State** Allows you to view the state of monitored objects.
- **Performance** Allows you to view performance metrics.
- **Alert** Allows you to view alert information.
- **Details** The properties of the item that is highlighted in the dashboard.
- **Instance Details** Provides details of the instances related to the object.
- **Objects By Performance** Performance counter data in tabular format for the selected object.

You create dashboards in the My Workspace view. For example, to create a grid layout dashboard view named Domain Controller Availability And Alerts in Operations Manager, perform the following tasks:

1. In the My Workspace view of the Operations Manager console, right-click Favorite View, click New, and then click Dashboard View.

2. On the Template page, click Grid Layout, and then click Next.

3. On the General Properties page, type the name **Domain Controller Availability and Alerts,** and click Next.

4. On the Layout page, click 2 Cells, and then click the layout on the left, as shown in Figure 2-41, and click Next.

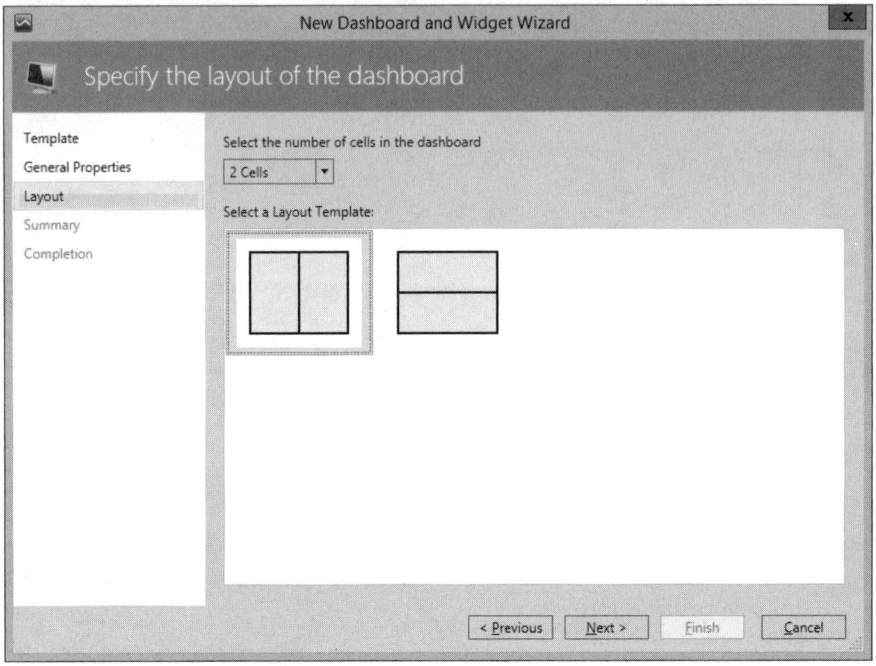

FIGURE 2-41 Dashboard cells

5. On the Summary page, click Create, and then click Close.

6. The new Dashboard will appear under the Favorite Views node. Click the new dashboard, in this case named Domain Controller Availability And Alerts, and then click the text Click To Add Widget. This will open the New Dashboard And Widget Wizard. Click State Widget, as shown in Figure 2-42, and click Next.

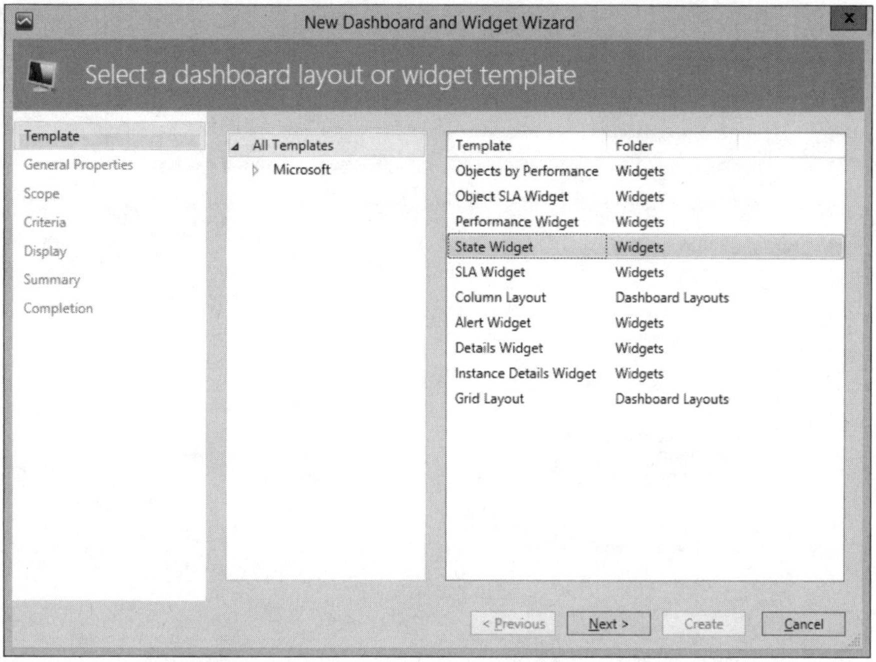

FIGURE 2-42 Dashboard widget

7. On the General Properties page, type **Domain Controller State,** and then click Next.

8. On the Scope page, click Add. On the Add Groups Or Objects dialog box, click Show All Objects And Groups. Type the domain suffix to limit the displayed items, and then navigate to the object that represents one of your organization's domain controllers. Figure 2-43 shows MEL-DC.adatum.internal selected. Click Add, and then click OK.

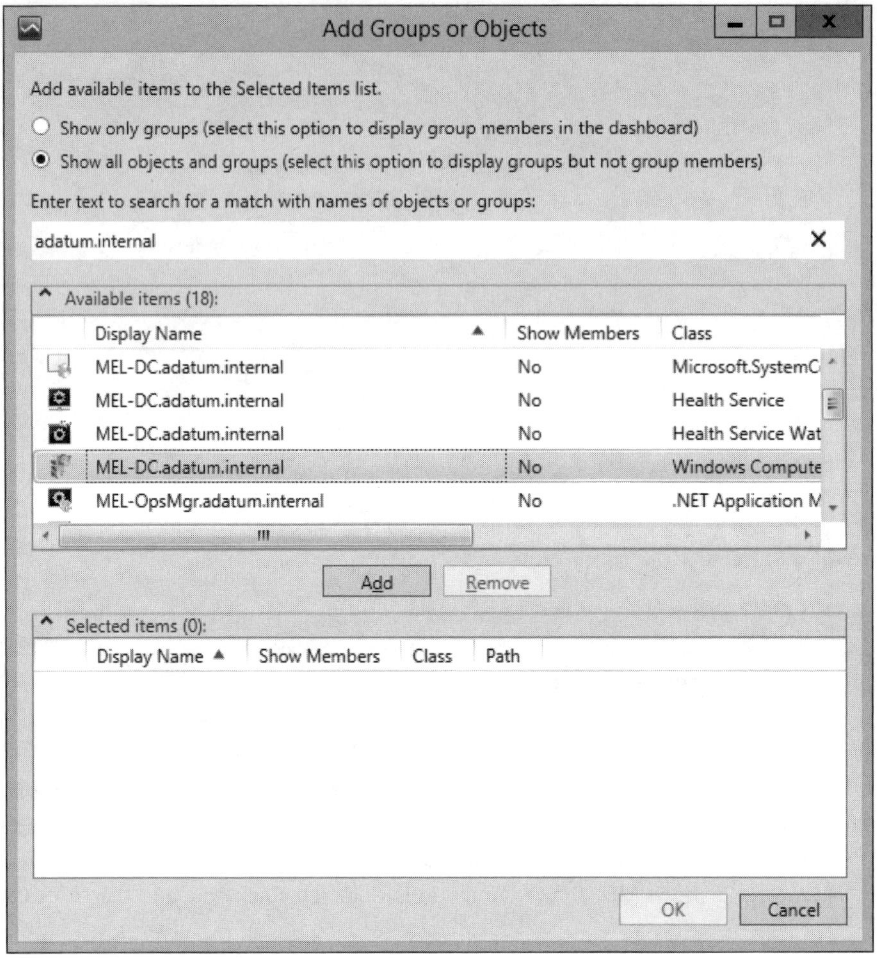

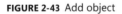

Add Groups or Objects

Add available items to the Selected Items list.

○ Show only groups (select this option to display group members in the dashboard)

◉ Show all objects and groups (select this option to display groups but not group members)

Enter text to search for a match with names of objects or groups:

adatum.internal   ✕

▲ Available items (18):

Display Name	▲	Show Members	Class
MEL-DC.adatum.internal		No	Microsoft.SystemC
MEL-DC.adatum.internal		No	Health Service
MEL-DC.adatum.internal		No	Health Service Wat
MEL-DC.adatum.internal		No	Windows Compute
MEL-OpsMgr.adatum.internal		No	.NET Application M

[Add]   [Remove]

▲ Selected items (0):

Display Name ▲	Show Members	Class	Path

[OK]   [Cancel]

FIGURE 2-43 Add object

9. On the Scope page, verify that the domain controller's computer object is listed.

10. On the Criteria page, select all of the available criteria except Display Only Objects In Maintenance Mode, as shown in Figure 2-44.

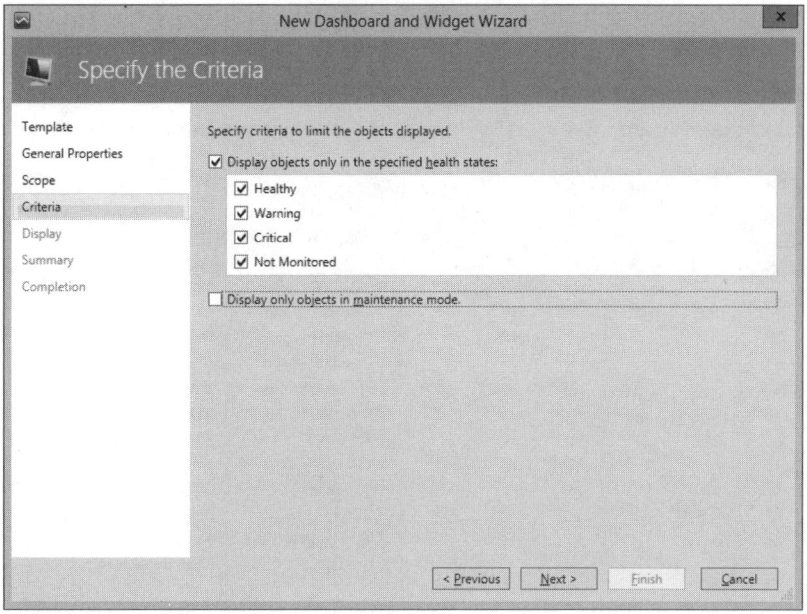

FIGURE 2-44 Dashboard criteria

11. On the Display page, select the Columns To Display, as shown in Figure 2-45, and then click Next.

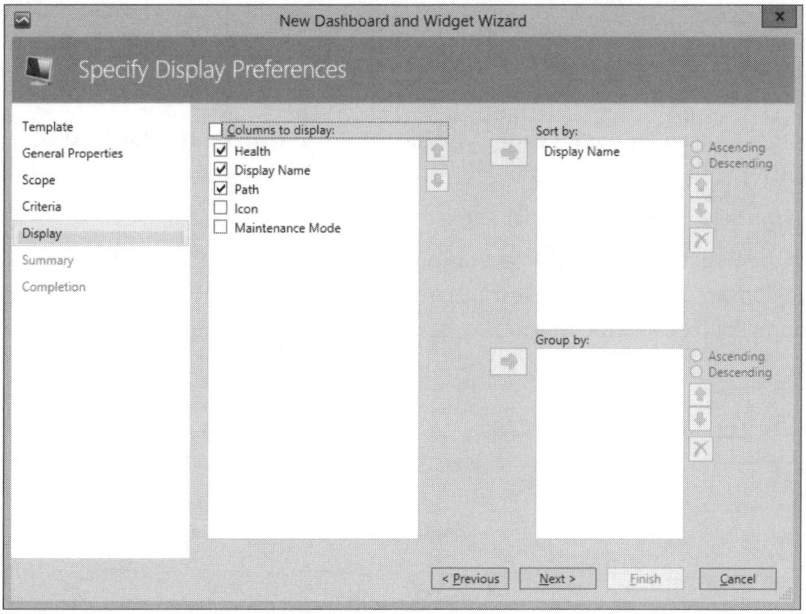

FIGURE 2-45 Display configuration

12. On the Summary page, click Create, and then click Close.

13. With the Domain Controller Availability And Alerts node selected, click the Click To Add Widget text.

14. On the Select A Dashboard Layout Or Widget template page of the New Dashboard And Widget Wizard, click Alert Widget, as shown in Figure 2-46, and click Next.

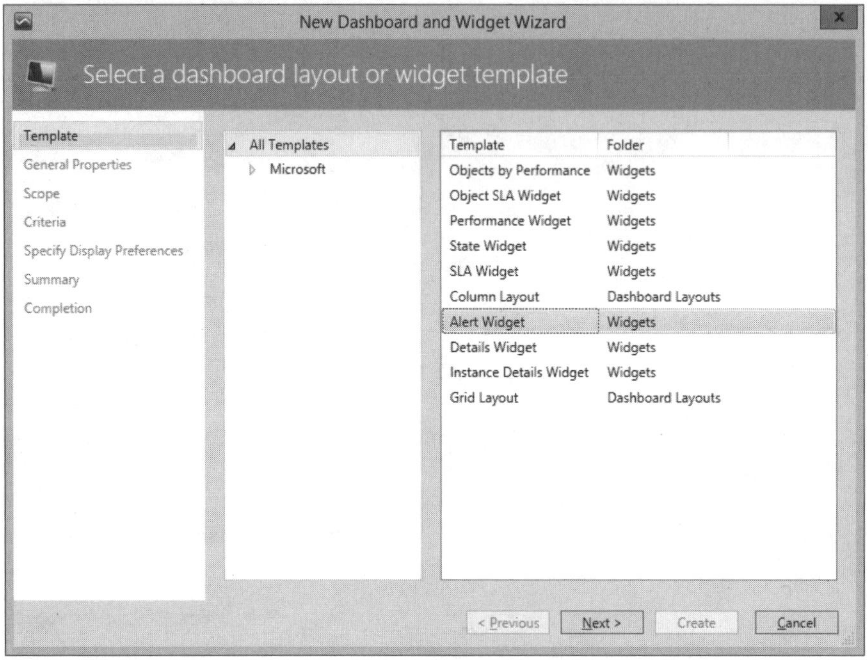

FIGURE 2-46 Alert widget

15. On the General Properties page, type the name, **Domain Controller Host Alerts,** and click Next.

16. On the Select Group Or Object page, click the ellipsis button (...).

17. On the Select A Group Or Object dialog box, click Groups And Objects, and then type the domain name suffix, and click Search. Figure 2-47 shows the MEL-DC.tailspintoys. internal object, and the Health Service Watcher Class is selected. Click OK.

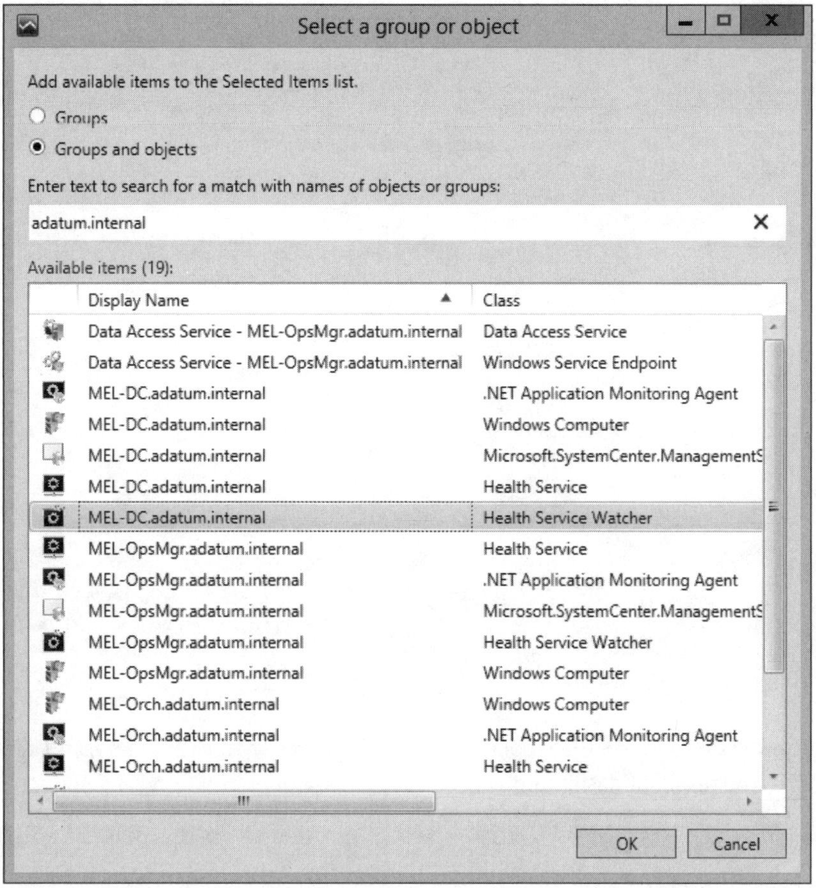

FIGURE 2-47 Health Service Watcher object

18. On the Criteria page, select the following check boxes, as shown in Figure 2-48.

- Display Alerts Only With The Specified Severities
- Critical
- Warning

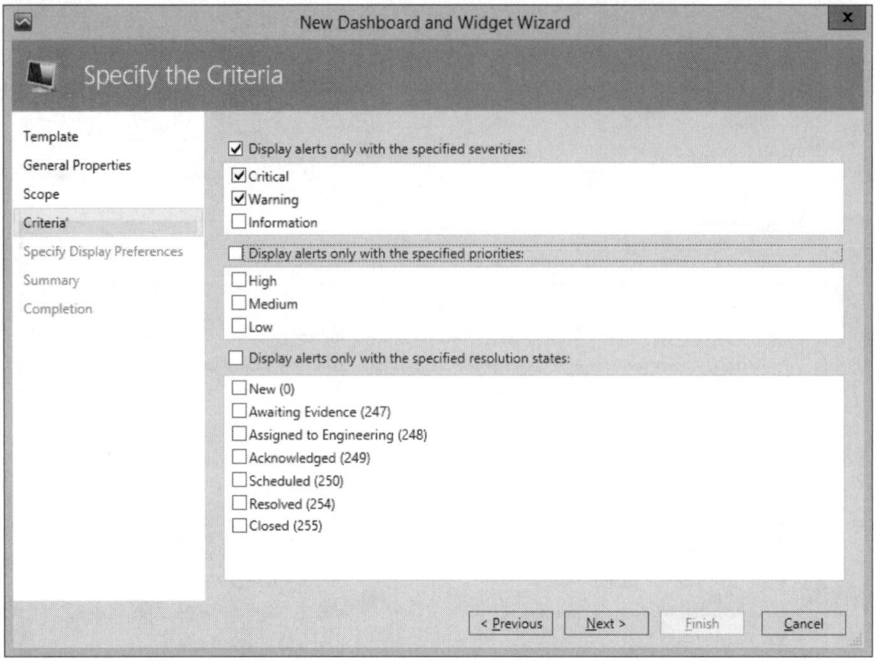

FIGURE 2-48 Criteria selection

19. Review the options on the Display tab, and click Next. Then click Create, and click Close. The resultant dashboard will look similar to Figure 2-49.

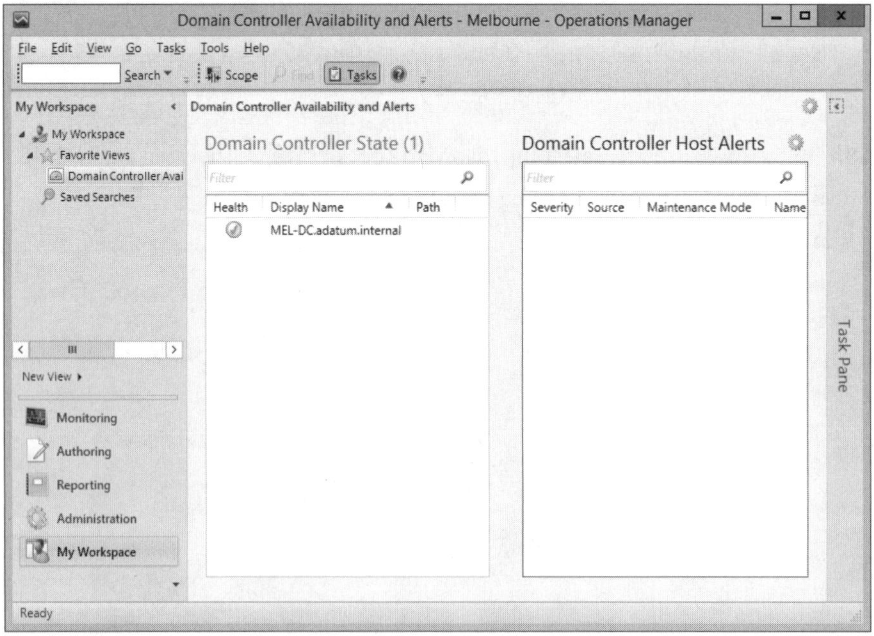

FIGURE 2-49 Dashboard view

To be able to display a dashboard in SharePoint, you need to have installed the Operations Manager SharePoint Web Part on the SharePoint server. A user that has administrative permissions on the SharePoint server must install the Operations Manager SharePoint Web Part.

> **MORE INFO OPERATIONS MANAGER DASHBOARDS**
>
> You can learn more about Operations Manager dashboards at *http://blogs.technet.com/b/momteam/archive/2011/09/27/introducing-operations-manager-2012-dashboards.aspx*.

Application Performance Monitoring

You can use Application Performance Monitoring (APM) to monitor Internet Information Services (IIS) hosted .NET and Windows Communication Foundation (WCF) applications from both the perspective of the server that hosts the application, and the client that is interacting with the application. APM allows you to use Operations Manager to collect detailed information about a specific application's performance and reliability.

You configure Application Performance Monitoring using the .NET Application Performance Monitoring Template that is available through the Authoring workspace of the Operations console.

To view Application Performance Monitoring event details, you'll need the Operations Manger web console. It's also necessary to import the following management packs and their dependencies into Operations Manager:

- Windows Server 2008 IIS 7.0
- Operations Manager APM Web IIS 7

If you need to monitor applications hosted on Windows Server 2012 or Windows Server 2012 R2, you'll need to import the following management packs and their dependencies:

- Microsoft Windows Server 2012 IIS 8
- Microsoft System Center APM Web IIS 8

Once you have installed these management packs, you can view the ASP.NET applications that Operations Manager finds in the Monitoring workspace, under Application Monitoring, under the .NET Monitoring node in the ASP.NET Web Application Inventory node. You'll be able to view WCF applications under the IIS Hosted WCF Web Service Inventory node.

When APM discovers an application, you'll usually need to restart IIS before you can start monitoring. You need to restart IIS so that the application pools recycle. This enables the APM extensions, and allows the APM function to register with the application.

The server-side monitoring capabilities of APM include:

- Performance event monitoring and alerting.
- Exception event monitoring and alerting.
- Modifying performance event threshold.

- Configuring performance event monitoring thresholds and sensitivity on a per-namespace or per-method basis.
- Configuring exception event monitoring types on a per-exception or per-exception handler basis.

The client-side monitoring capabilities of APM include:

- Performance event monitoring and alerting.
- Exception event monitoring and alerting.
- Performance event thresholds for:
- Page load
- Asynchronous JavaScript and XML
- WCF
- Collecting data related to images, scripts, CSS, HTML components, global variables, and exception stack.
- Collecting load balancer header data.

To configure Application Performance Monitoring, perform the following steps:

1. In the Authoring workspace of the Operations Manager console, click Management Pack Templates, and then click Add Monitoring Wizard on the ribbon.

2. On the Monitoring Type page, shown in Figure 2-50, click .NET Application Performance Monitoring.

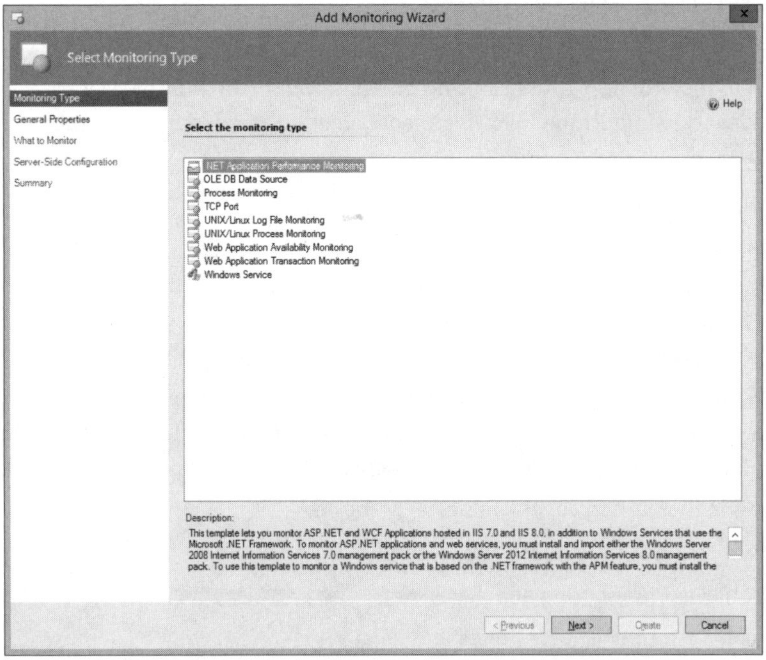

FIGURE 2-50 .NET Application Performance Monitoring template

3. On the General Properties page, provide a name for the monitor, and choose an unsealed management pack in which to store the monitor files.

4. On the What To Monitor page, click Add. On the Object Search page, click Search. A list of web applications and services that Operations Manager has discovered will be displayed. Select the applications that you want to manage, and click Add. This dialog box is shown in Figure 2-51.

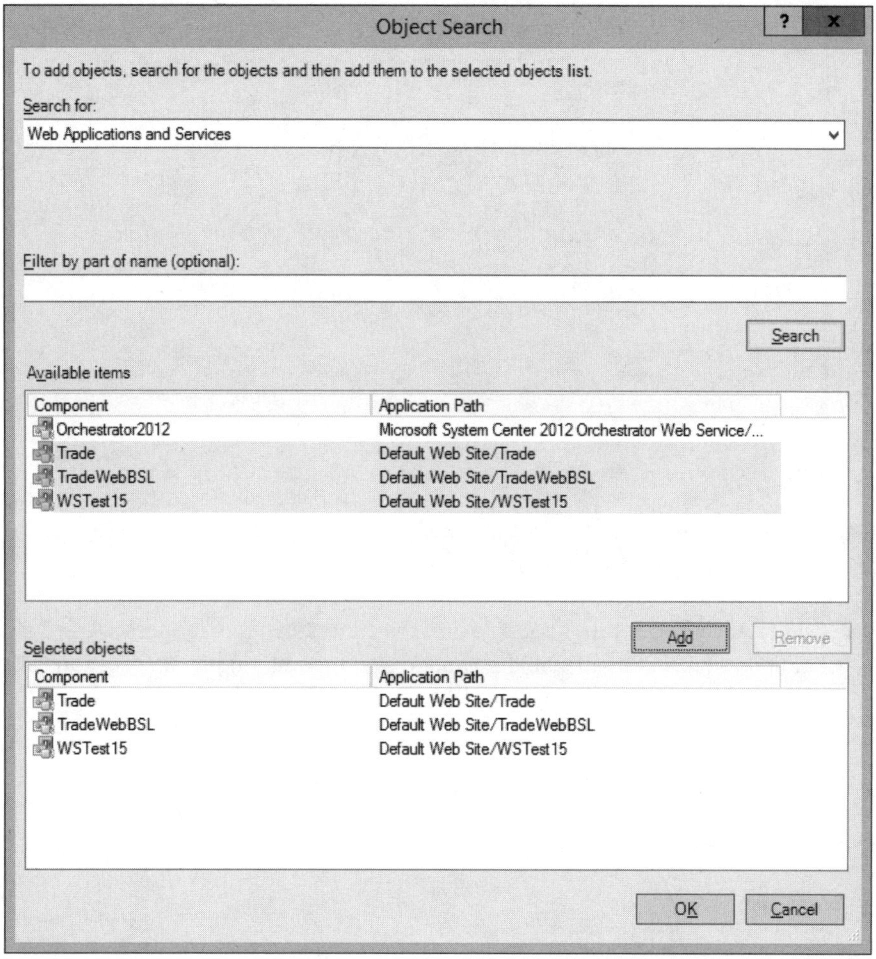

FIGURE 2-51 Web application search

5. On the Server-Side Configuration, select Enable Additional Configuration Options For Server-Side And Client-Side Monitoring, as shown in Figure 2-52, and then click Advanced Settings.

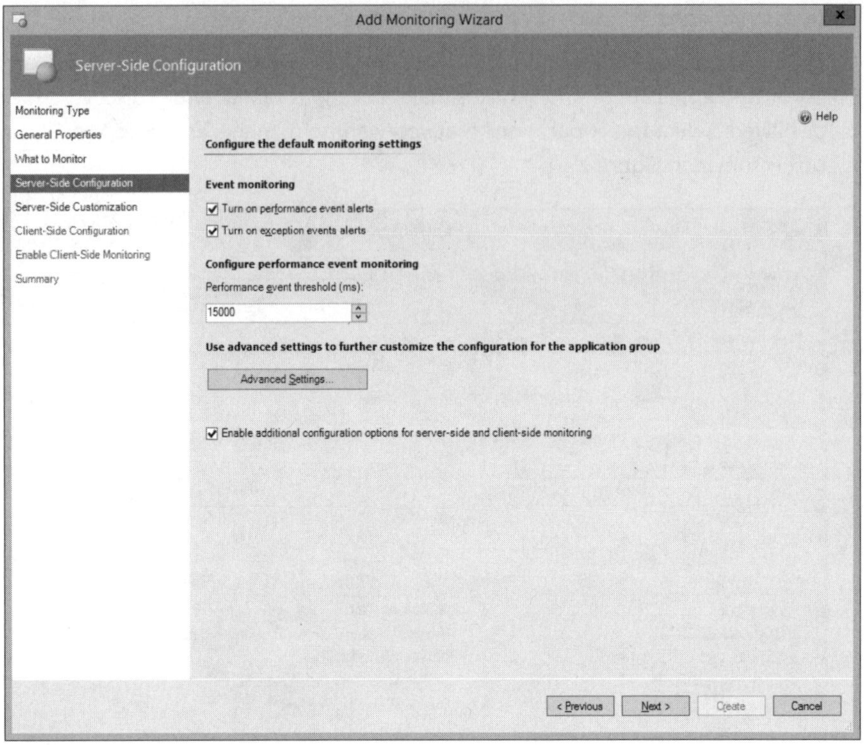

FIGURE 2-52 Server-side configuration

6. On the Advanced Settings page, review the current configuration, click Use Default Configuration, and then enable exception event monitoring for Application Failure Alerts, as shown in Figure 2-53.

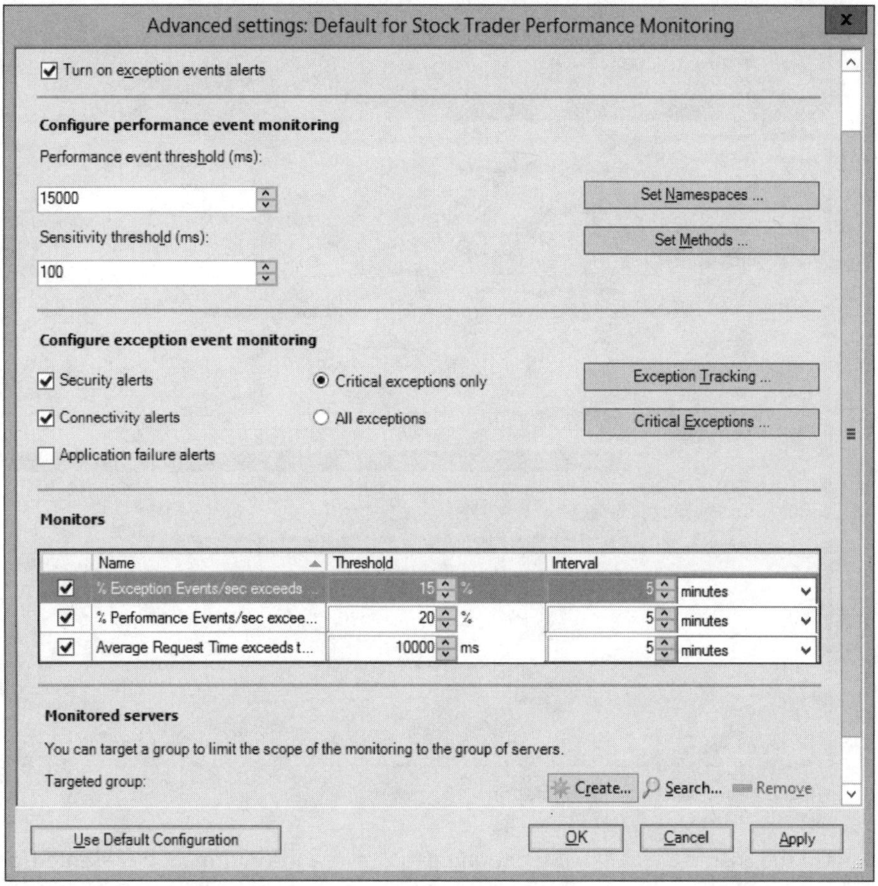

FIGURE 2-53 Advanced monitoring settings

7. On the Server-Side Customization page, select the first component, and click Customize. Verify that you can configure separate performance event monitoring settings for each application component, and then click OK.

8. On the Client-Side Configuration page, enable performance event alerts and exception event alerts, as shown in Figure 2-54. Review the page load threshold, and Ajax and WCF threshold settings.

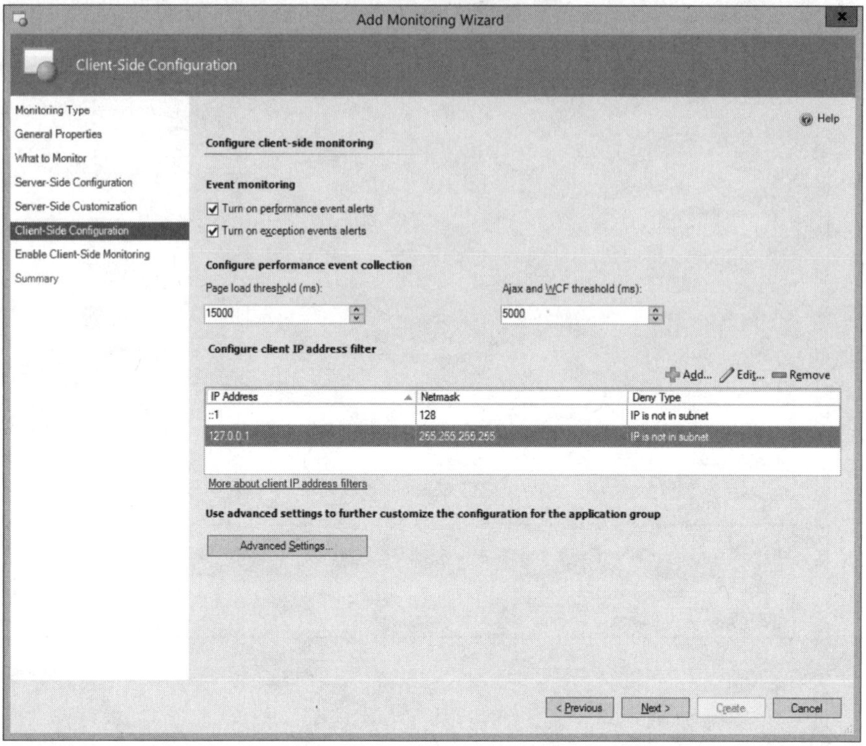

FIGURE 2-54 Client-side configuration

9. On the Enable Client-Side Monitoring page, review the information presented, and then complete the wizard. Note that it is likely that you'll need to restart IIS on the server that hosts the web application.

> **MORE INFO APPLICATION PERFORMANCE MONITORING**
>
> You can learn more about Application Performance Monitoring at *http://technet.microsoft. com/en-us/library/hh457578.aspx*.

Objective summary

- App Controller functions as a Self-Service Portal for VMM. It allows you to manage up to four separate VMM deployments. App Controller can also be used to manage Microsoft Azure private clouds.

- The Service Manager Self-Service Portal runs on SharePoint 2010 and allows Service Manager self-service users to interact with Service Manager service offerings.

- Operations Manager dashboards are customized views of Operations Manager information.

- You can use Application Performance Monitoring (APM) to monitor Internet Information Services (IIS) hosted .NET and Windows Communication Foundation (WCF) applications from both the perspective of the server that hosts the application, and the client that is interacting with the application.

Objective review

Answer the following questions to test your knowledge of the information in this objective. You can find the answers to these questions and explanations of why each answer choice is correct or incorrect in the "Answers" section at the end of this chapter.

1. You have configured App Controller to function as the Self-Service Portal for your organization's VMM 2012 R2 deployment. Which VMM role has the minimum required permissions to start and stop VMs in a VMM cloud to which it has been assigned permissions when used through App Controller?

   A. Tenant Administrator

   B. Fabric Administrator

   C. Application Administrator

   D. Read-Only Administrator

2. Which version of SharePoint can you deploy on Windows Server 2012 R2 to support the System Center 2012 R2 Service Manager Self-Service Portal?

   A. SharePoint 2010 SP2

   B. SharePoint 2013

   C. SharePoint 2007

   D. SharePoint 2010

3. You are creating an Operations Manager dashboard. Which of the following dashboard templates would you choose when creating a dashboard if you wanted to display the top 20 performance counters for chosen values? (choose the best answer)

   A. Service Level Dashboard

   B. Grid Layout

   C. Summary Dashboard

   D. Column Layout

Answers

This section contains the solutions to the thought experiments and answers to the objective review questions in this chapter.

Objective 2.1: Thought experiment

1. You should assign Oksana the Application Administrator role for the Contoso_Production as this will allow her to create and deploy virtual machines within the Contoso_Production cloud.

2. You should assign Rooslan the Fabric Administrator user role for the Contoso_Test cloud. This will allow Rooslan to perform administrative tasks within the Contoso_Test cloud, but not within the Contoso_Production cloud.

3. You should assign Nestor the read-only administrator role for the Contoso_Production cloud. This will allow Nestor to view all settings related to the Contoso_Production cloud, but not to modify those settings.

Objective 2.1: Review

1. **Correct answer:** A

   A. **Correct:** A DPM storage pool requires a minimum of a single disk.

   B. **Incorrect:** A DPM storage pool requires a minimum of a single disk.

   C. **Incorrect:** A DPM storage pool requires a minimum of a single disk.

   D. **Incorrect:** A DPM storage pool requires a minimum of a single disk.

2. **Correct answer:** C

   A. **Incorrect:** The Operations Manager agent can report to four separate management groups.

   B. **Incorrect:** The Operations Manager agent can report to four separate management groups.

   C. **Correct:** The Operations Manager agent can report to four separate management groups.

   D. **Incorrect:** The Operations Manager agent can report to four separate management groups.

3. **Correct answers:** A and B

   A. **Correct:** You can remotely deploy the Configuration Manager client using a client push installation.

   B. **Correct:** You can remotely deploy the Configuration Manager client using Windows Server Update Services.

C. Incorrect: The Configuration Manager client cannot be deployed using Windows Intune.

D. Incorrect: Manual installation requires a logon to the local computer.

4. **Correct answer:** C

 A. Incorrect: This role provides permission to interact with alerts, run tasks, and access views within their designated scope.

 B. Incorrect: This role provides the ability to control access to reports.

 C. Correct: This role provides access to alerts, views and tasks, and the ability to override the configuration of rules and monitors within the configured scope.

 D. Incorrect: This role can create and manage monitoring configuration for targets and groups of targets within configured scope.

5. **Correct answer:** D

 A. Incorrect: Users assigned to this role can create and edit service requests and activity work items in their queue scope. Have read access to work items in their queue scope. Have read access to configuration items in their queue scope.

 B. Incorrect: Users assigned to this role have read-only access to work items in their queue scope. Have read-only access to configuration items in their group scope.

 C. Incorrect: Users assigned this role can manage problems in their queue scope. Have read-only access to other work items in their queue scope. Have read-only access to configuration items in their group scope.

 D. Correct: Users that are members of this role can create change requests and activities for configuration items in their group scope. Have read access to work items in their queue scope.

Objective 2.2: Thought experiment

1. You would add the Alert widget to the dashboard to view alert information.

2. You would add the Objects By Performance widget as this displays performance counter data in tabular format for the selected object.

Objective 2.2: Review

1. **Correct answer:** C

   A. **Incorrect:** The Tenant Administrator has more permissions than the Application Administrator role and can make configuration changes.

   B. **Incorrect:** The Fabric Administrator has more permissions than the Application Administrator role and can make configuration changes.

   C. **Correct:** The Application Administrator role, formerly known as the self-service user role, has the minimum necessary required permissions to start and stop VMs in a VMM cloud to which it has been assigned permissions.

   D. **Incorrect:** The read-only administrator cannot start and stop virtual machines.

2. **Correct answer:** A

   A. **Correct:** SharePoint 2010 SP2 is the only version of SharePoint that you can deploy on Windows Server 2012 R2 that supports System Center 2012 R2 Service Manager.

   B. **Incorrect:** While SharePoint 2013 will deploy on Windows Server 2012 R2, it is not supported by System Center 2012 R2 Service Manager.

   C. **Incorrect:** You cannot deploy SharePoint 2007 on Windows Server 2012 R2.

   D. **Incorrect:** You can only deploy SharePoint 2010 SP2 on Windows Server 2012 R2.

3. **Correct answer:** C

   A. **Incorrect:** A service level dashboard allows you to display information related to service level tracking.

   B. **Incorrect:** Grid layouts consist of multiple cells, each of which contains separate information.

   C. **Correct:** The summary dashboard will display the top selected number of performance counters for chosen values.

   D. **Incorrect:** Column layouts consist of multiple columns of information.

CHAPTER 3

Configure the fabric

Fabric is the term used to describe a variety of resources that are available to support the private cloud. This includes storage, network, and infrastructure resources. In this chapter you'll learn about configuring the storage fabric, the network fabric, how to integrate PXE deployment with a VMM server, how to integrate a software update server with VMM, and how to configure virtualization hosts and private clouds.

Objectives in this chapter:

- Objective 3.1: Configure the storage fabric
- Objective 3.2: Configure the network fabric
- Objective 3.3: Configure and manage the deployment and update servers
- Objective 3.4: Configure clouds and virtualization hosts

Objective 3.1: Configure the storage fabric

This objective deals with managing the storage that VMM can provision to virtualization hosts and virtualization host clusters. This includes coverage of storage classifications, how VMM can use file shares, how you can provision logical units, and create storage pools.

> **This objective covers the following topics:**
> - VMM storage
> - Storage classifications
> - File shares and VMM
> - Storage pools from physical disks
> - Provision storage logical units

Understanding VMM storage

VMM can use local and remote storage, with local storage being storage devices that are directly attached to the server, and remote storage being storage available through a storage area network. VMM can use:

- **File storage** VMM can use file shares that support the SMB 3.0 protocol. This protocol is supported by file shares on computers running Windows Server 2012 and Windows Server 2012 R2. Third-party vendors of network-attached storage (NAS) devices also support SMB 3.0..

- **Block storage** VMM can use block-level storage devices that host LUNs (logical unit numbers) for storage using either the iSCSI, Serial Attached SCSI (SAS), or Fibre Channel protocols.

VMM supports automatically discovering local and remote storage. This includes automatic discovery of:

- Storage arrays
- Storage pools
- Storage volumes
- LUNs
- Disks
- Virtual disks

Using VMM, you can create new storage from capacity discovered by VMM and assign that storage to a Hyper-V virtualization host or host cluster. You can use VMM to provision storage to Hyper-V virtualization hosts, or host clusters using the following methods:

- **From available capacity** Allows you to create storage volumes or LUNs from an existing storage pool.
- **From writable snapshot of a virtual disk** VMM supports creating storage from writable snapshots of existing virtual disks.
- **From a clone of a virtual disk** You can provision storage by creating a copy of a virtual disk. This uses storage space less efficiently than creating storage from snapshots.
- **From SMB 3.0 file shares** You can provision storage from SMB 3.0 file shares.

VMM supports the creation of a thin provisioned logical unit on a storage pool. This allows you to allocate a greater amount of capacity than is currently available in the pool and is only possible when:

- The storage array supports thin provisioning.
- The storage administrator has enabled thin provisioning for the storage pool.

MORE INFO STORAGE IN VMM

You can learn more about storage in VMM at *http://technet.microsoft.com/en-us/library/gg610600.aspx.*

Understanding storage classifications

Storage classifications allow you to assign a metadata label to a type of storage. For example, you might name a classification used with a storage pool that consists of solid state disks as Alpha, a classification used with Fibre Channel RAID 5 SAS storage as Beta, and iSCSI SATA RAID 5 as Gamma. The labels that you use should be appropriate to your environment. Some organizations use the labels Gold, Silver, and Bronze, but the drawback of this approach is that it makes it challenging to add additional meaningful classifications. For example, while possible you could add Platinum storage, you'd have to start getting creative in naming a classification that was better than Platinum. The more creative you get, the less comprehensible your storage classifications will be to other people. Generally you classify based on speed and reliability, with expensive high speed reliable storage getting a higher classification.

To configure storage classifications in VMM, perform the following steps:

1. In the Fabric workspace of the VMM console, click Classifications And Pools under the Storage node.

2. On the VMM console ribbon, click Create Storage Classification.

3. In the New Classification dialog box, provide a name and a description for the storage classification. Figure 3-1 shows the new classification Alpha for Solid State Disks.

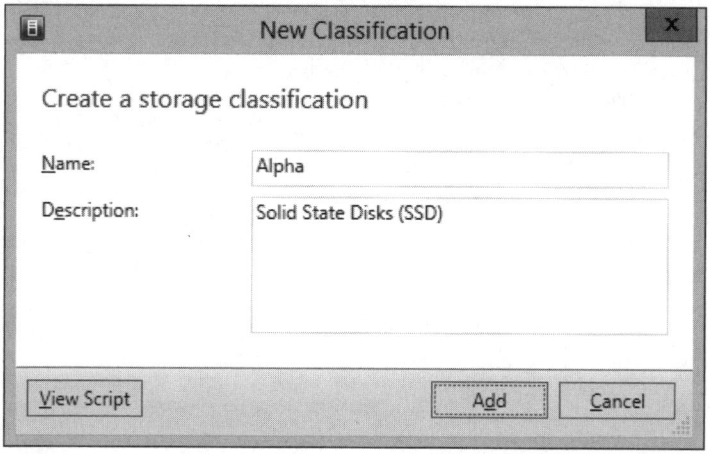

FIGURE 3-1 New classification

MORE INFO STORAGE CLASSIFICATIONS

You can learn more about storage classifications at *http://technet.microsoft.com/en-us/library/gg610685.aspx.*

Understanding file shares and VMM

You can add a remote file server as a storage device in VMM. To perform this action requires that you have an account that is a member of the Administrator or the Delegated Administrator user role. You must also have a Run As account configured that has administrative permissions on the file server.

To add the remote file server to VMM as a storage device, perform the following steps:

1. In the Fabric workspace of the VMM console, select File Servers under the Storage node.

2. On the VMM console ribbon, click Add Resources, and then click Storage Devices.

3. On the Select A Storage Provider Type page, select Windows-Based File Server, as shown in Figure 3-2.

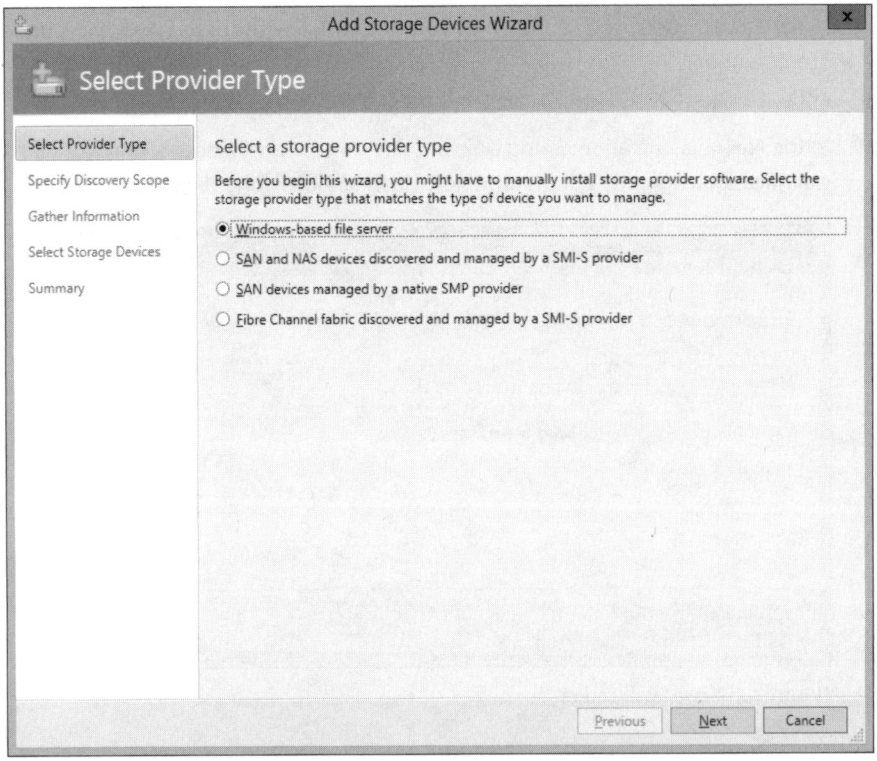

FIGURE 3-2 Add Storage Devices Wizard

4. On the Specify Discovery Scope page, provide the IP address or FQDN of the file server. Specify whether the server is in an untrusted Active Directory domain, and choose a Run As account that has local Administrator privileges on the target computer. Figure 3-3 shows a connection to the server MEL-STORAGE.adatum.internal using the Administrator Run As account.

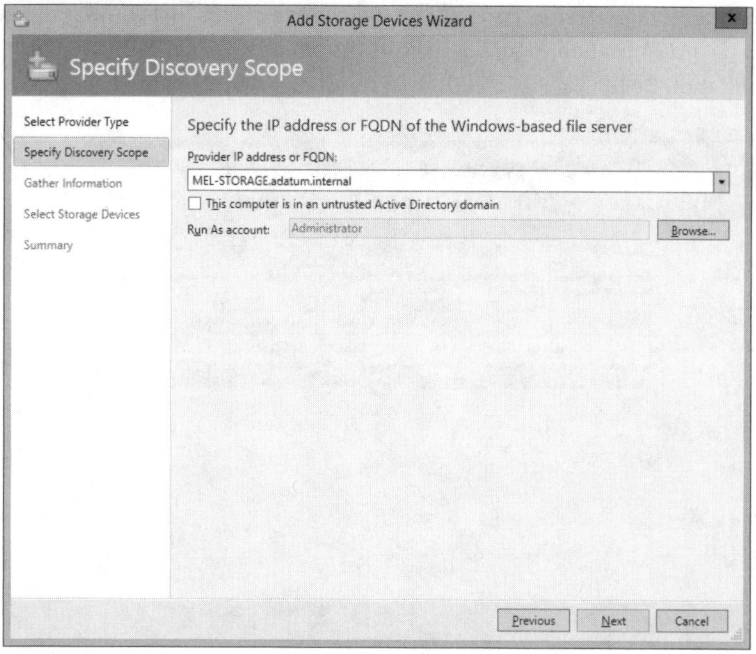

FIGURE 3-3 Specify discovery scope

5. VMM will then scan the targeted server and discover information about it, as shown in Figure 3-4.

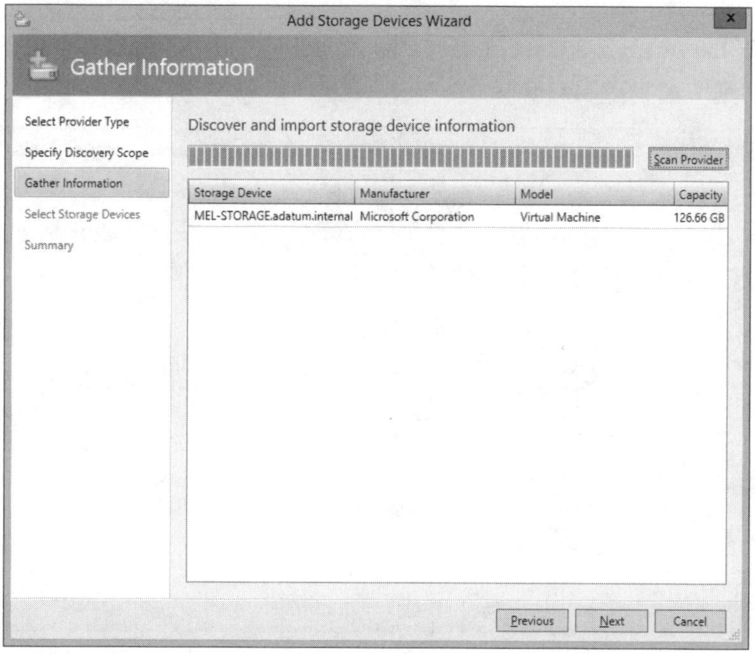

FIGURE 3-4 Discover storage device information

6. On the Select Storage Devices page, select the storage device that you want to add, and provide a classification. Figure 3-5 shows the storage device FILESHARE assigned the classification Delta.

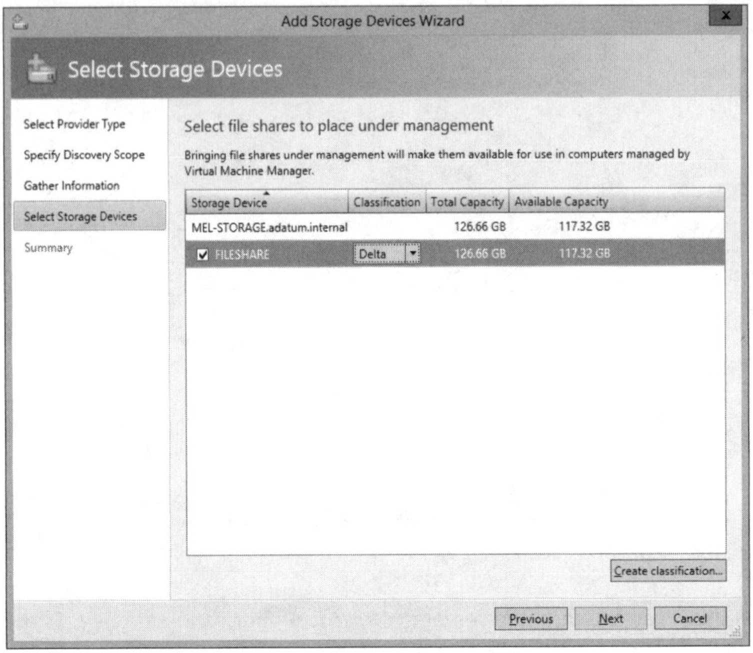

FIGURE 3-5 Select storage devices

7. Complete the wizard to add the storage. The storage will now be visible within the VMM console, as shown in Figure 3-6.

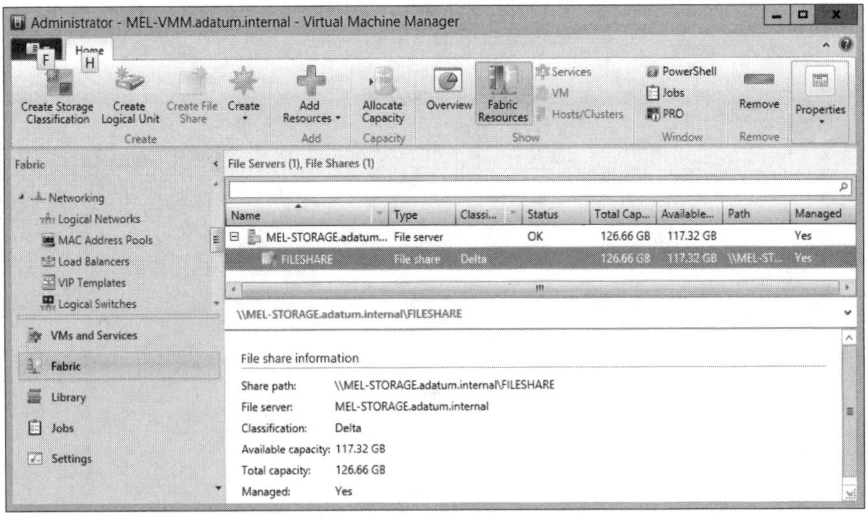

FIGURE 3-6 Storage in VMM console

To assign file share storage to a Hyper-V virtualization host, perform the following steps:

1. In the Fabric workspace, click All Hosts under Servers, and select the Hyper-V virtualization host to which you want to allocate the file server storage.

2. On the VMM console ribbon, click Properties.

3. On the Host Access tab of the virtualization host's properties, specify a Run As account that has local Administrator access on the file server that you want to provision as storage for the virtualization host. Figure 3-7 shows this set to the Administrator Run As account.

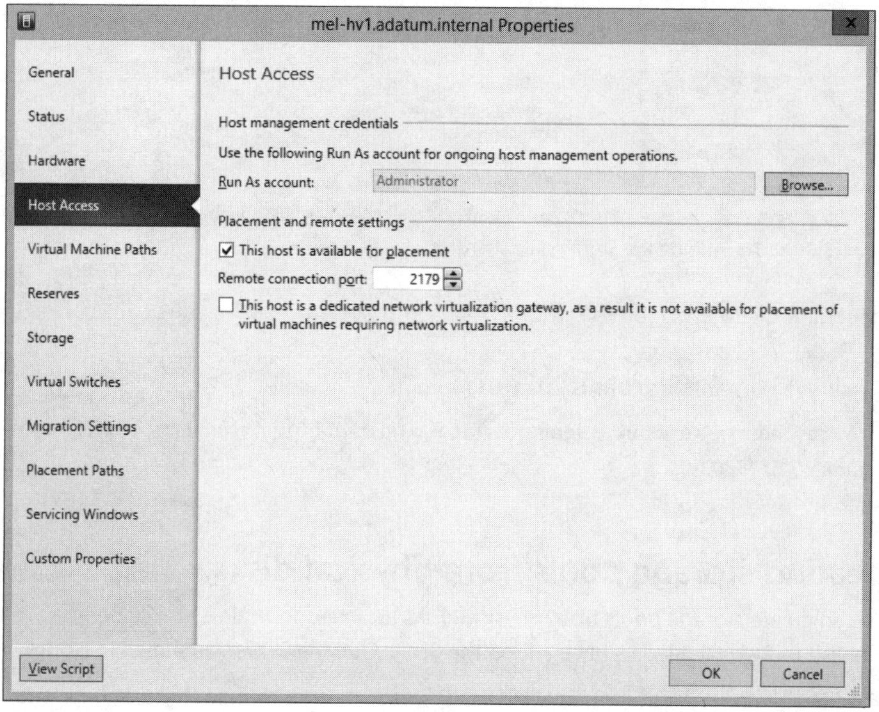

FIGURE 3-7 Host access

4. On the Storage tab of the virtualization host's properties, click Add, and then click Add File Share.

5. On the File Share Path drop-down, specify the file share that you want to provision to the virtualization host. Figure 3-8 shows the File Share Path \\MEL-STORAGE.adatum. internal\FILESHARE.

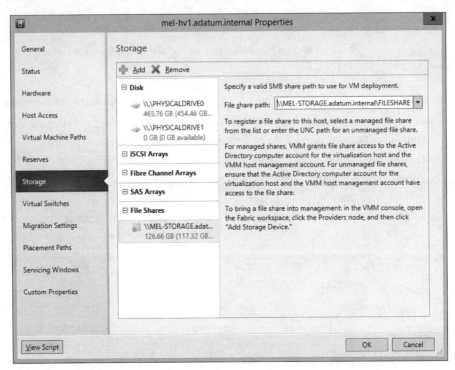

FIGURE 3-8 Adding the Storage file share

6. Click OK to provision the storage.

MORE INFO **ASSIGN STORAGE TO HOSTS**

You can learn more about assigning storage to hosts at *http://technet.microsoft.com/en-us/ library/jj614620.aspx*.

Creating storage pools from physical disks

You can create storage pools from physical disks attached to Scale-Out File Servers. To ac-complish this, you'll need to have added the Scale-Out File Server, as shown in Figure 3-9.

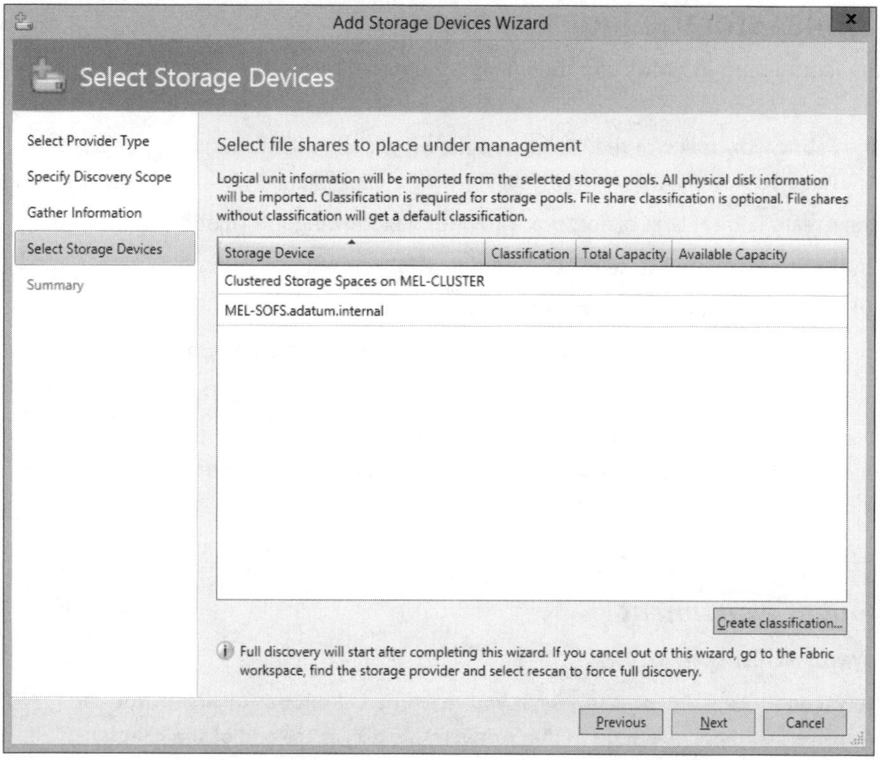

FIGURE 3-9 Select storage devices

To create the new storage pools, perform the following steps:

1. In the Fabric pane of the VMM console, select the Scale-Out File Server in the list of file servers.

2. On the VMM console ribbon, click Manage Pools.

3. On the Storage Pools dialog box, click New.

4. In the Create Storage Pool dialog box, provide a Pool Name and Classification, and click Create.

> **MORE INFO** **PROVISIONING STORAGE LOGICAL UNITS**
>
> You can learn more about provisioning storage logical units at *http://technet.microsoft. com/en-us/library/gg696973.aspx*.

Provisioning storage logical units

To provision logical units in VMM, and then assign them to a host group, perform the following steps:

1. In the Fabric workspace of the VMM console, right-click Classification And Pools, and click Create Logical Unit.

2. In the Create Logical Unit dialog box, provide the following information:

   - In the Storage Pool list, select the storage pool you will use.
   - In the Name text box, provide a name for the logical unit.
   - In the Size (GB) box, provide the size of the logical unit in gigabytes.

3. On the Home tab of the VMM console ribbon, click Allocate Capacity.

4. In the Allocate Storage Capacity dialog box, specify the host group that you want to allocate storage to, and the storage pools and logical units that you want to allocate to that host group.

Thought experiment
Storage at Tailspin Toys

In this thought experiment, apply what you've learned about this objective. You can find answers to these questions in the "Answers" section at the end of this chapter.

You are preparing a schema to classify storage that will be used with your organization's VMM deployment. You have tested the performance of the available storage and want to use this as the basis for the classification scheme.

In order from highest to lowest performance these are:

- Directly attached solid-state disk array
- Fibre Channel RAID 5 SAS
- Mirrored iSCSI storage
- SMB 3.0 file share storage

With this information in mind, answer the following questions:

1. What classification could you create to apply to the solid-state disk array?

2. What classification could you create to apply to the Fibre Channel RAID 5 SAS storage?

3. What classification could you create to apply to the SMB 3.0 file share storage?

4. If higher performance storage became available for use with VMM, what classification could you create to apply to that storage?

Objective summary

- VMM can use file storage on SMB 3.0 file shares or block-level storage devices that host LUNS.
- Using VMM, you can create new storage from capacity discovered by VMM and assign that storage to a Hyper-V virtualization host or host cluster.
- VMM supports the creation of a thin provisioned logical unit on a storage pool.
- Storage classifications allow you to assign a metadata label to a type of storage.
- You can add a remote file server as a storage device in VMM.
- You can create storage pools from physical disks attached to Scale-Out File Servers.

Objective review

Answer the following questions to test your knowledge of the information in this objective. You can find the answers to these questions and explanations of why each answer choice is correct or incorrect in the "Answers" section at the end of this chapter.

1. You are creating a private cloud test environment. You have yet to deploy any storage area network appliances or Scale-Out File Servers. Given these constraints, from which of the following sources can you use VMM to provision storage to Hyper-V virtualization hosts? (choose the best answer)

   A. Available capacity

   B. Writable snapshot of a virtual disk

   C. Clone of virtual disk

   D. SMB 3.0 file shares

2. Which of the following operating systems can provide file share storage that can be provisioned to virtualization hosts through VMM?

   A. Windows Server 2012 R2

   B. Windows Server 2008 R2

   C. Windows Server 2003

   D. Windows Server 2012

3. Which of the following conditions exist on creating thin provisioned logical units on a storage pool?

   A. Storage array must support for SMB 3.0.

   B. Storage array supports thin provisioning.

   C. Storage Administrator must have enabled thin provisioning.

   D. Storage Administrator must have enabled cluster shared volumes.

Objective 3.2: Configure the network fabric

This objective deals with how you can use VMM to manage network resources. It covers the different types of network resources that VMM can manage, and how these interrelate with each other.

> **This objective covers the following topics:**
> - VMM logical networks
> - Logical switches
> - Network virtualization
> - Virtual machine networks
> - MAC address pools
> - Static IP address pools
> - Private VLANs
> - Windows Server Gateway

Understanding VMM logical networks

A VMM logical network is a collection of network sites, VLAN information, and IP subnet information. A VMM deployment needs to have at least one logical network before you can use it to deploy VMs or services. When you add a Hyper-V based virtualization host to VMM, one of the following happens:

- If the physical adapter is associated with an existing logical network, it remains associated with that network once added to VMM.
- If the physical adapter is not already associated with a logical network, VMM will create a new logical network, associating it with the physical adapter's DNS suffix.

To create a logical network, perform the following steps:

1. In the Fabric workspace of the VMM console, click Logical Network under the Networking node.
2. On the ribbon of the VMM console, click Create Logical Network.
3. On the Name page of the Create Logical Network Wizard, shown in Figure 3-10, provide a name, and select one of the following options:
   - **One Connected Network**   Choose this option when network sites that comprise this network can route traffic to each other and you can use this logical network as a single connected network. You have the additional option of allowing VM networks created on this logical network to use network virtualization. You can also select the option of having VMM automatically create.

- **VLAN-Based Independent Networks** The sites in this logical network are independent networks. The network sites that comprise this network can, but do not require, the ability to route traffic to each other.
- **Private VLAN (PVLAN) Networks** Choose this option when you want network sites within the logical network to be isolated independent networks.

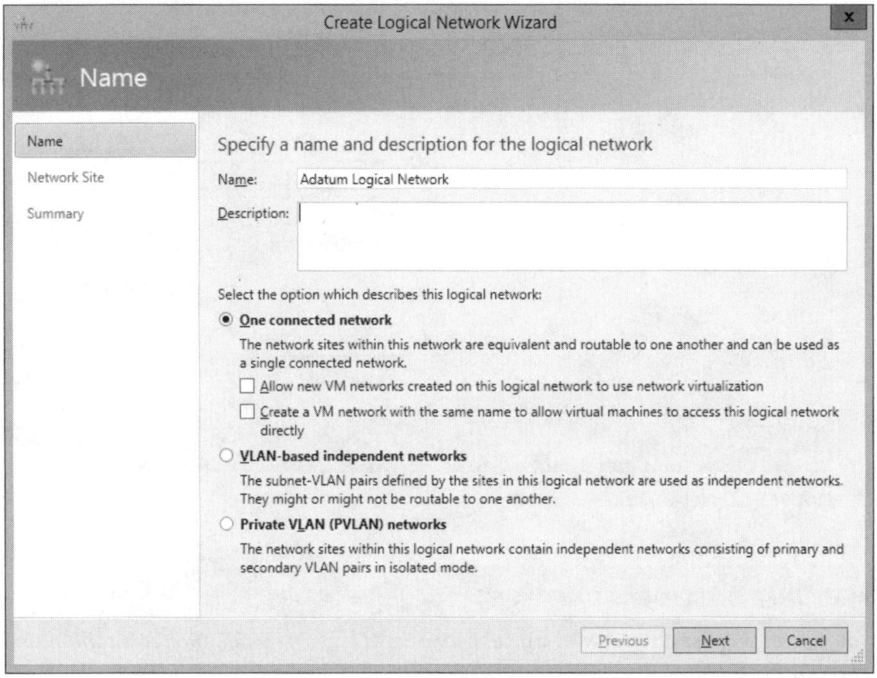

FIGURE 3-10 Network name

4. On the Network Sites page you can configure which network sites are associated with the logical network.

You can create network sites after (or during if using the Create Logical Network Wizard) you have created a VMM logical network. You use network sites to associate IP subnets, VLANs, and PVLANs with a VMM logical network.

To create a network site, perform the following steps:

1. In the Logical Networks node of the Fabric workspace of the VMM console, select the VMM logical network that will host the network site.

2. On the VMM console ribbon, click Properties.

3. On the Network Site page of the Logical Network Properties dialog box, click Add. As Figure 3-11 shows, this will create a new network site and will enable you to specify which host groups can use the network site and allow you to add VLANs and IP subnets to the site.

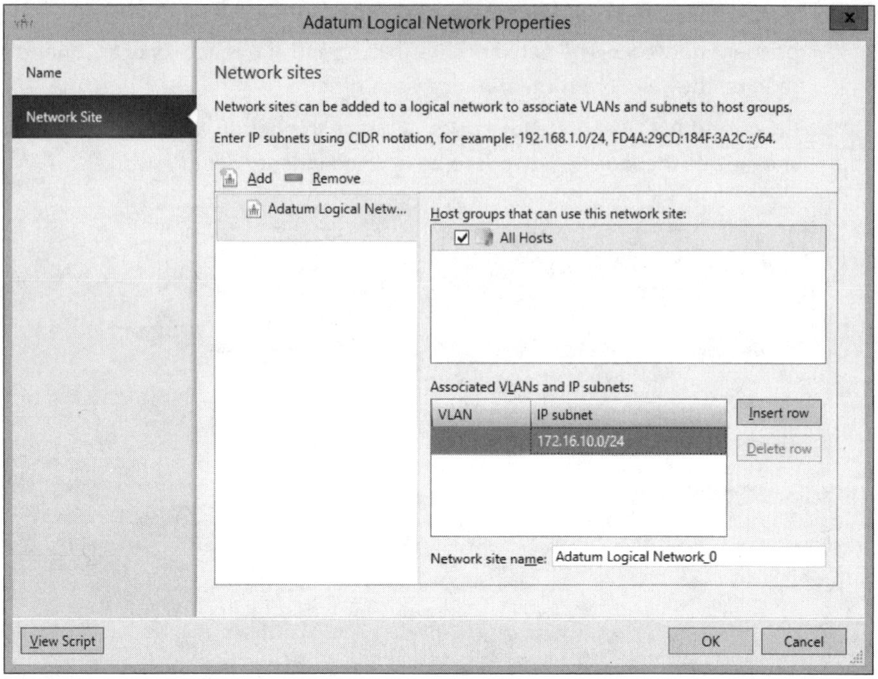

FIGURE 3-11 Network site

> **MORE INFO** **VMM LOGICAL NETWORK**
>
> You can learn more about VMM logical networks at *http://technet.microsoft.com/en-us/library/jj721568.aspx*.

Applying logical switches

VMM logical switches store network adapter configuration settings for use with VMM managed virtualization hosts. You configure the properties of one or more virtualization host's network adapters by applying the logical switch configuration information.

You should perform the following tasks before creating a logical switch:

- Create logical networks and define network sites.

- Install the providers for any Hyper-V extensible virtual switch extensions.
- Create any required native port profiles for virtual adapters that you will use to define port settings for the native Hyper-V virtual switch.

When you configure a VMM logical switch, you configure the following:

- Extensions
- Uplinks
- Virtual Ports

Extensions

You use logical switch extensions to configure how the logical switch interacts with network traffic. VMM includes the following switch extensions:

- **Monitoring**   Allows the logical switch to monitor, but not modify, network traffic.
- **Capturing**   Allows the logical switch to inspect, but not modify, network traffic.
- **Filtering**   Allows the logical switch to modify, defragment, or block packets.
- **Forwarding**   Allows the logical switch to alter the destination of network traffic based on the properties of that traffic.

In Figure 3-12, you can see that the Microsoft Windows Filtering Platform virtual switch extension is selected by default when you create a logical switch.

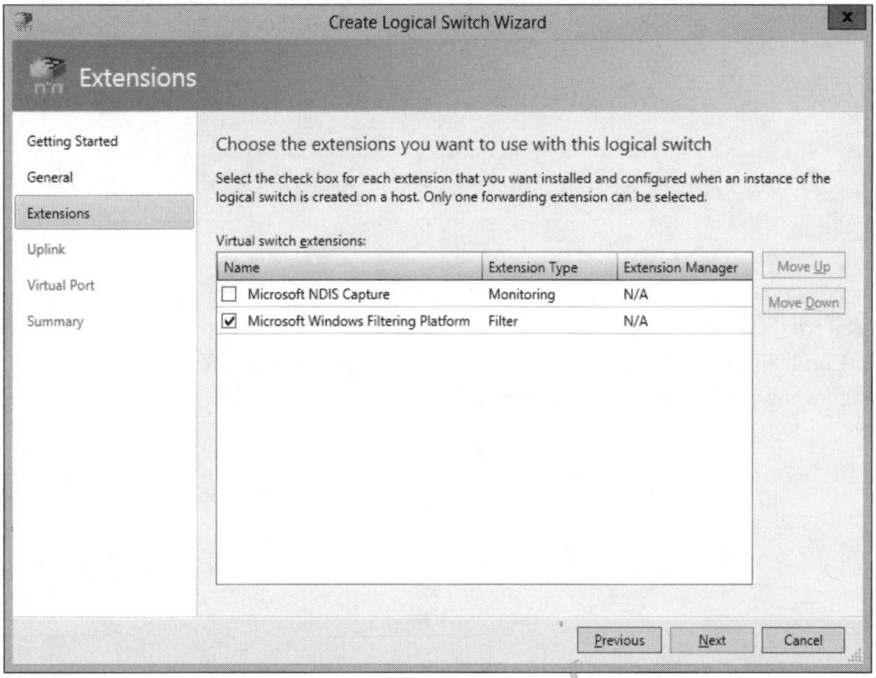

FIGURE 3-12 Logical switch Extension

Uplink port profiles

Uplink port profiles specify which set of logical networks should be associated with physical network adapters. In the event that there are multiple network adapters on a virtualization host, an uplink port profile specifies whether and how those adapters should participate in teaming. Teaming allows network adapters to aggregate bandwidth and provide redundancy for network connections. Figure 3-13 shows the Uplink page of the Create Logical Switch Wizard.

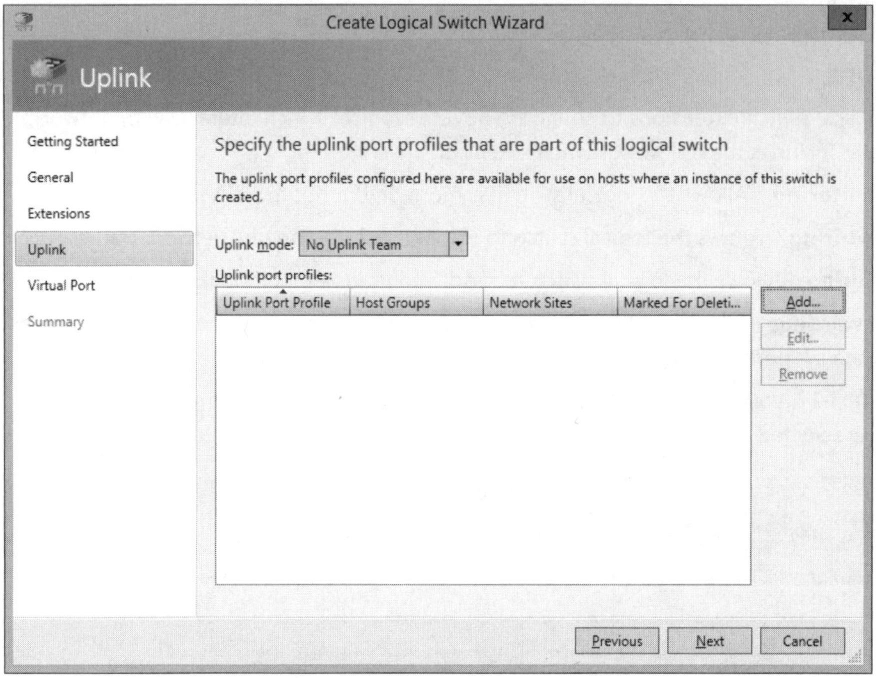

FIGURE 3-13 Uplink

Virtual port profiles

You use port profile classifications to apply configurations based on functionality. VMM includes the following port classifications shown in Figure 3-14.

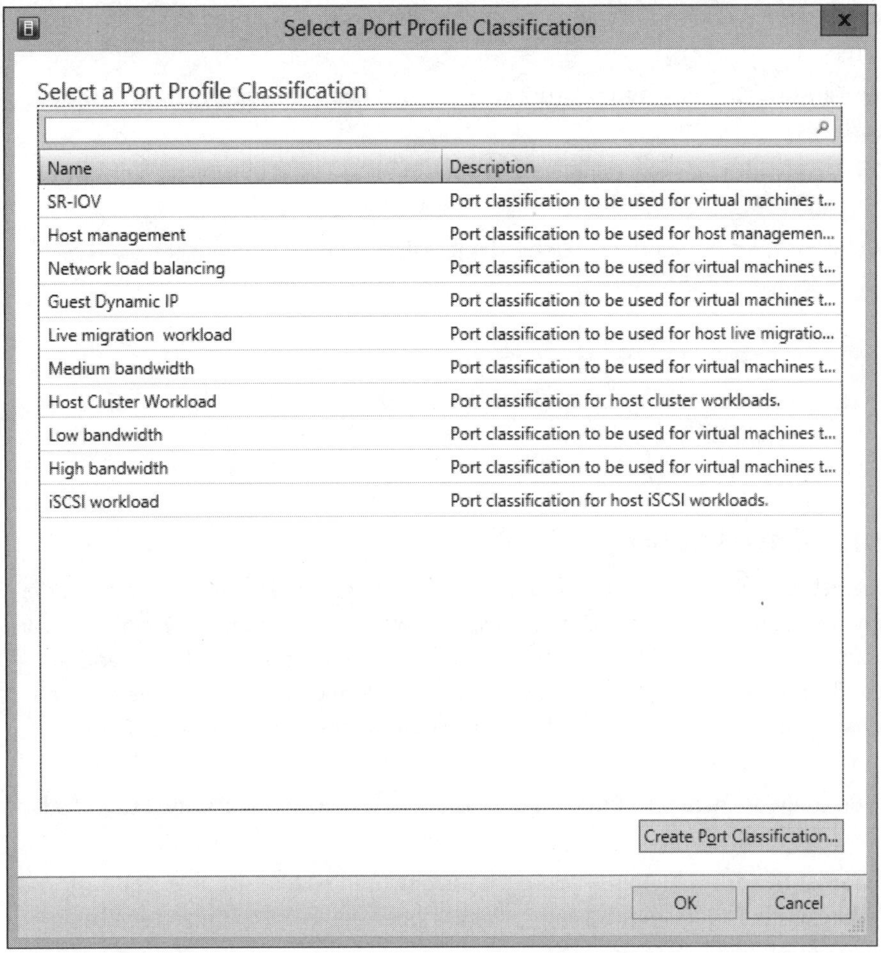

FIGURE 3-14 Port profiles

- **SR-IOV** Allows a virtual network adapter to use SR-IOV (Single Root Input Output Virtualization).
- **Host Management** For network adapters used to manage the virtualization host using RDP, PowerShell, or another management technology.
- **Network Load Balancing** Used with network adapters that participate in Microsoft Network Load Balancing.
- **Guest Dynamic IP** Used with network adapters that require guest dynamic IP addresses such as those provided by DHCP.
- **Live Migration Workload** Used with network adapters that support VM live migration workloads between virtualization hosts.
- **Medium Bandwidth** Assign to network adapters that need to support medium bandwidth workloads.

- **Host Cluster Workload**   Assign to network adapters that are used to support host clusters.
- **Low Bandwidth**   Assign to network adapters that need to support low bandwidth workloads.
- **High Bandwidth**   Assign to network adapters that are used to support high bandwidth workloads.
- **iSCSI Workload**   Assign to network adapters that are used to connect to SAN resources using the iSCSI protocol.

> **MORE INFO PORT PROFILES AND LOGICAL SWITCHES**
>
> You can learn more about port profiles and logical switches at *http://technet.microsoft.com/en-us/library/jj721570.aspx*.

Network virtualization

You can use network virtualization to configure logical networks in such a manner that different VM tenants can utilize the same IP address space on the same virtualization host without collisions occurring. For example, tenant alpha and tenant beta use the 172.16.10.x address space when their workloads are hosted on the same virtualization host cluster. Even though tenant alpha and tenant beta have virtual machines that use the same IPv4 address, network virtualization ensures that conflicts do not occur.

When you configure network virtualization, each network adapter is assigned two IP addresses.

- **Customer IP address**   This IP address is the one used by the customer. The customer IP address is the address visible within the VM when you run a command such as ipconfig or Get-NetIPConfiguration.
- **Provider IP address**   This IP address is used by and is visible to VMM. It is not visible within the VM operating system.

You can enable network virtualization when you create a VMM logical network and select the Allow New VM Networks Created On This Logical Network to use network virtualization on the Name page of the Create New Logical Network Wizard, as shown in Figure 3-15.

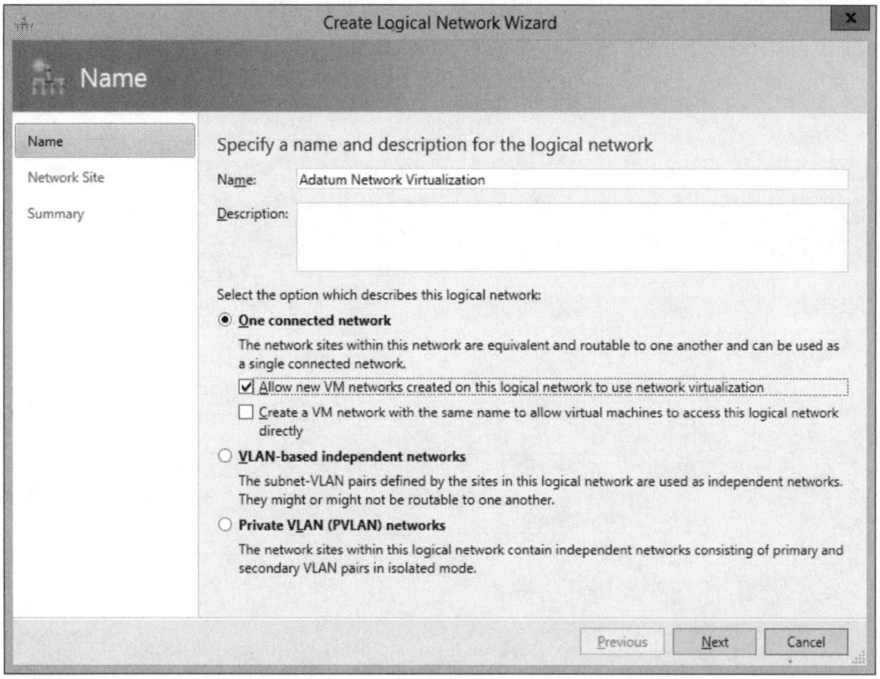

FIGURE 3-15 Logical network name

> **MORE INFO NETWORK VIRTUALIZATION**
>
> You can learn more about network virtualization at *http://blogs.technet.com/b/scvmm/ archive/2013/11/27/adopting-network-virtualization-part-ii.aspx*.

Virtual machine networks

In VMM, virtual machines connect to a VMM logical network through a VMM virtual machine network. You connect a virtual machine's network adapter to the virtual machine network rather than the logical network. You can have VMM automatically create an associated virtual machine network when you create a logical network. If you have configured a logical network to support network virtualization, you can connect multiple VM networks to the logical network and they will be isolated from each other.

To create a virtual machine network, perform the following steps:

1. In the Fabric workspace of the VMM console, click Logical Networks under Networking.

2. On the VMM console ribbon, click Create VM Network.

3. On the Name page of the Create VM Network Wizard, provide a name, and specify a logical network. Figure 3-16 shows the creation of a new network named Adatum Virtual Machine Network that connects to the logical network named Adatum Logical Network.

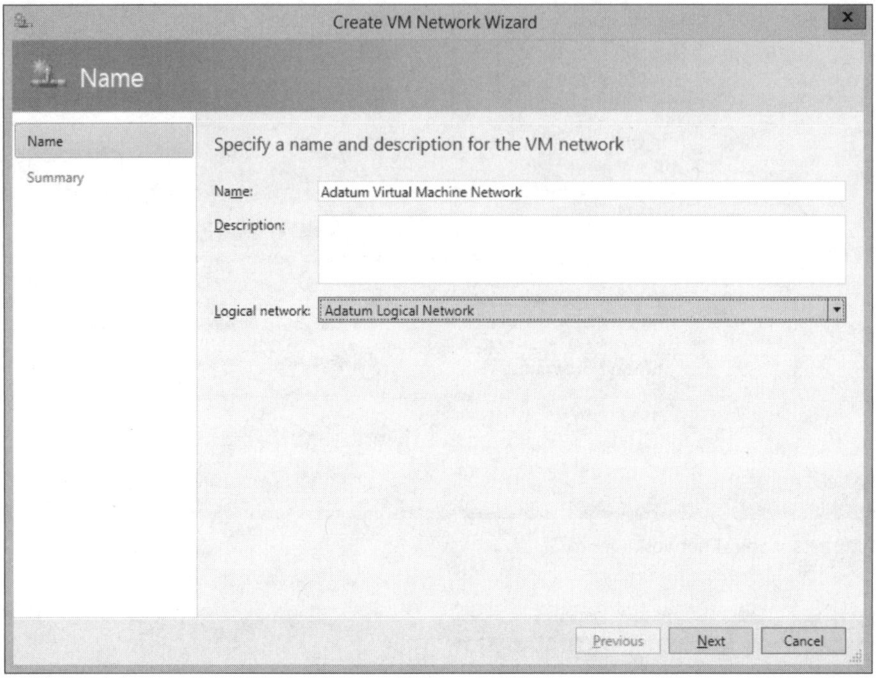

FIGURE 3-16 VM network name

> **MORE INFO** **VIRTUAL MACHINE NETWORKS**
>
> You can learn more about virtual machine networks at *http://technet.microsoft.com/en-us/library/jj983727.aspx.*

Understanding MAC address pools

A MAC address pool gives you a pool of MAC addresses that can be assigned to virtual machine network adapters across a group of virtualization hosts. Without MAC address pools, virtual machines are assigned MAC addresses on a per-virtualization host basis. While unlikely, it is possible that in environments with a very large number of virtualization hosts, that the same MAC address may be assigned by separate virtualization hosts. Using a central MAC address pool ensures that doesn't happen.

When creating a MAC address pool, you specify a starting and an ending MAC address range. Figure 3-17 shows the MAC address range in the default VMM MAC address pool.

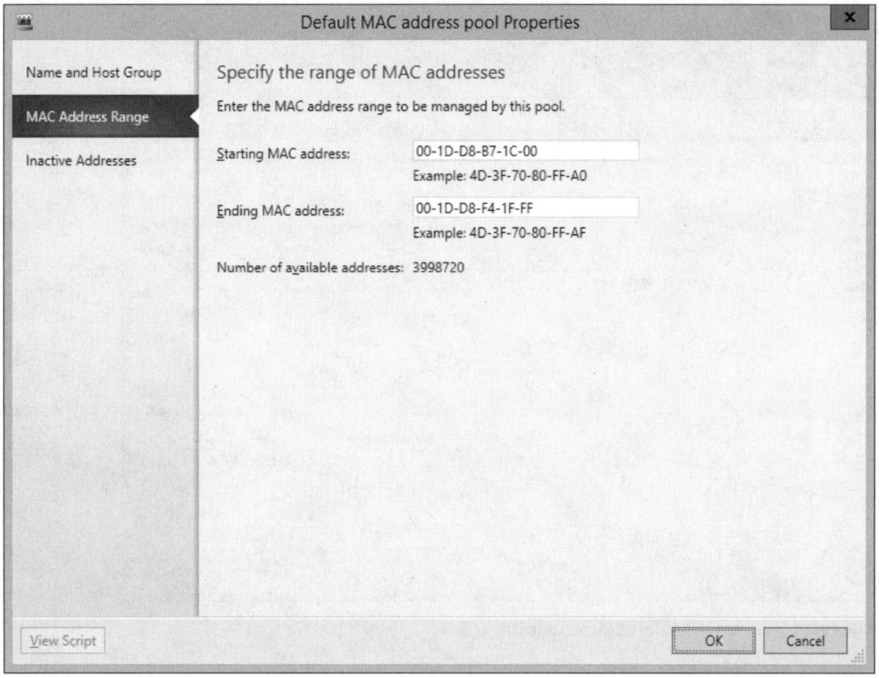

FIGURE 3-17 MAC address range

> **MORE INFO MAC ADDRESS POOLS**
>
> You can learn more about MAC address pools at *http://technet.microsoft.com/en-us/library/gg610632.aspx*.

Creating static IP address pools

An IP address pool is a collection of IP addresses that, through an IP subnet, is associated with a network site. VMM can assign IP addresses from the static IP address pool to virtual machines running Windows operating systems if those virtual machines use the logical network associated with the pool. Static IP address pools can contain default gateway, DNS server, and WINS server information. Static IP address pools aren't necessary as VMs can be assigned IP address information from DHCP servers running on the network.

To create a static IP address pool, perform the following steps.

1. In the Fabric workspace of the VMM console, click Create IP Pool on the console ribbon.

2. On the Name page of the Create Static IP Address Pool Wizard, provide a name for the IP address pool and specify the logical network with which the pool will be associated. Figure 3-18 shows the IP address pool named Adatum IP Address Pool Alpha associated with the logical network Adatum Logical Network.

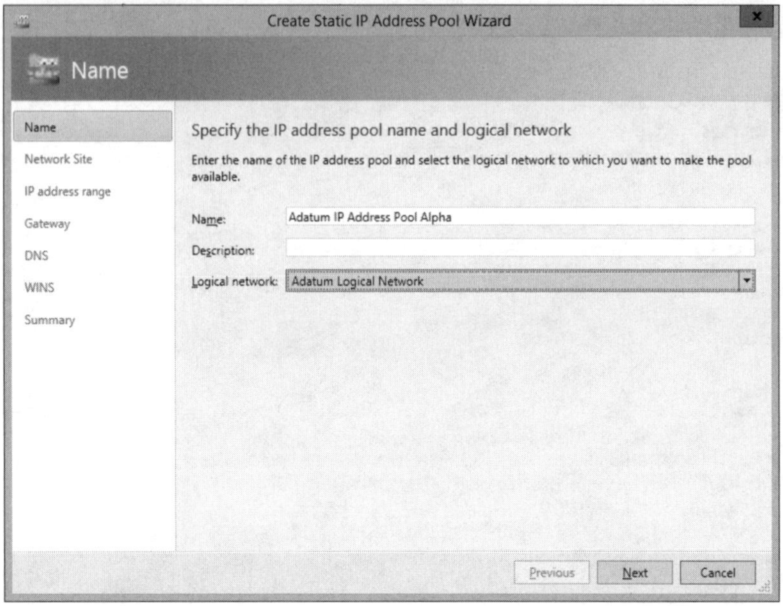

FIGURE 3-18 Adatum IP Address Pool Alpha

3. On the Network Site page, select whether you want to use an existing network site and an associated IP subnet, or to create a new site. Figure 3-19 shows selection of the Adatum Logical Network_0 network site, which is configured with the IP subnet 172.16.10.0/24. This subnet will define the range of the IP address pool.

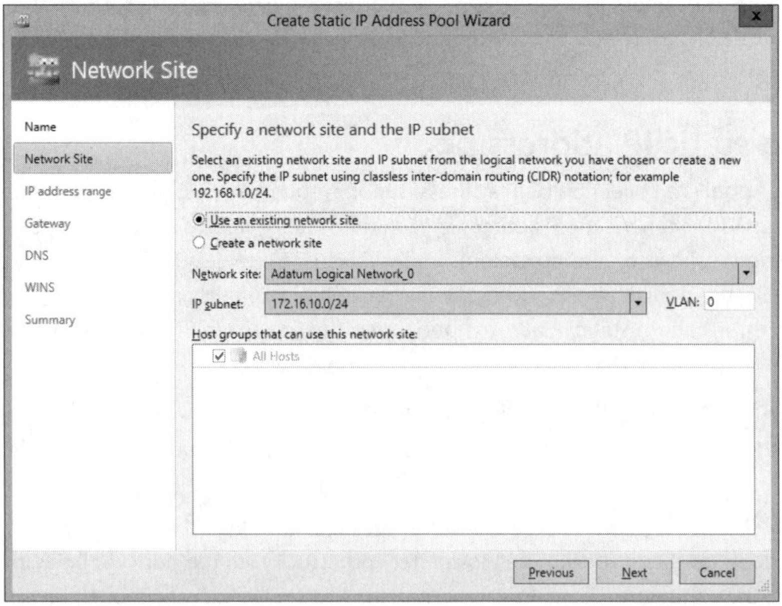

FIGURE 3-19 Network site

4. On the IP Address range page, specify the starting and ending IP address ranges. You can also specify the IP addresses to be reserved for load balances and other uses. Figure 3-20 shows the IP address range starting at 172.16.10.50 and ending at 172.16.10.254, with IP addresses between 172.16.10.50 and 172.16.10.60 reserved for load balancer VIPs and IP addresses between 172.16.10.61 and 172.16.10.80 reserved for other uses.

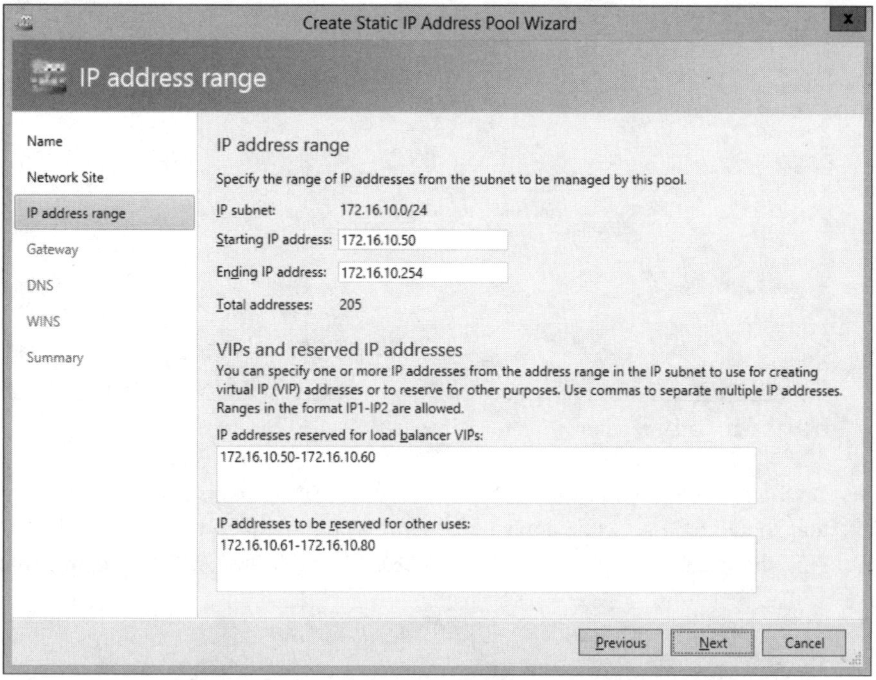

FIGURE 3-20 IP address range

5. On the Gateway page, you can add gateway address information. Figure 3-21 shows the Gateway Address 172.16.10.1 configured.

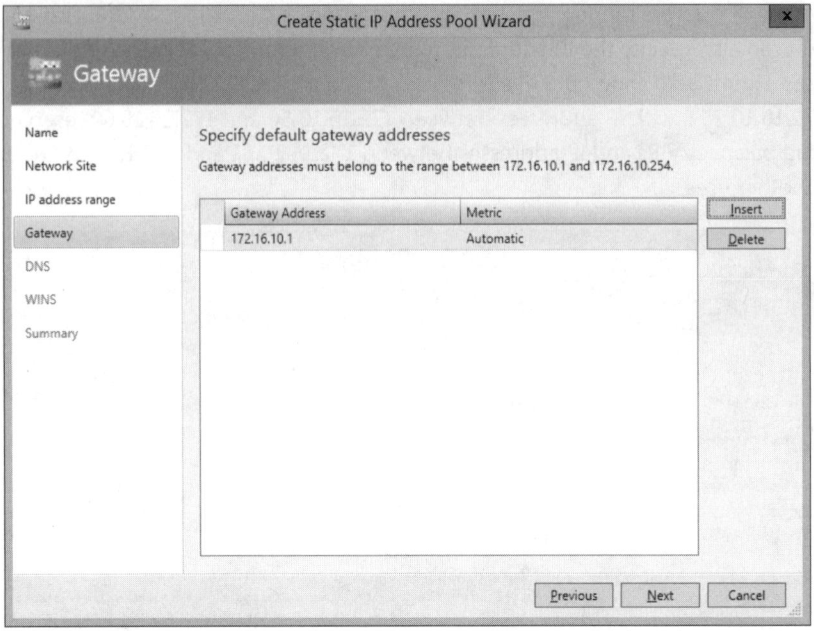

FIGURE 3-21 Gateway address

6. On the DHS page, you can specify the address of DNS servers and any DNS suffixes that should be used when applying IP address configuration to virtual machines. Figure 3-22 shows a DNS server address of 172.16.0.10, and a DNS Suffix of Adatum.internal.

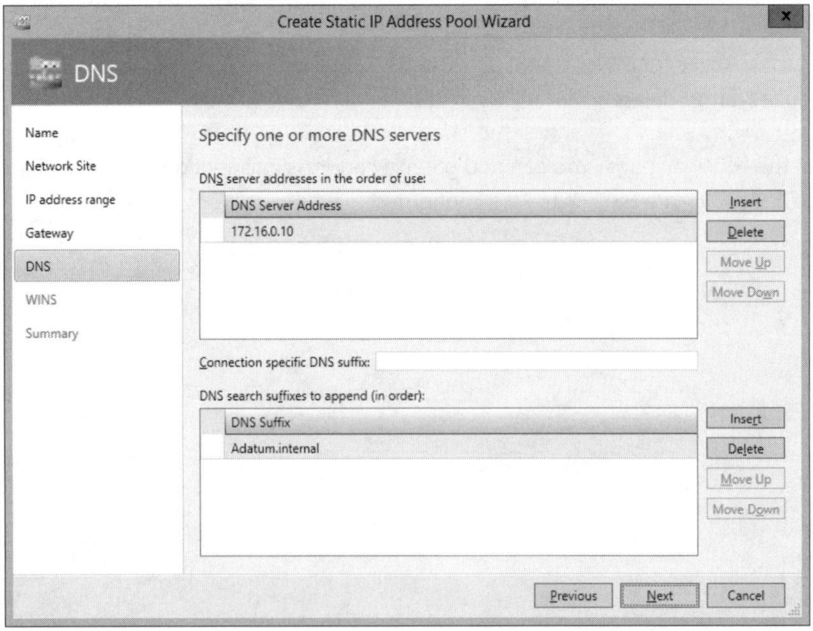

FIGURE 3-22 DNS

7. If your organization is still using WINS, you can enter the address of any WINS servers on the WINS page of the Create Static IP Address Pool Wizard.

8. Complete the wizard to create the static IP address pool.

> **MORE INFO IP ADDRESS POOLS**
>
> You can learn more about IP address pools at *http://technet.microsoft.com/en-us/library/gg610590.aspx*.

Implementing private VLANS

VLANs segment network traffic by adding tags to packets. A VLAN ID is a 12-bit number, allowing you to configure VLAN IDS between the numbers 1 and 4095. While this is more than adequate for the majority of on premises deployments, large hosting providers often have more than 5000 clients, so have to use an alternate method to segment network traffic. A PVLAN is an extension to VLANS that uses a secondary VLAN ID with the original VLAN ID to segment a VLAN into isolated sub networks.

You can implement VLANs and PVLANs in VMM by creating a logical network of the Private VLAN type, as shown in Figure 3-23.

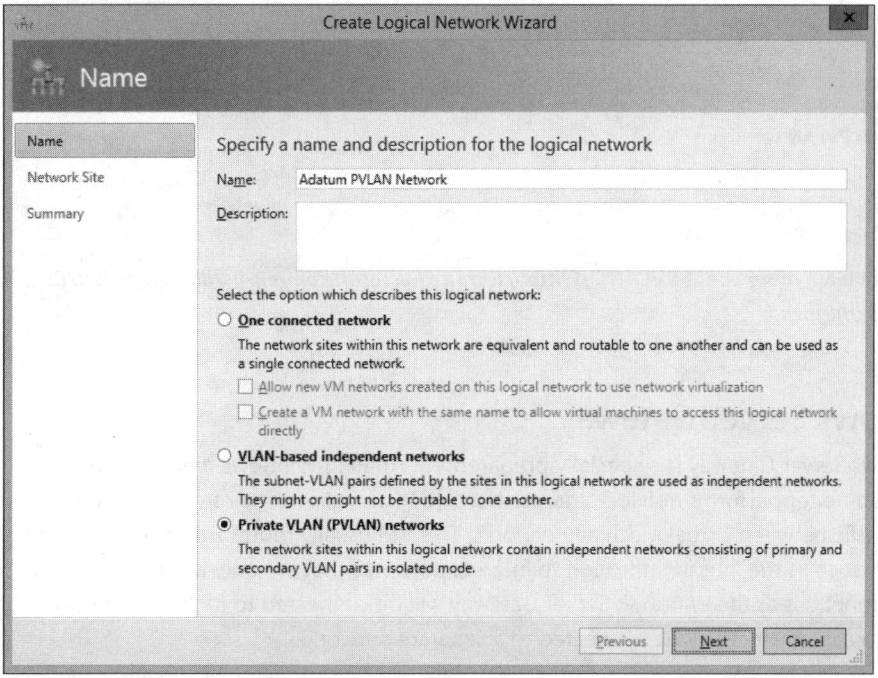

FIGURE 3-23 PVLAN network

When you create a logical network of this type you have the option, when adding a network site, of specifying the VLAN and/or PVLAN ID as well as the IPv4 or IPv6 network as shown in Figure 3-24.

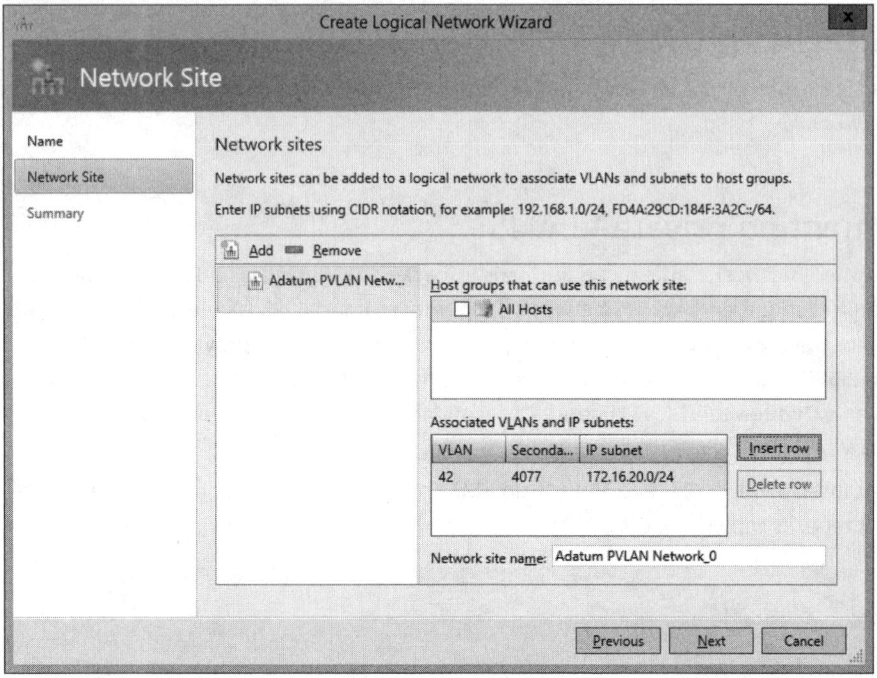

FIGURE 3-24 PVLAN settings

> **MORE INFO PVLANS**
>
> You can learn more about PVLANs at *http://technet.microsoft.com/en-us/library/jj679878. aspx#bkmk_pvlan*.

Windows Server Gateway

A Windows Server Gateway is a specially prepared VM running Windows that functions as a virtual router or performs network address translation and allows the routing or transla-tion of traffic between virtual machine networks. This VM usually routes traffic from external networks, such as the Internet, through to internal networks that are only used by VMs. The VM that functions as the Windows Server Gateway will be connected to multiple network adapters, each of which will be connected to a separate network.

To deploy a Windows Server Gateway, perform the following high-level steps:

1. Install the Remote Access role on the VM that will function as the Windows Server Gateway. Include the Direct Access and VPN (RAS) and Routing role services.

2. On the Hyper-V virtualization host that will host the Windows Server Gateway virtual machine:

- Enable multi-tenancy mode for the virtual machine network adapter. You can do this using the Set-VMNetworkAdapterIsolation Windows PowerShell cmdlet.

- Add the tenant routing domains and virtual subnets to the adapter using the Add-VmNetworkAdapterRoutingDomain Windows PowerShell cmdlet.

- Configure network virtualization settings with the New-NetVirtualizationProviderAddress, New-NetVirtualizationLookupRecord, and NewNetVirtualizationCustomerRoute Windows PowerShell cmdlets.

3. On the Windows Server Gateway virtual machine, configure IP address and network routes for each tenant network.

4. On other Hyper-V hosts that will host tenant virtual machines that the Windows Server Gateway virtual machine will route traffic to, configure network virtualization using the New-NetVirtualizationProviderAddress, New-NetVirtualizationLookupRecord, and New-NetVirtualizationCustomerRoute Windows PowerShell cmdlets.

5. In the VMM console, add the Gateway in the Network Service section of the Fabric workspace.

> **MORE INFO WINDOWS SERVER GATEWAY**
>
> You can learn more about Windows Server Gateway at *http://technet.microsoft.com/en-us/library/dn313101.aspx*.

EXAM TIP

Remember that virtual machines connect to a logical network through a virtual machine network.

Objective summary

- A VMM logical network is a collection of network sites, VLAN information, and IP subnet information.

- A VMM deployment needs to have at least one logical network before you can use it to deploy VMs or services.

- VMM logical switches store network adapter configuration settings for use with VMM managed virtualization hosts.

- You use logical switch extensions to configure how the logical switch interacts with network traffic.

- Uplink port profiles specify which set of logical networks should be associated with physical network adapters.

- In the event that there are multiple network adapters on a virtualization host, an uplink port profile specifies whether and how those adapters should participate in teaming.

- You use port classifications to apply configurations based on functionality.

- You can use network virtualization to configure logical networks in such a manner that different VM tenants can utilize the same IP address space on the same virtualization host without collisions occurring.

- Virtual machines connect to a VMM logical network through a VMM virtual machine network.

- A MAC address pool gives you a pool of MAC addresses that can be assigned to virtual machine network adapters across a group of virtualization hosts.

- An IP address pool is a collection of IP addresses that, through an IP subnet, is associated with a network site.

- A PVLAN is an extension to VLANS that uses a secondary VLAN ID with the original VLAN ID to segment a VLAN into isolated sub networks.
- A Windows Server Gateway is a specially prepared VM running Windows that functions as a virtual router or performs network address translation and allows the routing or translation of traffic between virtual machine networks.

Objective review

Answer the following questions to test your knowledge of the information in this objective. You can find the answers to these questions and explanations of why each answer choice is correct or incorrect in the "Answers" section at the end of this chapter.

1. To which of the following do you connect a virtual machine network adapter?

   A. Logical network

   B. Logical switch

   C. Virtual machine network

   D. MAC address pool

2. You need to create a logical network that will host 5000 separate tenants. Which of the following logical network types should you configure if you want to ensure that virtual machine networks within the logical network are isolated with a minimum of administrative effort? (Choose the best answer.)

   A. One connected network

   B. VLAN network

   C. PVLAN network

   D. MAC address pool

3. You have a group of virtualization hosts that contain numerous host clusters that between them, host more a very large number of virtual machines. Which of the following should you configure to assume that the hardware address assigned by VMM to virtual machine network adapters is always unique?

   A. MAC address pool

   B. Logical network

   C. Logical switch

   D. Virtual machine network

Objective 3.3: Configure and manage the deployment and update servers

This objective deals with integrating VMM with the Windows Server Update Services and Windows Deployment Services role that are included with the Windows Server operating system.

> **This objective covers the following topics:**
> - Adding a PXE server to VMM
> - Adding a WSUS server to VMM

Adding a PXE server to VMM

In a scalable private cloud, you'll need to add additional Hyper-V host servers on a frequent basis as either a standalone server or as part of a failover cluster to increase your capacity. While it's possible to use another technology to deploy new Hyper-V host servers to bare metal, the advantage of integrating virtualization host deployment with VMM is that you can fully automate the process. The process works in the following general manner:

1. Discovery of the chassis occurs. This may be through providing the MAC address of the chassis network adapter to VMM.

2. The chassis performs a PXE boot and locates the Windows Deployment Services (WDS) server that you have integrated with VMM as a managed server role. When you integrate WDS with VMM, the WDS server hosts a VMM provider that will handle PXE traffic from bare metal chassis started using the VMM provisioning tool.

3. The VMM provider on the WDS server queries the VMM server to verify that the bare metal chassis is an authorized target for managed virtualization host deployment.

4. In the event that the bare metal chassis isn't authorized, WDS will attempt to deploy another OS to the chassis. If that isn't possible, PXE deployment fails.

5. If the bare metal chassis is authorized, a special Windows PE (Preinstallation Environment) image is transmitted to the bare metal chassis. This special Windows PE image includes a VMM agent that manages the operating system deployment process.

6. Depending on how you configure it, the VMM agent in the Windows PE image can run scripts to update firmware on the bare metal chassis, configure RAID volumes, and prepare local storage.

7. A specially prepared virtual hard disk (in either .vhdx or .vhd format) containing the virtualization host operating system, is copied to the bare metal chassis from a VMM library server.

8. The VMM agent in the Windows PE image configures the bare metal chassis to boot from the newly placed virtual hard disk.

9. The bare metal chassis boots into the virtual hard disk. If necessary, the newly deployed operating system can obtain additional drivers not included in the virtual hard disk from a VMM library server.

10. Post deployment customization of the newly deployed operating system occurs. This includes setting a name for the new host and joining an Active Directory Domain Services domain.

11. The Hyper-V server role is deployed and the newly deployed virtualization host is connected to VMM and placed in a host group.

> **MORE INFO** ADDING PXE SERVER TO VMM
>
> You can learn more about adding a PXE server to VMM at: *http://technet.microsoft.com/en-us/library/gg610651.aspx/*.

Virtualization host requirements

To be able to configure a bare metal hardware chassis so that it can function as a VMM managed Hyper-V virtualization host, the hardware chassis needs to meet the following requirements:

- X64 processor that supports hardware assisted virtualization and hardware-enforced Data Execution Prevention (DEP). In some cases, it may be necessary to enable this support in BIOS.

- PXE boot support. The hardware chassis must be able to PXE boot off a PXE enabled network adapter. The PXE enabled network adapter needs to be configured as a boot device.

- Out of band (OOB) management support. System Center 2012 R2 VMM is able to discover and manage the power states of hardware chassis that support BMC (Baseboard Management Controller). This version of VMM supports the following protocols:

- SMASH (Systems Management Architecture for Server Hardware) version 1 over WS-Management

- DCMI (Datacenter Management Interface) version 1.0

- IPMI (Microsoft Intelligent Platform Management Interface) version 1.5 or version 2.0

PXE server requirements

The PXE server needs to provide the PXE service through Windows Deployment Services. When you add the VMM agent to an existing Windows Deployment Services server, VMM will only manage the deployment process if the computer making the request is designated as a new virtualization host by VMM.

The PXE server needs to be on the same subnet as the bare metal chassis to which it will deploy the virtualization host operating system.

To configure a PXE server to support VMM, perform the following steps:

1. On the Manage menu of the Server Manager console, click Add Roles And Features.

2. On the Select Installation Type page of the Add Roles And Features Wizard, choose Role-Based Or Feature-Based Installation, as shown in Figure 3-25.

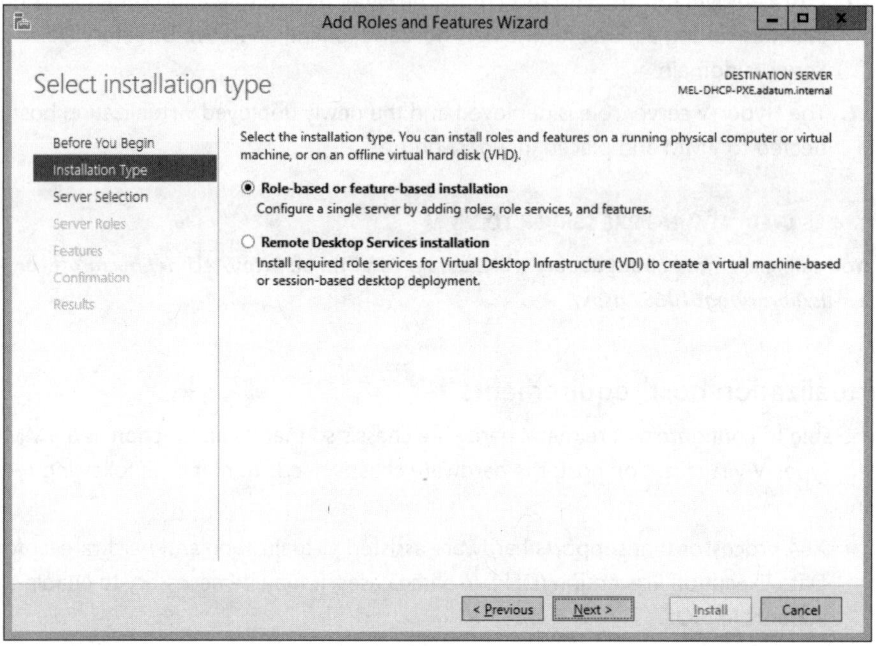

FIGURE 3-25 Installation type

3. On the Server Selection page of the Add Roles And Features Wizard, ensure that the server that you want to deploy the PXE role on is selected.

4. On the Server Roles page, select Windows Deployment Services, as shown in Figure 3-26. On the Add Roles And Features Wizard pop-up that queries you about adding the necessary management tools, click Add Features.

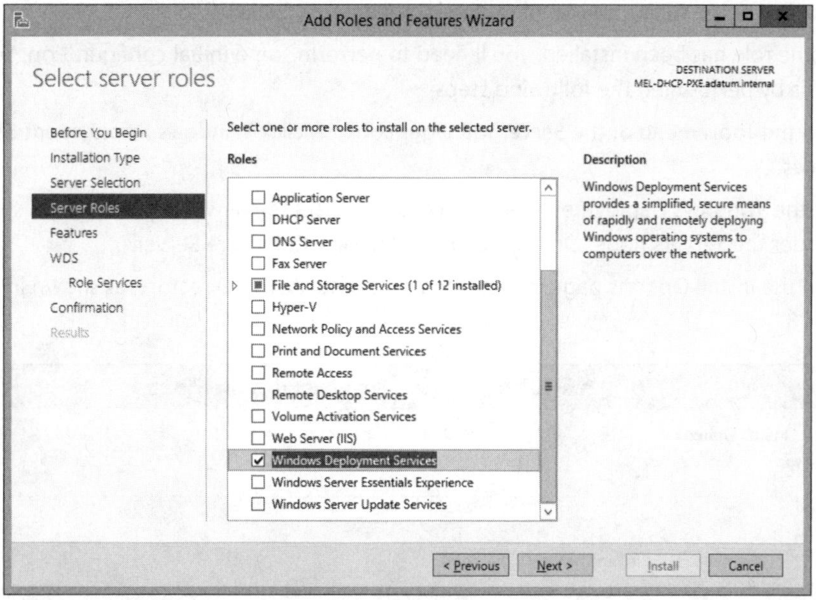

FIGURE 3-26 Windows Deployment Services

5. It is not necessary to select any additional features on the Features page to support a VMM manage PXE server.

6. On the Role Services page of the Add Roles And Features Wizard, ensure that both Deployment Server and Transport Server are selected, as shown in Figure 3-27.

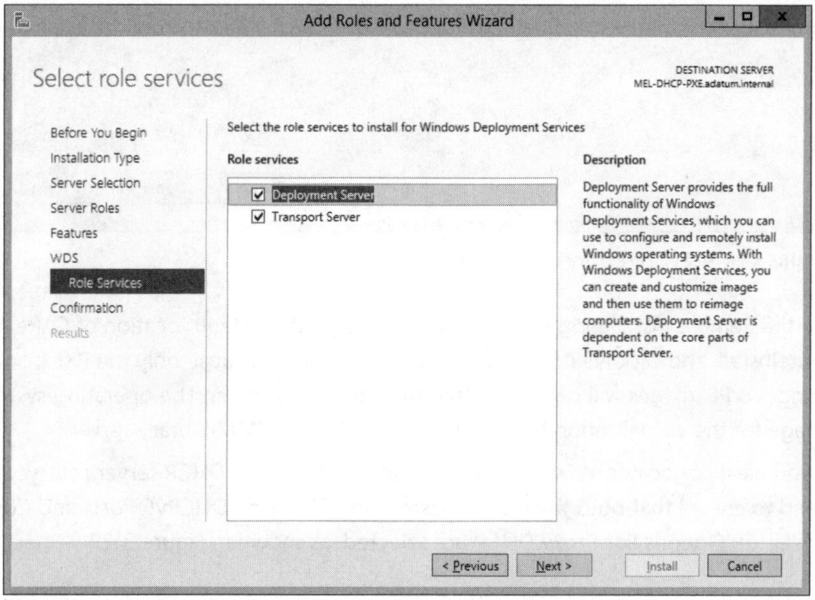

FIGURE 3-27 Role services

7. Complete the wizard to complete the installation of the WDS role.

Once the role has been installed, you'll need to perform some initial configuration. You can do this by performing the following steps:

1. On the Tools menu of the Server Manager console, click Windows Deployment Services.

2. In the Windows Deployment Services console, select the newly deployed WDS server under the Servers node. On the Action menu, click Configure Server.

3. On the Install Options page, select Integrated With Active Directory, as shown in Figure 3-28.

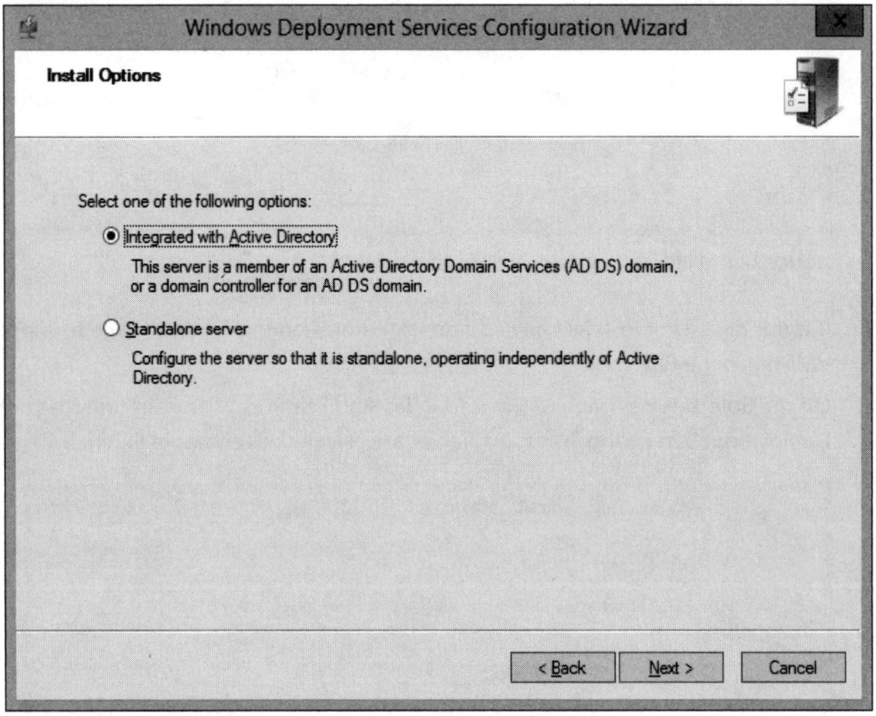

FIGURE 3-28 Active Directory integration

4. On the Remote Installation Folder Location, accept the default location of C:\RemoteInstall, and click Next. The default location is fine because only the PXE boot and Windows PE images will be transmitted from the WDS server. The operating system image for the virtualization host will be copied from a VMM Library server.

5. If you have co-located WDS on a server that also hosts the DHCP server role, you'll need to ensure that both the Do Not Listen On DHCP And DHCPv6 Ports and Configure DHCP Options For Proxy DHCP are selected, as shown in Figure 3-29.

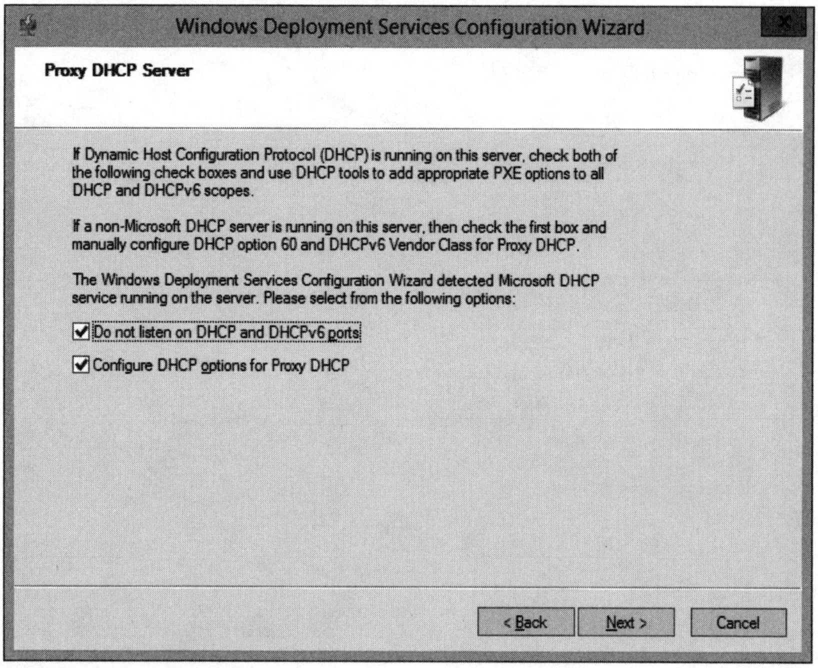

FIGURE 3-29 DHCP settings

6. On the PXE Server Initial Settings page, select Respond Only To Known Client Computers, as shown in Figure 3-30

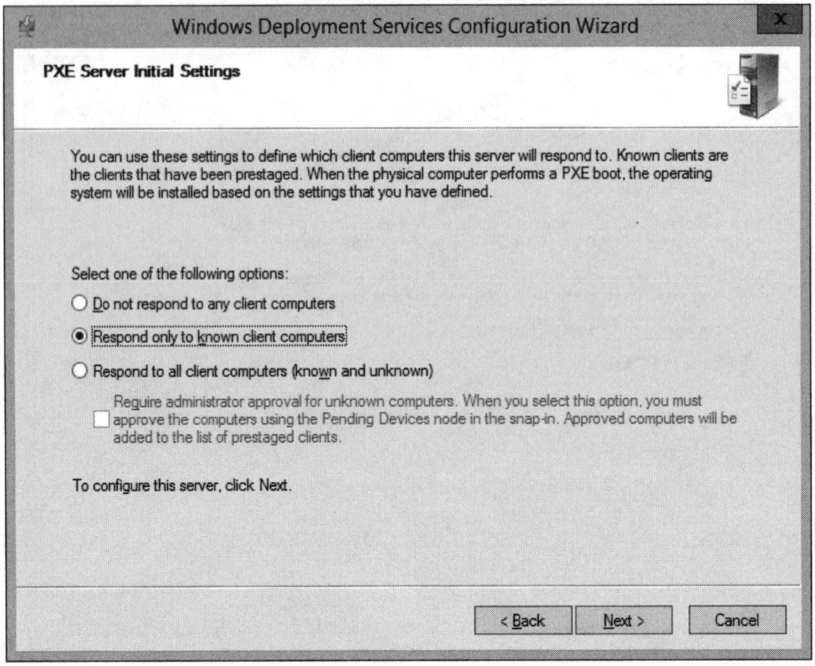

FIGURE 3-30 PXE response settings

7. Ensure that WDS starts before attempting to integrate the WDS server with VMM.

Integrating the WDS server with VMM

To integrate the WDS server with VMM to function as the VMM PXE server, you need to use an account on the VMM server that is a member of the local Administrators group on the WDS server.

To add an existing PXE server to VMM, perform the following steps:

1. In the Fabric workspace of the VMM console, expand the Infrastructure node, and select PXE Servers.

2. On the VMM console ribbon, click Add Resources, and then click PXE Server.

3. On the Add PXE Server dialog box, provide the computer name and the credentials used to connect to the WDS server to install the VMM agent. Figure 3-31 shows the computer name set to MEL-DHCP-PXE, and the credentials of the Adatum\administrator account.

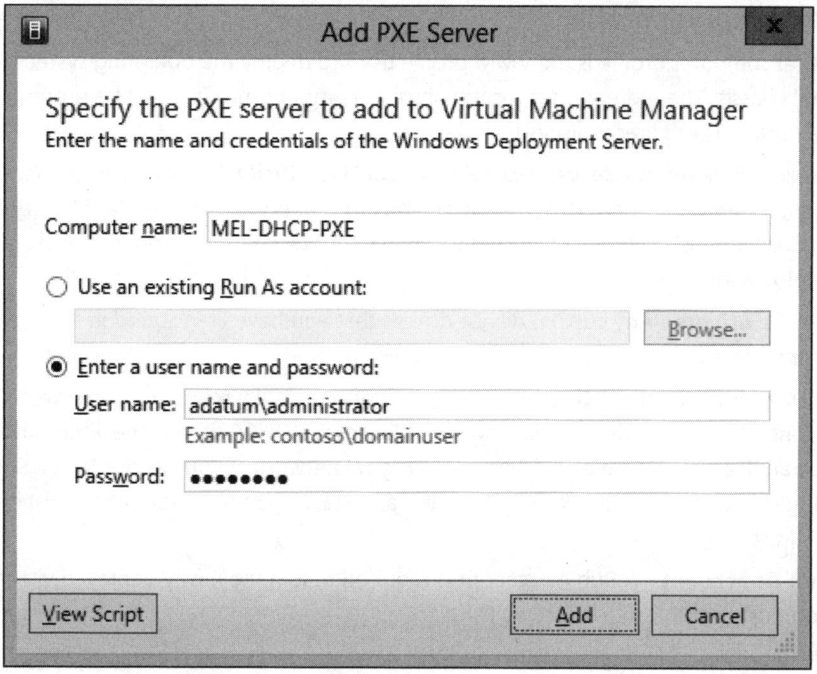

FIGURE 3-31 Setting the PXE server name and credentials

4. When the PXE server has been added, it will be visible in the VMM console in the PXE Servers node, as shown in Figure 3-32.

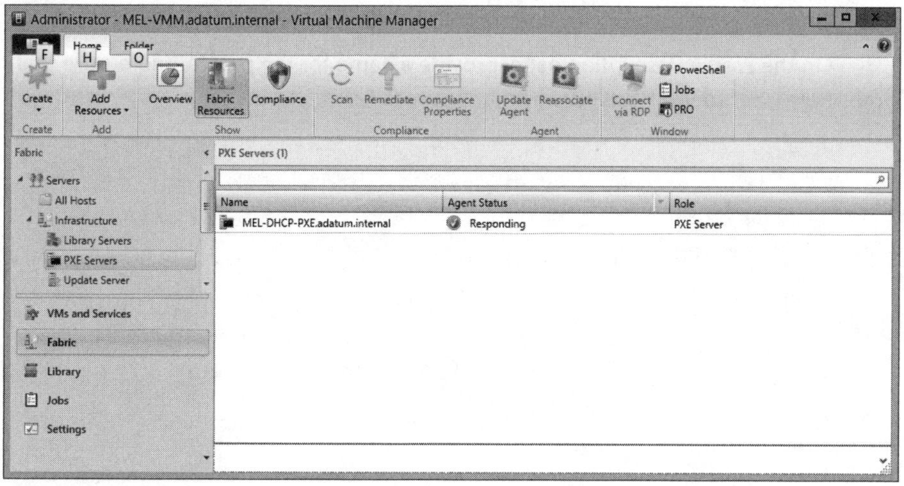

FIGURE 3-32 PXE server

Physical computer profile

The physical computer profile is the VMM profile used to deploy the operating system to the bare metal chassis. The prerequisites for the physical computer profile must be present within the VMM library. These prerequisites include:

- **Prepared Windows Server 2012 R2 Virtual Hard Disk File**   You need to have a Sysprepped virtual hard disk, in .vhd or .vhdx format present in the VMM library. This virtual hard disk will be transmitted to the bare metal chassis during virtualization host deployment.

- **Device drivers**   Any custom device drivers that you haven't included in the Sys-prepped virtual hard disk file must be added to VMM.

- **DHCP server or static IP address**   During profile deployment, the bare metal chassis will need an IP address. This can be obtained from a DHCP server. The alternative is to use an IP address from an existing VMM logical network. If you choose to use a VMM logical network, a network site, IP subnet, and static IP pool must already exist on the VMM server.

- **Run As account**   A Run As account is required to join the newly deployed virtualiza-tion host to the Active Directory Domain.

- **Networking**   The logical switch and VM network used when creating the Physical Profile must be available.

To create a physical computer profile, perform the following steps:

1. In the Library workspace of the VMM console, select Physical Computer Profiles under Profiles.

2. On the ribbon click Create, and then click Physical Computer Profile.

3. On the Profile Description page, provide a name for the profile, and ensure that the Role is set to VM Host, as shown in Figure 3-33.

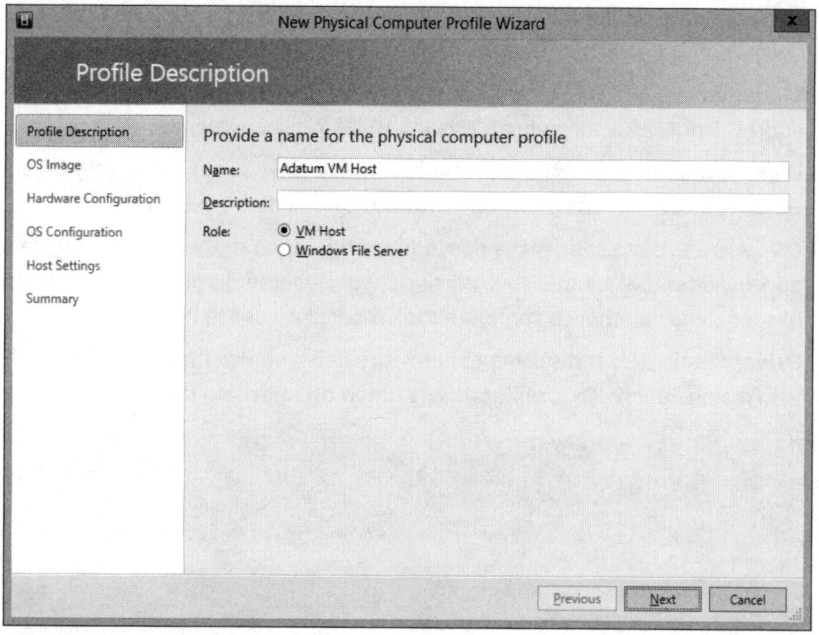

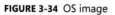

FIGURE 3-33 Profile description

4. On the OS Image page, select the prepared virtual hard disk. This virtual hard disk must already be present within the VMM library. Figure 3-34 shows a selected virtual hard disk.

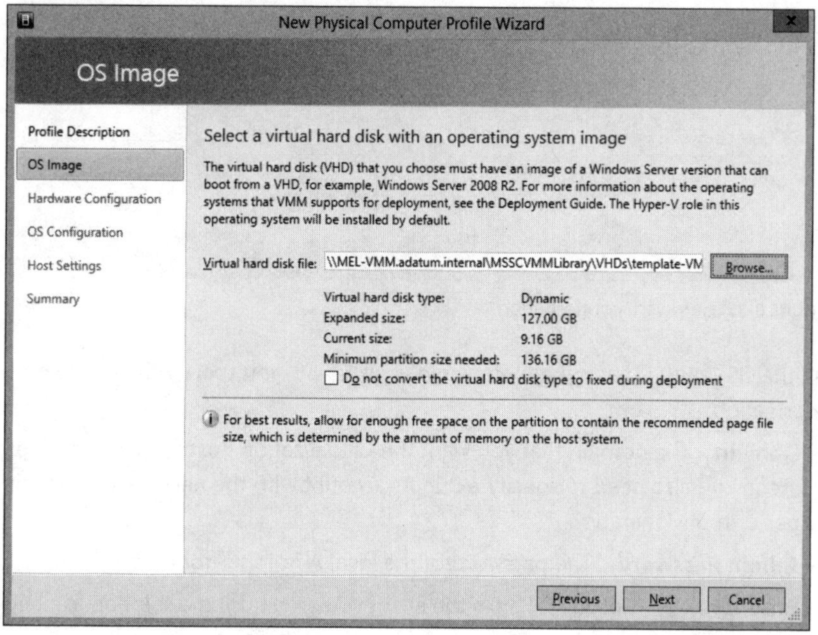

FIGURE 3-34 OS image

5. On the Hardware Configuration page, shown in Figure 3-35, configure the following settings:

- **Management NIC** You can choose to have the virtualization host obtain an IP address from DHCP, or from an existing VMM logical network.

- **Disk** Configure a partition scheme for the first disk. Select between MBR and GUID. You can only use GUID for hardware chassis that use UEFI.

- **OS** Allows you to specify the partition configuration of the operating system partition. Includes the volume label, partition type, whether to allocate a specific amount of space, and whether to configure the OS partition as the boot partition.

- **Driver Filter** Use this setting to configure between whether you will filter drivers with matching PnP IDs, or filter drivers based on matching tags.

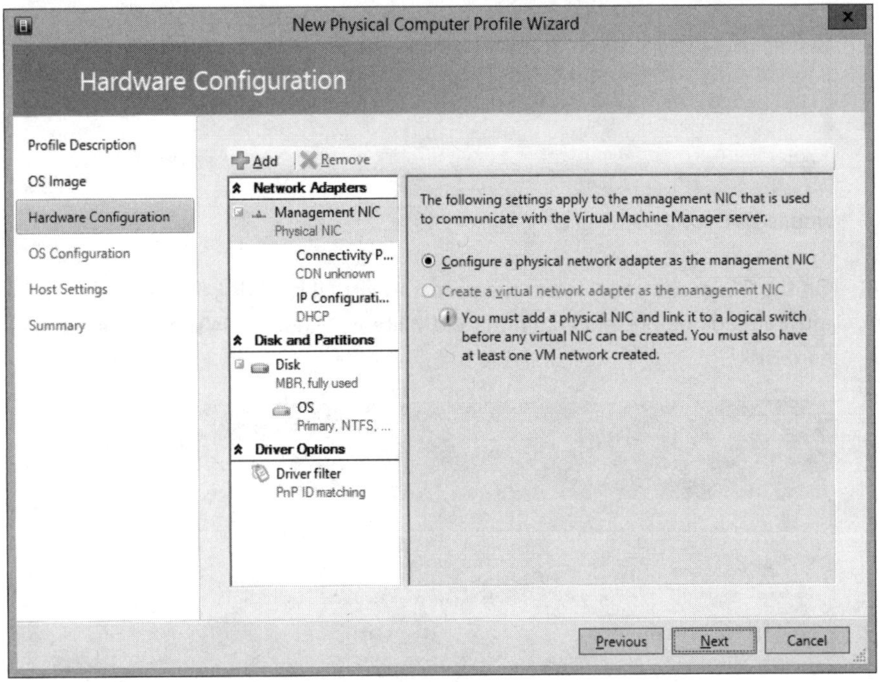

FIGURE 3-35 Hardware configuration

6. On the OS Configuration page, shown in Figure 3-36, you specify the following information:

- **Domain** The domain that you want the virtualization host to join after deployment. You also need to specify a Run As account with the necessary permissions to perform this operation.

- **Admin Password** The password of the local Administrator account.

- **Product Key** A product key in the event you aren't using a solution like Key Management Services or Active Directory based activation.

- **Time Zone**   Time zone that the virtualization host will be configured to use.
- **Answer File**   Any answer file that will be used as part of the deployment.
- **[GUIRunOnce] Command**   Any commands that should be run once after initial deployment is complete.

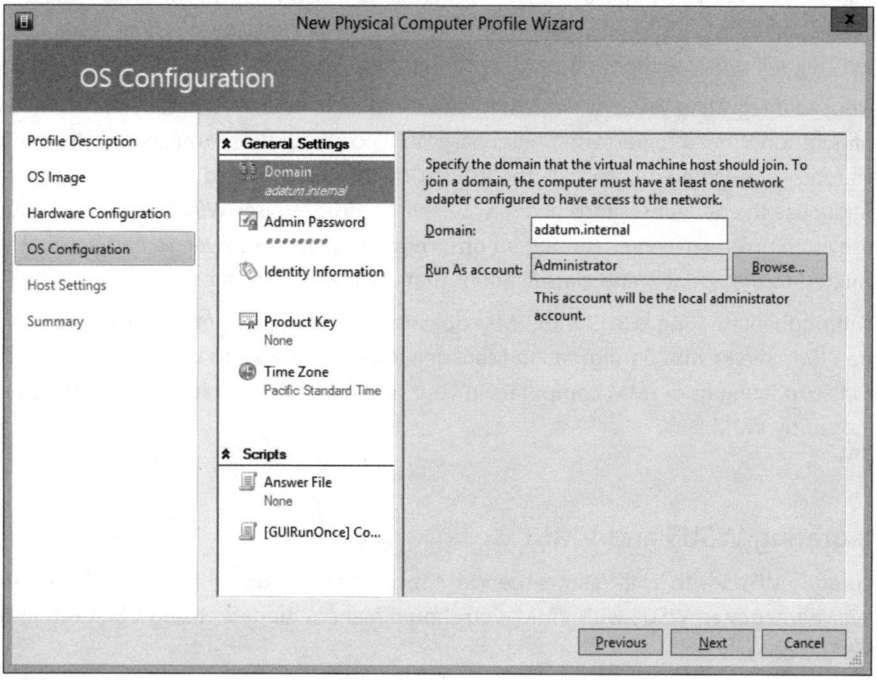

FIGURE 3-36 OS Configuration

7. On the Host Settings page, specify the placement paths to be used for virtual machines on the host. If you don't specify a path, VMM will determine the best location on the virtualization host.

Adding an WSUS server to VMM

Integrating WSUS with VMM allows you to use VMM to manage updates for computers that host VMM resources, including VMM management servers, library servers, PXE servers, as well as Hyper-V hosts and Hyper-V host clusters. By integrating VMM with WSUS, you can:

- Collect updates together in baselines
- Determine update compliance
- Remediate update compliance
- Automatically evacuate VMs from host cluster nodes that require a reboot to install updates.

WSUS server prerequisites

You can use a WSUS server running WSUS 3.0 SP2, which you can install on computers running the Windows Server 2008 or Windows Server 2008 R2 operating system, or WSUS 4.0, which is included as a role service for computers that have the Windows Server 2012 and Windows Server 2012 R2 operating systems. While you could deploy the WSUS role on the computer that hosts VMM, Microsoft recommends that you deploy WSUS on a separate computer. This will separate the workloads, ensuring that they don't conflict with each other.

Prior to integrating WSUS with VMM, you should install the WSUS role and run the WSUS Configuration Wizard to perform preliminary WSUS configuration. You should also perform synchronization. When running run the WSUS Configuration Wizard and performing synchronization, use the default settings unless you have an on-premises WSUS server that you want to use as an upstream server. If using an on-premises upstream server, remember that you'll be limited to the updates and classifications that are present on that server.

Although integrating WSUS with VMM doesn't preclude you from also integrating the same WSUS server with Configuration Manager, it's a better idea to keep the WSUS server used for updating non-VMM computers in your organization separate from the WSUS server managed by VMM.

Integrating WSUS and VMM

Integrating WSUS with VMM allows the VMM server to take control of the WSUS server. Once you have integrated WSUS with VMM, you should manage updates using VMM rather than the WSUS console.

To integrate WSUS with VMM, perform the following steps:

1. In the Fabric workspace of the VMM console, click the Update Server Node under Infrastructure, as shown in Figure 3-37.

FIGURE 3-37 Update Server

2. On the Ribbon, click Add Resources, and then click Update Server. This will launch the Add Windows Server Update Services Server dialog box.

3. In the Add Windows Server Update Services Server dialog box, provide the following information, as shown in Figure 3-38, and then click Add.

   - **Computer Name** The FQDN of the WSUS server.

   - **TCP Port** The WSUS server's TCP port. By default, this is port 8530 (or port 8531 if using SSL) when you deploy WSUS on computers running Windows Server 2012 or Windows Server 2012 R2.

   - **Credentials** An account with local Administrator privileges on the WSUS server. You can also use a Run As account for this task.

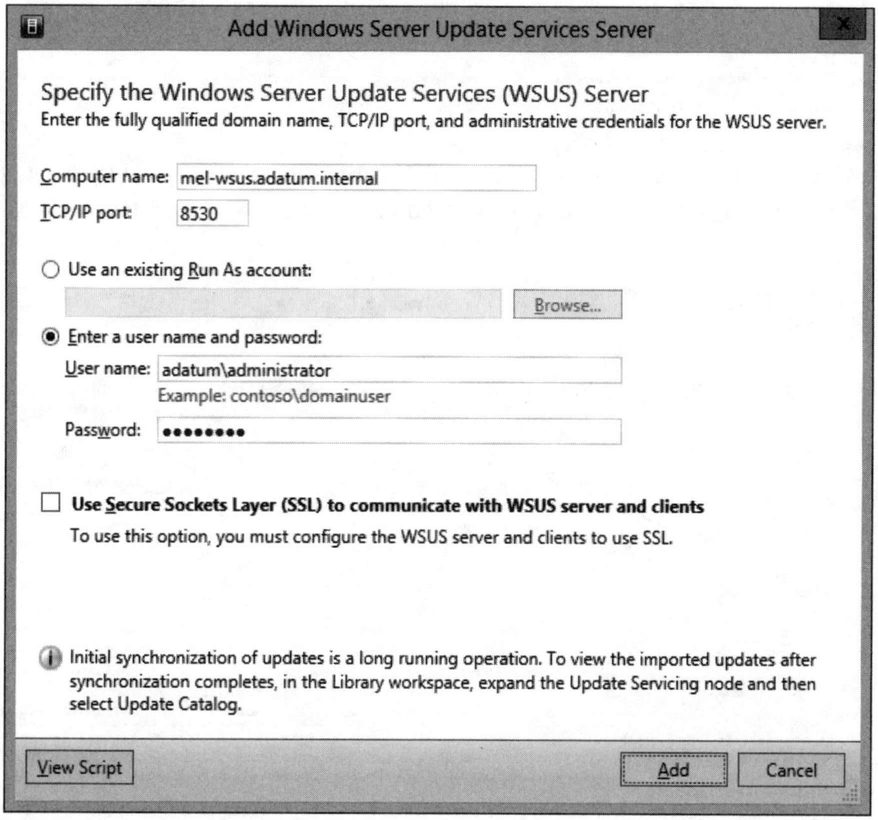

FIGURE 3-38 Add Update Server

4. Once the installation completes, verify that the update server is listed when the Update Server node is selected. The Agent Status is set to Responding, and Synchronization Result is listed as Succeeded, as shown in Figure 3-39.

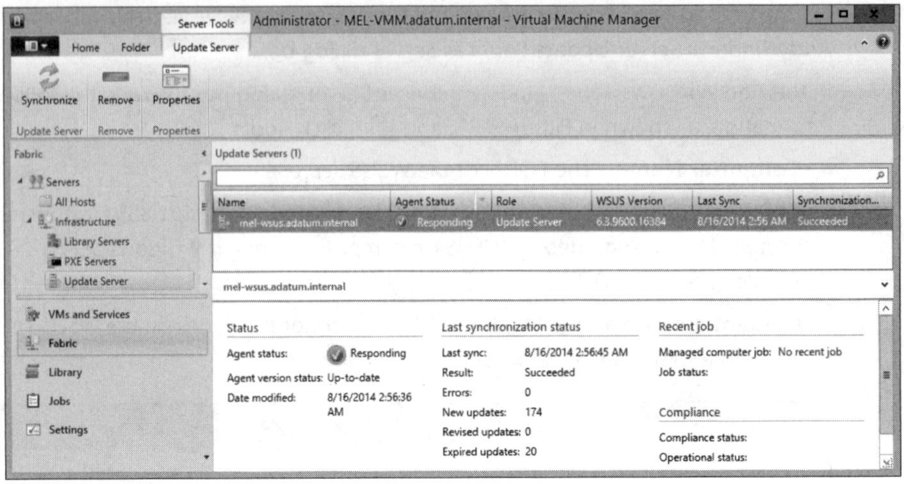

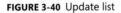

FIGURE 3-39 Update Server

5. To check which updates are available, in the Library workspace, select Update Catalog under Update Catalog And Baselines, and verify that updates are listed, as shown in Figure 3-40.

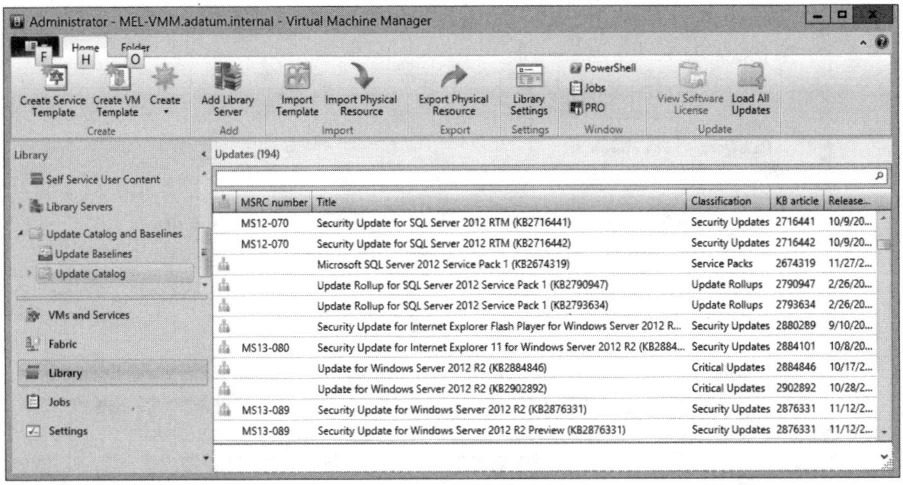

FIGURE 3-40 Update list

After you perform the initial synchronization between VMM and the WSUS server to gather the current list of available updates, VMM will not perform subsequent synchronizations automatically. This means that you need to either perform them manually, or configure a scheduled task using the Start-SCUpdateServerSynchronization Windows PowerShell cmdlet. To trigger a synchronization using the VMM console, perform the following steps:

1. In the Fabric workspace of the VMM console, select Update Server under the Servers\ Infrastructure node.

2. Select the WSUS server that you want VMM to synchronize.

3. On the ribbon, click the Synchronize icon.

To trigger synchronization from the Virtual Machine Manager Command Shell, issue the following command, where WSUSServerName is the name of the WSUS server.

```
SCUpdateServerSynchronization WSUSServerName
```

> **MORE INFO INTEGRATING WSUS WITH VMM**
>
> You can learn more about integrating WSUS with VMM at *http://technet.microsoft.com/en-us/library/gg675099.aspx*.

 EXAM TIP

Remember the permissions required to integrate WSUS with VMM.

Thought experiment

WSUS and VMM integration at Adatum

You are preparing the integration of WSUS and VMM at Adatum. You have deployed a new WSUS installation on a computer named MEL-WSUS.adatum.internal by using the Windows PowerShell command:

```
install-windowsfeature UpdateServices -IncludeAllSubFeature
-IncludeManagementTools
```

You are researching additional steps that you must take. With this in mind, you need answers to the following questions before you can proceed:

1. What steps must you take on MEL-WSUS.adatum.internal before attempting integration from VMM?

2. What permissions must the Run As account used to integrate the WSUS server with VMM have on MEL-WSUS.adatum.internal?

Objective summary

- The advantage of integrating virtualization host deployment with VMM is that you can fully automate the process of deploying a VMM managed virtualization host to bare metal.

- When you integrate WDS with VMM, the WDS server hosts a VMM provider that will handle PXE traffic from bare metal chassis started using the VMM provisioning tool.

- During deployment, a specially prepared virtual hard disk containing the virtualization host operating system is copied to the bare metal chassis from a VMM library server.

- The PXE server needs to provide the PXE service through Windows Deployment Services.
- To integrate the WDS server with VMM to function as the VMM PXE server, you need to use an account on the VMM server that is a member of the local Administrators group on the WDS server.
- The physical computer profile is the VMM profile used to deploy the operating system to the bare metal chassis.
- Integrating WSUS with VMM allows you to use VMM to manage updates for computers that host VMM resources, including VMM management servers, library servers, PXE servers, as well as Hyper-V hosts, and Hyper-V host clusters.

Objective review

Answer the following questions to test your knowledge of the information in this objective. You can find the answers to these questions and explanations of why each answer choice is correct or incorrect in the "Answers" section at the end of this chapter.

1. Which of the following must you create before you can use a PXE server integrated with VMM to deploy an operating system to a bare metal chassis to so that it can be used as a VMM managed virtualization host?

    A. Capability profile

    B. Guest OS profile

    C. Hardware profile

    D. Physical computer profile

2. Which port does a WSUS server deployed on Windows Server 2012 R2 use by default if configured to use SSL?

    A. 80

    B. 443

    C. 8530

    D. 8531

3. Which of the following must you have deployed to a VMM library server when configuring a physical computer profile?

    A. PXE boot image in WIM format

    B. Capture image in WIM format

    C. Sysprepped operating system image in WIM format

    D. Sysprepped operating system image in VHD or VHDX format

Objective 3.4: Configure clouds and virtualization hosts

Virtualization hosts, running Hyper-V or a supported third-party virtualization solution, are the bread and butter of a private cloud fabric. While storage and network resources are obviously required, the foundation of any cloud deployment is the ability to virtualize workloads.

> **This objective covers the following topics:**
> - VMM host groups
> - VMM private clouds

Creating VMM host groups

Host groups allow you to simplify the management of virtualization hosts by allowing you to apply the same settings across multiple hosts. VMM includes the All Hosts group by default. You can create additional host groups as required in a hierarchical structure. Child host groups inherit settings from the parent host group. However, if you move a child host group to a new host group, the child host group will retain its original settings with the exception of any PRO configuration. When you configure changes to a parent host group, VMM will provide a dialog box asking if you would like to apply the changed settings to child host groups.

To create a host group, perform the following steps:

1. In the Fabric workspace of the VMM console, click the All Hosts node under Servers.
2. On the Folders tab of the VMM console ribbon, click Create Host Group.
3. Provide the new host group name.

To move a virtualization host to a new host group, perform the following steps:

1. In the Fabric workspace of the VMM console, click the All Hosts node under Servers, and then click on the virtualization host that you want to move to a new host group.
2. On the Host tab of the VMM console ribbon, click Move To Host Group.
3. In the Move Host Group dialog box, shown in Figure 3-41, specify the new parent host group, and click OK.

When you move one host group into another host group, the child host group inherits properties from the parent host group.

Name:

mel-hv1.adatum.internal

Current location:

All Hosts\MEL-HOST-GROUP

Parent host group:

MEL-HOST-GROUP ▾

ⓘ If this host group is used for virtual machine self-service, to avoid service interruptions for self-service users, review self-service user roles for the parent host group carefully before you move the host group.

OK   Cancel

FIGURE 3-41 Move host group

MORE INFO **VMM HOST GROUPS**

You can learn more about VMM host groups at http://technet.microsoft.com/en-au/library/gg610645.aspx.

Placement rules

Placement rules allow you to configure how VMM identifies a suitable host for a VM deployment. Usually this is based on the available resources on the virtualization host or the host cluster. By configuring host group placement rules, you can create rules that dictate the conditions under which a new VM can be placed on a virtualization host in the host group.

To add a placement rule, edit the properties of the host group, and on the placement tab click Add. You then specify a custom property, and one of the following requirements:

- Virtual Machine Must Match Host
- Virtual Machine Should Match Host
- Virtual Machine Must Not Match Host
- Virtual Machine Should Not Match Host

Host reserves

Host reserves allow you to configure the resources that VMM should set aside for the host operating system. When VMM is going to place a new VM on a host, that host must be able to meet the VM's resource requirements without exceeding the configured host reserves. As Figure 3-42 shows, you can configure host reserves for:

- CPU
- Memory
- Disk I/O
- Disk Space
- Network I/O

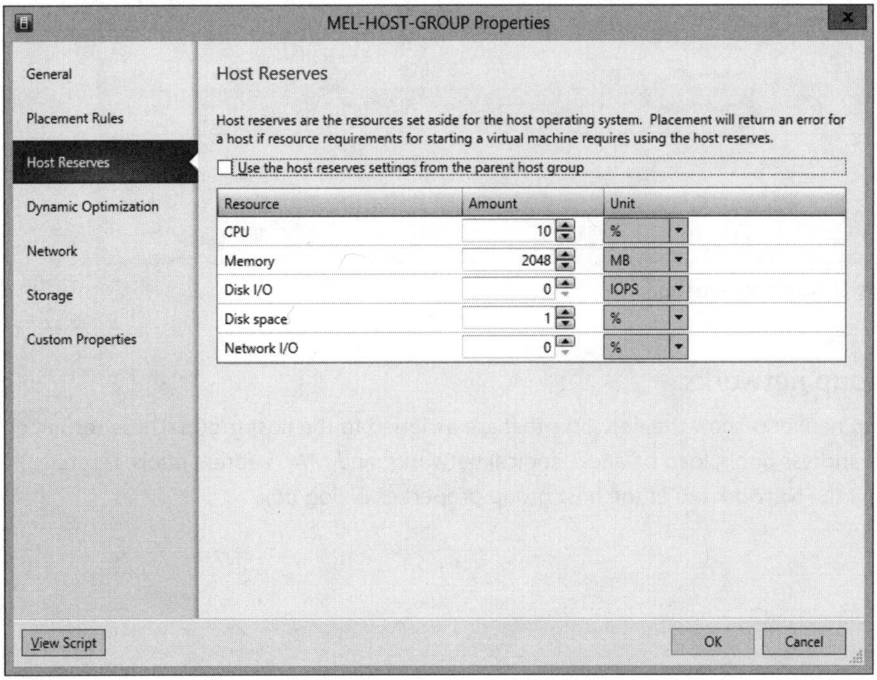

FIGURE 3-42 Host reserves

Dynamic optimization

Dynamic optimization allows virtualization host clusters to balance workloads by transferring VMs between nodes according to the settings configured at the host group level. Whether or not the transfer occurs depends on whether the hardware resources on a node in the virtualization host cluster fall below the configured settings shown in Figure 3-43. Dynamic optimization only applies to clustered virtualization hosts and does not apply hosts that are not members of a cluster.

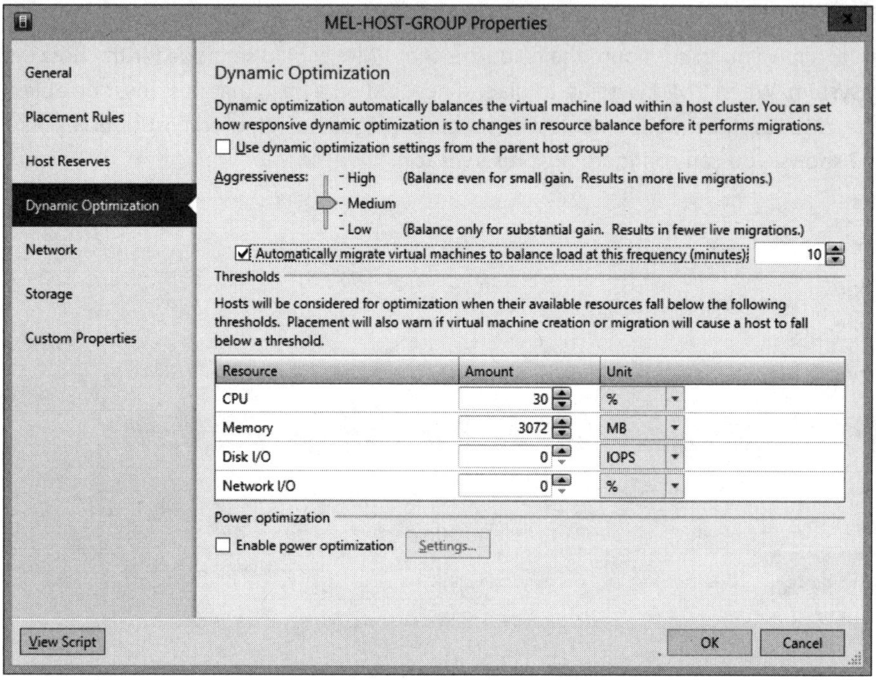

FIGURE 3-43 Dynamic optimization

Host group networks

Host group networks show the networks that are assigned to the host group. These resources include IP address pools, load balances, logical networks, and MAC address pools. Figure 3-44 shows the Network tab of the host group properties dialog box.

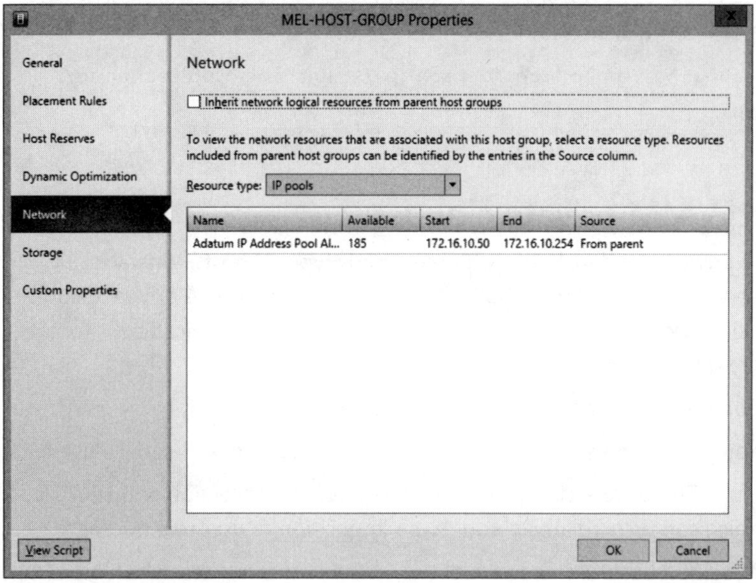

FIGURE 3-44 Network

Host group storage

Through host group storage, you can allocate logical units or storage pools that are accessible to the VMM server to a specific host group. Figure 3-45 shows the Storage tab of the Host Group Properties dialog box.

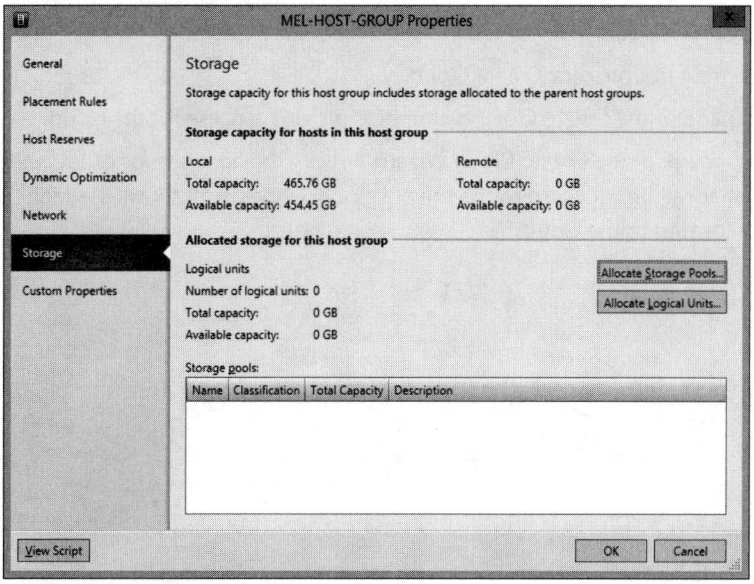

FIGURE 3-45 Storage

MORE INFO **HOST GROUP PROPERTIES**

You can learn more about host group properties at http://technet.microsoft.com/en-us/library/hh335101.aspx.

Understanding VMM private clouds

In VMM, the basis of a private cloud includes resources from Hyper-V hosts, VMware ESX hosts, and Citrix XenServer host, or, alternatively, a VMware resource pool. A private cloud can also include logical networks, load balancers, VIP templates, port classifications, storage, VMM libraries, capacity settings, and capability profiles.

A VMM private cloud provides the following to an organization:

- Self-service   You can delegate management of a private cloud to self-service users.
- Resource pooling   The private cloud allows you to present a collection of resources, utilization of which can be mediated through the imposition of user role quotas.
- Opacity   Private cloud users are unaware of the underlying resources, which are managed by VMM administrators.
- Elasticity   VMM administrators can add resources to increase the capacity of a private cloud.
- Optimization   VMM administrators can optimize the private cloud's underlying resources on an ongoing basis without adversely affecting the private cloud user experience.

To create a private cloud, perform the following steps:

1. In the VMs And Services workspace of the VMM console, click Clouds.
2. On the VMM console ribbon, click Create Cloud.
3. On the General page of the Create Cloud dialog box, provide a name for the cloud.
4. On the Resources page of the Create Cloud Wizard, specify the host groups or VMware resource pools that will be allocated to the private cloud. Figure 3-46 shows the MEL-HOST-GROUP allocated to the cloud.

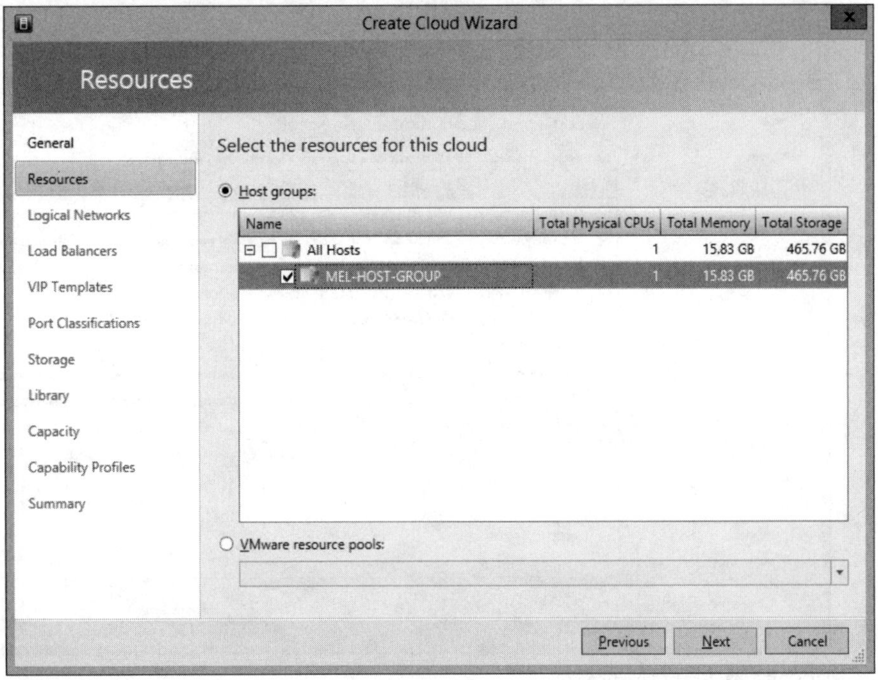

FIGURE 3-46 Resources

5. On the Logical Networks page, specify which logical networks will be included in the private cloud.

6. On the Load Balancers page, specify which load balancers will be allocated to the private cloud.

7. On the VIP Templates page, specify which VIP templates will be allocated to the private cloud.

8. On the Port Classifications page, specify which port classifications will be available to VMs deployed to the private cloud. Figure 3-47 shows all port classifications selected.

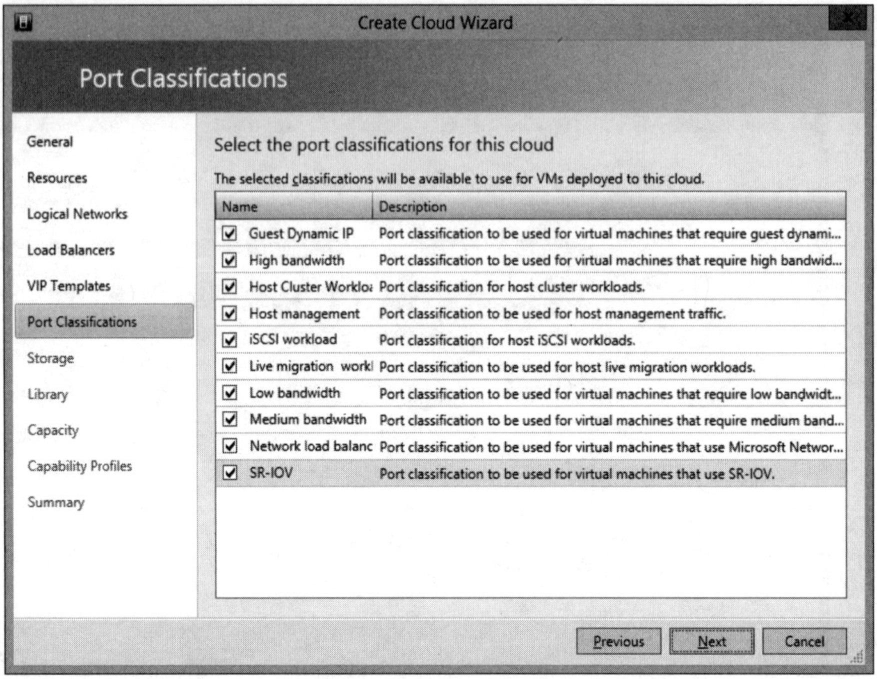

FIGURE 3-47 Port Classifications

9. On the Storage page, specify which storage classifications will be assigned to the cloud. Figure 3-48 shows the Local Storage classification assigned to the cloud.

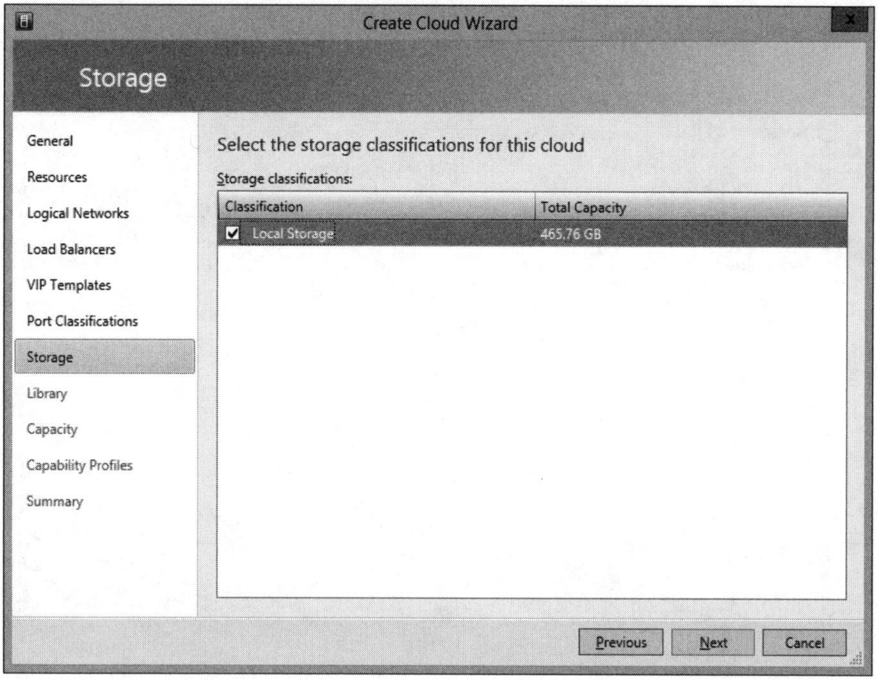

FIGURE 3-48 Storage

10. On the Library page, specify the stored VM path and read-only library share information.

11. On the Capacity page, specify the capacity of the cloud in terms of Virtual CPUs, Memory, Storage, Quota Points, and Virtual Machines. Figure 3-49 shows this page where the assigned capacity, rather than the use maximum, option is selected.

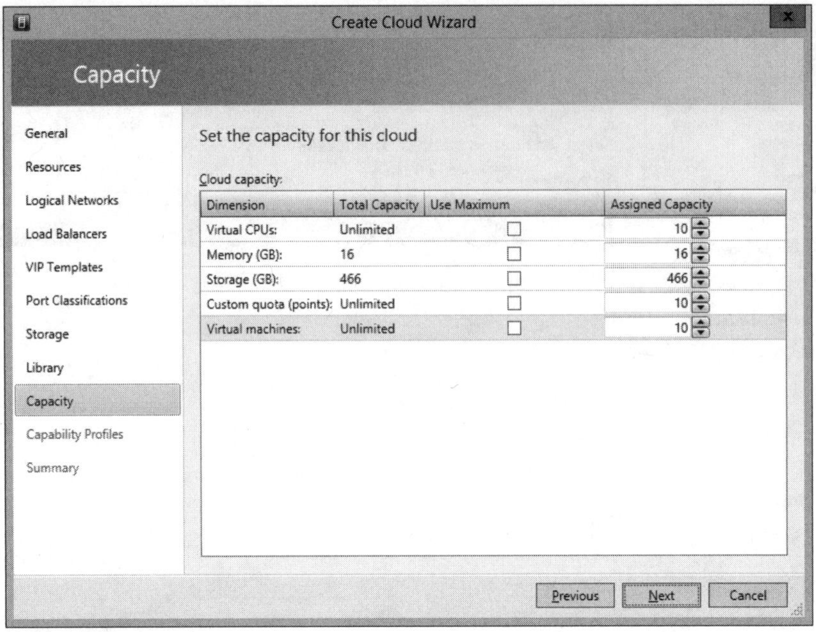

FIGURE 3-49 Capacity

12. On the Capability Profiles page, specify which capability profiles can be used with this cloud. Figure 3-50 shows the Hyper-V capability profile selected.

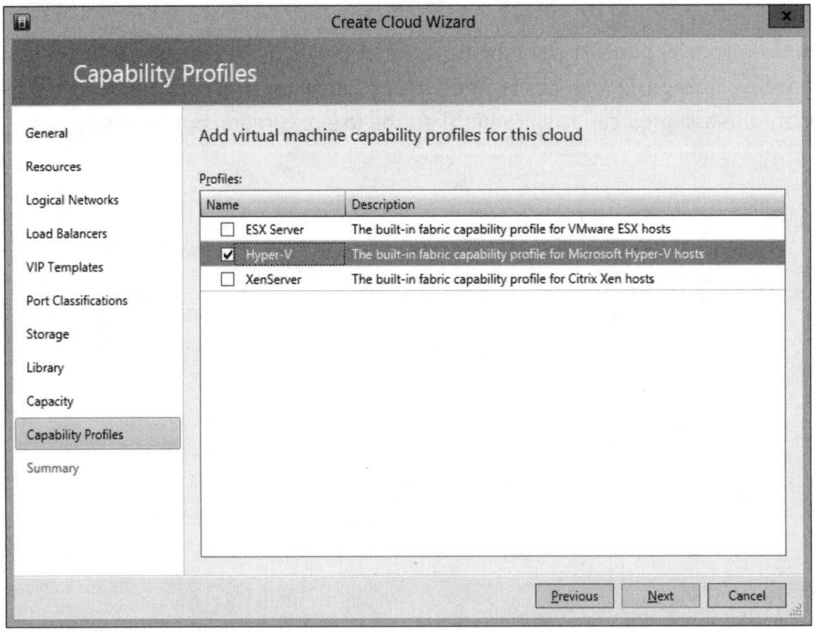

FIGURE 3-50 Capability profile

13. Review the summary, and click Finish to create the private cloud.

MORE INFO **VMM PRIVATE CLOUDS**

You can learn more about VMM private clouds at http://technet.microsoft.com/en-au/library/gg610625.aspx.

EXAM TIP

Remember that dynamic optimization only allows movement of virtual machines between cluster nodes in a host group. It does not allow automatic movement of VMs between non-clustered virtualization hosts.

Thought experiment
Host group settings at Wingtip Toys

In this thought experiment, apply what you've learned about this objective. You can find answers to these questions in the "Answers" section at the end of this chapter.

You are in the process of configuring host group settings for collections of Hyper-V virtualization hosts located in the Wingtip Toys Melbourne and Sydney datacenter. The virtualization hosts in the Melbourne datacenter have more powerful hardware than the virtualization hosts in Sydney, so should have different settings applied.

1. How can you apply a different set of host reserves rules for the Hyper-V hosts in Melbourne and the Hyper-V hosts in Sydney?

2. How would you make a storage pool available in the Sydney datacenter available only to Hyper-V hosts in Sydney?

Objective summary

- Host groups allow you to simplify the management of virtualization hosts by allowing you to apply the same settings across multiple hosts.
- Child host groups inherit settings from the parent host group.
- Placement rules allow you to configure how VMM identifies a suitable host for a VM deployment.
- Host reserves allow you to configure the resources that VMM should set aside for the host operating system.
- Dynamic optimization allows virtualization host clusters to balance workloads by transferring VMs between nodes according to the settings configured at the host group level.
- Host group networks show the networks that are assigned to the host group.

- Through host group storage, you can allocate logical units or storage pools that are accessible to the VMM server to a specific host group.

- In VMM, the basis of a private cloud is resources from Hyper-V hosts, VMware ESX hosts, and Citrix XenServer host, or, alternatively, a VMware resource pool.

- A private cloud can also include logical networks, load balancers, VIP templates, port classifications, storage, VMM libraries, capacity settings, and capability profiles.

Objective review

Answer the following questions to test your knowledge of the information in this objective. You can find the answers to these questions and explanations of why each answer choice is correct or incorrect in the "Answers" section at the end of this chapter.

1. Which of the following would you configure on a host group's properties to allocate logical units to the host group?

   A. Host reserves

   B. Dynamic optimization

   C. Placement rules

   D. Host group storage

2. You have a host group that contains five 8-node Hyper-V failover clusters. You want to ensure that VMs are moved off nodes that are under resource pressure and onto nodes that are not under as much resource duress. Which of the following would you configure on a host group's properties to accomplish this goal?

   A. Host group storage

   B. Placement rules

   C. Dynamic optimization

   D. Host reserves

3. Which of the following should you configure at the host group level to ensure that enough RAM is available to run the virtualization host operating system?

   A. Host group storage

   B. Host reserves

   C. Dynamic optimization

   D. Placement rules

Answers

This section contains the solutions to the thought experiments and answers to the objective review questions in this chapter.

Objective 3.1: Thought Experiment

1. The answer will depend on the scheme you develop. If you've reviewed all of the question, you know that you have to leave room for a classification to indicate that there may be better storage available in future. You could choose Gold here, and use Platinum with question four.

2. The classification for this storage should indicate that the performance is below that of the directly attached solid-state disk array

3. The classification for this storage should indicate that the performance is below the solid-state disk array, the Fibre Channel RAID 5 SAS, and the mirrored iSCSI storage.

4. Depending on what you chose, it would have to be thematically consistent with the other classifications. That means that if you chose Gold/Silver/Bronze/Tin that this would be something like Platinum, rather than Alpha or A1

Objective 3.1: Review

1. **Correct answer:** D

   A. **Incorrect:** Available capacity requires a storage pool, which is available either through a SAN device or a Scale-Out File Server.

   B. **Incorrect:** Writable snapshot of a virtual disk requires block-level storage, either through a SAN device or a Scale-Out File Server.

   C. **Incorrect:** Clone of a virtual disk requires block-level storage, either through a SAN device or a Scale-Out File Server.

   D. **Correct:** File level storage is available on SMB 3.0 file shares. You can deploy this type of storage when you haven't deployed block-level storage.

2. **Correct answer:** A and D

   A. **Correct:** Windows Server 2012 and Windows Server 2012 R2 support SMB 3.0, which is required when providing file share storage for use by VMM.

   B. **Incorrect:** SMB 3.0 support is required for a file server to be able to provide storage to VMM. Windows Server 2008 R2 doesn't support SMB 3.0

   C. **Incorrect:** SMB 3.0 support is required for a file server to be able to provide storage to VMM. Windows Server 2003 doesn't support SMB 3.0.

   D. **Correct:** Windows Server 2012 and Windows Server 2012 R2 support SMB 3.0, which is required when providing file share storage for use by VMM.

3. **Correct answer:** B and C

    A. Incorrect: Logical units are created on storage pools, not file shares.

    B. Correct: The storage array must support thin provisioning to use it to create thin provisioned logical units.

    C. Correct: The storage administrator must have enabled thin provisioning before it can be used with VMM.

    D. Incorrect: Cluster shared volumes are not required for thin provisioned logical units.

Objective 3.2: Thought experiment

1. You would use network virtualization to meet the goal of allowing VMs from different tenants to use the same local IP address.

2. You would deploy Windows Server Gateway to allow access from remote client sites to VMs hosted on the failover cluster where network virtualization is implemented.

Objective 3.2: Review

1. **Correct answer:** C

    A. Incorrect: A logical network is a collection of network sites, VLAN information, and IP subnet information.

    B. Incorrect: A logical switch stores network adapter configuration settings for use with VMM managed virtualization hosts.

    C. Correct: A VM connects to a VMM logical network through a virtual machine network.

    D. Incorrect: The MAC address pool is a range of MAC addresses that is allocated so that no two VMs use the same MAC address.

2. **Correct answer:** C

    A. Incorrect: The virtual machine networks in this logical network are routable to one another and can be used as a single connected network. Although you can use network virtualization, this requires more administrative effort than using a PVLAN network.

    B. Incorrect: The VLAN network type supports a maximum of 4096 clients in isolated configurations.

    C. Correct: The PVLAN logical network type supports more than 4096 tenants in an isolated configuration.

    D. Incorrect: The MAC address pool is a range of MAC addresses that are allocated so that no two VMs use the same MAC address. You can't use it to ensure network isolation.

3. **Correct answer:** A

- A. **Correct:** The MAC address pool is a range of MAC addresses that is allocated so that no two VMs use the same MAC address.
- B. **Incorrect:** A logical network is a collection of network sites, VLAN information, and IP subnet information.
- C. **Incorrect:** A logical switch stores network adapter configuration settings for use with VMM managed virtualization hosts.]
- D. **Incorrect:** A VM connects to a VMM logical network through a virtual machine network.

Objective 3.3: Thought Experiment

1. You will need to run the configuration wizard and perform an initial synchronization before attempting integration from VMM.
2. The Run As account must be a member of the local Administrators group on MEL-WSUS.adatum.internal.

Objective 3.3: Review

1. **Correct answer:** D

- A. **Incorrect:** A capability profile is used with a VM. You use a physical computer profile with bare metal chassis deployment.
- B. **Incorrect:** A guest OS profile is used with a VM. You use a physical computer profile with bare metal chassis deployment.
- C. **Incorrect:** A hardware profile is used with a VM. You use a physical computer profile with bare metal chassis deployment.
- D. **Correct:** You must create a physical computer profile before you can deploy an OS to a bare metal chassis from VMM.

2. **Correct answer:** D

- A. **Incorrect:** 80, WSUS deployed on Windows Server 2012 R2 and configured to use SSL uses port 8531.
- B. **Incorrect:** 443, WSUS deployed on Windows Server 2012 R2 and configured to use SSL uses port 8531.
- C. **Incorrect:** 8530, WSUS deployed on Windows Server 2012 R2 and configured to use SSL uses port 8531. Port 8530 is used for non-secure traffic.
- D. **Correct:** 8531, WSUS deployed on Windows Server 2012 R2 and configured to use SSL uses port 8531.

3. **Correct answer:** D

    A. **Incorrect:** The PXE boot image is stored on the WDS server.

    B. **Incorrect:** You do not perform captures using a WDS server in a VMM deployment.

    C. **Incorrect:** When preparing a physical computer profile, you need a virtual hard disk with a Sysprepped image.

    D. **Correct:** The Sysprepped virtual hard disk must be present on the VMM library server when creating a physical computer profile.

Objective 3.4: Thought experiment

1. Place the Hyper-V hosts in Melbourne in one host group, and place the Hyper-V hosts from Sydney in another host group.

2. You'd configure the Sydney host group's storage settings and specify the Sydney storage pool.

Objective 3.4: Review

1. **Correct answer:** D

    A. **Incorrect:** Host reserves allow you to reserve a minimum amount of hardware resources for the host operating system.

    B. **Incorrect:** Dynamic optimization allows you to configure thresholds that will trigger workloads to be moved between nodes in a Hyper-V failover cluster.

    C. **Incorrect:** Placement rules allow you to specify rules that determine whether a VM is eligible to be placed on host or host cluster within a host group

    D. **Correct:** Host group storage allows you to allocate logical units or storage pools that are accessible to the VMM server to the host group.

2. **Correct answer:** C

    A. **Incorrect:** Host group storage allows you to allocate logical units or storage pools that are accessible to the VMM server to the host group.

    B. **Incorrect:** Placement rules allow you to specify rules that determine whether a VM is eligible to be placed on host or host cluster within a host group. It does not trigger automatic VM movement.

    C. **Correct:** Dynamic optimization allows you to configure thresholds that will trigger workloads to be moved between nodes in a Hyper-V failover cluster.

    D. **Incorrect:** Host reserves allow you to reserve a minimum amount of hardware resources for the host operating system.

3. **Correct answer:** B

   A. **Incorrect:** Host group storage allows you to allocate logical units or storage pools that are accessible to the VMM server to the host group.

   B. **Correct:** Host reserves allow you to reserve a minimum amount of hardware resources for the host operating system.

   C. **Incorrect:** Dynamic optimization allows you to configure thresholds that will trigger workloads to be moved between nodes in a Hyper-V failover cluster.

   D. **Incorrect:** Placement rules allow you to specify rules that determine whether a VM is eligible to be placed on host or host cluster within a host group. It does not trigger automatic VM movement.

CHAPTER 4

Configure System Center Integration

The System Center products integrate with one another. You can leverage the functionality of one product, such as Operations Manager's performance and availability monitoring, with the automation capabilities of Orchestrator, and the incident and problem management functionality of Service Manager. In this chapter you'll learn how to integrate several different System Center products, allowing them to build off each other's functionality. You'll also learn about Service Provider Foundation, and Microsoft Azure Pack for Windows Server, which allow you to customize the way that users of your private cloud interact with the infrastructure.

Objectives in this chapter:

- Objective 4.1: Configure private cloud integration
- Objective 4.2: Configure integration of private and public clouds

Objective 4.1: Configure private cloud integration

This objective deals with integrating Operations Manager with Service Manager, and Virtual Machine Manager. You'll also learn about the Orchestrator integration packs (IPs), which allow you to use each System Center product's functionality when building automation runbooks. You'll learn about other non-Operations Manager connectors that are available, as well as how to integrate VMM with the new IP address management feature of Windows Server 2012.

> **This section covers the following topics:**
> - Integrating Operations Manager
> - Orchestrator integration packs
> - Other System Center connectors
> - Integrating IPAM with VMM

Integrating Operations Manager

Operations Manager is Microsoft's enterprise monitoring solution. When integrated with other products in the System Center suite, you can use it as a source of incidents and problems for Service Manager, and to extend the management and monitoring functionality of VMM. You can also use Operations Manager events to trigger Orchestrator runbook automation.

Integrating Operations Manager with Service Manager

The Operations Manager alert connector for Service Manager allows you to automatically create Service Manager incidents based on Operations Manager alerts. An Operations Manager alert is created in Operations Manager when an object that Operations Manager monitors experiences a change that is deemed worthy of attention, such as a hardware or software failure occurring on a monitored server. There are two types of Operations Manager connectors for Service Manager: the alert connector, and the configuration item (CI) connector. The CI connector imports objects that Operations Manager has discovered into the Service Manager database. Alert connectors bring alert information into Service Manager.

To create the alert connector, perform the following steps:

1. In the Administration workspace of the Server Manager console, click Connectors.

2. On the Tasks pane, click Create Connector, and then click Operations Manager Alert Connector.

3. On the General page of the Operations Manager Alert Connector Wizard, provide a name for the alert connector.

4. On the Server Details page, shown in Figure 4-1, specify the name of the Operations Manager server and a Run As account that has permission to connect to Operations Manager. Ensure that you use the Test Connection button to verify that the account works and has appropriate permissions.

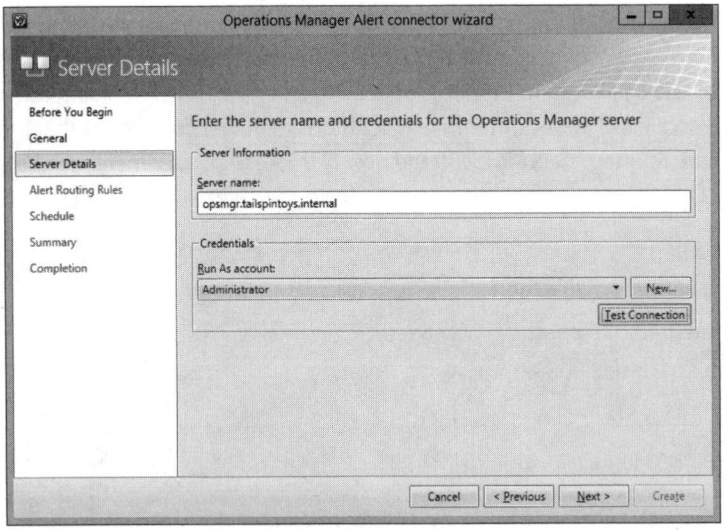

FIGURE 4-1 Alert connector configuration

5. On the Alert Routing Rules page, click Add to add an alert routing rule. An alert routing rule allows you to specify which Service Manager incident template will be used to create an incident based on an Operations Manager alert.

6. In the Add Alert Routing Rule dialog box, shown in Figure 4-2, provide the following information:

   - **Rule Name**   The name of the alert routing rule.

   - **Template**   The Service Manager incident template that will be used when creating the Service Manager incident.

   - **Criteria Type**   Here you can select the conditions that trigger the alert routing rule. You can choose between the alert being generated by a specific Operations Manager management pack, being generated by a specific computer or security group, a custom field, or an Operations Manager monitoring class.

   - **Select Alert Severity And Priority**   Allows you to specify the alert priorities and severities that will trigger the alert routing rule.

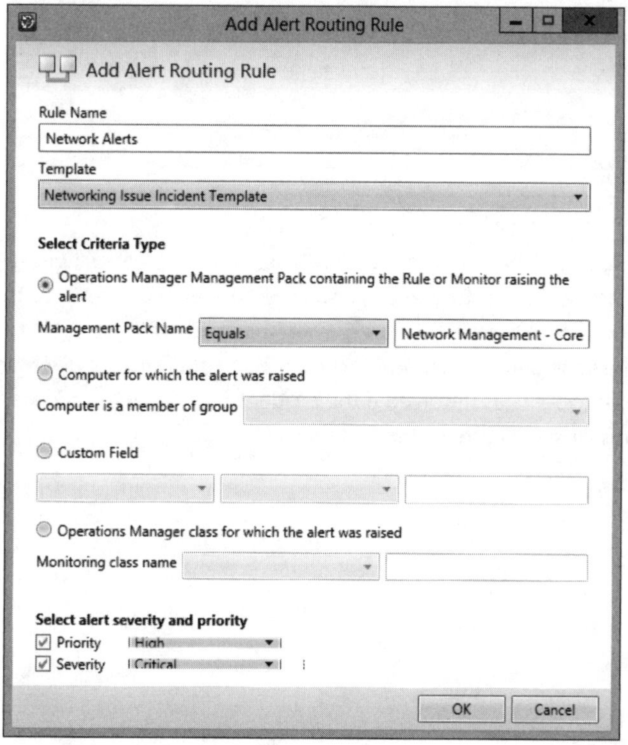

FIGURE 4-2   Alert routing rule

7. As Figure 4-3 shows, alerts that don't match any of your configured rules will automatically be created as incidents using the Operations Manager Incident Template.

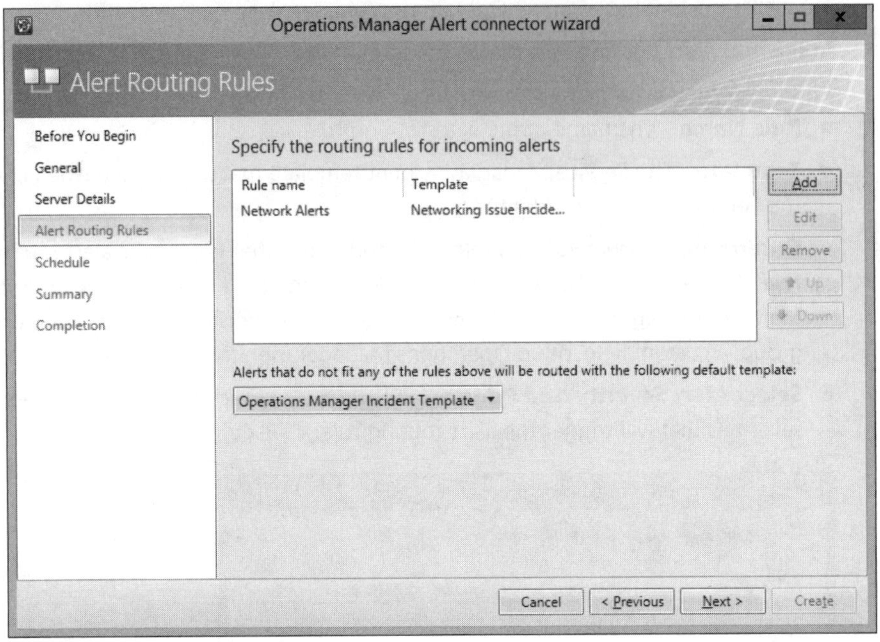

FIGURE 4-3 Routing rules

8. On the Schedule page, select the frequency at which Service Manager will query the Operations Manager server for alerts. You can also configure the connector so that alerts within Operations Manager will be closed when the incident that relates to the alert is resolved or closed in Service Manager. You can also configure Service Manager to automatically mark incidents as Resolved if the incident that triggered the alert in Operations Manager is closed. Figure 4-4 shows these settings.

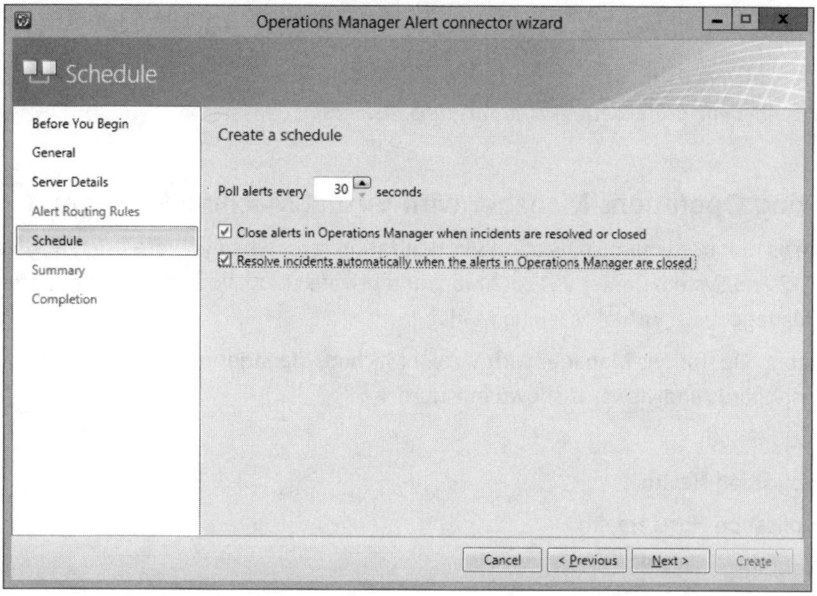

FIGURE 4-4 Schedule settings

9. On the Summary page, review the connector setup, and then create the connector.

10. Once the connector is created, you can modify the alert routing rules by editing the properties of the connector, as shown in Figure 4-5.

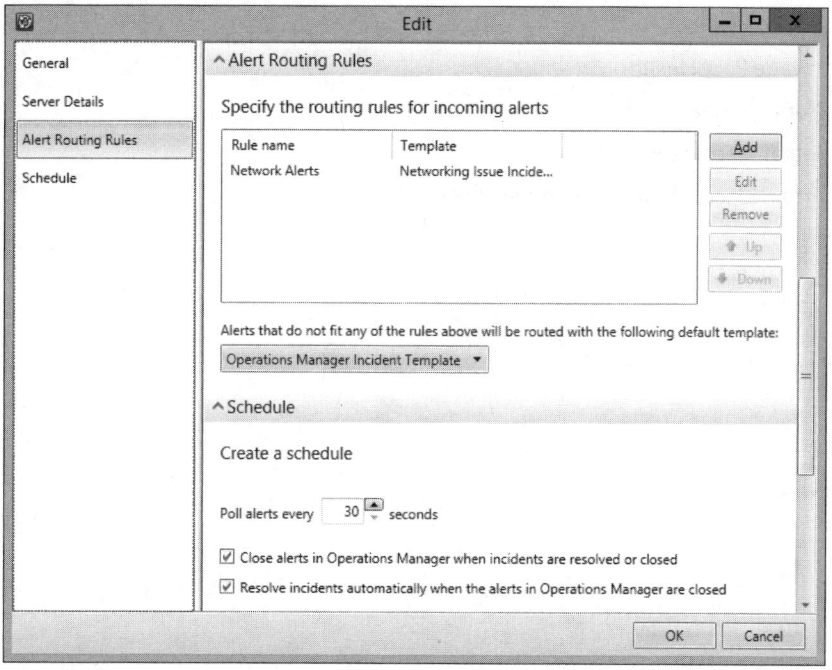

FIGURE 4-5 Connector properties

Integrating Operations Manager with Virtual Machine Manager

To be able to monitor your organization's virtualization layer when you are using a System Center 2012 and System Center 2012 R2 managed private cloud, you need to integrate Operations Manager with Virtual Machine Manager.

Integrating Operations Manager with Virtual Machine Manager provides you with the following dashboards and views, as shown in Figure 4-6:

- Cloud Health
- Application Health
- Application Hosts Health
- Host Cluster Health
- Host Health
- IP Address Pool Health
- Library Server Health
- Load Balancer Health
- MAC Address Pool Health
- Service Health
- Storage Pool Health
- User Role Health
- Virtual Machine Health
- Virtual Machine Manager Server Health

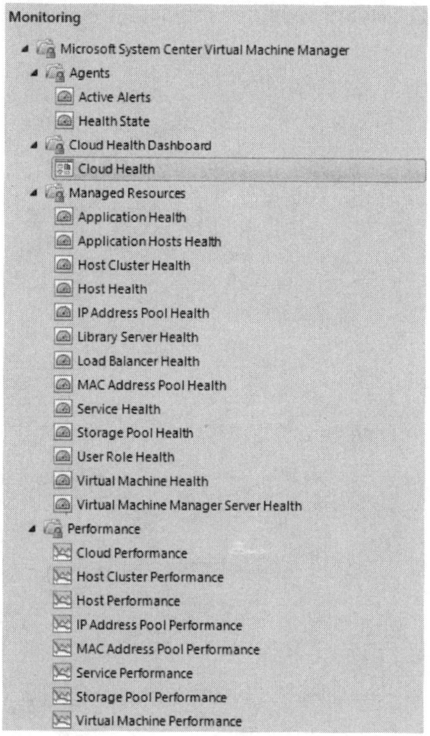

FIGURE 4-6 Virtualization dashboards and views

The Virtual Machine Health dashboard is shown in Figure 4-7.

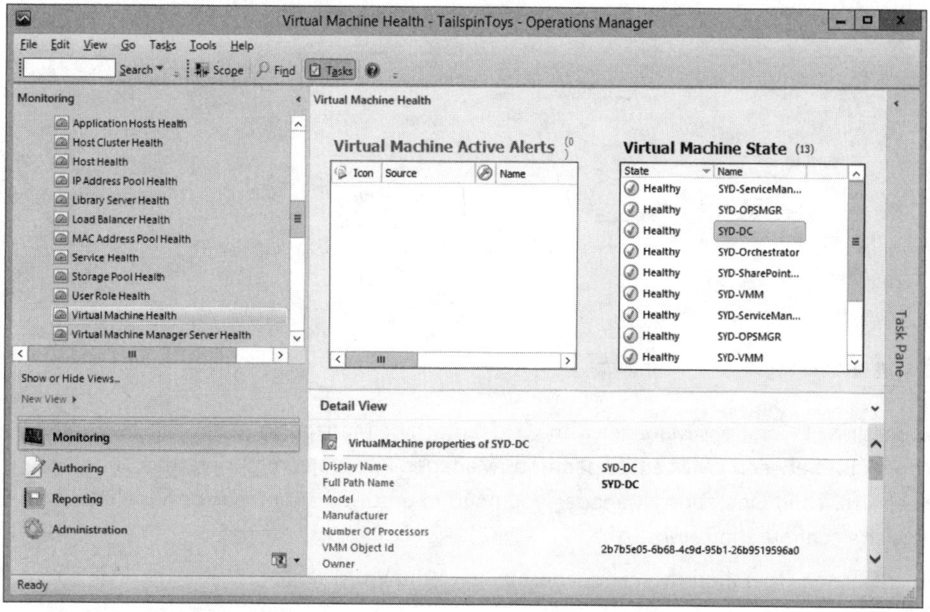

FIGURE 4-7 Virtual Machine Health

Integrating Operations Manager and Virtual Machine Manager also allows you to view the following performance information:

- Cloud Performance
- Host Cluster Performance
- Host Performance
- IP Address Pool Performance
- MAC Address Pool Performance
- Service Performance
- Storage Pool Performance
- Virtual Machine Performance

Figure 4-8 shows the Virtual Machine Performance view.

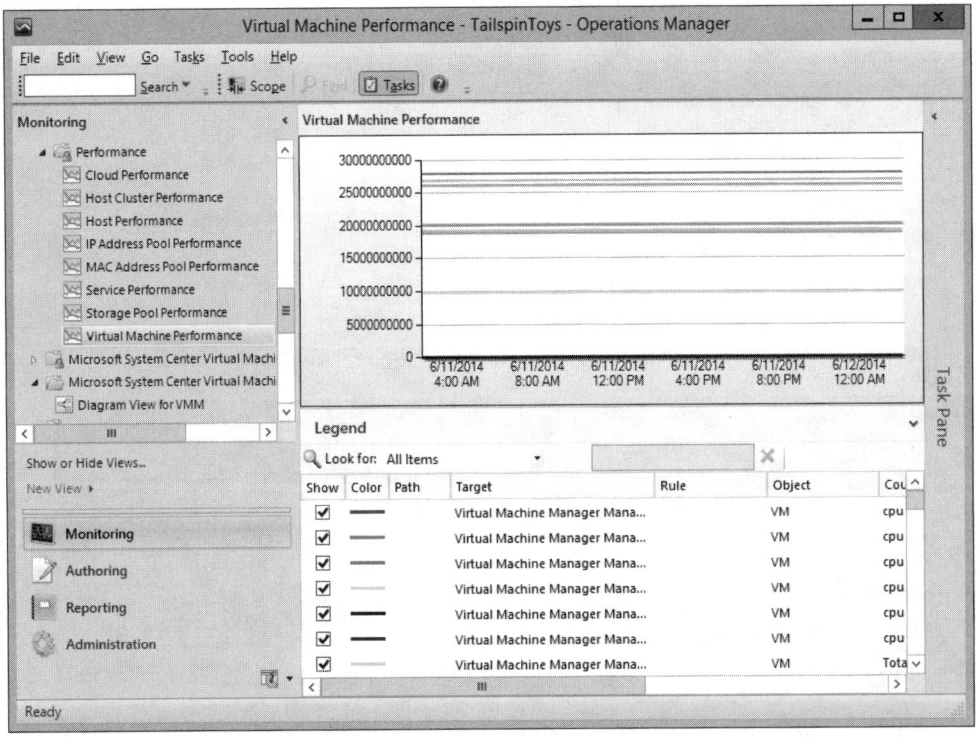

FIGURE 4-8 Virtual Machine Performance

To integrate Operations Manager with Virtual Machine Manager, you need to configure the connector between VMM and Operations Manager. Prior to configuring the connection between VMM and Operations Manager, you need to ensure that you perform the following prerequisite configuration steps:

- Install the Operations Manager console on to the VMM server.

- Install the following Operations Manager management packs on the Operations Manager server:

- SQL Server Core Library version 6.0.5000.0 or later

- Windows Server Internet Information Services Library version 6.0.5000.0 or later

- Windows Server Internet Information Services 2003 version 6.0.5000.0 or later

- Windows Server 2008 Internet Information Services 7 version 6.0.6539.0 or later

To link VMM and Operations Manager, you need the credentials of an account that is a member of the Operations Manager Administrators user role, and the credentials of an account that is a member of the VMM Administrator user role. These can be separate accounts or the same accounts. To configure a connection between VMM and Operations Manager, perform the following steps:

1. In the Settings workspace of the VMM console, click System Center Settings, and then click Operations Manager Server.

2. On the ribbon, click Properties.

3. On the Connection To...page of the Add Operations Manager Wizard, type the name of the Operations Manager server and a Run As account that has the appropriate permissions, as shown in Figure 4-9.

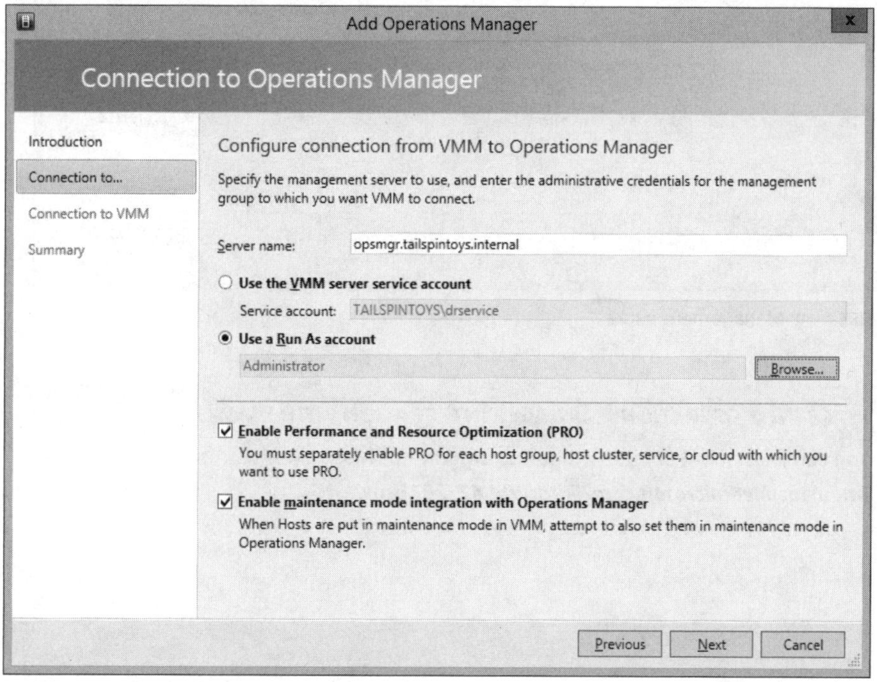

FIGURE 4-9 Connection to Operations Manager

4. On the Connection To VMM page, specify the credentials of the account that will be used by Operations Manger to connect to the VMM server.

5. Complete the wizard.

Configuring the connection between Operations Manager and VMM automatically loads the Management Packs, shown in Figure 4-10, which allow you to monitor the health and performance of your private cloud's virtualization layer.

Operations Manager Settings

Management Packs

The following is the list of currently installed VMM management packs

Management Pack	Installed Version
Microsoft System Center Virtual Machine Manager 2008 R2 PRO Library	3.2.7510.0
Microsoft System Center Virtual Machine Manager 2012 R2 Discovery	3.2.7510.0
Microsoft System Center Virtual Machine Manager 2012 R2 Monitoring	3.2.7510.0
Microsoft System Center Virtual Machine Manager 2012 R2 PRO Diagnostics	3.2.7510.0
Microsoft System Center Virtual Machine Manager 2012 R2 Reports	3.2.7510.0
Microsoft System Center Virtual Machine Manager Library	3.2.7510.0
Microsoft System Center Virtual Machine Manager Overrides	3.2.7510.0
Microsoft System Center Virtual Machine Manager PRO Library	3.2.7510.0
Microsoft System Center Virtual Machine Manager PRO V2 HyperV Host Performance	3.2.7510.0
Microsoft System Center Virtual Machine Manager PRO V2 Library	3.2.7510.0
Microsoft System Center Virtual Machine Manager Storage 2012 R2 Discovery	7.1.10125.0
Microsoft System Center Virtual Machine Manager Storage 2012 R2 Monitoring	7.1.10125.0
Microsoft System Center Virtual Machine Manager Storage Library	7.1.10125.0

FIGURE 4-10 Management packs

> **MORE INFO OPERATIONS MANAGER INTEGRATION WITH VMM**
>
> You can learn more about configuring Operations Manager integration with VMM at *http://technet.microsoft.com/library/hh427287.aspx*.

Orchestrator integration packs

Orchestrator integration packs are collections of tasks that allow you to automate activities with different System Center products. You can download the integration packs for the System Center 2012 R2 suite of products from Microsoft's website. Once you've downloaded the integration packs and extracted them to a temporary directory, you can install them by performing the following steps:

1. In the Orchestrator Deployment Manager, select the Integration Packs node.

2. Right-click the Integration Packs node and click Register IP With The Orchestrator Management Server. This will launch the Integration Pack Registration Wizard.

3. On the Select Integration Packs Or Hotfixes dialog, click Add.

4. Navigate to the location where you extracted the integration packs. You'll need to add one at a time as you can't add multiple integration packs using this interface. Figure 4-11 shows the integration packs that are available for the System Center 2012 R2 products.

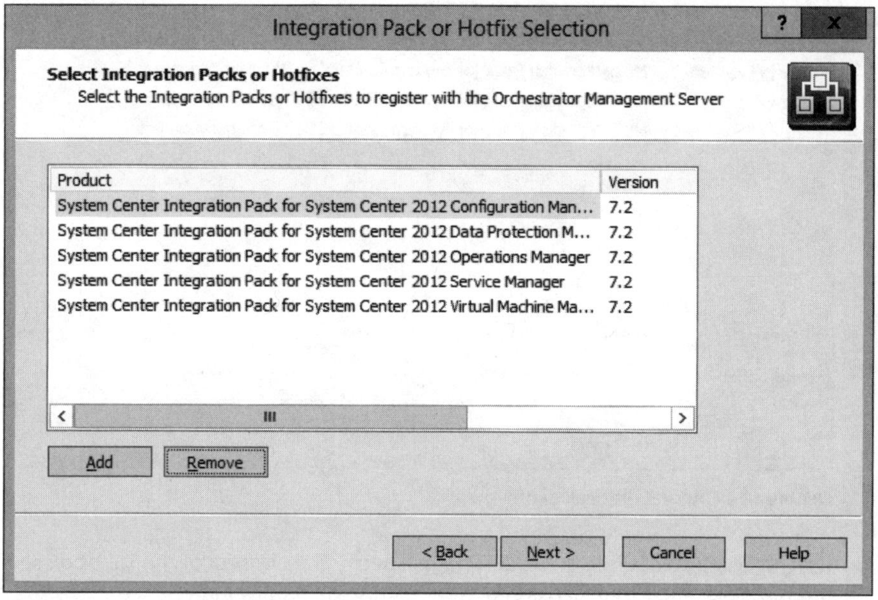

FIGURE 4-11 Integration packs

5. Complete the wizard to add the integration packs. This will involve agreeing to the license terms for each integration pack.

Once the integration packs have been registered, you need to deploy them to the runbook server. To deploy integration packs to the runbook server, perform he following tasks.

1. In the Deployment Manager console, select the Integration Packs node and then select all of the integration packs that you want to deploy to the runbook server.

2. Right-click on the selected integration packs and click Deploy IP To Runbook Server Or Runbook Designer. This will launch the Integration Pack Deployment Wizard.

3. On the Deploy Integration Packs Or Hotfixes page, select all of the integration packs that you want to deploy to the runbook server, as shown in Figure 4-12.

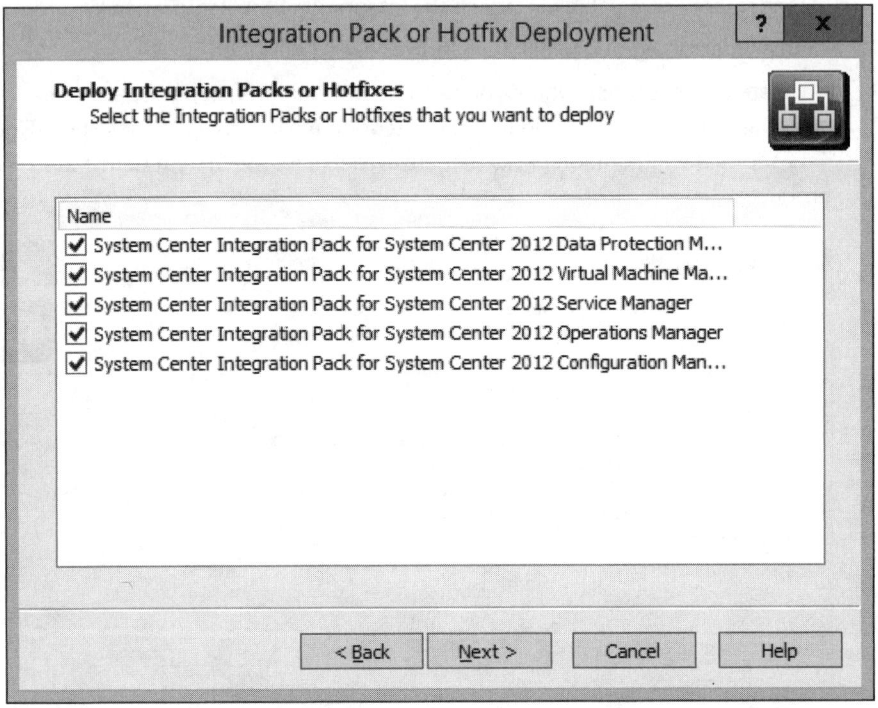

FIGURE 4-12 Integration pack deployment

4. On the Computer Selection Details page, specify the address of the runbook server or Runbook Designer to which you wish to deploy the integration packs.

5. On the Installation Options page, specify when to perform the installation. The default option, shown in Figure 4-13, is to install the integration packs immediately upon completion of the wizard.

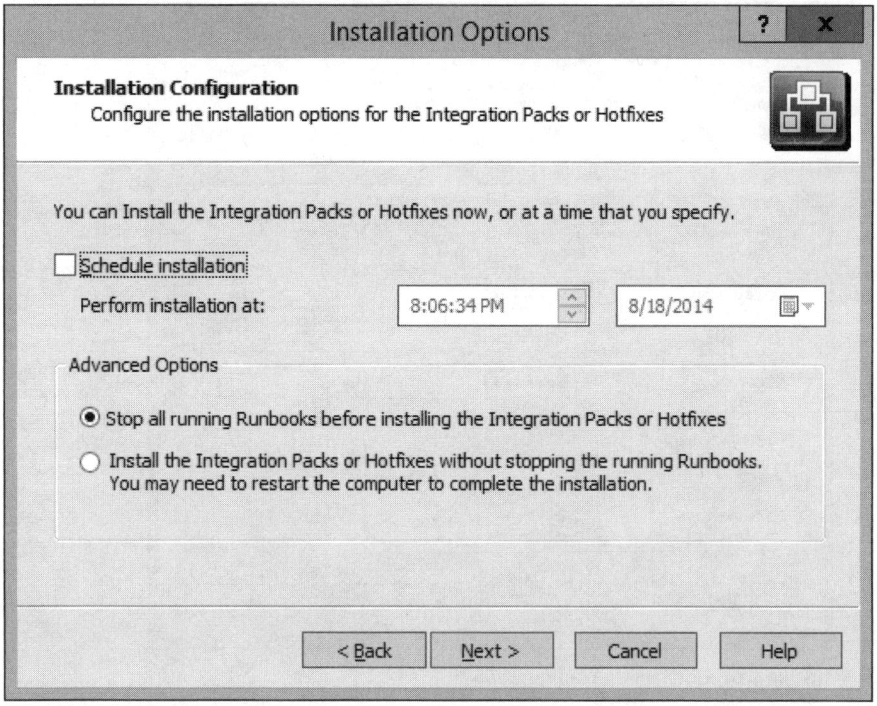

FIGURE 4-13 Installation Options

6. Complete the wizard to deploy the integration packs.

Operations Manager integration pack

You can configure Orchestrator to integrate with Operations Manager by configuring a connection to the Operations Manager server from the Orchestrator Management server. When you do this, you can monitor and collect information from Operations Manager alerts, which you can use when building Orchestrator runbooks. To integrate Orchestrator with Operations Manager, first install the Operations Manager integration pack. You can download this integration pack from Microsoft's website. You'll also need to install the Operations Manager console on the server that hosts the Runbook Designer, and verify that you can use it to make a connection to the Operations Manager server.

Once you've performed that step, you configure a connection from the Orchestrator Management server to the Operations Manager Management Group by performing the following steps:

1. In the Runbook Designer's Options menu, click SC 2012 Operations Manager.

2. On the Connections tab of the SC 2012 Operations Manager dialog box, click Add.

3. In the Connection dialog box, shown in Figure 4-14, type the name of the connection, IP address or FQDN of the Operations Manager server, and then provide the credentials of an account that has access to the Operations Manager server.

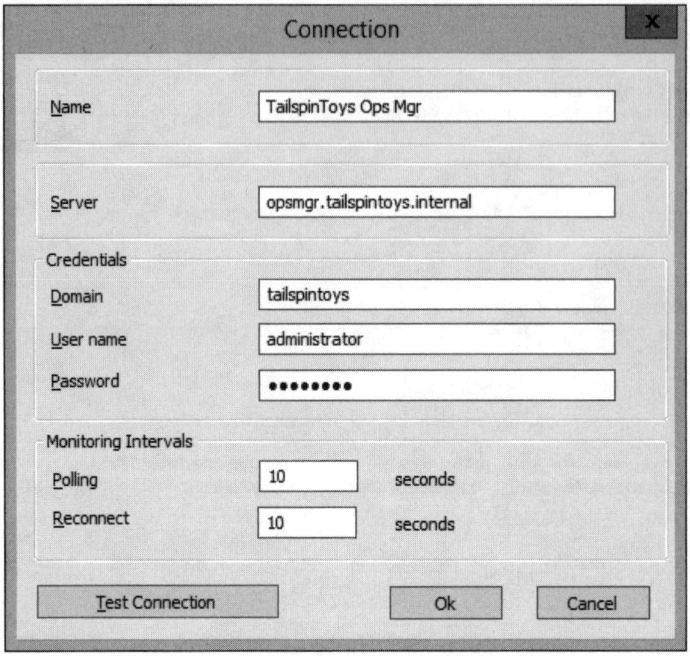

FIGURE 4-14 Connection configuration

4. On the SC 2012 Operations Manager dialog box, shown in Figure 4-15, click Finish.

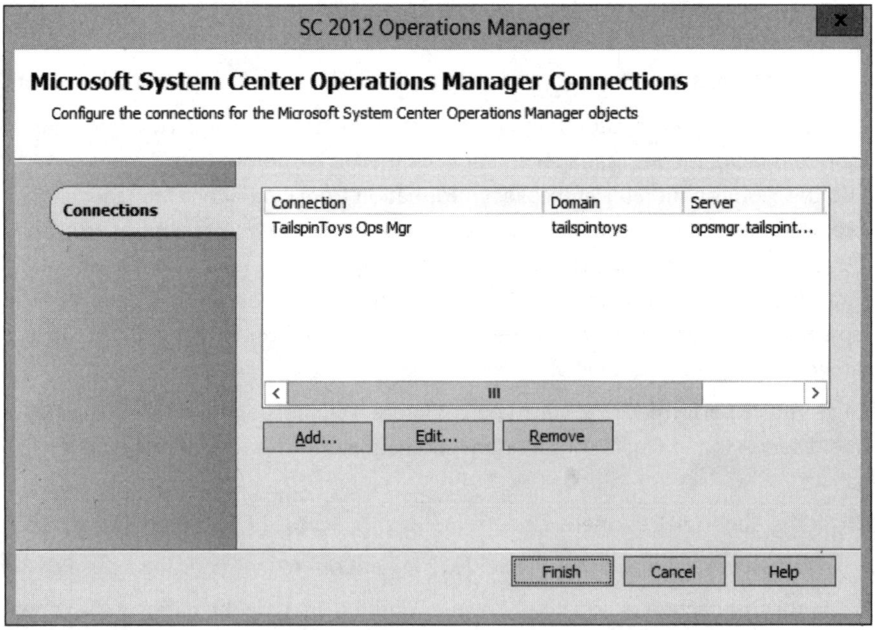

FIGURE 4-15 Operations Manager connections

Once you have configured the connection, you'll be able to use the activities that are included in the Operations Manager integration pack when building Orchestrator runbooks. These activities are shown in Figure 4-16, and have the following functionality:

- **Create Alert**   This activity allows you to create an alert in Operations Manager.
- **Get Alert**   This activity allows you to extract data from an Operations Manager alert. Use this activity as the basis of creating runbooks that create incidents in Service Manager by extracting relevant information from alerts and using that information when creating incidents.
- **Get Monitor**   Use this activity to collect monitoring data. You can take the data extracted from this activity and use it to populate incidents in Service Manager.
- **Monitor Alert**   Use this activity to watch for specific new or updated Operations Manager alerts. You might use this when configuring a runbook to have additional steps taken when specific alerts are raised in Operations Manager during runbook execution.
- **Monitor State**   Use this activity to monitor and run when an object managed by Operations Manager has its state changed to Warning or Critical. You might use this when configuring a runbook to have additional steps taken when the state of specific Operations Manager monitored objects changes during runbook execution.
- **Start Maintenance Mode**   This activity allows you to put an Operations Manager managed object into maintenance mode. Maintenance mode is a special state that suppresses alerting. For example, you would put a server into maintenance mode when applying software updates so that Operations Manager alerts aren't generated by the software update process.
- **Stop Maintenance Mode**   This activity allows you to take an Operations Manager managed object out of maintenance mode, so that Operations Manager alerts are no longer suppressed.
- **Update Alert**   Use this activity to update an Operations Manager alert with data. For example, you could update an Operations Manager alert with information provided in a Service Manager incident.

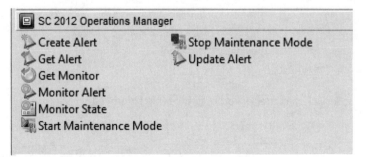

FIGURE 4-16 Operations Manager activities

Service Manager integration pack

You configure integration between Orchestrator and Service Manager by performing the following steps:

1. Ensure that the Service Manager integration pack is installed on the management server.

2. Click SC 2012 Service Manager in the Options menu of the Orchestrator Runbook Designer console.

3. On the Connections tab of the SC 2012 Service Manager dialog box, click Add.

4. In the Connection dialog box, shown in Figure 4-17, provide the following information. Ensure that you click Test Connection to verify that the connection to the Service Manager server functions correctly.

   - **Name** Name of the connection to the Service Manager server
   - **Server** FQDN of the Service Manager server
   - **Credentials** Credentials of an account that has permission to access the Service Manager server

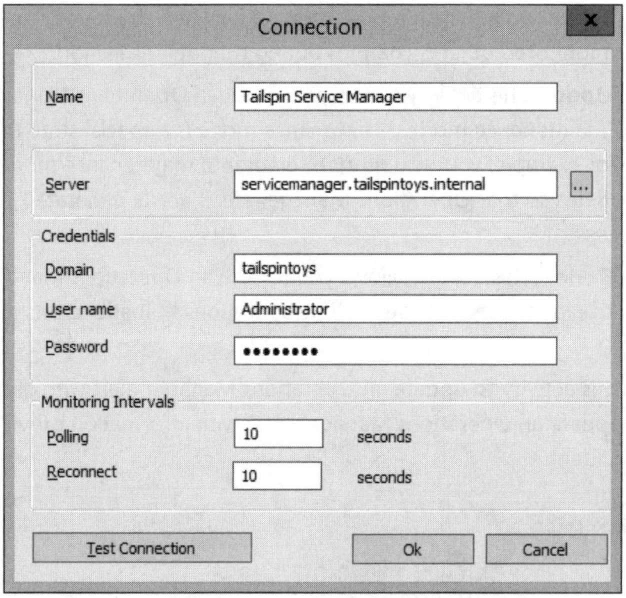

FIGURE 4-17 Connection properties

5. On the SC 2012 Service Manager dialog box, shown in Figure 4-18, click Finish.

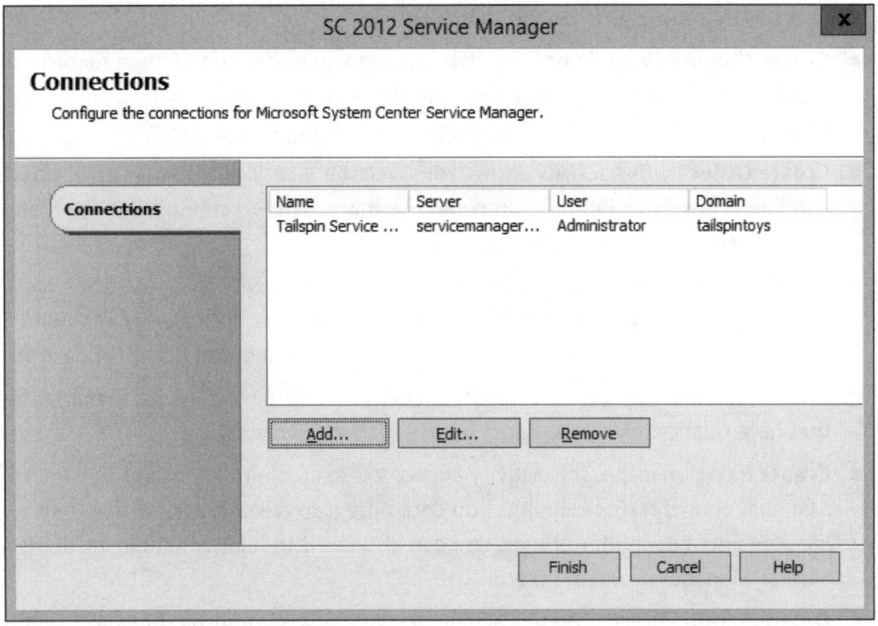

FIGURE 4-18 Service Manager connection

Once the connection between the Orchestrator and Service Manager server is established, you can use the integration pack activities, shown in Figure 4-19, to build workflows.

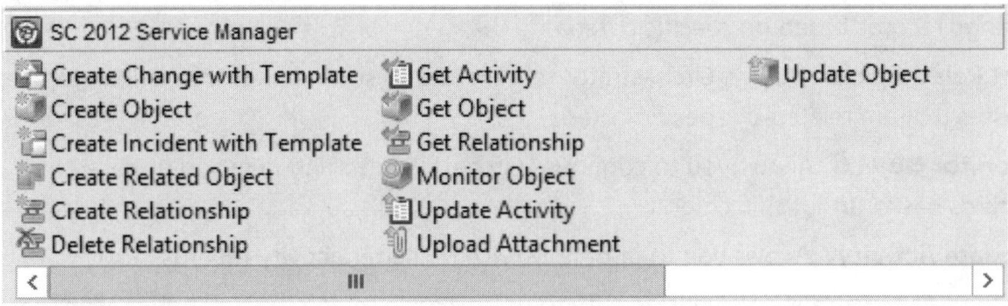

FIGURE 4-19 Service Manager integration pack activities

These activities allow you to do the following:

- **Create Change With Template**   Use this activity to create a change record using an existing change template. When you use this activity, mandatory fields in the service manager change record need to be configured using Orchestrator.

- **Create Object**   This activity allows you to create a Service Manager object based on a defined class. For example, you could use this activity to create a Service Manager incident, change, or problem record.

- **Create Incident With Template**   You can use this activity to create a Service Manager incident based on an existing template. When you use this activity, mandatory fields in the Service Manager incident record need to be configured using Orchestrator.

- **Create Related Object**   You use this activity to create new Service Manager objects that have relationships to existing Service Manager objects.

- **Create Relationship**   This activity allows you to create relationships between Service Manager elements. For example, you could use it to create a relationship between an incident and a computer or user. You can also use it to relate multiple incidents with a Service Manager problem record.

- **Delete Relationship**   Use this activity to remove a relationship between Service Manager elements.

- **Get Activity**   Allows an Orchestrator runbook to collect activity records based on specific criteria.

- **Get Object**   Use this activity to search for a Service Manager activity, incident, or change records based on specific criteria.

- **Get Relationship**   Allows Orchestrator to generate a list of objects from separate classes that are related by specific criteria.

- **Monitor Object**   Allows you to configure Orchestrator to find new and updated records based on specific criteria.

- **Update Activity**   Allows you to update Service Manager activity records.

- **Upload Attachment**   Use this activity to upload a file to an existing Service Manager object. For example, you might use this activity to upload a log file so that it can be stored with the incident generated automatically by an Operations Manager alert.

- **Update Object**   You can use this activity to modify the values of a Service Manager object's properties.

VMM integration pack

As shown in Figure 4-20, the VMM integration pack contains 45 activities.

SC 2012 Virtual Machine Manager		
Apply Pending Service Update	Get Service Configuration	Scale Tier In
Configure Service Deployment	Get Service Template	Scale Tier Out
Create Checkpoint	Get Tier	Set Pending Service Update
Create New Disk	Get User Role	Shut Down VM
Create New Disk From VHD	Get User Role Quota	Start VM
Create Network Adapter	Get VM	Stop Service
Create User Role	Get VM Host	Stop VM
Create VM From Template	Get VM Network	Suspend VM
Create VM from VHD	Get VM Subnet	Update Disk
Create VM from VM	Manage Checkpoint	Update Network Adapter
Deploy Service	Move VM	Update User Role Property
Get Checkpoint	Remove User Role	Update User Role Quota
Get Cloud	Remove VM	Update VM
Get Disk	Repair VM	
Get Network Adapter	Resume VM	
Get Service	Run VMM PowerShell Script	

FIGURE 4-20 VMM activities for Orchestrator

These activities allow you to do the following:

- **Apply Pending Service Update**   Apply a pending service update to a VMM service.

- **Configure Service Deployment**   Configure a VMM service for deployment. Requires the service configuration name, service template name, and deployment target.

- **Create Checkpoint**   Create a VM checkpoint. Requires the GUID of the VM.

- **Create New Disk**   Creates a new virtual hard disk. Requires you specify IDE/SCSI, Dynamic or Fixed, File Name, Size, and VM GUID of VM to which the disk should be attached.

- **Create New Disk From VHD**   Creates a new virtual hard disk from an existing virtual hard disk. Requires you specify IDE/SCSI, Dynamic or Fixed, file name of new disk, path to original disk, VM GUID of VM to which the disk should be attached.

- **Create Network Adapter**   Creates a new network adapter and attaches it to a VM. Requires the VM GUID. You can also configure additional network adapter properties such as MAC Address, MAC Address Pool, Network Tag, Virtual Network ID, VLAN ID, and Logical Network.

- **Create User Role**   Creates a VMM user role. Requires that you specify a role name and the VMM user role profile that the role will use.

- **Create VM From Template**   Allows you to create a VM from an existing VMM template. Requires the Type Of VM, Destination, Path, Source Template Name, Cloud Capability Profile, and VM Name.

- **Create VM From VHD**   Use this activity to create a VM from an existing virtual hard disk. Requires you to specify IDE or SCI, name of destination VHD, path, location of VHD from which you will be creating the VM, the name of the VM host, and the VM name.

- **Create VM From VM**   Use this activity to create a new VM from an existing VM. Requires that you specify the type of VM to create, destination, VM path, the VM GUID of the source VM, and the name to apply to the newly created VM.

- **Deploy Service**   Use this activity to create a VMM service using a VMM service template. Requires that you specify the new service's name, and the VMM template name.

- **Get Checkpoint**   Use this activity to retrieve VM checkpoint information.

- **Get Cloud**   Get information to view information about clouds on the VMM management server.

- **Get Network Adapter**   View information about VMM virtual network adapters.

- **Get Service**   Use this activity to return data on all services on the VMM management server.

- **Get Service Configuration**   You use this activity to generate information about service configurations on the VMM management server.

- **Get Service Template**   This activity allows you to generate a list of all VMM service templates.

- **Get Tier**   Provides information about all VMM tiers.

- **Get User Role**   Use this activity to extract information about VMM user roles.

- **Get User Role Quota**   Use this activity to return information about all user role quotas on VMM management server.

- **Get VM**   This activity provides information on a specific VM.

- **Get VM Host**   Use this activity to extract information about a virtualization host.

- **Get VM Network**   This activity allows you to extract information about a VMM VM network.

- **Get VM Subnet**   Use this activity to provide Orchestrator with information about a VMM VM subnet.

- **Manage Checkpoint**   You can use this activity in an Orchestrator runbook to revert a VMM VM to a specific checkpoint, or to remove checkpoints that are no longer required.

- **Move VM**   This activity allows you to move a VM to a new location.

- **Remove User Role**   This activity deletes a user role from VMM.

- **Remove VM**   Use this activity to delete a VM. This activity can only target a VM that is in a shutdown state.

- **Repair VM**   Use this activity to issue a retry, undo, or dismiss action on a VMM VM.

- **Resume VM**   This activity allows Orchestrator to resume a VM that is in a paused state.
- **Run VMM PowerShell Script**   Use this activity to trigger a PowerShell script.
- **Scale Tier In**   This activity allows Orchestrator to remove a virtual machine instance from a specific service tier.
- **Scale Tier Out**   This activity allows Orchestrator to add a virtual machine instance to a specific service tier.
- **Set Pending Service Update**   Use this activity to set a specific VMM service template as the pending service update.
- **Shut Down VM**   This activity allows Orchestrator to shut down a stopped VM, taking the VM offline.
- **Start VM**   Use this activity in an Orchestrator runbook to start a VM that has been paused, shut down, or stopped.
- **Stop Service**   This activity will stop a VMM service.
- **Stop VM**   Use this activity in an Orchestrator runbook to place a VM into a stopped state.
- **Suspend VM**   This activity will place a VM into a suspended state.
- **Update Disk**   This activity allows an Orchestrator runbook to change the properties of an existing disk.
- **Update Network Adapter**   Use this activity to update the properties of an existing network adapter.
- **Update User Role Property**   Updates the properties of a VMM user role.
- **Update User Role Quota**   Updates the quota for a user role.
- **Update VM**   Use this activity in an Orchestrator runbook to update a VM.

MORE INFO VMM INTEGRATION PACK

Learn more about the VMM integration pack for Orchestrator by consulting the following article at *http://technet.microsoft.com/en-us/library/hh830704.aspx*.

To create Orchestrator runbooks that can use activities that perform tasks in VMM, you configure VMM integration for Orchestrator. To configure the VMM connector for Orchestrator, perform the following steps:

1. Ensure that the VMM integration pack is installed on the Orchestrator server.

2. Ensure that the VMM Administration console is installed on the Orchestrator server. It is possible to configure the connector without a local deployment of the VMM console, but this is a more complicated process than installing the console on the Orchestrator server.

3. Ensure that the Windows PowerShell execution policy on the Orchestrator server is set to Remote Signed.

4. In the Options menu of the Orchestrator Runbook Designer, click SC 2012 Virtual Machine Manager.

5. On the SC 2012 Virtual Machine Manager dialog box, click Add.

6. On the Add Configuration dialog box, specify the name of the connection. Next to type, click the ellipsis (...).

7. On the Item Selection page, click System Center Virtual Machine Manager.

8. In the Properties section of the Add Configuration dialog box, shown in Figure 4-21, configure the following settings:

   - **VMM Administrator Console**   Address of the server with the VMM console.

   - **VMM Server**   Address of the VMM server.

   - **User**   User account of the user with permissions to the VMM server.

   - **Domain**   Domain that hosts the user account.

   - **Password**   Password associated with the account.

   - **Authentication Type (Remote Only)**   Needs to be configured if the VMM Administrator console is not installed on the Orchestrator server. You need to enable the authentication method for WinRM using Group Policy.

   - **Port (Remote Only)**   Only required if the Orchestrator runbook server doesn't have an instance of the VMM Administrator console.

   - **Use SSL (Remote Only)**   Only required if the Orchestrator runbook server doesn't have an instance of the VMM Administrator console.

   - **Cache Timeout**   Amount of time in minutes before the session times out.

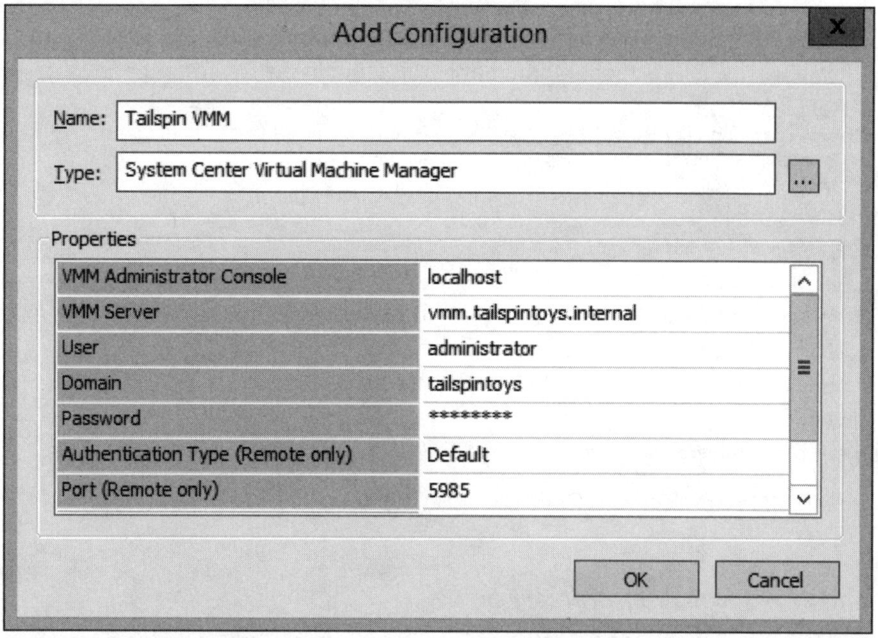

FIGURE 4-21 Connect VMM to Orchestrator

9. Click OK on the Add Configuration dialog box, and the SC 2012 Virtual Machine Manager dialog box.

DPM Orchestrator integration pack

You can use the DPM integration pack for Orchestrator, shown in Figure 4-22, to create DPM-specific runbook automation. These activities allow you to automate the following tasks when creating an Orchestrator runbook:

- **Create Recovery Point** Use this activity to create a recovery point for a specific data source.
- **Get Data Source** Use this activity to determine information about available data sources.
- **Get Recovery Point** Use this activity to determine which recovery points exist for a specific protected data source.
- **Get DPM Server Capacity** Use this activity to determine a DPM server's capacity.
- **Protect Data Source** Use this activity to put a data source into protection. Use the Get Data Source activity to determine the identity of eligible data sources.
- **Recover SharePoint** Use this activity to recover SharePoint data.
- **Recover SQL** Use this activity to recover SQL data.
- **Recover VM** Use this activity to recover a protected virtual machine.

- **Run DPM PowerShell Script**   Use this activity to run a DPM PowerShell script. You can use the information returned from this script in the Orchestrator runbook.

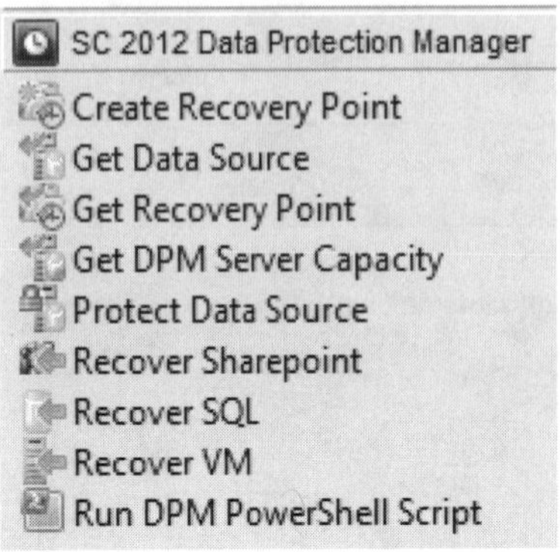

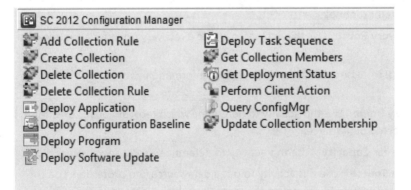

Figure 4-22 DPM activities for Orchestrator

> **MORE INFO** **DPM INTEGRATION PACK**
>
> You can learn more about the DPM integration pack at *http://technet.microsoft.com/en-us/ library/hh830694.aspx*.

Configuration Manager integration pack

The Configuration Manager integration pack includes a number of activities that allow you to automate Configuration Manager processes using Orchestrator. The integration pack is shown in Figure 4-23.

FIGURE 4-23 Configuration Manager integration pack activities

The Configuration Manager integration pack includes the following activities:

- **Add Collection Rule**   This activity allows you to add membership rules to a collection.
- **Create Collection**   Use this activity to automate the creation of a collection.
- **Delete Collection**   This activity allows you to remove a collection.
- **Delete Collection Rule**   This activity allows you to delete a collection rule.
- **Deploy Application**   Use this activity to deploy an application to a collection.
- **Deploy Configuration Baseline**   This activity allows you to deploy an existing configuration baseline to an existing collection.
- **Deploy Program**   Use this activity to deploy an existing program, including a script that you want to run, to a collection.
- **Deploy Software Update**   Use this activity to deploy an existing software update to a collection.
- **Deploy Task Sequence**   This activity assigns an existing task sequence to a collection.
- **Get Collection Members**   Use this activity to view the membership of a collection.
- **Get Deployment Status**   This activity allows you to view the deployment status of an application, program, task sequence, or software update deployment.
- **Perform Client Action**   This activity allows you to trigger client actions such as the Machine Policy Retrieval & Evaluation Cycle or File Collection Cycle.
- **Query ConfigMgr**   Use this activity to query the Configuration Manager database.
- **Update Collection Membership**   Use this activity to trigger an update of a collection's membership.

> **MORE INFO** **CONFIGURATION MANAGER INTEGRATION PACK**
>
> You can learn more about the Configuration Manager integration pack at *http://technet. microsoft.com/en-us/library/hh967525.aspx.*

Configuring other System Center connectors

While this objective focuses on connecting Operations Manager with other System Center products and Orchestrator integration packs, it's also possible to configure integration between other products in the System Center suite.

Orchestrator and Service Manager

Earlier in this chapter you learned how to connect Orchestrator to Service Manager, which allows you to use Orchestrator runbooks to perform tasks in Service Manager. You can also configure a connector that works the other way, between Service Manager and Orchestrator, which allows Service Manager to make reference to and utilize Orchestrator runbooks. To configure the connector between Service Manager and Orchestrator, perform the following steps:

1. In the Administration workspace of the Service Manager console, click Connectors.

2. In the Tasks pane, click Create Connector, and then click Orchestrator Connector.

3. On the General page of the Orchestrator Connector Wizard, enter a name for the connector.

4. On the Connection page, specify the Orchestrator Web Service URL as shown in Figure 4-24, and the operational database account. The URL of the Orchestrator web service will be *http://computer.fqdn:81/Orchestrator2012/Orchestrator.svc*. The Run As account you use must have the right to connect to Orchestrator. Ensure that you click Test Connection to verify that the connection is successful.

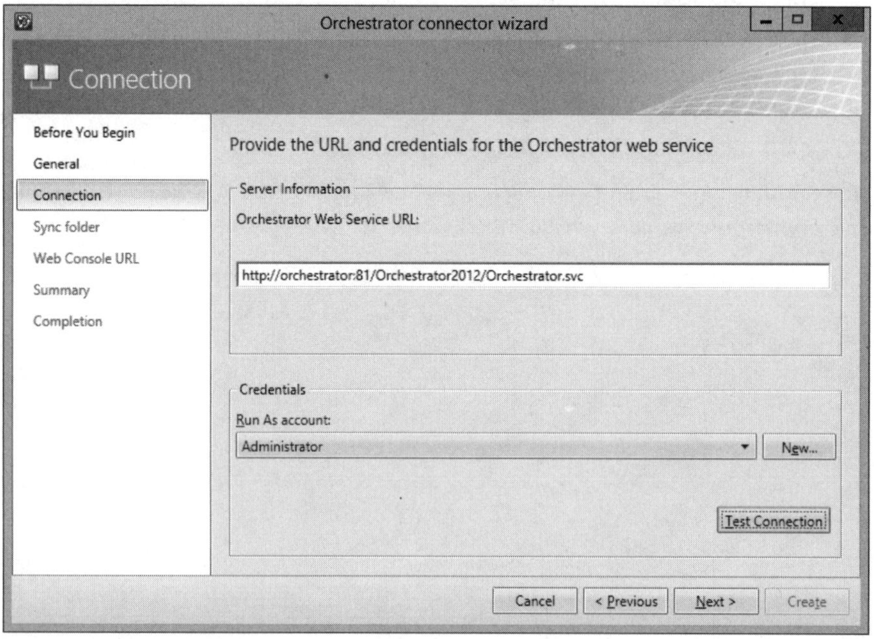

FIGURE 4-24 Orchestrator connector

5. On the Sync Folder page, select a Sync Folder, and click Next.

6. On the Web Console URL page, shown in Figure 4-25, specify the URL for the Orchestrator web console. The URL will be *http://computer.fqdn:92*.

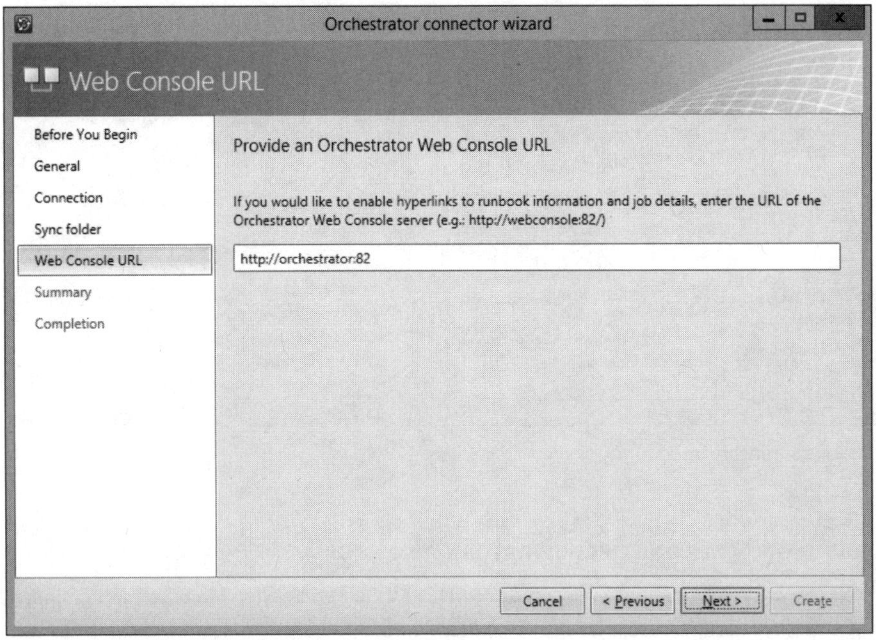

FIGURE 4-25 Web console URL

7. On the Summary page, review the settings, and click Create.

You will be able to verify that the process has worked by navigating to the Library workspace, and clicking the Runbooks node. Any runbooks that you've created on the Orchestrator will be present in this node. Figure 4-26 shows this node with a runbook present.

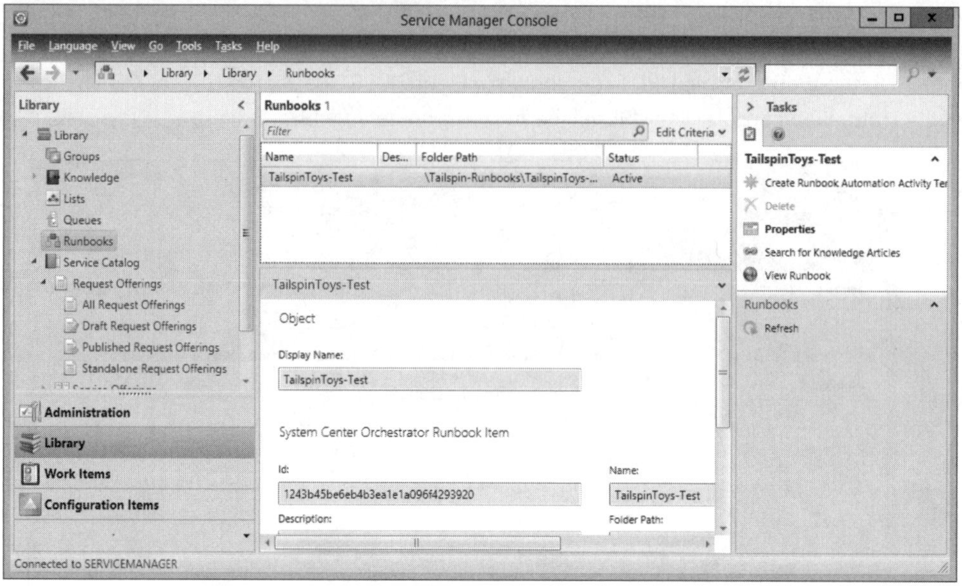

FIGURE 4-26 Synchronized runbooks

> **MORE INFO CREATING ORCHESTRATOR CONNECTOR**
>
> You can learn more about creating a connector between Service Manager and Orchestrator at *http://technet.microsoft.com/en-us/library/hh519779.aspx*.

VMM Connector for Service Manager

Configuring the VMM connector for Service Manager will provide Service Manager with information about the VMM environment. To configure the VMM connector for Service Manager, perform the following steps:

1. In the Administration workspace of the Service Manager console, click Connectors.

2. In the Tasks pane, click Create Connector, and then click Virtual Machine Manager Connector.

3. On the General page of the Virtual Machine Manager Connector Wizard, type the connector name.

4. On the Connection page, shown in Figure 4-27, type the FQDN of the VMM server, and specify a Run As account. This account needs to have permissions to access VMM. Click Test Connection to verify this account.

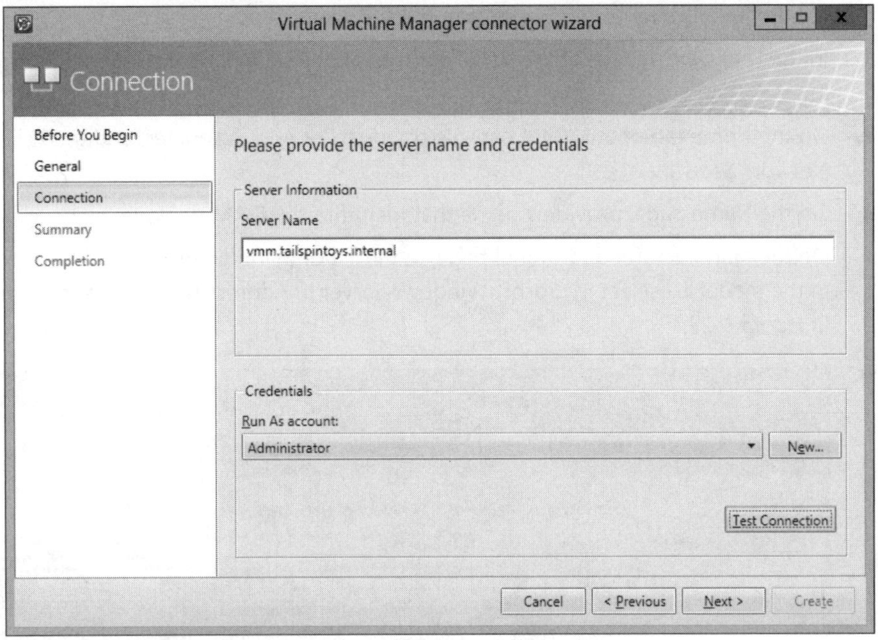

FIGURE 4-27 VMM connector

5. On the Summary page, review the configuration information, and click Create.

Integrating IPAM with VMM

IPAM is a Windows Server 2012 and Windows Server 2012 R2 role service that allows you to centralize the management of DHCP and DNS servers. You can use a single IPAM server to manage up to 150 separate DHCP servers, and up to 500 individual DNS servers. A single IPAM server is able to manage 6,000 separate DHCP scopes and 150 separate DNS zones. You can perform tasks such as creating address scopes, configuring address reservations, and managing DHCP and DNS options globally, rather than having to perform these tasks on a server-by-server basis.

You can integrate the IPAM role with VMM. When you do this, VMM synchronizes IP address settings associated with logical networks and virtual machine networks with the IPAM database. After you integrate IPAM with VMM, VMM administrators use IPAM to configure and monitor logical networks and their associated network sites and IP address pools. Tenants, however, must continue to use VMM to manage and configure any virtual machine networks that use network virtualization. Put another way, you cannot use IPAM to manage the tenant address space.

To add the IPAM server to VMM, perform the following steps:

1. In the Fabric workspace of the VMM console, click Network Services under Networking.

2. On the Home tab of the VMM console ribbon, click Add Resources, and then click Network Services.

3. On the Name page, provide a name that identifies the IPAM deployment.

4. On the Manufacturer and Model page, in the list of manufacturers click Microsoft, and in the model list select Microsoft Windows Server IP Address Management, as shown in Figure 4-28.

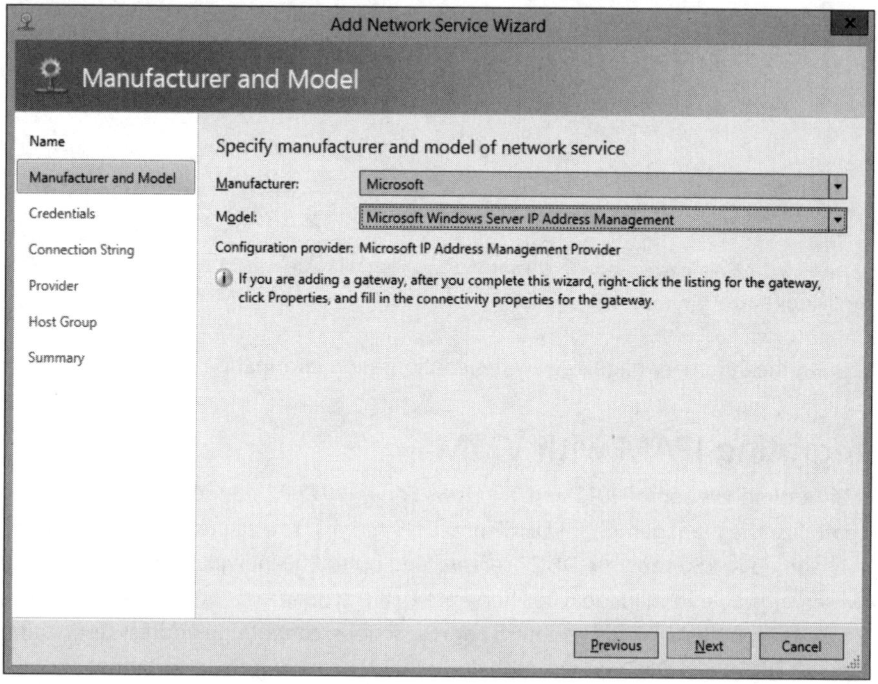

FIGURE 4-28 Add Network Service Wizard

5. On the Credentials page, select a Run As account that is a member of the IPAM ASM Administrators and Remote Management Users security groups.

6. On the Connection String page, provide the FQDN of the IPAM server.

7. On the Provider page, ensure that Microsoft IP Address Management Provider is selected, as shown in Figure 4-29, and click Test.

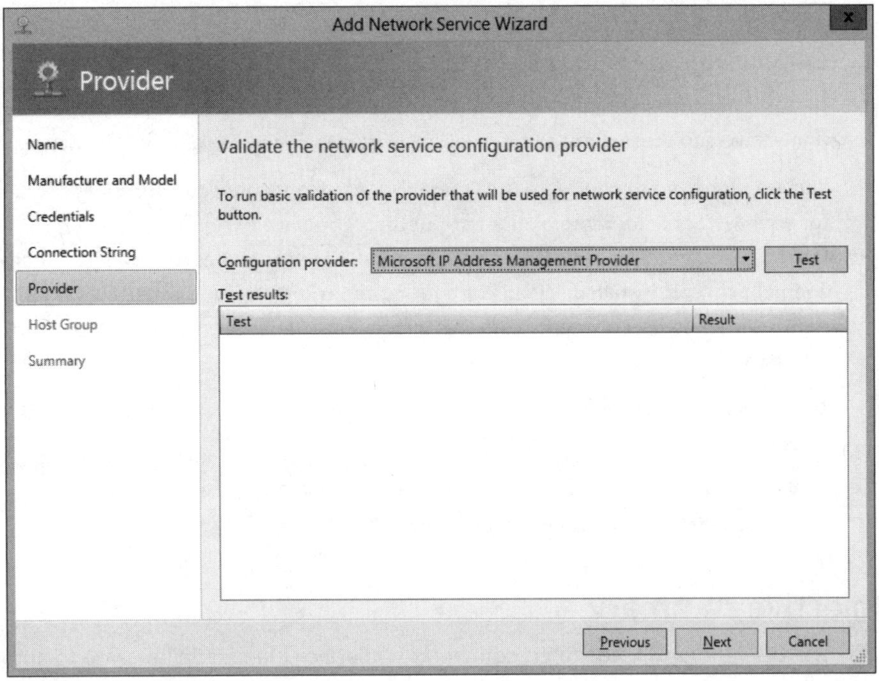

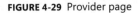

FIGURE 4-29 Provider page

8. On the Host Group page, select which host groups you want to have IPAM manage the address space for.

9. Complete the wizard.

> **MORE INFO IPAM AND VMM**
>
> You can learn more about integrating IPAM and VMM at *http://technet.microsoft.com/en-us/library/dn249418.aspx*.

EXAM TIP

Understand the steps required to configure integration between Operations Manager and VMM.

Objective summary

- The Operations Manager alert connector for Service Manager allows you to automatically create Service Manager incidents based on Operations Manager alerts.

- Integrating Operations Manager with Virtual Machine Manager allows you to monitor your organization's virtualization layer when you are using a System Center 2012 and System Center 2012 R2 managed private cloud.

- The Operations Manager connector for VMM prerequisite requirements include the Operations Manager console to be installed on the VMM server and the installation of several management packs.

- To link VMM and Operations Manager, you need the credentials of an account that is a member of the Operations Manager Administrators user role, and the credentials of an account that is a member of the VMM Administrator user role.

- Orchestrator integration packs are collections of tasks that allow you to automate activities with different System Center products.

- You can import integration packs for Service Manager, Operations Manager, VMM, DPM, and Configuration Manager.

Objective review

Answer the following questions to test your knowledge of the information in this objective. You can find the answers to these questions and explanations of why each answer choice is correct or incorrect in the "Answers" section at the end of this chapter.

1. Which of the following Operations Manager integration pack tasks would you use to extract data from an existing Operations Manager alert for use in an Orchestrator runbook?

   A. Create Alert

   B. Get Alert

   C. Get Monitor

   D. Monitor Alert

2. Which of the following activities from the VMM Orchestrator integration pack would you use to create a clone of an existing virtual machine hosted on a VMM managed virtualization host? (Choose the best answer.)

   A. Deploy Service

   B. Create VM From VM

   C. Create VM From VHD

   D. Create VM From Template

3. Which of the following activities from the DPM integration pack for Orchestrator could you use in an Orchestrator runbook to create a recovery point for a virtual machine hosted on a protected Hyper-V host?

   A. Recover VM

   B. Create Recovery Point

   C. Get Recovery Point

   D. Protect Data Source

4. Which of the following activities from the Configuration Manager integration pack for Orchestrator would you use to deploy a script to a virtual machine that has the Configuration Manager client installed? (Choose the most correct answer.)

   A. Deploy Application

   B. Deploy Configuration Baseline

   C. Deploy Program

   D. Deploy Task Sequence

Objective 4.2: Configure integration of private and public clouds

This objective deals with Service Provider Foundation and Microsoft Azure Pack for Windows Server, which are add-ons that allow you to extend your organization's private cloud infrastructure. Service Provider Foundation allows you to build a multi-tenant self-service private cloud. Microsoft Azure Pack for Windows Server allows you to use the Microsoft Azure public cloud interface as a way of allowing your on-premises users to interact with your organization's private cloud.

> **This section covers the following topics:**
> - Understanding Service Provider Foundation
> - Deploying Service Provider Foundation
> - Understanding Microsoft Azure Pack for Windows Server

Understanding Service Provider Foundation

Service Provider Foundation allows you to build a multi-tenant self-service private cloud that includes the following features:

- **Multi-Tenancy**   Supports multiple separate tenants. Each tenant is isolated from other tenants.
- **Usage Monitoring**   Monitor how cloud resources are being utilized through Operations Manager.
- **Usage Billing**   Service Provider Foundation supports chargeback, which is where organizations charge tenants fees based on how they utilize resources.
- **Usage Metering**   Measure resource utilization.
- **Management Stamps**   A scalable unit of virtualized platform infrastructure.

A management stamp represents a unit of virtualized platform infrastructure that includes a VMM deployment, one or more virtualization hosts, the VMs that are managed by VMM, and the unique service accounts and user roles that are individual to that stamp.

Stamps are monitored through Operations Manager, though one instance of Operations Manager may monitor many stamps. Stamps allow service providers to spread tenants and services across System Center elements in separate datacenters. For example, if your organization has datacenters in Melbourne, Sydney, and Brisbane, a stamp can be configured to allow a tenant seamless access to resources in all three locations.

Stamps are scalable. This means that as a tenant's capacity requirements increase, additional stamps can be allocated to meet that demand. For example, if a tenant needs 10,000 additional VMs in the Melbourne datacenter, additional stamps can be allocated to the tenant.

Service Provider Foundation allows organizations to use industry standard web service interfaces to connect their own web based management interfaces to a System Center cloud through the REST (Representational State Transfer) web service and the Odata (Open Data Protocol) API. Service Provider Foundation provides a programmatic web-based management interface to a large number of VMM scenarios. Rather than being restricted to using one of Microsoft's self-service portal implementations, a tenant can use their own Self-Service Portal to interface with the System Center backend resources.

Service Provider Foundation has the following elements:

- **Web Services** These provide tenants with portal applications and administration tools and include the following:
  - **Admin Web Service** This web service generates User Roles, Servers, management stamps and other objects required for administrative tasks
  - **VMM Web Service** This web service interacts with VMM to create and manage virtual machines, virtual networks, and tenants
  - **Usage Web Service** This web service collects usage data from tenant virtual machines and other parts of the fabric such as storage and networking

> **MORE INFO** SERVICE PROVIDER FOUNDATION
>
> You can learn more about Service Provider Foundation at *http://technet.microsoft.com/en-us/library/jj642895.aspx*.

Deploying Service Provider Foundation

The Service Provider Foundation installation files are located on the System Center 2012 R2 Orchestrator installation media. Service Provider Foundation has the following prerequisites as shown in Figure 4-30:

- Windows Server 2012 or Windows Server 2012 R2
- PowerShell 4.0
- IIS Version 7.5 or later
- IIS Management Scripts and Tools role service
- IIS Security Basic Authentication

- IIS Security Windows Authentication

- IIS Application Development ASP.NET 4.5

- WCF Data Services 4.0 for OData V3

- ASP.NET MVC 4

- Management OData IIS Extension

- Virtual Machine Manager 2012 R2 Administrator Console

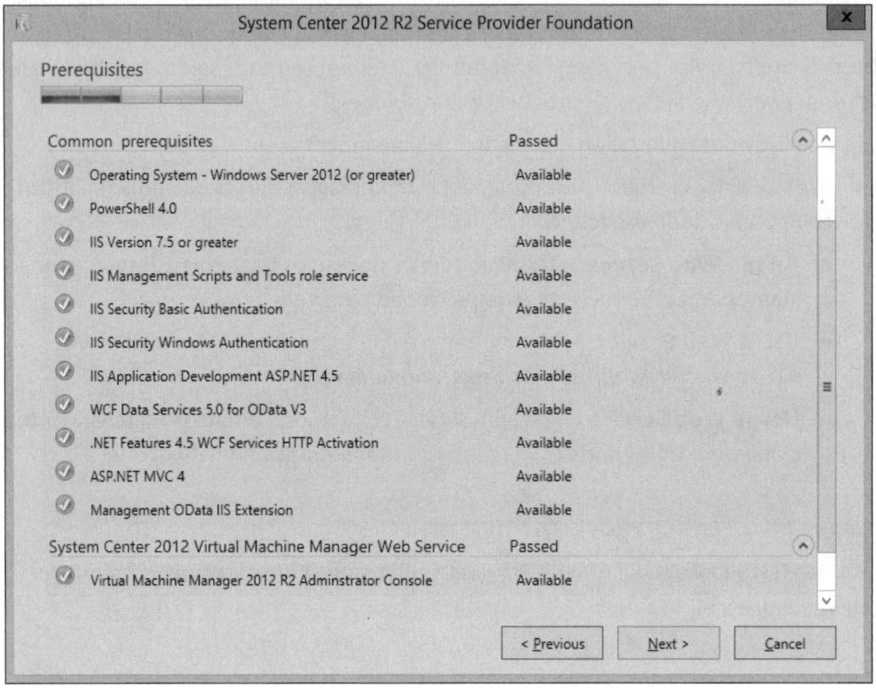

FIGURE 4-30 SPF prerequisites

You deploy Service Provider Foundation from the Orchestrator installation media. To deploy Service Provider Foundation, perform the following steps:

1. On the System Center 2012 R2 Orchestrator Setup dialog box, shown in Figure 4-31, click Service Provider Foundation.

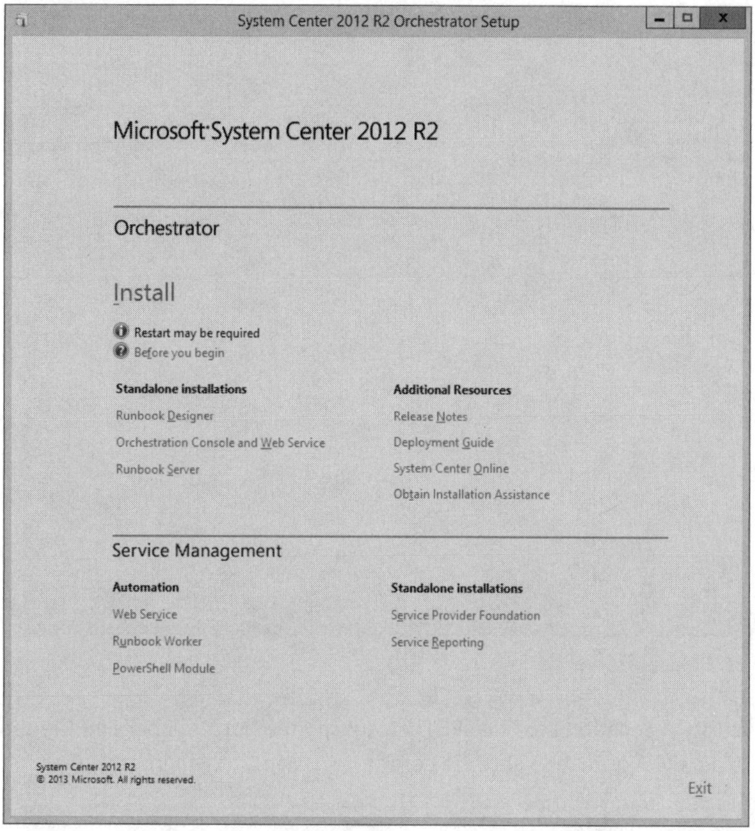

FIGURE 4-31 Installation splash screen

2. On the Service Provider Foundation dialog box, click Install.

3. On the License Terms page, agree to the license terms.

4. On the Prerequisites page, verify that all prerequisites are available.

5. On the Configure The Database page, review the database settings. Figure 4-32 shows the default database name is SCSPFDB.

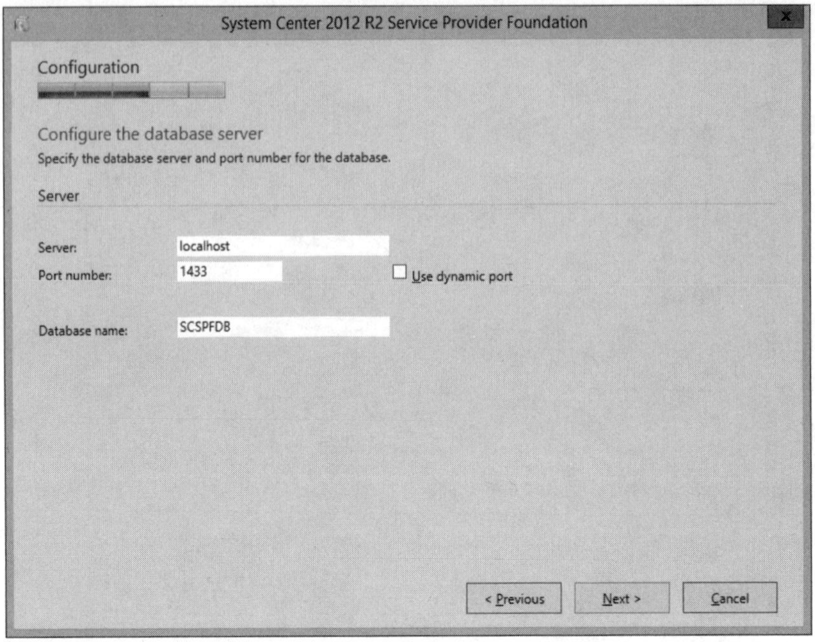

FIGURE 4-32 Database server settings

6. On the Specify A Location For The SPF Files, specify the port number and the server certificate details. Figure 4-33 shows a certificate issued from an internal CA.

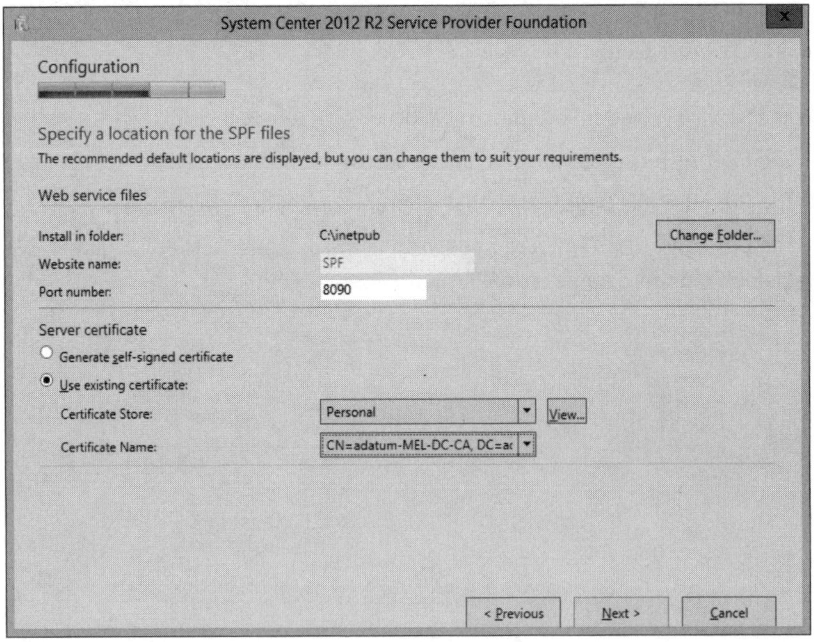

FIGURE 4-33 SPF file location

7. On the Configure The Admin Web Service page, specify the domain credentials of the System Center Administrator web service and the credentials of the related application pool service account.

8. On the Provider Web Service page, you specify domain credentials for the System Center Provider web service and the application pool credentials for the related application pool.

9. On the VMM Web Service page, specify domain credentials for the VMM web service and service account credentials for the VMM web service application pool.

10. On the Usage Web Service page, specify domain credentials for the Usage web service and service account credentials for the Usage web service.

11. On the CEIP and Microsoft Update page, choose whether to opt in to the Customer Experience Improvement Program, and whether to enable Microsoft Update.

12. On the Installation Summary page, review the installation settings, and click Install. Verify that Setup Is Complete, as shown in Figure 4-34.

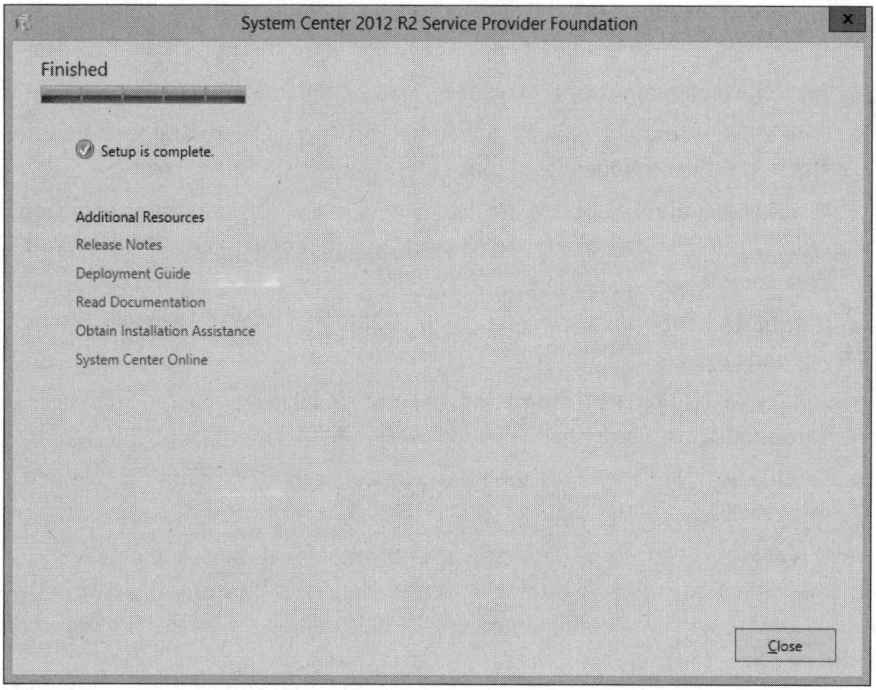

FIGURE 4-34 Verify setup is complete

> **MORE INFO DEPLOY SERVICE PROVIDER FOUNDATION**
>
> You can learn more about Service Provider Foundation deployment at *http://technet.microsoft.com/en-us/library/jj642900.aspx.*

Understanding Microsoft Azure Pack for Windows Server

Microsoft Azure Pack provides an on-premises replica of Microsoft Azure services that you can deploy in your datacenter, including Virtual Machine and website provisioning. The advantage of Microsoft Azure Pack is that it provides a replica of the experience that a user would get if they used the online Microsoft Azure portal to perform tasks.

Microsoft Azure Pack provides Self-Service IT through a Self-Service Portal that allows hybrid cloud scenarios. A hybrid cloud is spread across private, public, and hosted clouds.

Microsoft Azure Pack includes the following:

- **End User Portal**   The end user portal is designed to replicate the Microsoft Azure portal. Like the Microsoft Azure portal, the end user portal allows end users to access their resources in the private cloud. Administrators can configure separate offerings for each tenant.

- **Management Portal**   This portal is for cloud administrators. It allows them to manage the offerings and services that end users access through the end user portal.

- **Management API**   Web service that handles requests from the management portal. Can also be used by third party management portals through OData REST standards.

- **Service Management API Database**   Stores configuration data.

- **Web Sites**   Provides a scalable shared web hosting platform. Supports sites that host ASP.NET, PHP, and Node.js applications.

- **Virtual Machines**   Supports the deployment of any VM that can be managed using VMM. Supports software defined networking and remote access connections to each VM's console.

- **Databases**   Supports Microsoft SQL 2008/2012 and MySQL 5.x in Platform as a Service configuration.

- **Service Management Automation**   Allows the building of automation based on Orchestrator and PowerShell 3.0 workflows.

- **Service Bus**   Provides a messaging service between applications running in the private cloud.

VMM is able to collect usage data, such as CPU, memory, storage, and network utilization, for all of the VMs and virtualization hosts it manages. VMM stores this data in the VMM database for 30 days. If you've integrated VMM with Operations Manager, this data can be transferred across to the Operations Manager data warehouse.

The Service Provider Foundation element of Microsoft Azure Pack is able to utilize this data when stored in the Operations Manager data warehouse, providing it to authorized users to view through interfaces such as the management portal for administrators. Service Provider Foundation is able to collect metric data from multiple VMM instances and aggregate them so that you can use that data for billing, or for overall infrastructure analysis.

> **MORE INFO** **MICROSOFT AZURE PACK FOR WINDOWS SERVER**
>
> You can learn more about Microsoft Azure Pack for Windows Server at *http://technet.microsoft.com/en-au/library/dn296432.aspx*.

Microsoft Azure Pack VM clouds

To add a VMM cloud to Microsoft Azure Pack, perform the following general steps:

1. On the server that hosts the Microsoft Azure Pack Management Portal for Administrators, start the Management Portal by navigating to *https://localhost:30091*.

2. In the Management Portal, click VM Cloud.

3. Click Register System Center Service Provider Foundation Server. This will be in the form *https://server.fqdn:8090*. You'll need to provide the credentials used for the following Application Pool identities on the Service Provider Foundation server:

   - VMM
   - Usage
   - Admin
   - Provider

4. Once registration is complete, all of the VMM instances (or stamps) associated with the Service Provider Foundation endpoint will be listed.

All clouds present on the VMM server (or stamp) will be listed under the Clouds tab of the portal. You can add stamps or VMM servers in the management portal for Administrators by clicking New, click VM Clouds, and click Connect to, and specify the FQDN of the VMM server or stamp.

Microsoft Azure Pack web clouds

A Microsoft Azure Pack web cloud deployment has the following roles:

- **Web Sites Controller**   This role is used by Microsoft Azure Pack to provision and manage other web sites role.

- **Management Server**   This role hosts a REST endpoint. It routes management traffic to the Microsoft Azure Pack Web Sites Management API.

- **Web Workers**   The web servers that will process client web requests. Can be configured as either Shared or Reserved. One of each is required. Reserved web workers are categorized as small, medium, and large.
- **Front End**   This role accepts client web requests, provides clients with responses from web workers, routes web worker requests, and provides load balancing and SSL termination.
- **File server**   Hosts web site content for every web site that runs on the web cloud.
- **Publisher**   Allows content publishing to the web sites in the cloud for FTP clients, Visual Studio, and WebMatrix through the Web Deploy and FTP protocols.
- **Web Sites Runtime Database**   Database that Microsoft Azure Pack web clouds uses for operations.
- **Service Management API Database**   Stores configuration data for the Microsoft Azure Pack Service Management API. This role will have already been installed during the deployment of Microsoft Azure Pack.
- **Application Databases**   If supported usage scenarios include providing back end database functionality for the websites hosted through Microsoft Azure Pack for Windows Server, it's necessary to install databases instances for one or both of Microsoft SQL Server or MySQL.

> **MORE INFO** **AZURE PACK WEB CLOUDS**
>
> You can learn more about Microsoft Azure Pack web clouds at *http://technet.microsoft. com/en-us/library/dn457747.aspx.*

Microsoft Azure Pack SQL clouds

The SQL Server and MySQL resource providers for Microsoft Azure Pack enable users to have the use of Microsoft SQL and MySQL databases. To support this usage scenario, it is necessary for you to install the separate SQL server and MySQL databases that underpin this service. It is only necessary to install MySQL if you want to offer MySQL through Microsoft Azure Pack.

To install a SQL Server or MySQL resource provider:

1. Sign on to the computer on which you are going to install the SQL Server or MySQL resource provider, and launch the Web Platform Installer.
2. On the Products tab of the Web Platform Installer, click Microsoft Azure.
3. Depending on whether you are deploying a SQL Server provider or MySQL provider, click Add next to one of the following, and then click Install:
   - Microsoft Azure Pack: SQL Server Extension
   - Microsoft Azure Pack: MySQL Extension

4. When the installation completes, click Continue. This will launch the Configuration site. On this site, enter the following information using the settings specified when you deployed Microsoft Azure Pack for Windows Server:

   ■ Address of the database server configured when you deployed Microsoft Azure Pack

   ■ Azure Pack database authentication details

   ■ Azure Pack Configuration Store passphrase.

5. Once these steps are complete, you'll be able to register the database endpoints for the Microsoft SQL or the MySQL instances you have deployed.

Once you have registered the appropriate resource provider, you can register database endpoints. You'll need to have deployed the database instance prior to attempting endpoint registration.

REGISTER MICROSOFT SQL DATABASE ENDPOINT

To register a Microsoft SQL database endpoint, perform the following steps:

1. Sign on to the server that hosts the Microsoft Azure Pack Management Portal for Administrators, and launch the portal.

2. Click SQL Servers in the navigation pane, and then click New or Add. Click Connect.

3. Provide the following SQL Server instance name:

   ■ **Group Name** The name of the group that you want the instance to belong to in Microsoft Azure Pack.

   ■ **Server Name** The name of the server that hosts the instance. Usually this will be just the name of the server, but can also include the instance name in the Servername\instancename format if you have deployed multiple instances on a computer.

   ■ **Administrator User Name** Name of a user with administrative privileges on the instance.

   ■ **Administrator Password** Password of the user account specified that has administrative privileges on the instance.

   ■ **Size Of The Hosting Server (GB)** Specify the amount of disk space available on the hosting server.

4. Click Connect to register the Microsoft SQL instance.

REGISTER MYSQL INSTANCE

To connect an existing MySQL instance to Microsoft Azure Pack, perform the following steps:

1. Sign on to the server on which you deployed the Microsoft Azure Pack Management Portal for Administrators and launch the management portal.

2. In the Microsoft Azure Pack Management Portal for Administrators, click MySQL Servers, click New or Add, and then click Connect.

3. Provide the following information about the MySQL instance:

   - **Group Name**   Name of the Microsoft Azure Pack group to which you want to add the MySQL server.
   - **Server Name**   Name of the MySQL server instance.
   - **Administrator User Name**   Name of a user account that has administrative privileges on the MySQL instance.
   - **Administrator Password**   Password of the user account that has administrative privileges on the MySQL instance.
   - **Size Of The Hosting Server (in GBs)**   Provide the amount of available space.

4. Click Connect to register the MySQL instance.

   - Enter the MySQL server instance information: group name, server name, administrator user name, administrator password, and the size of the hosting server (in GBs).
   - Click Connect. When you receive a message indicating that registration was successful, close the message.

> **MORE INFO SQL CLOUDS WITH MICROSOFT AZURE PACK**
>
> You can learn more about Microsoft Azure Pack SQL clouds at *http://technet.microsoft.com/en-us/library/dn469317.aspx*.

> **EXAM TIP**
>
> Remember that Service Provider Foundation provides a framework for multi-tenant self-service clouds where custom portals are used. Microsoft Azure Pack for Windows Server provides portals that replicate the Microsoft Azure experience, though these can also be customized.

Objective summary

- Service Provider Foundation allows you to build a multi-tenant self-service private cloud.

- Service Provider Foundation clouds support multi-tenancy, usage monitoring, usage billing, usage metering, and management stamps.

- A management stamp represents a unit of virtualized platform infrastructure that includes a VMM deployment, one or more virtualization hosts, the VMs that are managed by VMM, and the unique service accounts and user roles that are individual to that stamp.

- Stamps allow service providers to spread tenants and services across System Center elements in separate datacenters.

- As a tenant's capacity requirements increase, additional stamps can be allocated to meet that demand.

- Microsoft Azure Pack provides an on-premises replica of Microsoft Azure services that you can deploy in your datacenter, including Virtual Machine and website provisioning.

- When deploying Microsoft Azure Pack, you need to provide credentials for the VMM, Usage, Admin and Provider Application Pool identities on the Service Provider Foundation server.

Objective review

Answer the following questions to test your knowledge of the information in this objective. You can find the answers to these questions and explanations of why each answer choice is correct or incorrect in the "Answers" section at the end of this chapter.

1. You are installing Microsoft Azure Pack for Windows Server. Service Provider Foundation is already deployed in your organization's environment. During the installation of Service Provider Foundation, you used domain accounts when configuring each application pool service account. Which of these credentials are required when deploying Microsoft Azure Pack for Windows Server? (Choose all that apply.)

   A. Provider web service application pool.

   B. Admin web service application pool.

   C. VMM web service application pool.

   D. Orchestrator web service application pool.

2. Which of the following database products can you install to provide as a service to users after installing Microsoft Azure Pack for Windows Server.

   A. PostgreSQL.

   B. MySQL.

   C. Microsoft SQL Server.

   D. Oracle.

3. Which of the following elements are included in a Service Provider Foundation management stamp? (Choose all that apply.)

   A. One or more virtualization hosts.

   B. Orchestrator runbook server.

   C. Operations Manager management group.

   D. VMs managed by VMM.

Answers

This section contains the solutions to the thought experiments and answers to the objective review questions in this chapter.

Objective 4.1: Thought experiment

1. You must install the Operations Manager console on the VMM server.

2. To link VMM and Operations Manager, you need the credentials of an account that is a member of the Operations Manager Administrators user role, and the credentials of an account that is a member of the VMM Administrator user role.

Objective 4.1: Review

1. **Correct answer:** B
   A. **Incorrect:** This activity allows you to extract data from an Operations Manager alert.
   B. **Correct:** This activity allows you to extract data from an Operations Manager alert.
   C. **Incorrect:** Orchestrator integration packs are collections of tasks that allow you to automate activities with different System Center products.
   D. **Incorrect:** Orchestrator integration packs are collections of tasks that allow you to automate activities with different System Center products.

2. **Correct answer:** B
   A. **Incorrect:** Use this activity to create a VMM service using a VMM service template.
   B. **Correct:** You use this activity to create a new VM from an existing VM that is on a VMM managed virtualization host.
   C. **Incorrect:** Use this activity to create a VM from an existing virtual hard disk in the VMM library.
   D. **Incorrect:** This cmdlet allows you to create a VM from an existing VMM template.

3. **Correct answer:** B
   A. **Incorrect:** You use this activity to recover a protected virtual machine.
   B. **Correct:** You use this activity to create a recovery point for a specific data source.
   C. **Incorrect:** You use this activity to determine which recovery points exist for a specific protected data source.
   D. **Incorrect:** You use this activity to put a data source into protection. Use the Get Data Source activity to determine the identity of eligible data sources.

4. **Correct answer:** C

   A. **Incorrect:** You use this activity to deploy an application to a collection. In Configuration Manager, you use a Program rather than an Application to deploy scripts.

   B. **Incorrect:** This activity allows you to deploy an existing configuration baseline to an existing collection.

   C. **Correct:** You use this activity to deploy an existing program, including a script that you want to run, to a collection.

   D. **Incorrect:** This activity assigns an existing task sequence to a collection. While task sequences can run scripts, the "more correct" answer is to use a Program to deploy the script. Task sequences are most commonly used in Operating System Deployment (OSD) type activities.

Objective 4.2: Thought experiment

1. Microsoft Azure Pack for Windows Server supports any operating system that can be managed through VMM. This means that it is possible to deploy VMs running supported versions of the Windows and Linux operating systems.

2. Both Microsoft SQL Server and MySQL can be used to host the databases that store the data for web applications deployed in a Microsoft Azure Pack for Windows Server web cloud.

Objective 4.2: Review

1. **Correct answers:** A, B and C

   A. **Correct:** You need to specify credentials for the VMM, Provider, Admin, and Usage web service application pool when installing Microsoft Azure Pack for Windows Server.

   B. **Correct:** You need to specify credentials for the VMM, Provider, Admin, and Usage web service application pool when installing Microsoft Azure Pack for Windows Server.

   C. **Correct:** You need to specify credentials for the VMM, Provider, Admin, and Usage web service application pool when installing Microsoft Azure Pack for Windows Server.

   D. **Incorrect:** You do not need to specify credentials for the Orchestrator web service application pool when installing Microsoft Azure Pack for Windows Server.

2. **Correct answers:** B and C

A. **Incorrect:** You cannot provision PostgreSQL database to users through Microsoft Azure Pack for Windows Server.

B. **Correct:** You can install MySQL databases and provide them as a service to users through Microsoft Azure Pack for Windows Server.

C. **Correct:** You can install Microsoft SQL Server databases and provide them as a service to users through Microsoft Azure Pack for Windows Server.

D. **Incorrect:** While it is possible to deploy Oracle in the cloud version of Microsoft Azure, Oracle is not supported for deployment through Microsoft Azure Pack.

3. **Correct Answers:** A and D

A. **Correct:** A management stamp represents a unit of virtualized platform infrastructure that includes a VMM deployment, one or more virtualization hosts, the VMs that are managed by VMM, and the unique service accounts and user roles that are individual to that stamp.

B. **Incorrect:** While a Service Provider Foundation management stamp may utilize Orchestrator and Service Provider Foundation is installed from the Orchestrator installation media, there is no direct relationship between a management stamp and Orchestrator.

C. **Incorrect.** A single Operations Manager management group can monitor multiple Service Provider Foundation management stamps.

D. **Correct:** A management stamp represents a unit of virtualized platform infrastructure that includes a VMM deployment, one or more virtualization hosts, the VMs that are managed by VMM, and the unique service accounts and user roles that are indi

CHAPTER 5

Configure and deploy virtual machines and services

VMM allows you to rapidly deploy virtual machines, applications, and services by leveraging profiles, virtualized applications, and templates. In this chapter you will learn how to configure profiles, and how to virtualize applications. You'll then learn how you can use templates and packages to deploy a service, as well as how to update a service that you have already deployed to your organization's private cloud.

Objectives in this chapter:

- Objective 5.1: Configure profiles
- Objective 5.2: Create and configure Server App-V packages
- Objective 5.3: Configure and deploy a service
- Objective 5.4: Update a service

Objective 5.1: Configure profiles

This objective deals with configuring the various profile types supported by VMM. In this section you will learn how to use hardware profiles, guest operating system profiles, application profiles, and SQL Server profiles.

> **This section covers the following topics:**
> - Hardware profiles
> - Guest operating system profiles
> - Application profiles
> - SQL Server profiles

Creating hardware profiles

A VMM hardware profile allows you to create a representation of a virtual machine's hardware configuration that can be used by VMM. Hardware profiles include information about the number of processors, the amount of RAM available to the virtual machine, as well as the IDE and SCSI configuration that the VM will use. You can also use a VMM hardware profile configuration to specify whether a virtual machine will use generation 1, or generation 2 virtual hardware. While you could configure virtual machine hardware settings manually each time you use VMM to create a virtual machine, a VMM hardware profile allows you to create VMs that have a standardized virtual hardware configuration.

To create a hardware profile, perform the following steps:

1. In the Library workspace of the VMM console, right-click the Profiles node, and click Create Hardware Profile.

2. On the General page of the New Hardware Profile dialog box, shown in Figure 5-1, provide a name for the profile and select which VM generation you want to use. This can be Generation 1 or Generation 2. Remember that Generation 2 VMs can only be used with virtualization hosts running Windows Server 2012 R2 or later.

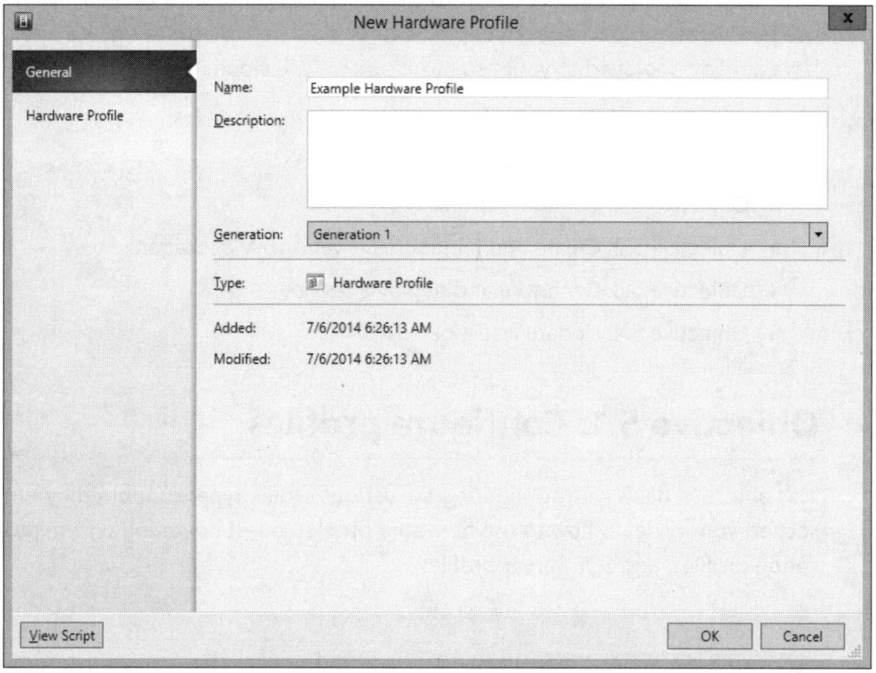

FIGURE 5-1 New Hardware Profile

3. On the Hardware Profile page, you can configure the following settings:

   - **Cloud Capability Profiles** Allows you to specify which capability profile to use with the hardware profile. You can choose between XenServer, ESX Server, and Hyper-V. Figure 5-2 shows the selection of the Hyper-V profile.

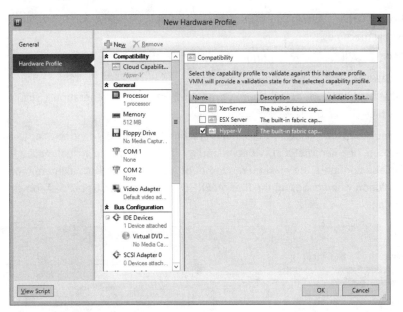

FIGURE 5-2 Cloud compatibility

- **Processor** Allows you to configure the number of processors to be used by the VM. This also allows you to configure whether you want to allow migration to occur to a virtual machine host running a different processor version.

- **Memory** Allows you to configure the amount of memory that will be allocated to the VM. You can choose to statically assign memory, or to allow the use of dynamic memory. Figure 5-3 shows the memory settings.

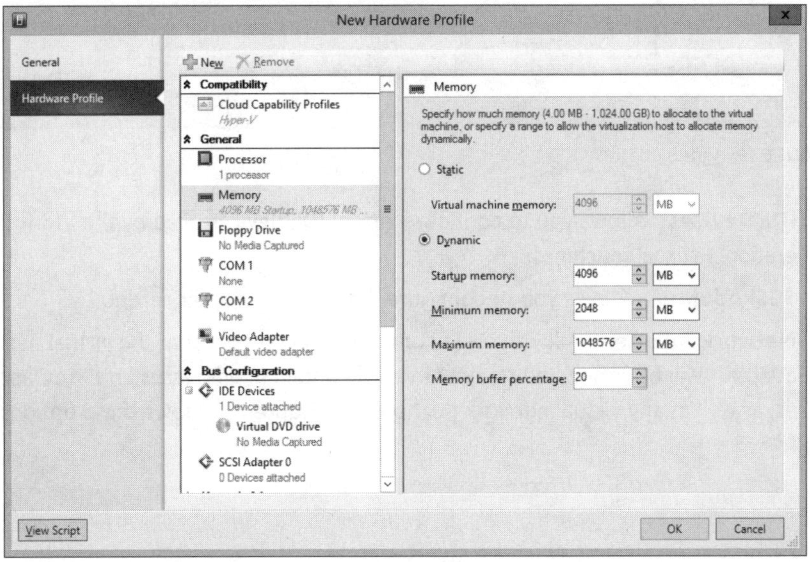

FIGURE 5-3 Memory

- **Floppy Drive** Allows you to configure a virtual floppy drive for generation 1 virtual machines.
- **COM 1** Allows you to configure Com Port 1 settings for generation 1 virtual machines.
- **COM 2** Allows you to configure Com Port 2 settings for generation 1 virtual machines.
- **Video Adapter** Allows you to configure whether a standard video adapter will be used, or a RemoteFX 3D video adapter will be available to virtual machines. You can also configure the maximum number of monitors and the maximum monitor resolution when choosing the RemoteFX 3D video adapter. Figure 5-4 shows this setting.

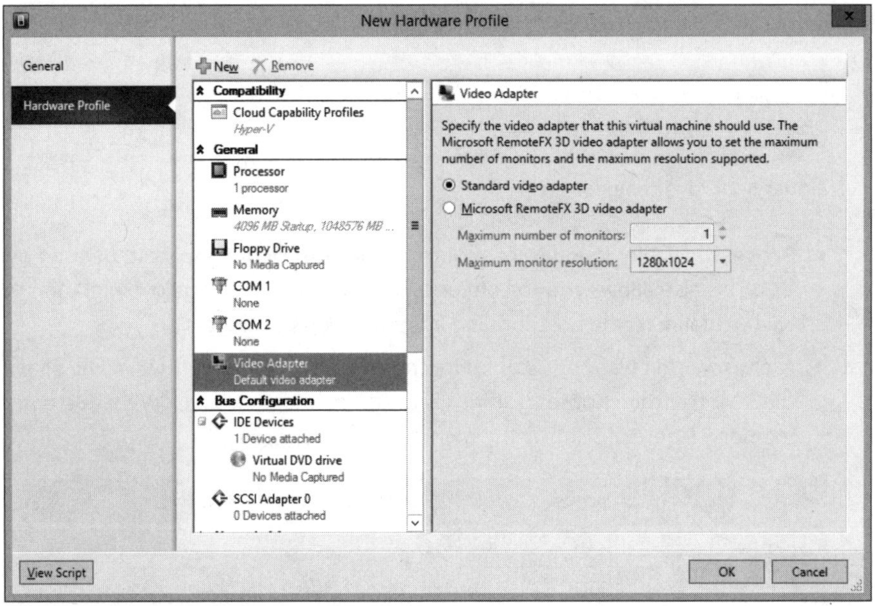

FIGURE 5-4 Video adapter

- **IDE Devices** Allows you to configure virtual IDE devices used by the VM for generation 1 virtual machines.
- **SCSI Adapter** Allows you to configure virtual SCSI adapter settings.
- **Network Adapter** Allows you to configure the network that the virtual network adapters will be connected to, how they will obtain IP addresses and MAC addresses, as well as any virtual network port profiles. Figure 5-5 shows these options.

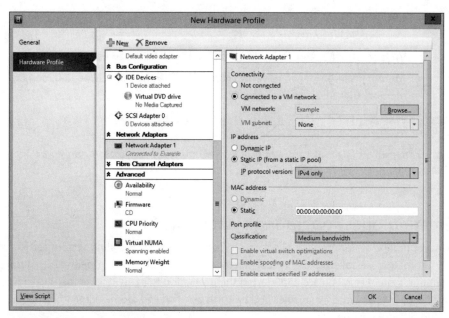

FIGURE 5-5 Network adapter settings

- **Availability** This option is for virtual machines that should be placed on highly available host clusters and ensures the VM is made highly available.

- **Firmware** Allows you to configure VM startup order, as shown in Figure 5-6.

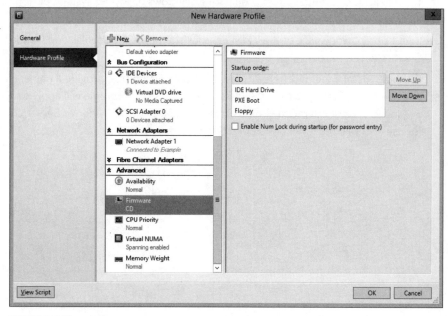

FIGURE 5-6 Firmware

- **CPU Priority** Allows you to configure the priority for the VM when the host is allocating CPU resources.
- **Virtual NUMA** Allows you to configure the VM to span hardware NUMA nodes.
- **Memory Weight** Allows you to configure how the VM is allocated memory when memory utilization on the virtualization host is high.

> *MORE INFO* **HARDWARE PROFILES**
>
> You can learn more about hardware profiles at *http://technet.microsoft.com/en-us/library/ hh427289.aspx.*

Creating guest operating system profiles

Guest operating system profiles allow you to configure guest operating system settings that are automatically applied to the virtual machine during deployment. Depending on the guest operating system that you are configuring the profile for, this can include the local administrator account password, what roles and features are installed, domain join information, and how to name the computer.

Guest operating system profiles aren't limited to VMs running Windows. You can also configure a guest operating system profile for VMs running Linux operating systems. Using a guest operating system profile saves you from having to perform configuration steps manually on an operating system each time you deploy a virtual machine.

To create a guest operating system profile for a Windows operating system, perform the following steps:

1. In the Library workspace of the VMM console, right-click the Profiles node, and click Create Guest OS Profile.

2. On the General page of the New Guest OS Profile dialog box, provide a name, and select which operating system the guest operating system profile will apply to. Figure 5-7 shows a guest operating system profile named Example Windows Server 2012 R2 for use with Microsoft Windows operating systems.

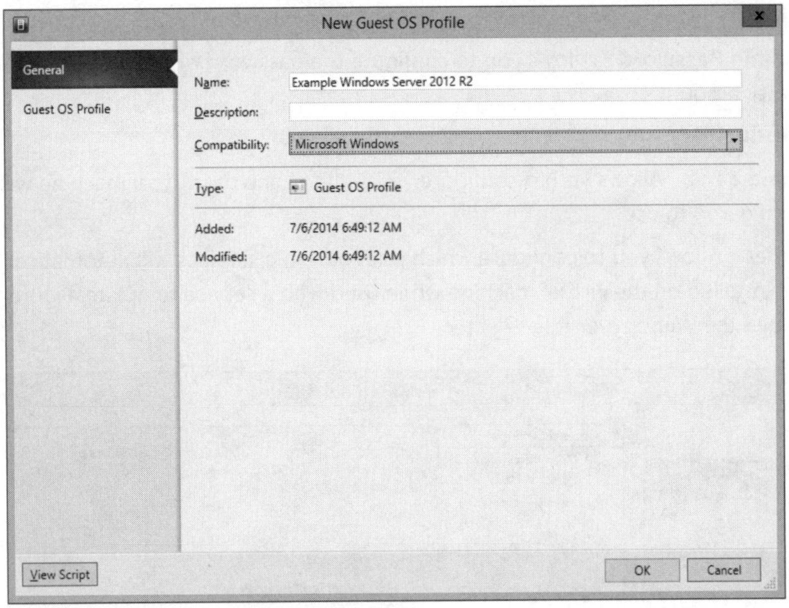

New Guest OS Profile

General

Guest OS Profile

Name: Example Windows Server 2012 R2

Description:

Compatibility: Microsoft Windows

Type: Guest OS Profile

Added: 7/6/2014 6:49:12 AM

Modified: 7/6/2014 6:49:12 AM

View Script   OK   Cancel

FIGURE 5-7 Guest operating system profile

3. On the Guest OS Profile page, specify the following settings:

   ■ **Operating System** Allows you to select which operating system the guest operating system profile applies to. Figure 5-8 shows some of the options that can be selected using the drop-down menu.

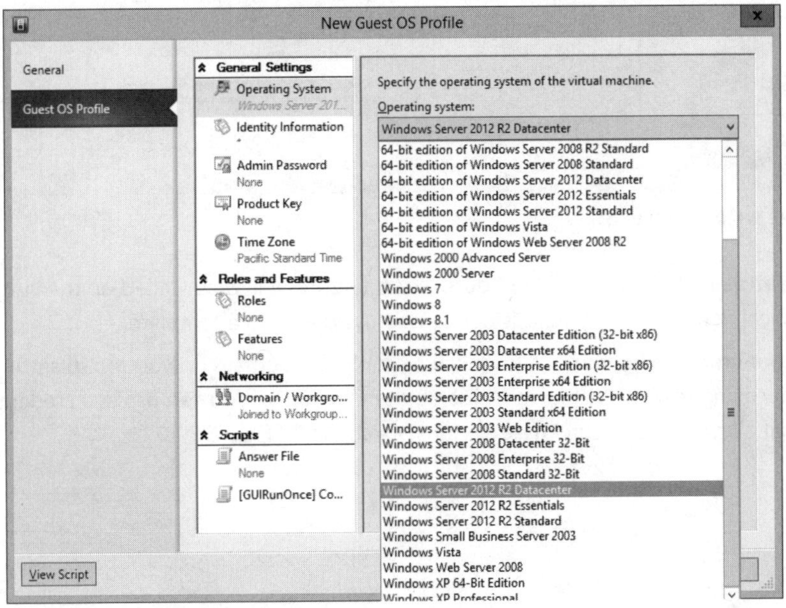

New Guest OS Profile

General

Guest OS Profile

General Settings

Operating System
Windows Server 201...

Identity Information

Admin Password
None

Product Key
None

Time Zone
Pacific Standard Time

Roles and Features

Roles
None

Features
None

Networking

Domain / Workgro...
Joined to Workgroup...

Scripts

Answer File
None

[GUIRunOnce] Co...

Specify the operating system of the virtual machine.

Operating system:

Windows Server 2012 R2 Datacenter

64-bit edition of Windows Server 2008 R2 Standard
64-bit edition of Windows Server 2008 Standard
64-bit edition of Windows Server 2012 Datacenter
64-bit edition of Windows Server 2012 Essentials
64-bit edition of Windows Server 2012 Standard
64-bit edition of Windows Vista
64-bit edition of Windows Web Server 2008 R2
Windows 2000 Advanced Server
Windows 2000 Server
Windows 7
Windows 8
Windows 8.1
Windows Server 2003 Datacenter Edition (32-bit x86)
Windows Server 2003 Datacenter x64 Edition
Windows Server 2003 Enterprise Edition (32-bit x86)
Windows Server 2003 Enterprise x64 Edition
Windows Server 2003 Standard Edition (32-bit x86)
Windows Server 2003 Standard x64 Edition
Windows Server 2003 Web Edition
Windows Server 2008 Datacenter 32-Bit
Windows Server 2008 Enterprise 32-Bit
Windows Server 2008 Standard 32-Bit
Windows Server 2012 R2 Datacenter
Windows Server 2012 R2 Essentials
Windows Server 2012 R2 Standard
Windows Small Business Server 2003
Windows Vista
Windows Web Server 2008
Windows XP 64-Bit Edition
Windows XP Professional

View Script

FIGURE 5-8 Operating system

- **Identity Information** Allows you to configure how the VM will be named.
- **Admin Password** Allows you to configure the password of the built-in Administrator account.
- **Product Key** Allows you to specify a product key.
- **Time Zone** Allows you to configure which time zone the virtual machine will be configured to use.
- **Roles** Allows you to configure which roles and role services will automatically be installed on the virtual machine when used with a service template. Figure 5-9 shows the Web Server role selected.

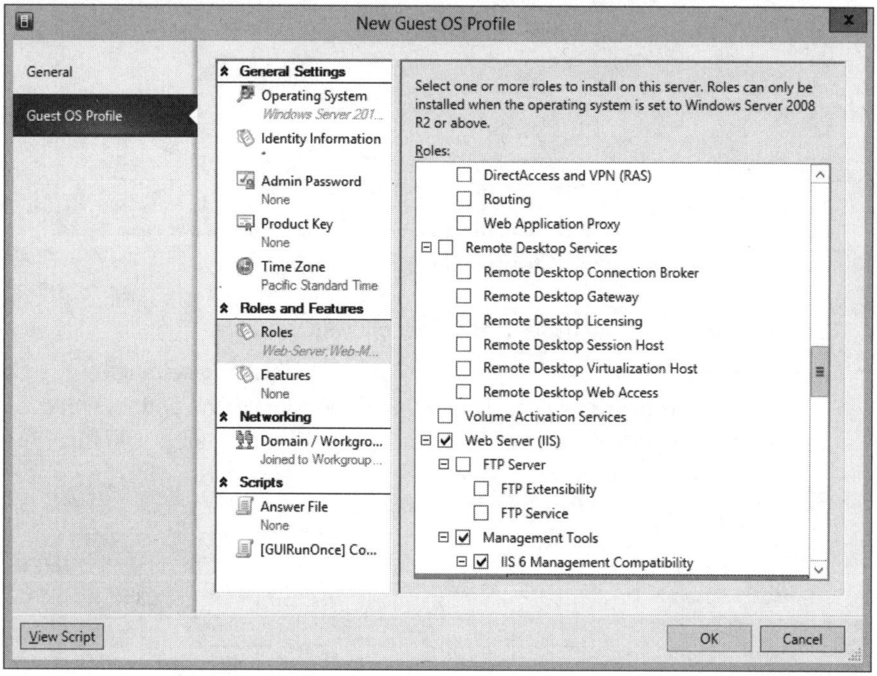

FIGURE 5-9 Roles section

- **Features** Allows you to configure which features will be installed on the virtual machine when deployment is performed using a service template.
- **Domain / Workgroup** Allows you to configure domain or workgroup settings. If specifying that the virtual machine be domain joined, you can provide credentials that allow this to occur. These options are shown in Figure 5-10.

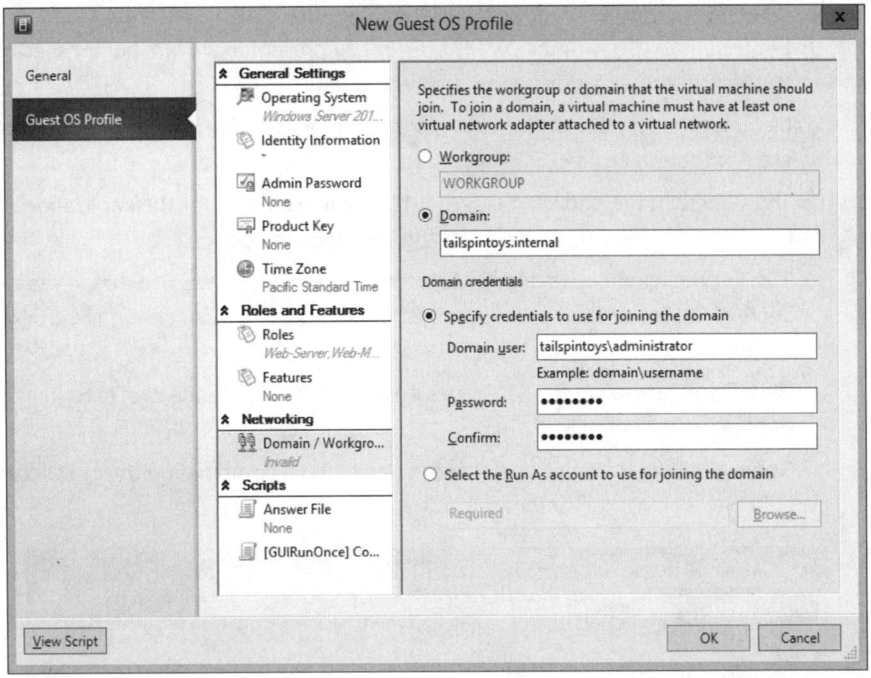

FIGURE 5-10 Domain information

- **Answer File**   Allows you to specify an answer file to automatically configure the virtual machine.
- **[GUIRunOnce] Command**   Allows you to specify a set of commands that will be run automatically the first time a user logs on to the virtual machine.

> **MORE INFO** **GUEST OPERATING SYSTEM PROFILES**
>
> You can learn more about guest operating system profiles at *http://technet.microsoft.com/en-us/library/hh427296.aspx.*

Creating application profiles

Application profiles include information that VMM can use for installing Microsoft Web Deploy applications, SQL Server data-tier applications, Microsoft Server App-V applications, and instructions for running scripts when you deploy a VM as part of a service. You only use application profiles if you are going to deploy a VM as part of a service, and don't use them when deploying standalone VMs. You can add multiple applications of the same type, or applications of different types to the same profile. You will learn more about services later in this chapter.

Before creating an application profile, you should ensure that all of the packages and scripts that you want to use with the profile are already present in a VMM library share. To create an application profile, perform the following steps:

1. In the Library workspace of the VMM console, right-click the Profiles node, and click Create Application Profile.

2. On the General page, shown in Figure 5-11, provide a name for the application profile and choose between one of the following compatibility options:

    - **SQL Server Application Host**   Select this option if you will use the profile to deploy SQL Server DAC packages or SQL Server scripts to an existing SQL Server instance.

    - **Web Application Host**   Select this option if you will use the profile to deploy Web Deploy packages to IIS.

    - **General**   Select this option if you are deploying a combination of application types or Server App-V applications.

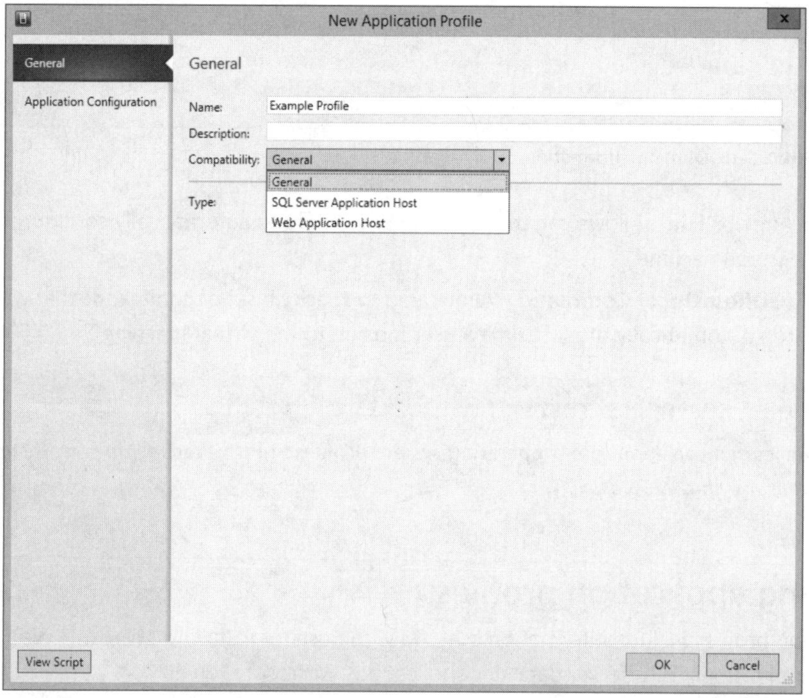

FIGURE 5-11 Application profile

3. On the Application Configuration page, select the operating system compatibility, as shown in Figure 5-12.

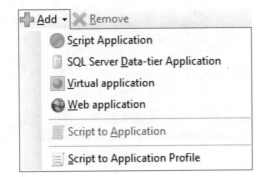

FIGURE 5-12 Operating system compatibility

4. Click Add, as shown in Figure 5-13, to add one of the following:

- Script Application
- SQL Server Data-Tier Application
- Virtual Application
- Web Application
- Script To Application Profile

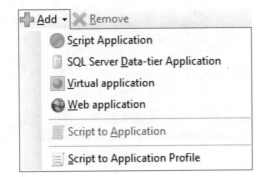

FIGURE 5-13 Add application

MORE INFO APPLICATION PROFILES

You can learn more about application profiles at *http://technet.microsoft.com/en-us/library/hh427291.aspx*.

Configuring SQL Server profiles

A SQL Server profile allows you to configure a sysprepped instance of SQL Server 2008 R2, SQL Server 2012, or SQL Server 2014 for deployment through VMM. You use SQL Server profiles when deploying VMs that are part of a service. The SQL Server profile configures SQL Server according to the profile settings.

To configure a SQL Server profile, perform the following steps:

1. In the Library workspace of the VMM console, right-click the Profiles node, and click Create SQL Server Profile.
2. On the General page of the New SQL Server Profile dialog box, provide a name for the SQL Server profile.
3. On the SQL Server Configuration page, click Add SQL Server Deployment, and provide the following information, as shown in Figure 5-14.

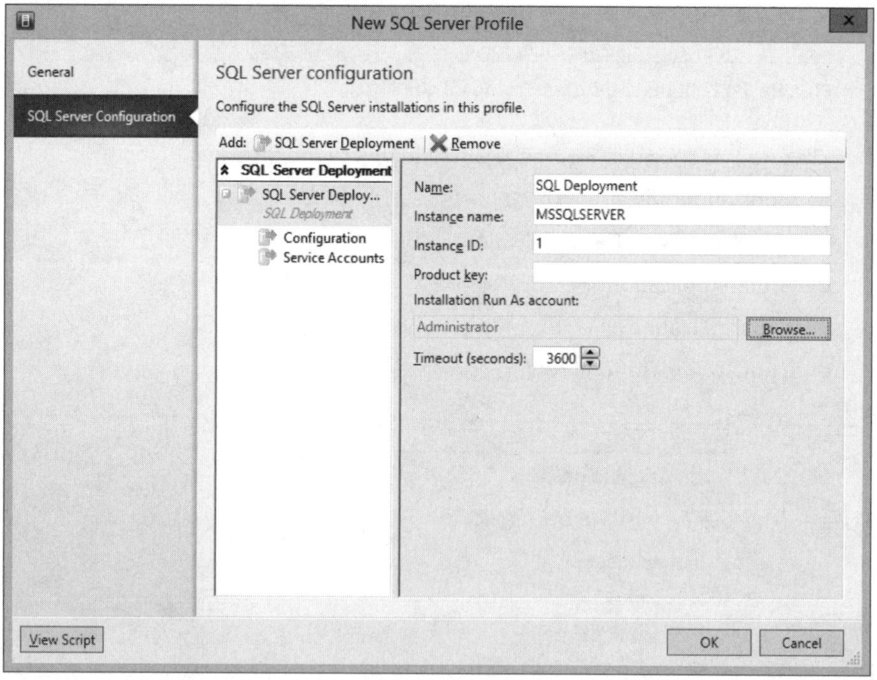

FIGURE 5-14 SQL Deployment

- **Name**   Name for the SQL Server deployment.
- **Instance Name**   The instance name. If left blank, it will use the default name MSSQLSERVER.
- **Instance ID**   The instance ID used when you sysprepped the SQL instance.
- **Installation Run As Account**   Account with the permission to deploy SQL Server.
- **Media Source**   Location of the SQL Server installation media, such as a VMM Library share.
- **SQL Server Administrators**   Users or groups that will be configured as SQL Server Administrators. You must specify at least one account.
- **Security Mode**   Select Windows or SQL Server authentication.
- **Service Accounts**   Configuration for the SQL Server service, SQL Server agent, and Reporting Services service accounts. You must select a Run As account for all three services.

> ***MORE INFO*** **SQL SERVER PROFILES**
>
> You can learn more about SQL Server profiles at *http://technet.microsoft.com/en-us/ library/hh427294.aspx*.

Thought experiment
Profiles at Wingtip Toys

In this thought experiment, apply what you've learned about this objective. You can find answers to these questions in the "Answers" section at the end of this chapter.

You are the virtualization administrator at Wingtip Toys. You are experimenting with VMM profiles and templates as a part of a private cloud pilot project. With this information in mind, answer the following questions:

1. What is the limitation, in terms of virtualization hosts, when using the generation 2 option in a hardware profile?

2. In what circumstances will the role and feature configuration of the guest operating system profile you are experimenting will be enacted?

Objective summary

- Hardware profiles allow you to configure virtual machine hardware settings.
- Guest operating system profiles allow you to configure operating system settings, including settings for local administrator accounts, computer name, and domain join information.
- Application profiles allow you to configure Server App-V, SQL DAC, and Web Deploy settings for when you deploy services.
- SQL Server profiles allow you to configure SQL Server settings for when you deploy services.

Objective review

Answer the following questions to test your knowledge of the information in this objective. You can find the answers to these questions and explanations of why each answer choice is correct or incorrect in the "Answers" section at the end of this chapter.

1. Which of the following do you use to configure the service account used by a SQL Server instance's SQL Server service?

   A. SQL Server profile

   B. Hardware profile

   C. Guest operating system profile

   D. Application profile

2. Which of the following do you use to configure a virtual machine's memory configuration?

   A. Application profile

   B. Guest operating system profile

   C. Hardware profile

   D. SQL Server profile

3. Which of the following do you use to configure the local administrator account password on a virtual machine?

   A. SQL Server profile

   B. Hardware profile

   C. Guest operating system profile

   D. Application profile

Objective 5.2: Create and configure Server App-V packages

Server App-V is an application virtualization technology that allows you to virtualize applications, usually web applications that run on server platforms. Once virtualized and packaged, application deployment and removal is simple, minimizing the amount of work required to add instances of an application as you scale out a service across additional VMs as a way of increasing capacity.

> **This section covers the following topics:**
> - Server App-V
> - Server App-V packages
> - Sequencing applications
> - Deploying a Server App-V package

Server App-V

Server App-V allows you to create virtual application packages through a process termed sequencing. You can deploy sequenced applications to a computer that has the Server App-V agent installed. These sequenced applications will run without requiring local installation.

You create a virtual application package using Server App-V by capturing the following elements of an application running on Windows Server:

- Information required to install the application
  - Application binary files
  - Registry settings
- Runtime state of the deployed application
  - Registry settings
  - Log files
  - Application data

You can deploy sequenced Server App-V applications to a new server with the application's last runtime state intact, which means you don't need to go through installation and configuration steps when deploying the application.

Primarily, Server App-V will be used with custom in-house applications, and you'll need to test whether Server App-V works with your organization's applications. In general, you can use Server App-V to sequence applications that have the following characteristics:

- Stores runtime state on a local disk
- Adds services to Windows
- Creates IIS applications
- Adds or modifies registry settings
- Installs or uses COM+ and DCOM
- Uses text-format configuration files
- Adds WMI providers
- Uses SQL Server Reporting Services
- Modifies local user and group accounts
- Installs and uses Java-based applications

If the sequenced application is designed to function in a load-balanced configuration, you can use VMM to deploy the application across additional servers as a way of scaling out capacity.

Server App-V uses the following elements:

- **Application**   This is the binaries, configuration, and settings to be virtualized.
- **Server App-V Sequencer**   This tool allows you to virtualize the application. It functions by monitoring and storing every change that the application makes during the deployment process.
- **Server App-V Agent**   Software deployed on the server that will run the sequenced application.
- **Package**   A package contains the virtualized application and includes the binary files, configuration, and runtime state data.
- **Server App-V Virtual Drive (Q:\)**   This virtual drive stores the virtualized application's binaries and settings. The App-V agent creates and will maintain the virtual drive using a folder on the host computer's system drive.

> **MORE INFO SERVER APP-V OVERVIEW**
>
> You can learn more about Server App-V at *http://technet.microsoft.com/en-us/library/gg703262.aspx.*

Understanding Server App-V packages

A Server App-V package contains the following files:

- **.SFT file** The package payload file. This binary file is created by the Server App-V sequencer and stores the deployed files, folders, registry settings, and any other package data.

- **.OSD files** Open Software Descriptor files. These XML-based files provide information to the Server App-V agent on how to import the package.

- **.SPRJ file** The sequencer project file. This XML-based file is used by the Server App-V sequencer to modify or upgrade the package.

- **_Manifest.xml** The Packagename_manifest.xml file stores information that describes the package. The Server App-V agent uses this file, in conjunction with the .OSD files, to import the package. The Packagename_manifest.xml file also includes information on how to run the package.

- **DeploymentConfig.xml** This file stores data used to customize package settings that were specific to the environment in which the application was sequenced. For example, database connection strings, server names, and passwords for a specific deployment.

Sequencing applications

At a high level, sequencing an application involves performing the following steps:

1. Deploy the Server App-V sequencer to the computer that will host the application.
2. Start the Server App-V sequencer by running the New Virtual Application Package Wizard.
3. Install the application that you want to virtualize to the Server App-V virtual drive (Q:\).
4. Run any other installers necessary to finalize application configuration.
5. Once installation completes, stop the Server App-V sequencer.
6. Save the virtualized application as a package to a location external to the server used to perform the sequencing.

When preparing the server on which you will be sequencing the application, consider the following best practices:

- Prepare the computer that will host the Server App-V sequencer to have a configuration as similar as possible to the computers that will host the sequenced application in a production environment.

- Verify that the default sequencing drive is available. Server App-V uses volume Q: by default. If servers in your environment already map volume Q: for other purposes, adjust the default sequencing drive prior to attempting to sequence the application.

- Disable unused applications. The computer that hosts the sequencer should have no anti-malware software active and no Windows Update activity pending.

- If you are planning on deploying the virtualized application to multiple server operating systems, sequence the application on the earliest version of the operating system. For example, if you are deploying to servers running the Windows Server 2012 and Windows Server 2012 R2 operating systems, sequence the application on Windows Server 2012.

- Configure ODBC or printer connections prior to sequencing. You'll also need to configure ODBC and printer settings on computers with the Server App-V agent installed prior to importing the sequenced package.

- Use a virtual machine with checkpoints to perform sequencing. This way you can revert to the checkpoints to sequence new applications as necessary.

> **MORE INFO SERVER APP-V SEQUENCING**
>
> You can learn more about Server App-V sequencing at *http://technet.microsoft.com/en-us/library/gg703265.aspx.*

Deploying a Server App-V package

Before you deploy a Server App-V package to a server, you must first ensure that you have deployed the Server App-V agent. You also need to ensure that any roles, features, and other dependencies required by the application are also present. The dependencies that are required will depend on the application, with some being captured by the sequencing process, and others being required on the host computer.

The Server App-V PowerShell agent cmdlets allow you to test package deployment locally, including running tests to verify the functionality of a package. If you want to use the Server App-V PowerShell agent cmdlets, you need to set the execution policy on the computer that will host the virtualized application to RemoteSigned.

Server App-V has the following Windows PowerShell cmdlets:

- **Add-ServerAppvPackage**   Adds a new virtual application to a computer that has the Server App-V agent installed, or can be used to upgrade an existing virtual application.

- **Backup-ServerAppvPackageState**   Saves the runtime state of an existing Server App-V application to a designated location.

- **Get-ServerAppvAgent**   Provides information about the Server App-V agent.

- **Get-ServerAppvPackage**   Provides information about a deployed Server App-V package.

- **Remove-ServerAppvPackage**   Removes Server App-V package from a computer to which it has been deployed.

- **Remove-ServerAppvPackageState**   Removes the runtime state, returning the virtual application package to its initial state, but does not remove the virtual application package.

- **Restore-ServerAppvPackageState**   Restores the runtime state of a virtual application. You can only use this cmdlet if you have a backup of the application's runtime state.

- **Set-ServerAppvPackageConfiguration**   Configures an existing virtual application package to use a specific deployment configuration.

- **Start-ServerAppvPackage**   Starts an installed virtual application package and associated subsystem.

- **Stop-ServerAppvPackage**   Shuts down a virtual application package an associated subsystems.

The Server App-V sequencer uses the following Windows PowerShell cmdlets:

- **New-ServerAppVSequencerPackage**   This cmdlet is used to create a new virtual application package.

- **Protect-UpdateConfiguration**   This cmdlet encrypts sensitive values stored in the deployment configuration document.

- **Unprotect-UpdateConfiguration**   This cmdlet decrypts any encrypted sections of the deployment configuration document.

- **Update-ServerAppVSequencerPackage**   This cmdlet is used to update an existing virtual application package.

If you are going to use VMM to deploy the Server App-V package, ensure that you have copied the package to the VMM library as a custom resource. To do this, place the package contents in a folder that has the extension .CR, and copy the folder to the VMM library share.

MORE INFO **SERVER APP-V WINDOWS POWERSHELL CMDLETS**

You can learn more about Server App-V Windows PowerShell cmdlets at *http://technet. microsoft.com/en-us/library/hh393499.aspx.*

EXAM TIP

Remember what steps you need to take to add a Server App-V package to the VMM library.

Thought experiment

Server application virtualization at Tailspin Toys

In this thought experiment, apply what you've learned about this objective. You can find answers to these questions in the "Answers" section at the end of this chapter.

You are in the process of testing some virtualized applications. You need to be able to save the runtime state of these virtualized applications, so if there is a problem later on in the testing process, you can return them to a known state. With this information in mind, answer the following questions.

1. What Server App-V Windows PowerShell cmdlet would you use to save the runtime state of an existing Server App-V application to a designated location?

2. What Server App-V Windows PowerShell cmdlet would you use to restore the runtime state of an existing Server App-V application from a designated location?

Objective summary

- Server App-V allows you to create virtual application packages through a process termed sequencing.

- You can deploy sequenced Server App-V applications to a computer that has the Server App-V agent installed, and these sequenced applications will run without requiring local installation.

- You can deploy sequenced Server App-V applications to a new server with the application's last runtime state intact, which means you don't need to go through installation and configuration steps when deploying the application.

- An App-V package contains the virtualized application and includes the binaries, configuration, and runtime state data.

- Server App-V uses virtual drive Q:\ to store the virtualized application's binaries and settings. The App-V agent creates, and will maintain, the virtual drive using a folder on the host computer's system drive.

Objective review

Answer the following questions to test your knowledge of the information in this objective. You can find the answers to these questions and explanations of why each answer choice is correct or incorrect in the "Answers" section at the end of this chapter.

1. Which of the following Server App-V related Windows PowerShell cmdlets can you use to remote the runtime state of a virtualized application, returning the virtual application package to its initial state? (Choose the best answer.)

   A. Restore-ServerAppvPackageState

   B. Start-ServerAppvPackage.

   C. Remove-ServerAppvPackageState.

   D. Stop-ServerAppvPackage.

2. Which of the following Server App-V related Windows PowerShell cmdlets can you use to upgrade an existing virtual application?

   A. Remove-ServerAppvPackage.

   B. Remove-ServerAppvPackageState.

   C. Add-ServerAppvPackage.

   D. Restore-ServerAppvPackageState.

3. Which of the following cmdlets should you use to update the contents of an existing Server App-V virtual application package?

   A. Restore-ServerAppvPackageState.

   B. Add-ServerAppvPackage.

   C. Update-ServerAppVSequencerPackage

   D. Start-ServerAppvPackage.

4. You have created a Server App-V package and saved it in a folder named ContosoApp. To which of the following should you rename the ContosoApp folder prior to copying it the VMM library so that you can configure it as part of an application profile?

   A. ContosoApp.ZIP.

   B. ContosoApp.CR.

   C. ContosoApp.VMM.

   D. ContosoApp.App-V.

Objective 5.3: Configure and deploy a service

This objective deals with configuring virtual machine templates, service templates, web deploy packages, and SQL DAC packages. These all form the basis of being able to build scalable applications in a private cloud.

This section covers the following topics:

- Configuring virtual machine templates
- Creating service templates
- Web Deploy packages
- SQL DAC packages

Configuring virtual machine templates

A Virtual Machine Manager VM template allows you to deploy a single virtual machine with a consistent set of settings. A VMM VM template is an XML object that is stored with a VMM library, and includes one or more of the following components:

- **Guest Operating System Profile**   A guest operating system profile that includes operating system settings.
- **Hardware Profile**   A hardware profile that includes VM hardware settings.
- **Virtual Hard Disk**   This can be a blank hard disk, or a virtual hard disk that hosts a specially prepared, sysprepped in the case of Windows based operating systems, version of an operating system.

You can create VM templates based on existing virtual machines deployed on a virtualization host managed by VMM, based on virtual hard disks stored in a VMM library, or by using an existing VM template.

VM templates have the following limitations:

- A VM template allows you to customize IP address settings, but you can only configure a static IP address for a specific VM when deploying that VM from the template.
- Application and SQL Server deployment are only used when you deploy a VM as part of a service.
- When creating a template from an existing VM, ensure that the VM is a member of a workgroup and is not joined to a domain.
- You should create a separate local administrator account on a VM before using it as the basis of a template. Using the built-in administrator account will cause the sysprep operation to fail.
- You cannot create a virtual machine template for a Linux virtual machine based on an existing Linux VM deployed to a virtualization host.

To create a VM template based on an existing virtual hard disk (which can include a blank hard disk), or existing VM template, perform the following steps:

1. In the Library workspace of the VMM console, click Create VM Template on the ribbon.

2. On the Select Source page, click Browse next to Use An Existing VM Template For A Virtual Hard Disk Stored In The Library.

3. On the Select VM Template Source dialog box, select the hard disk that will serve as the basis for the VM template.

4. On the VM Template Identity page, provide a name for the VM template, and choose between a Generation 1 and a Generation 2 VM. This page is shown in Figure 5-15.

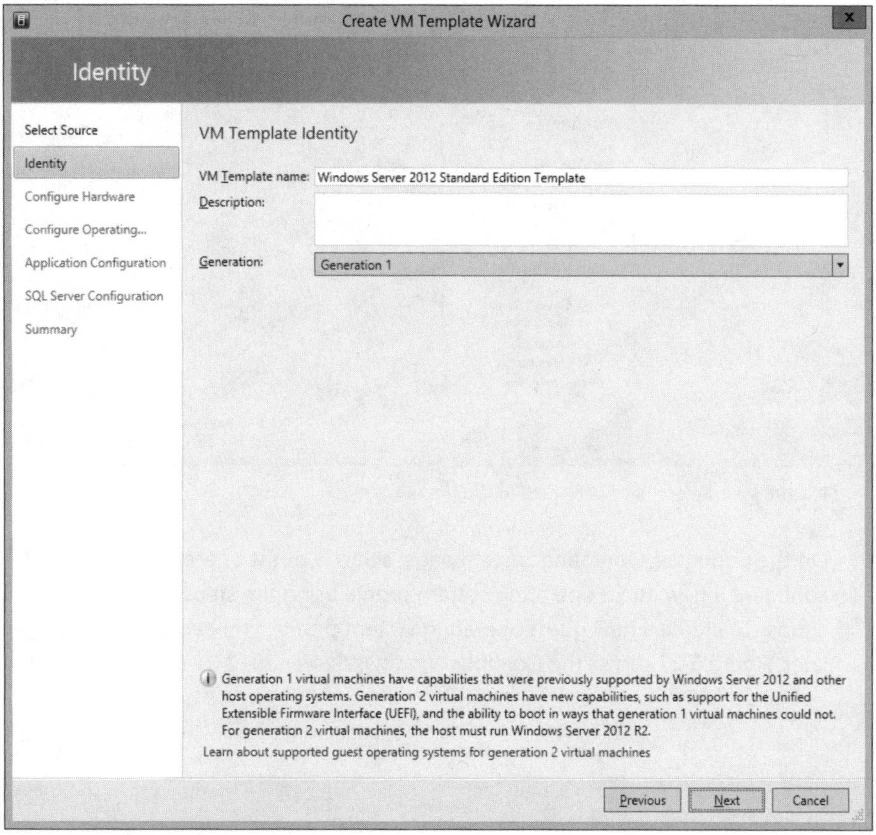

FIGURE 5-15 Template name

5. On the Configure Hardware page, you can select an existing hardware profile, or create a new hardware profile using the steps outlined earlier in this chapter. If you choose to create a new hardware profile, you can save this profile for use in the future. Figure 5-16 shows the selection of the Example Hardware Profile.

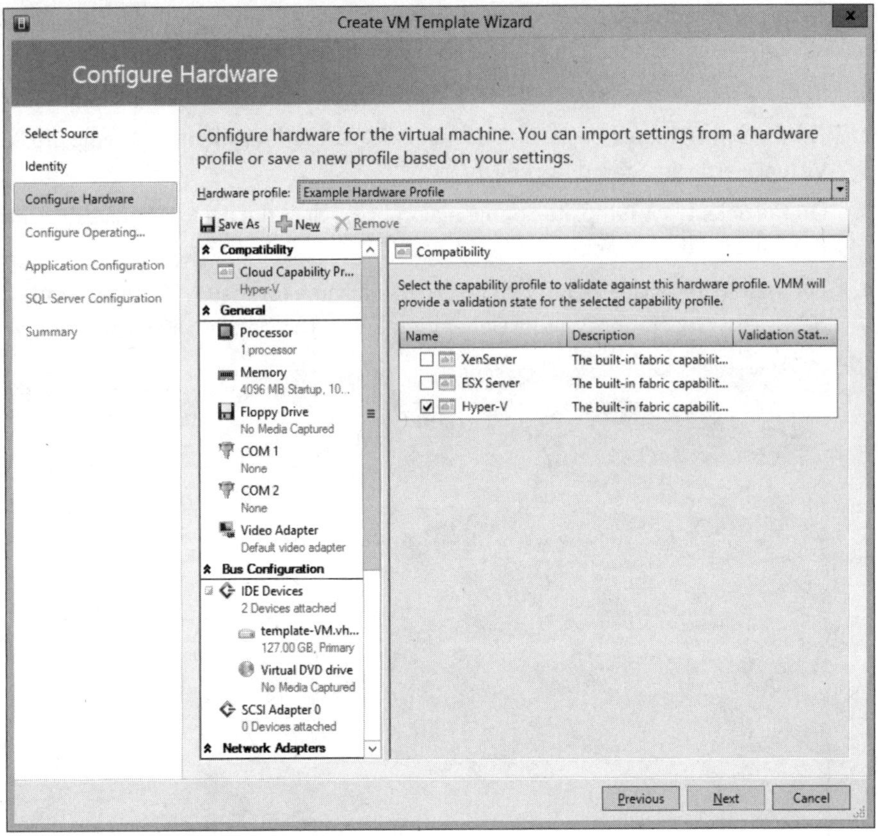

FIGURE 5-16 Select hardware profile

6. On the Configure Operating System page, select a guest operating system profile, or configure a new guest operating system profile using the steps outlined earlier. If you choose to create a new guest operating system profile, you can save it for use again later. Figure 5-17 shows the Example Windows Server 2012 R2 profile selected.

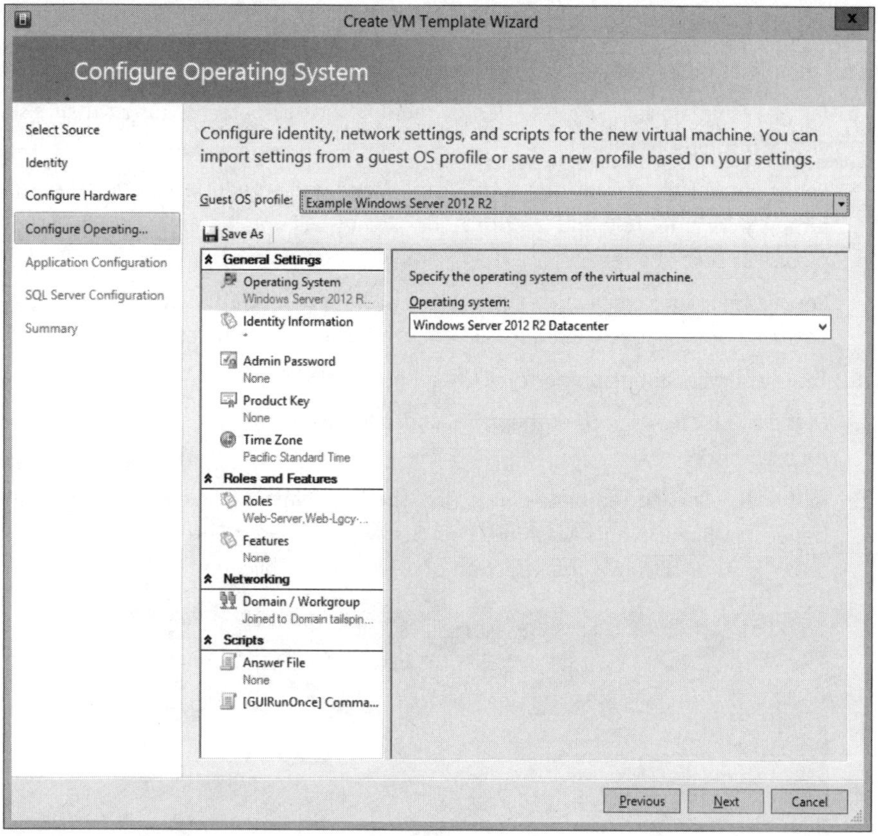

FIGURE 5-17 Select the guest operating system profile

7. On the Application Configuration page, you can select an existing application profile. This will only be used if the VM is deployed as a service, and you don't have to select an application profile when configuring a VM template.

8. On the SQL Server Configuration page, you can select an existing SQL Server profile. This will only be used if the VM is deployed as a service and you don't have to select a SQL Server profile when configuring a VM template.

9. Complete the wizard, which creates the profile.

When creating a VM template from a VM that is already deployed, you'll be asked to select an existing VM from a list of those that are deployed on a virtualization host managed by VMM.

MORE INFO **VIRTUAL MACHINE TEMPLATES**

You can learn more about virtual machine templates at *http://technet.microsoft.com/en-us/ library/hh427282.aspx.*

Creating service templates

Service templates differ from virtual machine templates in the following ways:

- Service templates allow you to deploy multiple virtual machines rather than a single virtual machine.

- Service templates can include settings for Windows Server roles and features. If a VM template includes role and feature settings, they will only be used if the VM is deployed as part of a service.

- Service templates can include application profiles and SQL server profiles. These profiles are not available when deploying a VM from a VM template.

To create a service template, perform the following steps:

1. In the Library workspace of the VMM console, click the Create Service Template item on the ribbon.

2. In the New Service Template dialog box, specify a Name, a Release version, and select between a Blank, Single Machine, Two Tier Application, or Three Tier Application pattern. Figure 5-18 shows the selection of a Two Tier Application.

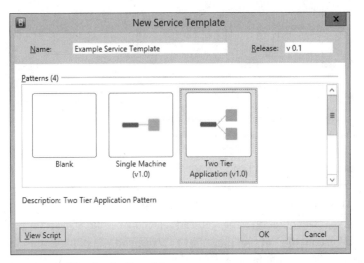

FIGURE 5-18 New Service Template

3. In the Virtual Machine Manager Service Template Designer, shown in Figure 5-19, use the drag-and-drop interface to add applications and configure which VM templates will be used with the multiple tier application. You can also add VM networks and load balancers, as well as adding additional machine tiers using the designer.

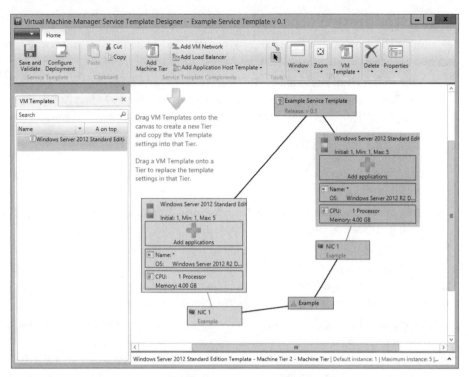

FIGURE 5-19 VMM Service Template Designer

4. When you have competed configuring the service template, click Save And Validate. This will check the service template for errors which must be resolved before the template can be saved and used for deployment.

MORE INFO **SERVICE TEMPLATES**

You can learn more about creating service templates at *http://technet.microsoft.com/en-us/ library/gg675105.aspx.*

Understanding Web Deploy packages

Microsoft Web Deploy allows you to deploy, migrate, and manage IIS websites, web servers, and web applications. Web Deploy has the following features:

- **Web application packaging**   This feature allows you to package a web application, complete websites, associated databases, registry settings including Access Control Lists (ACLs), Element Object Model (COM), and global assembly cache (GAC).

- **Web application deployment**   This feature allows you to deploy web applications without requiring local administrative privileges on the server hosting IIS and configure parameters to change how the package is deployed, such as modifying database connection strings.

- **Web server migration and synchronization**   This feature allows you to synchronize or migrate web servers, websites, or web applications from one host to another.

To create a web deploy package, you need to first install the Web Deployment Tool and the IIS Manager UI module on the server that hosts the website or web application you intend to package. Once the Web Deployment Tool is installed, you can use the IIS Manager console to export a website or web application as a Web Deploy package.

When exporting an application, you can choose which elements to export, whether to include an encryption password, and whether to include ACLs as part of the package. The package is exported to a .zip file, which you can then paste into the VMM library share. Once present in the library share, the Web Deploy package can be used with an application profile.

SQL DAC packages

Data-tier application (DAC) packages include database and SQL Server instance objects that can be used by an application. The advantage of a DAC is that it provides a single entity for authoring, managing, and deploying a data-tier object. A DAC package is a zip file that stores multiple XML files that describe the following elements:

- **DAC metadata**   This includes the name and version of the DAC.

- **Database object definitions**   This includes database schema, tables, views, and stored procedure.

- **Instance level object definitions**   Includes database login information.

- **Prerequisites**   A set of prerequisites for hosting the DAC, such as collation.

- **Scripts and files**   Can include application documents, data-generation plans, pre and post deployment scripts.

DACs are usually created in Visual Studio by developing a data-tier application.

> **MORE INFO UNDERSTANDING DATA-TIER APPLICATIONS**
>
> You can learn more about data-tier applications at *http://msdn.microsoft.com/en-us/ library/ee240739%28SQL.105%29.aspx*.

EXAM TIP

Remember what you use a SQL DAC and a Web Deploy package for.

> **Thought experiment**
>
> **VMM service deployment at Contoso**
>
> In this thought experiment, apply what you've learned about this objective. You can find answers to these questions in the "Answers" section at the end of this chapter.
>
> You are in the process of configuring service deployment using VMM at Contoso. You want to automate the deployment of VMs, applications, and multi-tier services using VMM profiles and templates. With this in mind, answer the following questions:
>
> 1. What should you configure to automate the deployment of Microsoft Server App-V applications to a virtual service in VMM?
>
> 2. What should you configure so that you can simplify the deployment of a multi-tier application using VMM?

Objective summary

- Virtual machine templates allow you to create templates that serve as the basis for virtual machine deployment. These include hardware and guest operating system settings. You can create VM templates based on an existing virtual hard disk, virtual machine, or existing VM template.

- Service templates allow you to deploy multiple virtual machines and applications in multi-tier configurations.

- Microsoft Web Deploy allows you to deploy, migrate, and manage IIS websites, web servers, and web applications.

- The web application packaging feature allows you to package a web application, complete websites, associated databases, registry settings including Access Control Lists (ACLs), Element Object Model (COM), and global assembly cache (GAC).

- Data-tier application (DAC) packages include database and SQL Server instance objects that can be used by an application.

Objective review

Answer the following questions to test your knowledge of the information in this objective. You can find the answers to these questions and explanations of why each answer choice is correct or incorrect in the "Answers" section at the end of this chapter.

1. Which of the following can you use as the basis for creating a virtual machine template?

   A. Deployed virtual machine

   B. VMM VM template

   C. Virtual hard disk

   D. Guest OS profile

2. In which format is a SQL DAC package stored in the VMM library?

   A. VHD

   B. ZIP

   C. CAB

   D. XML

3. Which of the following can you include in a VM template?

   A. Physical profile

   B. Application profile

   C. SQL Server profile

   D. Guest operating system profile

4. Which of the following can you include in a VMM service template?

   A. SQL Server profile

   B. VM template

   C. Physical profile

   D. Application profile

Objective 5.4: Update a service

Once deployed, a service is likely to need to be updated, either because there have been changes to the application it hosts, because you want to replace the underlying operating system, or another aspect of the service such as the SQL Server tier.

> **This section covers the following topics:**
> - Updating services in VMM
> - Scaling out a service tier

Updating Services in VMM

Each time you deploy a service using VMM, VMM will record which service template you used as the basis of that deployment. If you update that service template later, VMM allows you to update the service in deployment based on the changes that you made to the service template.

VMM supports the following methods of updating a deployed service:

- Apply updates to the in-place virtual machines that comprise the service.
- Deploy new virtual machines with updated settings to replace the existing virtual machines that comprise the service.

Performing an in-place upgrade is usually the quickest option. To reduce the chance of disruption when performing an in-place upgrade, you can configure multiple upgrade domains to segment each tier. When configuring upgrade domains, you specify the number of upgrade domains you want to use and VMM will arbitrarily sort virtual machines across that number of upgrade domains. When VMs are segmented into upgrade domains, VMM will apply updates to one upgrade domain at a time, only moving on to the next upgrade domain once the updates are applied to the current upgrade domain.

Deploying new VMs is usually more time consuming. You choose this method when you want to perform an operating system replacement. For example, you want to upgrade the operating system from Windows Server 2012 to Windows Server 2012 R2. This becomes more complicated if applications are installed on the virtual machines you want to replace. In this case, if the application has a method of saving and restoring application state, you can configure a script in the application profile to save that state to a separate location before replacing the VM. An additional script will then restore the application state once the replacement VM is running. If you are using Server App-V virtualized applications, the applications automatically support the saving and restoration of state data without requiring scripts.

> **MORE INFO** **UPDATING SERVICES IN VMM**
>
> You can learn more about updating services in VMM at *http://technet.microsoft.com/en-us/library/gg675089.aspx.*

Updating service templates

Updating the service template of a deployed service in VMM involves creating a copy of the original service template and specifying a new release value. You then make the appropriate updates to the service template.

To update an existing service template, perform the following steps:

1. In the Library workspace of the VMM console, click Service Templates under the Templates node.

2. Select the service template that you want to update. On the Service Template tab of the VMM console ribbon, click Create, and then click Copy.

3. Right-click the newly created copy, and click Properties.

4. On the General page of the Service Template Properties dialog box, specify a new release value.

5. Make the changes to update the template in the Service Template Designer.

If you are using Service Template Designer with a service template that is the basis for a service that is already deployed, you'll be prompted by VMM to save the service template with an incremented release value.

> **MORE INFO** UPDATING SERVICE TEMPLATES
>
> You can learn more about updating service templates at the following address: *http://technet.microsoft.com/en-us/library/gg675120.aspx.*

Modifying templates for updated resources

If you update a resource in VMM that is referenced by a service template, you'll need to copy and update the service template to reference the newly updated resource.

To update an existing service template to use an updated resource, perform the following steps:

1. In the Service templates node of the Library workspace of the VMM console, locate the service template that uses the resource that you have updated. Service templates that utilize outdated resource have "Outdated" listed in the Update Status column.

2. Right-click the service template and click View Updated Resources. This will display the most up-to-date version or resources referenced by the template.

3. Right-click the template, and select Copy And Update. The new copy will reference the updated resources.

4. Publish the updated template by selecting it, and in the Actions group of the VMM Console ribbon, click Publish.

Once published, you can then apply the updated template to the deployed service. You'll learn how to do this in the next section.

> **MORE INFO** UPDATING TEMPLATES FOR UPDATED RESOURCES
>
> You can learn more about updating service templates to use updated resources at *http://technet.microsoft.com/en-us/library/jj860435.aspx.*

Apply updates to deployed services

Once you've published an updated template, you can apply updates to an existing service using the updated service template.

To apply updates to a deployed service using an updated service template, perform the following steps:

1. In the VMs and Services workspace of the VMM console, select the service that you want to update using the updated service template.

2. On the Service tab of the Update group of the VMM console ribbon, click Set Template.

3. On the Updated Service Template page of the Change Service Template Wizard, select Replace The Current Template With An Updated Template For This Service.

4. Browse to, and select, the updated service template.

5. On the Settings page, configure any listed application settings.

6. On the Update Method page, select between applying the updates in-place to the existing VMs, or whether you want to deploy new VMs with updated settings.

7. Complete the wizard.

Once you have set the new template and configured the update method, you can click Apply Template on the ribbon to trigger the update job. When the update job completes, the Template Release value will have updated.

> **MORE INFO** **APPLY UPDATES TO DEPLOYED SERVICES**
>
> You can learn more about applying updates to deployed services at *http://technet. microsoft.com/en-us/library/gg675106.aspx*.

Scaling out a service tier

Scaling out a service tier is the process of adding additional virtual machines to a tier of a service as a method of increasing capacity. When creating a tier in a service template, you configure whether the tier can be scaled out. You also configure the minimum and maximum number of VMs that can be deployed in the tier. VMM will not prevent you from scaling out a tier beyond the number of VMs that you specify here, but once you exceed the limit you configured, the tier and the service will display a Needs Attention status in the VMM console's VMs And Services workspace.

To scale out a service tier, perform the following steps:

1. In the VMs And Services workspace of the VMM console, click the private cloud or host group to which you deployed the service.

2. On the VMM console ribbon, click Services.

3. In the Services pane, click the service that you wish to scale out.

4. In the Service tab of the VMM console ribbon, click Scale Out.

5. On the Select Tier page of the Scale Out Tier Wizard, in the list of tiers, select the tier that you want to scale out.

6. On the Specify Virtual Machine Identity page, provide a name for the new virtual machine that will join the tier.

   - If the tier is deployed to a private cloud, you only need to provide the computer name for the VM.

   - If the tier is deployed to a host group, you'll have to specify which host to deploy the VM to as well as provide the name to the VM.

7. On the Add Properties page, select what actions to perform on the VM if the virtualization host starts or stops.

8. Review the settings on the wizard and click Scale Out.

> **MORE INFO** **SCALE OUT A SERVICE TIER**
>
> You can learn more about scaling out a service tier at *http://technet.microsoft.com/en-us/library/gg675080.aspx*.

> **EXAM TIP**
>
> Remember that you need to publish an updated template before you can apply an updated template.

Thought experiment

Managing services at Contoso

In this thought experiment, apply what you've learned about this objective. You can find answers to these questions in the "Answers" section at the end of this chapter.

You are in the process of testing upgrade and scale out procedures at Contoso. You have noticed that when you scale out certain tiers of the service, the Needs Attention status is displayed for the tier and service in the VMM console. You are also interested in ensuring that tiers remain available during upgrade operations. With this information in mind, answer the following questions:

1. How can you ensure that some parts of each tier of the service remain available during upgrade operations?

2. How can you ensure that the Needs Attention status isn't displayed when you scale out a tier?

Objective summary

- If you update that service template that was used to deploy a service, VMM allows you to update the service in deployment based on the changes that you made to the service template.

- VMM supports updating a deployed service by either applying updates to the in-place virtual machines that comprise the service or deploy new virtual machines with up-dated settings to replace the existing virtual machines that comprise the service.

- When VMs are segmented into upgrade domains, VMM will apply updates to one up-grade domain at a time, only moving on to the next upgrade domain once the updates are applied to the current upgrade domain.

- Updating the service template of a deployed service in VMM involves creating a copy of the original service template and specifying a new release value.

- If you update a resource in VMM that is referenced by a service template, you'll need to copy and update the service template to reference the newly updated resource.

- Once you've published an updated template, you can apply updates to an existing service by configuring the service to use the updated service template.

Objective review

Answer the following questions to test your knowledge of the information in this objective. You can find the answers to these questions and explanations of why each answer choice is correct or incorrect in the "Answers" section at the end of this chapter.

1. You need to update the service template of a service you deployed in VMM. Which of the following steps do you need to take to accomplish this goal?

   A. Specify a new release value on the original template.

   B. Specify a new release value on the template copy.

   C. Create a copy of the original service template and make changes to the copy.

   D. Make changes to the original template.

2. You want to apply updates to a deployed service. On the Updated Service Template page of the Change Service Template Wizard, which step should you take?

   A. Edit the current template.

   B. Delete the current template.

   C. Replace the current template with the updated template for the service.

   D. Replace the updated template with the current template.

3. You've created an updated template that references updated resources. Which of the following steps must you take before you can apply updates to an existing service us-ing the updated service template?

   A. Delete the template.

   B. Publish the template.

   C. Export the template.

   D. Import the template.

Answers

This section contains the solutions to the thought experiments and answers to the objective review questions in this chapter.

Objective 5.1: Thought experiment

1. If you choose to use generation 2 in a hardware profile, you'll only be able to use virtualization hosts running Windows Server 2012 R2 or later.

2. In what circumstances will the role and feature configuration of the guest operating system profile you are experimenting will be enacted? [Role and feature configuration applies when the guest operating system profile is enacted as part of a service template.]

Objective 5.1: Review

1. **Correct answer:** A
   A. **Correct:** You can use the SQL Server profile to configure SQL Server configuration settings such as the SQL Server service account.
   B. **Incorrect:** You use a hardware profile to configure a VM's hardware configuration, including the VM's memory configuration.
   C. **Incorrect:** A guest operating system profile allows you to configure settings including the local administrator account password settings for a VM.
   D. **Incorrect:** Application profiles include information that VMM can use for installing Microsoft Web Deploy applications, SQL Server data-tier applications, Microsoft Server App-V applications, and instructions for running scripts when you deploy a VM as part of a service.

2. **Correct answer:** C
   A. **Incorrect:** Application profiles include information that VMM can use for installing Microsoft Web Deploy applications, SQL Server data-tier applications, Microsoft Server App-V applications, and instructions for running scripts when you deploy a VM as part of a service.
   B. **Incorrect:** A guest operating system profile allows you to configure settings, including the local administrator account password settings for a VM.
   C. **Correct:** You use a hardware profile to configure a VM's hardware configuration, including the VM's memory configuration.
   D. **Incorrect:** You can use the SQL Server profile to configure SQL Server configuration settings such as the SQL Server service account.

3. **Correct answer:** C

  A. **Incorrect:** You can use the SQL Server profile to configure SQL Server configuration settings such as the SQL Server service account.

  B. **Incorrect:** You use a hardware profile to configure a VM's hardware configuration, including the VM's memory configuration.

  C. **Correct:** A guest operating system profile allows you to configure settings including the local administrator account password settings for a VM.

  D. **Incorrect:** Application profiles include information that VMM can use for installing Microsoft Web Deploy applications, SQL Server data-tier applications, Microsoft Server App-V applications, and instructions for running scripts when you deploy a VM as part of a service.

Objective 5.2: Thought experiment

1. What Server App-V Windows PowerShell cmdlet would you use to save the The Backup-ServerAppvPackageState cmdlet saves the runtime state of an existing Server App-V application to a designated location.

2. The Restore-ServerAppvPackageState cmdlet restores the runtime state of a virtual application. You can only use this cmdlet if you have a backup of the application's runtime state.

Objective 5.2: Review

1. **Correct answer:** C

  A. **Incorrect:** This cmdlet restores the runtime state of a virtual application. You can only use this cmdlet if you have a backup of the application's runtime state. As the question did not state that such a backup existed, this is not the best answer.

  B. **Incorrect:** This cmdlet starts an installed virtual application package and associated subsystem.

  C. **Correct:** This cmdlet removes the runtime state, returning the virtual application package to its initial state, but does not remove the virtual application package.

  D. **Incorrect:** This cmdlet shuts down a virtual application package and associated subsystems.

2. **Correct answer:** C

   A. **Incorrect:** This cmdlet removes a Server App-V package from a computer to which it has been deployed.

   B. **Incorrect:** This cmdlet removes the runtime state, returning the virtual application package to its initial state, but does not remove the virtual application package.

   C. **Correct:** This cmdlet adds a new virtual application to a computer that has the Server App-V agent installed, or can be used to upgrade an existing virtual application.

   D. **Incorrect:** This cmdlet restores the runtime state of a virtual application. You can only use this cmdlet if you have a backup of the application's runtime state.

3. **Correct answer:** C

   A. **Incorrect:** This cmdlet restores the runtime state of a virtual application. You can only use this cmdlet if you have a backup of the application's runtime state.

   B. **Incorrect:** This cmdlet adds a new virtual application to a computer that has the Server App-V agent installed, or can be used to upgrade an existing virtual application.

   C. **Correct:** Use this cmdlet to update an existing virtual application package.

   D. **Incorrect:** This cmdlet starts an installed virtual application package and associated subsystem.

4. **Correct answer:** B

   A. **Incorrect:** To add a Server App-V application to a VMM library as a custom resource, which allows you to deploy it using VMM, place the package files in a folder with the extension .CR and copy that folder to the VMM library.

   B. **Correct:** To add a Server App-V application to a VMM library as a custom resource, which allows you to deploy it using VMM, place the package files in a folder with the extension .CR and copy that folder to the VMM library.

   C. **Incorrect:** To add a Server App-V application to a VMM library as a custom resource, which allows you to deploy it using VMM, place the package files in a folder with the extension .CR and copy that folder to the VMM library.

   D. **Incorrect:** To add a Server App-V application to a VMM Library as a custom resource, which allows you to deploy it using VMM, place the package files in a folder with the extension .CR and copy that folder to the VMM library.

Objective 5.3: Thought experiment

1. You should configure an Application Profile to automate the deployment to Microsoft Server App-V applications to virtual services.

2. You should configure a service template so that you can automate the deployment of multi-tier applications. Service templates include VM templates, application, and SQL Server profiles.

Objective 5.3: Review

1. **Correct answers:** A, B and C

   A. **Correct:** You can use a deployed virtual machine, an existing virtual machine template, or a virtual hard disk as the basis for a virtual machine template

   B. **Correct:** You can use a deployed virtual machine, an existing virtual machine template, or a virtual hard disk as the basis for a virtual machine template

   C. **Correct:** You can use a deployed virtual machine, an existing virtual machine template, or a virtual hard disk as the basis for a virtual machine template

   D. **Incorrect:** You can use a deployed virtual machine, an existing virtual machine template, or a virtual hard disk as the basis for a virtual machine template

2. **Correct answer:** B

   A. **Incorrect:** SQL DAC packages are stored in the VMM library in zip format.

   B. **Correct:** SQL DAC packages are stored in the VMM library in zip format.

   C. **Incorrect:** SQL DAC packages are stored in the VMM library in zip format.

   D. **Incorrect:** While SQL DAC data is written in XML format, the package itself is stored in the library as a zip file.

3. **Correct answer:** D

   A. **Incorrect:** Physical profiles are used with PXE deployment of virtualization hosts.

   B. **Incorrect:** Service templates can include application profiles and SQL server profiles. These profiles are not available when deploying a VM from a VM template.

   C. **Incorrect:** Service templates can include application profiles and SQL server profiles. These profiles are not available when deploying a VM from a VM template.

   D. **Correct:** You can include a guest operating system profile in a VM template.

4. **Correct answers:** A, B, and D

    A. **Correct:** Service templates can include VM templates, SQL Server profiles, and application profiles.

    B. **Correct:** Service templates can include VM templates, SQL Server profiles, and application profiles.

    C. **Incorrect:** Physical profiles are used with PXE deployment of virtualization hosts and cannot be included in VMM service templates.

    D. **Correct:** Service templates can include VM templates, SQL Server profiles, and application profiles.

Objective 5.4: Thought experiment

1. Configure upgrade domains so that only a portion of the servers in the tier are upgraded at any one time.

2. Adjust the tier settings and increase the maximum number of VMs that can be deployed in the tier.

Objective 5.4: Review

1. **Correct answers:** B and C

    A. **Incorrect:** Updating the service template of a deployed service in VMM involves creating a copy of the original service template and specifying a new release value. You then make the appropriate updates to the service template.

    B. **Correct:** Updating the service template of a deployed service in VMM involves creating a copy of the original service template and specifying a new release value. You then make the appropriate updates to the service template.

    C. **Correct:** Updating the service template of a deployed service in VMM involves creating a copy of the original service template and specifying a new release value. You then make the appropriate updates to the service template.

    D. **Incorrect:** Updating the service template of a deployed service in VMM involves creating a copy of the original service template and specifying a new release value. You then make the appropriate updates to the service template.

2. **Correct answer:** C

   A. **Incorrect:** To apply updates to a deployed service, on the Updated Service Template page of the Change Service Template Wizard, you need to select the option to Replace the current template with an updated template for this service.

   B. **Incorrect:** To apply updates to a deployed service, on the Updated Service Template page of the Change Service Template Wizard, you need to select the option to Replace the current template with an updated template for this service.

   C. **Correct:** To apply updates to a deployed service, on the Updated Service Template page of the Change Service Template Wizard, you need to select the option to Replace the current template with an updated template for this service.

   D. **Incorrect:** To apply updates to a deployed service, on the Updated Service Template page of the Change Service Template Wizard, you need to select the option to Replace the current template with an updated template for this service.

3. **Correct answer:** B

   A. **Incorrect:** Before you can apply updates to an existing service using an updated service template, you must publish the service template.]

   B. **Correct:** Before you can apply updates to an existing service using an updated service template, you must publish the service template.

   C. **Incorrect:** Before you can apply updates to an existing service using an updated service template, you must publish the service template.

   D. **Incorrect:** Before you can apply updates to an existing service using an updated service template, you must publish the service template.

Index

A

D

S

About the author

ORIN THOMAS is an MVP, an MCT and has a string of Microsoft MCSE and MCITP certifications. He has written more than 25 books for Microsoft Press and is a contributing editor at Windows IT Pro magazine. He has been working in IT since the early 1990's. He regularly speaks at events like TechED in Australia and around the world on Windows Server, Windows Client, System Center and security topics. Orin founded and runs the Melbourne System Center, Security, and Infrastructure Group. You can follow him on twitter at *http://twitter.com/orinthomas*.